Un/Translatables

Un/Translatables

New Maps for Germanic Literatures

✦

Edited by Bethany Wiggin
and Catriona MacLeod

NORTHWESTERN UNIVERSITY PRESS
EVANSTON, ILLINOIS

Northwestern University Press
www.nupress.northwestern.edu

Printed in the United States of America

10 9 8 7 6 5 4 3 2 1

Library of Congress Cataloging-in-Publication Data

Names: Wiggin, Bethany, 1972– editor. | MacLeod, Catriona, 1963– editor.
Title: Un/translatables : new maps for Germanic literatures / edited by Bethany Wiggin and Catriona MacLeod.
Description: Evanston, Illinois : Northwestern University Press, 2016. | "The contributions here originated in a conference in the spring of 2011 hosted by the Department of Germanic Languages and Literatures at the University of Pennsylvania"—Introduction.
Identifiers: LCCN 2016021661 | ISBN 9780810133433 (pbk. : alk. paper) | ISBN 9780810133440 (cloth : alk. paper) | ISBN 9780810133501 (e-book)
Subjects: LCSH: Translating and interpreting—History and criticism—Congresses. | German literature—Translations—History and criticism—Congresses. | Literature—Translations into German—History and criticism—Congresses.
Classification: LCC PT125 .U58 2016 | DDC 830.9—dc23
LC record available at https://lccn.loc.gov/2016021661

CONTENTS

ACKNOWLEDGMENTS

The seeds of *Un/Translatables* were planted at a conference at the University of Pennsylvania for which we received generous funding from the Mellon Cross-Cultural Fund, the German Academic Exchange Service (DAAD), the University Research Foundation, the School of Arts and Sciences, and the support of many departments and programs across the School of Arts and Sciences. We would especially like to thank our many colleagues who work in Germanic languages and literatures at Penn, several of whom are also authors of chapters in this volume.

Daniel DiMassa and Nicholas Theis were indispensable collaborators on every aspect of the conference and the book. Though we were unsuccessful in having their names placed on the title page, we regard them as co-editors. Two student assistants in the Department of Germanic Languages & Literatures, Andro Mathewson and Matthew Planesi, also deserve our thanks, as they provided crucial technical assistance in the collation of chapters and in preparing the final manuscript for the Press. We are indebted to Martina Bale for her practical help with many conference- and book-related issues.

Finally, we would like to acknowledge with deep gratitude Henry Carrigan, our editor at Northwestern University Press, for his interest in and stewardship of the project, as well as the helpful comments of two anonymous reviewers.

Prologue

✦

Laurel's Eyes

Each night is soul-bedeviled
As each frayed ship rigs sail
In journey's end sight falters
Where journey never ends

A draught so thin it's better
A ruin like the Rhine
That rips its fleece in kilter
Abandoned to its shine

The shone star yearns for light
Door opens, wonder barred
Ire's golden gate gets blistered
Seek comet, err in folded heart

Seek comet, err in folded heart
And drink a daft farewell
That has its blunder tendered
In quivering, feathered tar

Sifted in climate's sieve
Engrafts its festooned way
As spark ignites the weave
And shouts ordain the play

This globe spins on, verse lingers
A sail without a sigh
A song without a singer
Laurel's veil, Laurel's eyes

Charles Bernstein

Un/Translatables

Introduction

Bethany Wiggin, Catriona MacLeod,
Daniel DiMassa, and Nicholas Theis

Raphèl maí amècche zahí almi

—Dante Alighieri, *Inferno*

Wer das Dichten will verstehen,
Muß ins Land der Dichtung gehen;
Wer den Dichter will verstehen,
Muß in Dichters
Lande gehen.

—Goethe, *Zu besserem Verständnis des west-östlichen Divans* (1819)

So ist jeder Übersetzer ein Prophet in seinem Volke

—Goethe, Essay on "German Romance" (1827)

We find ourselves between a rock and a hard place: the distinctive poetic voices of Charles Bernstein and Yoko Tawada lend the prologue and epilogue for this volume. Posing as bookends, their contributions point toward what the essays show: the critical fruits gleaned when literary study circles around moments and figures of untranslatability. Bernstein, a contemporary American poet, wrote the mostly English-language libretto for the opera *Shadowlands*, an account of Walter Benjamin's final hours that premiered at Munich's Prinzregententheater on May 25, 2004. In the first of seven tableaux vivants, entitled "Laurel's Eyes," in the opera's sixth section, Bernstein invites play with *Die Loreley*, suggesting with his sound translation of the famous romantic ballad that a German sound remains essential to its English reworking: it is stubbornly untranslatable. Of course the Lorelei has been subject to various poetic and folkloric renditions and other versions in English, notably by Mark Twain as well as Sylvia Plath. Rather than foundering on the rock of untranslatablity, as so many fishermen sunk by the Lorelei, poets have seized this paradoxical topos as an engine of creativity. In Bernstein's suggestive phrasing, "This globe spins on, verse lingers."[1]

Tawada's "Vierundzwanzig," our volume's epilogue, translated by Susan Bernofsky in "Twentyfour," lingers among the *loci communes* of translation, including of course *the* figure of untranslatability, the tower of Babel. Tawada, also the subject of several essays in this volume, is a writer whose remarkable transitions between Japanese and German have earned her the prestigious Adelbert-von-Chamisso Prize (1996). In our epilogue, the lyric I swings through a series of fairy-tale infinitives, also the form of the imperative in German, pivoting between commanding herself and the reader, directing both to "ascend the sleepy tower" (den schläfrigen Turm besteigen). She, and we, find our perch here "nicht für die Bande des Bluts, sondern für die Band der Straßenmusiker mit ihren Hunden," or in Bernofsky's voice, "not for a bond of blood, but for the band of street musicians with their dogs." The lyric I then inserts herself, "ich spiele bedingungslos mit," and in the musical translation of Bernofsky, "I follow their lead." And yet, the I can only play along with these street players for so long before her own voice inevitably returns, "Ich springe vom Turm hinunter, lande unverletzt" (I leap down from the tower, landing uninjured). This oscillation—between the music of the street and one's own internal sound, between the word of the other and the word of a self—marks a central concern for this volume on untranslatability in Germanic cultures. It is very much, to speak with Tawada and Bernofsky, "eine Übung, Gleichgewicht zu halten" (an exercise in keeping my [and our] balance). And of course, to accomplish this balancing exercise, the stumbling blocks and *Stolpersteine* posed by Untranslatability are essential.

With the advent of hyper-globalism (globalism 2.0), critics and translators often bemoan the demise of literary vernaculars: rich traditions beset by a flavorless global prose. The strictures of the global market, dominated by global English and Chinese, are said to flatten local literary landscapes, towers of untranslation disappeared. The "dull new global novel," according to one would-be Cassandra, Tim Parks, will soon supplant deep, profoundly idiomatic literary traditions.[2] In short, the heterogeneous, organic cultures of the planet's various literary ecosystems must be added to the endangered list, their very existence imperiled by an aggressively invasive, alien monoculture.

Whatever one thinks of such recent warnings, the pressures of today's globalism have given the lie to translation as a transparent process. Increasingly visible, translation may well figure as a most efficient tool of empire. And yet it may also provide a deeply creative vehicle. Concerns that translation levels localities as it smooths over towering obstacles to cultural interchangeability may find that the supposed path to equivalence is paved unevenly, littered with rocks and hard places, so many "Laurel's Eyes."

Perhaps we find ourselves, like Dante and Virgil in the excerpt from *Inferno* XXXI taken as this introduction's first epigraph, confronted with Nimrod's incomprehensible language of Babel, "Raphèl maí amècche zahí almi."[3] As Virgil explains in the translation by Ciaran Carson, "This egomaniac / is

Nimrod, who built Babel; he's the cause / of all our tribulations linguistic."[4] Yet while Virgil urges Dante onward, decrying the heteroglossia to which the giant's towering ambition fated humankind, the poet of the Florentine vernacular, on the other hand, remains silent, as Allen and Bernofsky also emphasize, saying "nothing either to or about Nimrod."[5] Dante embraced many languages in the *Commedia*, including Nimrod's babble, and he left them in their vernaculars, including "not only many styles, but several languages, common and uncommon," as Matthew Reynolds notes in his review of Carson's translation.[6] Polyglot poet-translator Carson has taken Dante of the *Commedia*, not Dante's Virgil, as his guide, for he "does not attempt to overcome our 'tribulations linguistic,' but works imaginatively within them."[7] Perhaps, we might say, he sees with "Laurel's Eyes." As translation's etymology indicates, translation has always been about place—or, more precisely, about culture's (including agriculture's) movements between places. But in a world we recognize, for good and bad, as increasingly unified, what are the spaces and places that translation purports to cross? We need new maps.

The *Oxford English Dictionary* records translation entering English via Old French amidst what Charles Homer Haskins so influentially called the renaissance of the twelfth century.[8] For while translation always comes from place, it is also powerfully linked to time and to an age's sense of itself as new and different: in the twelfth century no less than today. Early modern literati on both sides of the Alps urged a break with the scholarly idiom of their day. From Lorenzo Valla to Johannes Reuchlin to Erasmus, men of letters labored to produce new translations, and their philological awareness of history's incursions ushered in the Renaissance. And, as work such as A. G. Coldiron's suggests, as we continue to examine the role of translation in the Renaissance, we will refine our account of its places and times.[9] We need new histories.

The past decade has witnessed an efflorescence of, if not a renaissance in, translation studies in connection with globalism. Contributors to the present volume, for example, have prompted us to follow the "translational turn" (Doris Bachmann-Medick), to re-vision the invisibility of the translator (Lawrence Venuti), and to read "writing outside the nation" (Azade Seyhan).[10] A review of additional key moments in the past decade's vibrant discussion of translation might also include a 2001 essay by Emily Apter urging a new hearing for Horkheimer and Adorno's critique of the culture industry with our ears newly attuned to the dictates of a "transnationally translatable monoculture."[11] A series of suggestive articles from the aughts by Rebecca Walkowitz innovatively argued for the creative potential of novels "born translated."[12]

2004 marked the appearance of the five-volume *Vocabulaire européen des philosophies, dictionnaire des intraduisibles*, edited by Barbara Cassin, a project deeply inspired by Derrida's insistence on "l'intraduisible corps des langues" (the untranslatable body of languages).[13] The space of translation itself provided the foundation of Apter's 2006 monograph, *The Translation Zone*, which urged the consideration of translation as "a significant medium of subject re-formation and political change."[14] Apter's 2008 article "Untranslatables" introduced Cassin's project to a North American audience, elaborating the term via Cassin so as to "mobilize this theoretical (un)translatability for theoretical and curricular ventures in literary comparatism that aim for geopolitical specificity and theoretical reach against the fine grain of aesthetic comparison."[15] Then, in 2009, the annual conference of the Modern Language Association took translation as its topic and Catherine Porter chose to devote her presidential address to the welcome topic, "English Is Not Enough." Porter also dedicated the Presidential Forum of *Profession* the following year to "The Tasks of Translation in the Global Context," publishing many essays from the conference, including the elegant essay by Venuti that launched the critique of empiricism and translation that he elaborates in the essay in our volume's first part.[16] Within the forum provided by the annual meetings of the American Comparative Literature Association (ACLA), David Damrosch and Gayatri Spivak have several times debated translation in conjunction with world literature. In their keynote debate at the ACLA conference in Vancouver in April 2011, for example, Damrosch advocated the adoption of pedagogies suitable for world literature taught in translation; Spivak, on the other hand, campaigned against easy notions of translatability in an extension of her 2003 obituary for comparative literature.[17]

The 2014–2015 *Report on the State of the Discipline of Comparative Literature* includes Untranslatables among its notable "Ideas of the Decade."[18] Writing for the *Report*, Shaden Tageldin explains how the term has been enlisted in battle against easy translatability and a global monoculture. Untranslatables are, as in the title of Apter's latest foray, a collection of essays (many of which have appeared previously), supposedly *Against World Literature*.[19] Pitting untranslatability against world literature strikes an adversarial pose that would certainly have surprised earlier interpreters of world literature, including Goethe. And Apter, relying on Jonathan Arac's not altogether convincing gloss of *Verkehr* in *The Communist Manifesto*, suggests how world literature might indeed be thought otherwise:

> Verkehrte Weltliteratur, or screwed-up literature, has precisely the right impertinent coding. For in standing the world on its head, it encourages the literature of the world to mess with World Literature, turning it into a process of translating untranslatability. It beckons one to run the experiment of imagining what a literary studies contoured around untranslatability might be.[20]

And here, in Apter's call to experiment with a study shaped by untranslatability, we have arrived precisely at the point where the present volume intervenes. Apter's citation of Arac, with her unfortunate misspelling, "Die verkehter Welt," betrays Apter's own reliance on an instrumental notion of translation. The typo indexes in fact her glancing attention to the Germanic tradition; while the names Schleiermacher, Goethe, and Benjamin receive mention in *Against World Literature*, more substantive discussion is missing. In one instance of a more sustained discussion, of Luther's *dolmetschen* (to interpret, to translate simultaneously), her reading evidences an overreliance on the *Vocabulaire* in its assertion that *dolmetschen* means to Germanicize.[21] In fact, as most German speakers know, Luther also used the verb "teutschen," and certainly this verb, not *dolmetschen*, would have better illustrated her point.

If a reliance on purportedly easy translatability has underpinned the propagation, ironically enough, of Apter's *Against World Literature* as well as of the "dull new" world literature, again to echo Tim Parks, then it is beyond time to return to that which resists translation—including the Germanic languages and literary and cultural contexts in which today's discussions of world literature and untranslatability take root. Untranslatability was surely a "ghostwritten word" of the century's first decade, as Tageldin reports, and it is quite certain to be "a watchword of the next." Its study, to return once more to Tawada, will require exercises in finding some balance. One cannot, we believe, be for or against world literature, or untranslatability. One can, however, retranslate them.

Even before scholars of the past decade rediscovered translation as an essential object of literary study and the emergence of new translation studies, a peculiar trait of translation theory began to express itself: its German-ness. André Lefevere, leaning on Andreas Huyssen, noted that, above all, German translation theorists remain "to a great extent still central to the theory of literary translation as such, whether that theory is formulated in German or not."[22] Thirty years later, in the second volume of *Übersetzung Translation Traduction* (2007), Armin Paul Frank reminded us all that

> German literature came to be considered a latecomer in Europe, which therefore owed a great deal to translation and other forms of interliterary transfer. As a consequence, reflection on translating and translation possessed an urgency and was carried to an intensity much greater than in other countries. Hence, it will make sense to pay careful attention to the German tradition, though certainly not at the expense of others.[23]

For Germanic literary and cultural history, perhaps more than for any other literary or cultural corpus, translation is innovation, key translations marking well-recognized renaissances in canonical literary history. Otfrid rendered the word and praise of God, previously restricted to Hebrew, Greek, and Latin, in his German dialect; Gottfried culled, he claimed, from Thomas of Britain, and Hartmann from Chrétien, while Wolfram apparently invented Kyôt, the source from which he purported to translate. Luther made the Bible German by lending voice to mothers in the kitchen, children in the streets, and men in the market. A "German" Shakespeare emerged in the eighteenth century; Goethe's Werther channeled the (apparently fake) Ossian translations of James Macpherson. Then Goethe expressed love anew via his study of the *ghazal*, while to render Pindar's Greek, Hölderlin had to make German monstrous. After the Second World War, Adorno urged that German must be made hospitable to "Wörter aus der Fremde" (words from abroad).[24] And the literary scene in today's Germany receives new energies from the contributions of and debates surrounding "Chamisso-Autoren," writers whose first language is not German but who, like the nineteenth-century French-born writer of German, Adalbert von Chamisso—and like volume contributor Yoko Tawada as well as Emine Sevgi Özdamar and Yusuf Yesilöz, all three authors' work treated in the following pages—have adopted it as their literary language.[25]

The present collection of essays unites two inescapable interventions in contemporary translation discourses: the concept of "Untranslatables" as points of productive resistance, and the Germanic tradition as the primary interlocutor for translation studies. The contributions here originated in a conference in the spring of 2011 hosted by the Department of Germanic Languages and Literatures at the University of Pennsylvania. (Selected talks appear in this volume, revised after the profound collaborative discussions our meeting generated; other essays were commissioned for this volume.) We, the conference organizers and collection's editors, were spurred on by Cassin's, Apter's, and Frank's projects. Germanists, we wanted to pursue the critical itineraries that would result if "Untranslatables" à la Cassin and Apter were returned, productively estranged, to their original German context as elucidated by Frank. Thus we set off to explore Untranslatables across Germanic literatures—German, Yiddish, Dutch, and Afrikaans—and ended up, as the essays here show, on trajectories into Hebrew, Arabic, Mandarin, Japanese, English, and Scots. But before we embark on these circuitous trajectories, it will be helpful to map out our place of departure.

The term "Untranslatables," as astute readers will have recognized, is rooted in two explorations of translation written originally in German: Walter Benjamin's now ubiquitous "The Task of the Translator" and Goethe's extensive notes to his "tradaptation" of mystical Persian poetry, from which our second epigraph hails. First published in 1819, these notes were appended to a reissued edition of the Weimar poet's *West-östlicher Divan*, produced at his publisher's behest.[26] Benjamin drew from the notes, particularly the final section on "Translations," quoting heavily and in places verbatim, for the "Task." In this section of Goethe's notes, he sketches three gradations of translation. Of the highest, Goethe concludes:

> Eine Übersetzung, die sich mit dem Original zu identifizieren strebt, nähert sich zuletzt der Interlinearversion und erleichtert höchlich das Verständnis des Originals; hiedurch werden wir an den Grundtext

> hinangeführt, ja getrieben, und so ist denn zuletzt der ganze Zirkel abgeschlossen, in welchem sich die Annäherung des Fremden und Einheimischen, des Bekannten und Unbekannten bewegt.[27]
>
> A translation that aims to be identical with the original approaches at the end an interlinear version and very much eases the comprehension of the original; through it we are led to the foundational text, indeed driven to it, and thus finally the whole circle is closed in which the approach of the foreign and domestic, the known and unknown are in motion.

The productivity of estranging native culture, of putting it "in motion" in a circle in which the "known and unknown" ceaselessly revolve, similarly structures Benjamin's thought. The "Task," written originally as a preface to his German translation of Baudelaire's *Tableaux parisiens*, proposes that the best translations estrange their native language.[28] The worst, on the other hand, attend to the letter of their native language while remaining ignorant of the spirit of the foreign. Or, as Benjamin quotes Rudolf Pannwitz, deeming Pannwitz's writings "neben Goethes Sätzen in den Noten zum 'Divan' leicht das Beste . . . , was in Deutschland zur Theorie der Übersetzung veröffentlicht wurde" (next to Goethe's pronouncement in the Notes to the *Divan* easily the best thing published in Germany on the theory of translation):

> Unsre übertragungen auch die besten gehn von einem falschen grundsatz aus sie wollen das indische griechische englische verdeutschen anstatt das deutsche zu verindischen vergriechischen verenglischen.[29]
>
> Even the best of our translations proceed from a false premise: they attempt to Germanicize Indian, Greek, and English instead of Indianizing, Greekicizing, and Englishizing German.

Together, Goethe's "Notes" and Benjamin's "Task" provide the "open sesame" to what is often called the "new translation studies" as represented in critical organs such as the journal *Translation Studies*.[30] Both essays have generated an enormous corpus in translation while providing a powerful optic for what is ineluctably lost in translation. Cassin captures the productive irony central to Untranslatables well, noting in her introduction to the *Vocabulaire*, "Parler d'*intraduisibles* n'implique nullement que les termes en question, ou les expressions, les tours syntaxiques et grammaticaux, ne soient pas traduits et ne puissent pas l'être—l'intraduisible, c'est plutôt ce qu'on ne cesse pas de (ne pas) traduire" (To speak of untranslatables hardly implies only that the terms in question, or the expressions, the syntactical and grammatical routes are not translated and cannot be—untranslatability is rather that you do not stop [not] translating).[31]

What serves as the backdrop for Goethe's remarks and for Benjamin's subsequent reading is a particularly German historical-conceptual moment that spans the early Enlightenment and romanticism. The rationalism of the Wolffian school determined translation theory for the first half of the eighteenth century. Contrary to the early modern belief that the clothes make the man, the rationalist system assumed the content of thought to be the unchanging "inner" core that simply donned a different "outer shell" when translated into another language.[32] This model's foundation in the pre-linguistic equivalence of thoughts with no room for linguistic idiosyncrasies found its most striking articulation in J. J. Breitinger's claim that proper synonyms exist only between languages, each having one equivalent way of expressing a particular thought's content.[33] This orderly one-to-one correspondence present in Breitinger's theory of translation, despite his vehement breaks from Gottsched and his followers, reflected the beauty of rational order, the underlying foundation of the divine mind since Leibniz and of rationalist aesthetics since Wolff, Gottsched, and Baumgarten.

The challenge posed to this rational order came from a translator and his translation, both of which changed the course of German letters: J. J. Bodmer and his more than fifty-year project of translating Milton's *Paradise Lost*. If the content of *Paradise Lost* pushed the envelope of rationalist aesthetics' beauty of order with its sublime scenes of angels battling in heaven and with contradictions of immaterial entities waging physical war, Milton's verse—with its syntactical inversions, twisted English, and frequent incorporations of Hebraisms, Latinisms, and Hellenisms—raised flags as to the propriety of appropriating the foreign in national literature.[34]

Bodmer's translations took this issue very seriously, resulting in an early argument for translation as enrichment through foreignization of the target language. The "translation" of foreign terms into "original" German writing proved that German's hospitality to other languages was at the same time the marker of its own improvement:

> Sie [die deutsche Sprache] hat nun Wörter empfangen, die ganz bequem, sanft, und poetisch sind. Man hat zuweilen Ausdrücke und sogar besondere Eigenschaften anderer Sprachen in unsere hunübergebracht, die ganz ungezwungen sind und uns mittelst der Neuigkeit und Verschiedenheit die sie mit sich führen, sehr belüstigen. Wir bewundern die Fremdlinge in dem einheimischen Gewande, und freuen uns, wenn wir sie so frey und munter um sich schauen sehen, als ob sie gebohrne Deutsche wären.[35]

> It [German] has now received words that are quite fitting, smooth, and poetic. At times poets have brought over expressions and even peculiar properties of other languages into our own, which, now comfortable in German, greatly amuse us on account of the novelty

> and variety that they bring with them. We marvel at the foreigners in our native garb and take pleasure whenever they look at their surroundings, blithe and free, as though they were born Germans.

But although Bodmer posed a challenge to the correspondence theory of translation by identifying that individual languages have their own locally developed and idiosyncratic means of expression, the hospitality and clothing tropes he employs still reveal a conception of translation at the level of individual words and expressions. It was not until Herder's cultural-historical relativism that translation theory began to conceptualize the movement of translation in terms not of individual words, works, or authors, but in terms of entire cultures and historical moments.

Herder's theory of language added another dimension to translation as movement—translation now figured as a means by which to guide a language's movement along the continuum of its historical development. In his exploration of the fitness of organic analogy in Herder, Frank notes that Herder positions German in the middle of the four ages of language, a most desirable location for its ability "'to steer into both directions'"—making German capable of youthful (language of poetic expression) as well as mature (language of philosophical clarity) development.[36] Older and newer languages, with an idiosyncratic genius unique to their cultural-historical development, constitute the spectrum of less and more suitable reservoirs from which to translate, while reflection provides a rational governor by which to help development in terms of clarity. This conception of translation rendered it a tool that necessarily enriched German through movements over distances and epochs.

Amidst the final throes of the Enlightenment, German romantics—whose translations popularized both Dante and Shakespeare—contributed to the discourse on translation and made a significant gesture toward Untranslatables by calling into question the textual practices of the German language's most famous translator, Martin Luther. The Protestant Reformer, whose *Sendbrief vom Dolmetschen* extolled his own "rein und klar teutsch" and boasted of having translated the Bible so smoothly as to have planed it of its knots, served as a precursor to linguistic globalism, donning what Lawrence Venuti has called the "translator's invisibility."[37] Luther's translation, spurred on by a drive toward popularization and aided by his recourse to the budding science of philology, was judged by the romantics to employ methods that would prove deleterious to the future of art, poetry, and religion. Thus in his essay *Die Christenheit, oder Europa* (*Christianity or Europe*), Novalis writes of the consequences of the canonization of Luther's translation, "bald nachher [nach dem Anfang des Protestantismus] ist schon die Vertrocknung des heiligen Sinns bemerklich; das Weltliche hat die Oberhand gewonnen, der Kunstsinn leidet sympathetisch mit . . ." (soon thereafter [after the beginning of Protestantism] is the drying out of the holy sense noticeable; the worldly has won the upper hand and the artistic sense suffers along with it . . .).[38] The holy and the artistic suffer, in Novalis's estimation, in that Luther's textual work subordinates a sacred text to an earthly science (philology) for the sake of "die absolute Popularität der Bibel" (the absolute popularity of the Bible).[39] For what Novalis perceives in Luther's Bible is the instrumentalization of translation: a utilitarian endeavor inseparable from German princes' and Protestant reformers' seizure of the medieval church's assets.[40] Just such a conception of Luther as utilitarian forerunner of the Enlightenment would inform Adorno and Horkheimer's choice to pair him with Francis Bacon as one of two forefathers of instrumental reason in their *Dialektik der Aufklärung*. Inasmuch as Novalis's assertions undercut the notion of scientistic translation, they even adumbrate Venuti's critique of instrumental translation.

In the wake of the Napoleonic Wars, Schleiermacher's "Methoden des Uebersetzens" combined an act of political and cultural resistance with a new theory of translation as two different kinds of movement.[41] As the romantic translation theorist famously wrote in a phrase discussed in Venuti's present essay, "Entweder der Uebersetzer läßt den Schriftsteller möglichst in Ruhe, und bewegt den Leser ihm entgegen; oder er läßt den Leser möglichst in Ruhe und bewegt den Schriftsteller ihm entgegen" (Either the translator leaves the author at home, as best as he can, and moves the reader towards him; or he leaves the reader at home, as best as he can, and moves the author towards him).[42]

This dichotomy brings us back to our epigraph from Goethe's notes to the *Divan*. After all, Goethe had noted only months before Schleiermacher:

> Es gibt zwei Übersetzungsmaximen: die eine verlangt daß der Autor einer fremden Nation zu uns herüber gebracht werde, dergestalt, daß wir ihn als den Unsrigen ansehen können; die andere hingegen macht an uns die Forderung, daß wir uns zu dem Fremden hinüber begeben und uns in seine Zustände, seine Sprachweise, seine Eigenheiten finden sollen.
>
> There are two maxims in translating: one requires that the author of a foreign nation be carried across to us in such a way as to make him appear as one of ours; the other demands of us to go abroad and adapt ourselves to the foreigner's conditions, his way with language, his peculiarities.[43]

Frank's analysis of Schleiermacher positions him contrary to Goethe: whereas Goethe grants the usefulness of both directions of movement, yet ultimately endorses bringing the author to the reader's home, in Schleiermacher's remarks on translation preceding the treatise, Schleiermacher rejects using both methods simultaneously and condemns moving the author to the reader.[44] But

Goethe's reformulation of movement and understanding in the *Divan* suggests that he realized something Schleiermacher had stressed the year before, namely that the value of a translation is predicated on its possessing an imprint of a perceptible *Fremdheit* (foreignness). For Schleiermacher, this detectable foreignness of the translation represented, among other things, a resistance to cultural and literary capitulation that mirrored resistance to the hegemony of France—and translation in the French style.[45] As the contributions to this volume show, two centuries after Schleiermacher's treatise, the resistance of foreign elements to complete assimilation in destinations foreign to them represents the space necessary for critical engagement.

This is the kind of critical space in which Cassin and Apter are active when they turn toward the Untranslatable. Let us return then to the moments of resistance in their formulations of the Untranslatable. Untranslatables—cultural moments that deny transfer—offer an analytic through which to conceive sites of local cultural production. Untranslatables refuse easy migration across languages, media, spaces, and histories. Even as they migrate abroad, Untranslatables retain a residue from their origins. Their trajectories produce intellectual property, without home or final destination. They elude claims of national or linguistic ownership, without resorting to the cant of globality. For Apter and Cassin, the Untranslatable provides a point of critical resistance to nation- or foreign-based epistemes, one that could enable a remapping of the humanities demarcated not along lines of national or foreign boundaries but "around hubs of irreducible singularity."[46] As the work of Cassin and Apter, not to mention Derrida, indicates, the concept of Untranslatability long ago took flight from its German origins—Benjamin thinking about Baudelaire and Goethe about Hafiz, origins necessarily *unheimlich* (uncanny) from the start. As the essays collected in the present volume document, Untranslatables offer enormous critical thrust to generate times and places for literary history beyond the frame of the nation. At the same time, they productively estrange our "own" Germanic history, engendering new readings of canonical materials. As Greg Carr has recently explored in his reflections on the need for other archives, translation is a twin of recovery; together they are central to renaissance.[47]

German's many, not always hospitable, translations today find new audiences. From the novel to film, poetry, and blogs, their futurity is based on their translatability. Untranslatables, ineluctable in all translations, provoke fresh consideration of German-ness. The following pages proceed along vectors other than those pointing always to the nation and its author-genius. No transparent process, translation—as the new translation studies remind us—is everywhere determined by relations of power. It demands our attention.

Untranslatability, as the essays gathered here demonstrate, may be the enabling condition of knowledge. It is predicated upon a hermeneutic model of translation, issuing from a materialist theory of language, as Lawrence Venuti outlines in his chapter here. Put most simply, language, including the language of translations, creates. Shaped to the core by its local situation, language constructs reality. Strictly speaking, translation is impossible. But this Untranslatability—or what Willi Goetschel discusses in the following pages as the text's alterity—is profoundly generative, since "translation is a creative process that preserves meaning by creating it, a conscious act of creative substitution whose supplementary aspect is a critical asset rather than a fatality."[48]

The range of critical assets afforded by Untranslatability is amply documented by the subsequent eighteen chapters. We have marshaled them into six parts according to the types of knowledge generated. As Azade Seyhan astutely observes in the conclusion to her chapter on the legacy of early German (Jena) romanticism (*die Frühromantik*) and the leverage it offers scholars, "critical reflection on the role of translation as a historical and a geographical site" of cultural creativity is "poised at the initial station(s) of an unmapped itinerary."[49] Our part titles draw attention to these new spaces of knowledge unfolding. We have labeled each with terms suggestive of the charts we will need as we consider the work of translation: Untranslatable Maps, Cosmopolitanisms, Mobile Peripheries, Intimate Geographies, Intermedial Itineraries, and Translingual Travels. The temporal range of essays included in each part witnesses our conviction that the work of translation requires new histories. Problems of Untranslatability are posed in a stunning array of local situations in these pages: from fourteenth-century Christian pilgrims who traveled from across Europe to the town of Wilsnack (near Braunschweig/Brunswick) and the souvenir badges that rendered their goals mutually intelligible (Rasmussen), to profoundly multilingual early modern translators (Scholz Williams), to "foreignizing" translators and their frequent triangulations of translation, be it German-French-English (Venuti), German-French-Turkish (Seyhan), German-Hebrew-Yiddish (Frieden), Yiddish-Chinese-English (Hellerstein), German-English-Scots (MacLeod), or German-Japanese-English (Brandt, Adelson).

We might have wished to include still other language itineraries. As Doris Bachmann- Medick reminds us in our volume's opening chapter, "the marginalization of many languages creates situations of interaction and transference that are characterized by asymmetricalities of far-reaching impact"; and as Seyhan warns, such asymmetries threaten "the culture that has less power to preserve its expressive legacy."[50] Or, as Lydia Liu cautions, "In thinking about the translatability between historical languages, one cannot but consider the actual power relations that dictate the degree and magnitude of sacrifice that one language must make in order to achieve some level of commensurability with the other."[51]

There are perhaps infinite local histories and spaces that will remain tasks for other translators. Important desiderata remain—to name just a few—questions of translation in debates between medieval nominalists and realists, translation and the iconoclasm of the radical Reformation, or, flipping the title of Yasemin Yildiz's recent book, what we have begun to call the history of "the premonolingual condition."[52]

Translation is the twin of cultural memory. Braced against the angel of history, these essays share a program of critical remembrance and reflection. This programmatic nature comes to the fore most acutely in the essays gathered in the first part. These essays consider the weave of translation and theory; theoretical reflections unfold into practical programs calling for other norms to measure a "good" translation. Bachmann-Medick's lead essay ranges widely across the work of now-canonical postcolonial fiction and criticism, asking us via readings of Salman Rushdie, Dipesh Chakrabarty, and others to consider the inflationary use of the language of translation, what she calls both here and in her monograph, the translational turn. In his essay, Lawrence Venuti contests the long dominance of instrumental measures of a good translation, posing Locke versus Schleiermacher so as to sketch instrumental versus hermeneutic theories of translations, predicated respectively upon empiricist and materialist conceptions of language. In practice, these mutually opposed theories of translation lead to an uncanny mix, as Venuti diagnoses both in the language of Schleiermacher and in that of his recent English translator, Susan Bernofsky (whose work translating Tawada concludes this volume). Derrida lurks at the edges of these essays, unsurprisingly, most visibly so in the genealogy worked out by Goetschel: the "family resemblance" (Wittgenstein) of Jewish philosophers whose patriarch would be Baruch de Spinoza. Concentrating on Spinoza and particularly Moses Mendelssohn, Goetschel extends materialist conceptions of language back in time, arguing too for Derrida's situation in a philosophical lineage including Buber, Rosenzweig, Benjamin, and others. And in this part's concluding chapter, Azade Seyhan returns us to early German romanticism, leveraging Schlegel and Schleiermacher to unpack two texts by Turkish-born authors of divergent degrees of fame: the Chamisso Prize-winning Emine Sevgi Özdamar and the less well-known Yusuf Yesilöz, who resides today in German-speaking Switzerland. Their work, in her perceptive readings, performs the foreignization of the target language (high German, Swiss German) as envisioned by the early romantics, while simultaneously liberating the repressed source language (Turkish, Kurdish) in an embrace offered by self-translation.

The second part, on "Cosmopolitanisms," attends to profoundly multilingual actors. Scholz Williams considers the language games played by two seventeenth-century men of letters, the erudite Johann Praetorius and the impresario Eberhard Werner Happel. Their delight in the wider world, but in particular in the Near East, importantly anticipates that of the early twentieth-century writer-adventurer Carl Raswan. His widely translated autobiography, *Im Land der schwarzen Zelte* (1934, variously translated into English, including as *The Black Tents of Arabia*), recounts his experiences among the Arab Bedouin he loved; and it propels Nina Berman's larger reflections on the critical assistance that translation studies might lend interpretations of cross-cultural representations. Xiaojue Wang's chapter takes us to the Far East and back, examining the influence of modern German poetry on the Chinese poet Feng Zhi. Feng Zhi, who wrote his doctoral paper in Heidelberg, is widely acknowledged among the first modernists to write Chinese poetry, and his engagement with German canonical figures allowed him to reinvent the status of the aesthetic subject.[53] Feng Zhi's long career spans the Cold War divide, and Wang's elaboration of the poet's various receptions of Rilke as well as the early and late Goethe provide us new critical avenues into even such well-known German writers.

In early medieval adaptations and translations of the Gospels, such as the *Heliand* and the *Evangelienbuch*, and humanists' scholarly involvement in *translatio imperii*, translation in the German tradition operated as a means of linguistic democratization, bearing writers of German across a sea of Latin. In the age of the Enlightenment, Bodmer's translation of Milton put Swiss literary criticism head-to-head with German criticism, while just a few decades later, A. W. Schlegel's translations of Shakespeare made canonical the work of a scholar otherwise less known than his more famous brother.

The chapters in part III, "Mobile Peripheries" trace a broader geography of Untranslatables by exploring uncharted moments in which translation bears those on the margins of the map to its very center. In "China in Two Yiddish Translations: Ethnographic and Modernist Appropriations," Kathryn Hellerstein offers an account of Yiddish translations of Chinese culture and poetry, first by examining a text that introduces China to Yiddish readers at the end of World War I, and second, by presenting a Yiddish modernist translation of a poem by Li Tai Po. In each moment, with Yiddish translators reconsidering their own traditions in light of those of the Chinese, Hellerstein asserts that translation comes to function as a means of overcoming the "perceived provincialism of the Jewish language." Ken Frieden, in "Translations from German in Yiddish Literary History," shows the way in which Hebrew-Yiddish writers Mendel Lefin and Haikl Hurwitz use translation through a peripheral language, Yiddish, in order to supersede the literary work of a more dominant language, German. Focusing on their renderings of J. H. Campe's travel narratives, Frieden argues that translation becomes a space of literary experimentation for Lefin and Hurwitz, who early on introduced radically new forms of colloquial language and realism while leaving behind prevailing trends in German literature. Catriona MacLeod's chapter, "Lost and Found in Translation: The Itinerant Kafka Translations of Edwin and Willa Muir," examines the Muirs' translation of Kafka's famous novel, *Der Verschollene* (*Amerika*), and shows the way in which two Scots, marginalized on account of their language, "powerfully enter the terrain of modernism in English" through the practice of translation. Highlighting the ways in which *Der Verschollene* displays Kafka's consideration of questions of untranslatability and linguistic marginalization, MacLeod argues compellingly that the Muirs' linguistic affinity to Kafka emerges at various moments in their translation, the long commercial success of which had led some critics erroneously to deem it unreflective.

Part IV, "Intimate Geographies," examines the difficulties of traversing even the most immediate and familiar of territories: our own bodies. To map the human body for translation would entail delineating regions whose boundaries are everywhere complicated by subjective experience, queer lines, and variously stacked yet incongruent topographies of language-specific idiom. And the contributions in this part are concerned with more than the ample stock of terms different languages exhibit for bodily parts, pains, pleasures, and practices. They remind us that, at least since Herder and A. W. Schlegel, the body figures in at least two major conceptions of translation's activity: snuggling (*sich anschmiegen*) and fidelity (*die Treue*). But if Herder and Schlegel point to the advantages of a translation snuggling as close as possible to the original, whether for the benefit of the target language or for the formal fidelity of poetic translation, the scholars whose work appears in "Intimate Geographies" focus on the barriers between bodies and language, and specifically the interruptions that frustrate embrace and lead to productive friction. Fidelity, it appears, stands in no easy relation to snuggling.

Heike Bauer, in "Staging Untranslatability: Magnus Hirschfeld Encounters Philadelphia," investigates the translation methods of the international sexology pioneer and sexual-freedom fighter Magnus Hirschfeld. Bauer's analysis includes Hirschfeld's practice of leaving German and English words side-by-side, literally *sich anschmiegend* (snuggling) yet untranslated, in his sexological work and in his attempts to thwart normative and homophobic discourses. Simon Richter's chapter, "Trans(fel)latio: Gerard Reve, Jürgen Hillner, Paul Verhoeven, and *De vierde man*," queries language's body and the possibility and implications of "trans(fel)lation" between languages (here Dutch and German) and media (film's adaptation of literature). But the ready imagery of the body, the mouth, and release that attends successful trans(fel)lation fails to arrive where linguistic and representational limits prevent original and translation from coming together. Nonetheless, as Richter argues, the inevitable missed connection might be central to an often overlooked criterion for good translation since Schleiermacher: pleasure (*Genuss*).

When Clemens Brentano announced in his early romantic novel *Godwi* that the essence of all romantic art is translation (*Übersetzung*), he intended to comprehend, as well, the bridging of a gulf between media that had been in play at least since Lessing's pivotal Laocoön essay of 1766. In that essay's subtitle, "oder über die Grenzen der Malerei und der Poesie," Lessing had deployed a spatial metaphor that indeed patrolled and policed—even barricaded—the boundaries between verbal and visual arts, and that installed a model of radical, even antagonistic untranslatability between media.[54] Yet even though Brentano's novel models romantic hybridity (containing poetry, epistolary sections, dialogue inserts, comic interludes, diary entries, geometric diagrams, songs, and footnotes), it also exhibits a poignant awareness of the intermedial gulf that would need to be overcome by the romantic translation project in the wake of classical theory. One of the protagonists, Molly Hodefeld, whose aesthetic ideals consist of "Übergang" (transition), "Wechsel" (change), and "Beweglichkeit" (mobility), expresses the belief in a former paradisiacal unity of art forms that has in the modern age fallen into categorization and fragmentation. Though she prizes the mediating potential of "Poesie" to animate the mute plastic arts, it is important to note the implicit limitations she sets on the linguistic project, which is conducted nervously (*ängstlich*) and with the awareness that there will always be visible fissures in the result: "Das sind nun die einzelnen Künste, deren Zusammenhang sie [die Menschen] ängstlich zusammensuchen, und sie mit den Resten des allmächtigen Verstandes zusammenkleben und beschreiben wollen" ("those are now the individual arts, whose connections they [humans] now anxiously seek to gather and to glue back together and describe with the remnants of omnipotent reason").[55]

Part V, "Intermedial Itineraries," destabilizes these representational boundaries between media and arts. Ann Marie Rasmussen, considers, as her subtitle plainly states, "What a Medieval Badge Can Tell Us about Translation in the Middle Ages." Exploring one important example of medieval pilgrimage badges, small tokens collected as souvenirs by Christian pilgrims, Rasmussen reminds us of a long-ago world where multilingualism was the rule, not the exception and in which various forms of translation—between languages, across media, and of relics from site to site—incorporated a polyglot world within a larger Christological body, itself the key figure of making the word flesh. Both Andrea Bachner and Barbara Kosta urge us to reconsider media that have in a century privileging the visual or pictorial often either been underemphasized (for Bachner, the sonic) or debased (for Kosta, the film subtitle). Bachner's essay, "Between the Visual and the Sonic: Rewriting Rilke's 'Ur-Geräusch,'" traces the notion of the corporeal inscription of a primary, ineffable sound by means of a "reverse" gramophone in Rilke (1919) and via the influential work on media and technology by Kittler to contemporary works by poet Durs Grünbein and novelist Marcel Beyer that foreground the traces of technology on stubbornly resistant, even victimized bodies. Rather than translation being a medium, Bachner reminds us, it is helpful to consider media themselves as translations, and in the case of inscription, to read it as a hybrid of matter and word. Barbara Kosta, in "Translating Lola: Multiple Language Versions of *The Blue Angel* and Subtitles," turns to a film that was originally an example of a genuinely multilingual, transnational art work (produced in 1930 in both a German and an English-language version), but that was subsequently released internationally in at least three English subtitled versions. These subtitled releases highlight the pitfalls and opportunities for film subtitling in either smoothing out and containing the original German (a dubious model of "fidelity," in Kosta's reading), or in bringing to the fore the essential foreignness of the film as untranslatable "other" to the ostensibly sutured viewer. Bachner is quick to remind us that the digital age seems to reduce the distance between media, turning everything—the visual, the sonic, the textual—into input and output, but thereby also to open the possibility of overcoming essentialist understandings of media. In "Five Maps of Translations of Shakespeare," Tom Cheesman and his colleagues emphasize the potential of digital humanities tools to render literary translation still more complex and differentiated, not less: by analyzing two lines from *Othello*, for example, across different periods and translations (including no fewer than thirty-five in German), it becomes possible to map out translations as consensus, versus idiosyncratic translations and to explore to what extent distinctiveness is produced by the source text or by the translating culture.

The dual semantic character of both *translation* and *Übersetzung*, each of which refers simultaneously to linguistic and spatial phenomena, lends itself especially well to poetic manipulation and finds unique expression in the work of Yoko Tawada. Alone in the title of her book *Überseezungen* (2002), a neologism that suggests both "tongues abroad" (*Übersee Zungen*) and "translations" (*Übersetzungen*), one glimpses the beginnings of a linguistic labyrinth paved by translation.

In part VI, "Translingual Travels," Leslie Adelson and Bettina Brandt track the lingual and spatial metaphorics of translation in two of Tawada's texts, *Das nackte Auge* (2004) and "Zungentanz" (in *Überseezungen*), by examining Tawada's treatment of movement and travel. In "Rusty Rails and Parallel Tracks: *Trans-latio* in Yoko Tawada's *Das nackte Auge* (2004)," Adelson focuses on the complex resonances of the rusty rail in Tawada's novel, *Das nackte Auge*, in order to explore the formal modes in which Tawada figures the network of translation, travel, and transformation. Asserting by the end of her chapter that Tawada's parallel tracks do not merely engage Benjamin's famous reference to what is "zwischen den Zeilen," but rather that they constitute a translation of it in their own right, Adelson demonstrates the manner in which translation often operates between the lines. Brandt, in her essay "Yoko Tawada's 'Tongue Dance,' or the Failed Domestication of a Tongue in Furs," analyzes what Tawada calls a *Wortknäuel*, or word knot, in an effort to unfurl an interpretive map to Tawada's "Zungentanz." Focusing her attention on lexical and metaphorical transformations in "Zungentanz," Brandt shows that word knots in the text reference famous psychoanalytic texts by Freud and Sacher- Masoch, while arguing that the narrator, a personified tongue, remains in the end an untamed, undomesticated speaker, despite various attempts to correct her speech.

Notes

1. Charles Bernstein, *Shadowtime* (Copenhagen: Green Integer Books, 2005), 102.

2. Tim Parks, "The Dull New Global Novel," *New York Review of Books Blog* (February 9, 2010), http://www.nybooks.com/blogs/nyrblog/2010/feb/09/the-dull-new-global-novel/.

3. Dante Alighieri, *The Inferno of Dante Alighieri*, trans. Ciaran Carson (New York: New York Review of Books, 2004), 290.

4. Ibid.

5. Esther Allen and Susan Bernofsky, "Introduction: A Culture of Translation," in *In Translation: Translators on Their Work and What It Means*, ed. Esther Allen and Susan Bernofsky (New York: Columbia University Press, 2013), xiv.

6. Matthew Reynolds, "Jamming up the Flax Machine," *London Review of Books* 25, no. 9 (May 8, 2003): 31–32.

7. Ibid.

8. Charles Homer Haskins, *The Renaissance of the Twelfth Century* (New York: New American Library, 1955).

9. A. G. Coldiron, *Canon, Period, and the Poetry of Charles of Orleans: Found in Translation* (Ann Arbor: University of Michigan Press, 2000).

10. Doris Bachmann-Medick, ed., *Translation Studies*. 2, no. 1 (2009); Lawrence Venuti, *The Translator's Invisibility: A History of Translation* (New York: Routledge, 1995); Azade Seyhan, *Writing Outside the Nation* (Princeton, N.J.: Princeton University Press, 2001).

11. Emily Apter, "On Translation in a Global Market," *Public Culture* 13, no. 1 (Winter 2001): 1–12, here 3.

12. Rebecca Walkowitz, "The Location of Literature: The Transnational Book and the Migrant Writer," *Contemporary Literature*, 47, no. 4 (Winter 2006): 527–45; Rebecca Walkowitz, "Unimaginable Largeness: Kazuo Ishiguro, Translation, and the New World Literature," *Novel* 40, no. 3 (Summer 2007): 216–39.

13. Barbara Cassin, ed., *Vocabulaire européen des philosophes: Dictionnaire des intraduisibles* (Paris: Seuil, 2004). The *Vocabulaire* has now also appeared in an English version under the guidance of Emily Apter. Other translations, such as Ukrainian, had already previously appeared. Cassin has also launched an extensive web platform for the *Vocabulaire* at http://intraduisibles.org/. She imagines a key audience for the *Vocabulaire* to be Anglo-American analytical philosophers. The project had been conceived, she explained, to rescue Derridean language theory from remaining an exclusive enclave of comparative literature: "C'est là une vraie différence avec la philosophie analytique anglo-saxonne qui suppose que Derrida n'est pas un philosophe et qu'il peut tout juste enseigner dans les départements de littérature comparée. Dans ce Dictionnaire, nous voulons voir ce que cela change de philosopher en langues (soulignons le s), en étant donc conscients qu'on emploie des mots et pas seulement des concepts." (This is a genuine difference with Anglo-American analytical philosophy, which does not hold Derrida to be a philosopher and believes he can teach only in departments of comparative literature. In the *Dictionnaire* we want to see what happens if one philosophizes in languages (stressing the plural), with the awareness that words are being used, not just concepts." The full text of the 2006 interview with Cassin is available at http://www.revue- texto.net/Dialogues/Cassin_interview.html#[1].)

Cassin's introduction to the *Vocabulaire* underscores the same point, suggesting that the twin ideas of language as a neutral tool and of the possibility of transparent translation are deeply grounded in English empiricism: "Toute la tradition anglo-saxonne s'est attachée à ne pas jargonner, à refuser le langage ésotérique, à dégonfler les baudruches de la métaphysique: l'anglais se présente, cette fois dans sa singularité de langue, comme celle du *common sense* et de l'expérience commune, y compris l'expérience commune de la langue. L'angélisme du rationnel et le militantisme du langage ordinaire se rejoignent pour étayer une prévalence de l'anglais, qui se traduit, dans le pire des cas, par le déni du statut de philosophie à cette philosophie continentale engluée dans les contingences de l'histoire et des langues." (The entire Anglo-American tradition is concerned with avoiding jargon, refusing esoteric language, debunking empty metaphysical theory: the English language presents itself, this time in its linguistic singularity, as the language of common sense and of common experience, including the common experience of language. The idealization of the rational and the militancy of ordinary language join together to spread the dominance of English, which results, in the worst case, in denying the status of philosophy to Continental philosophy caught up in the contingencies of history and languages.) (http://intraduisibles.org/index.php?option=com_content&view=article&id=95&Itemid=2&lang=en).

14. Emily Apter, *The Translation Zone: A New Comparative Literature* (Princeton, N.J.: Princeton University Press, 2006), 6.

15. Emily Apter, "Untranslatables: A World System," *New Literary History* 39, no. 3 (Summer 2008): 581–98, here 584.

16. Lawrence Venuti, "Translation, Empiricism, Ethics," *Profession* (2010): 72–81.

17. Gayatri Spivak, *Death of a Discipline* (New York: Columbia University Press, 2003).

18. *The 2014–15 Report on the State of the Discipline of Comparative Literature. Ideas of the Decade.* http://stateofthediscipline.acla.org/entry/untranslatability.

19. Emily Apter, *Against World Literature: On the Politics of Untranslatability* (New York: Verso, 2013).

20. Ibid., 18.

21. Ibid., 36.

22. André Lefevere, *Translating Literature: The German Tradition from Luther to Rosenzweig* (Assen: Van Gorcum, 1977), 1. See also Andreas Huyssen, cited in this context in Lefevere: "Schleiermacher's investigations into hermeneutics and Humboldt's interpretation of understanding are the basis of the whole modern theory of translation, even though this is very seldom so clearly stated" (1).

23. Armin Paul Frank, "Main Concepts of Translating: Transformations during the Enlightenment and Romantic periods in France, Great Britain, and the German Countries," in *Übersetzung = Translation = Traduction*, ed. Harald Kittel et al., vol. 2 (Berlin: de Gruyter, 2007), 1531–1609; here, 1535–36.

24. Theodor Adorno, "Wörter aus der Fremde," *Noten zur Literatur*, ed. Rolf Tiedemann et al. (Frankfurt am Main: Suhrkamp, 1974), 216–32.

25. Harald Weinrich, "Chamisso, Chamisso Authors, and Globalization," trans. Jane and Marshall Brown, *PMLA* 119, no. 5 (October 2004): 1336–46.

26. We refer here to the "Weimar poet" to return Goethe, following Pizer's useful work, to his local context. John Pizer, *The Idea of World Literature: History and Pedagogical Practice* (Baton Rouge: Louisiana State University Press, 2006).

27. Johann Wolfgang von Goethe, *Noten und Abhandlungen: Zu besserem Verständnis des west-östlichen Divans*, in *Werke*, vol. 2, *Gedichte und Epen II*, ed. Erich Trunz (Hamburger Ausgabe) (Munich: DTV, 2000), 126–267, here, 258.

28. Walter Benjamin, "Die Aufgabe des Übersetzers," in *Gesammelte Schriften*, vol. 4.1 (Frankfurt am Main: Suhrkamp, 1972), 9–21.

29. Ibid., 20.

30. See, in particular, that journal's second issue (2009), edited by volume contributor Doris Bachmann-Medick.

31. Cassin, "Introduction," *Vocabulaire*.

32. For discussion of the widespread early modern anxiety about translation, imitation, and cultural identity, see Bethany Wiggin, *Novel Translations: The European Novel and the German Book* (Ithaca, N.Y.: Cornell University Press, 2011), 24–57.

33. Frank, "Main Concepts of Translating," 1575–76.

34. We use the term "national literature" in order to reflect (1) the significance that Milton gave to English as a language of literature and the extent to which his use of unrhymed iambic pentameter was designed to help English find its way back to more exalted and refined expression, and (2) the national significance of the epic form in the vernacular and historical-political context of social and governmental upheaval in Milton's England.

35. Johann Jakob Bodmer, *Johann Miltons verlohrnes Paradies: Ein Episches Gedicht in zwölf Gesängen: Neu überarbeitet, und durchgehends mit Anmerkungen von dem Uebersezer und verschiednen andern Verfassern* (Zurich: Conrad Orell, 1754), preface to the second volume, 23.

36. Frank, "Main Concepts of Translating," 1588.

37. Martin Luther, *D. Martin Luthers Werke, Kritische Gesamtausgabe*, vol. 30, part 2 (Weimar: Hermann Böhlaus Nachfolger, 1909), 636.

38. Novalis (Friedrich von Hardenburg), "Die Christenheit, oder Europa," in *Novalis: Schriften, Die Werke Friedrich von Hardenbergs*, ed. Paul Kluckhohn and Richard Samuel, vol. 1 (Stuttgart: Kohlhammer, 1960-), 512.

39. Ibid.

40. Ibid., 513.

41. Frank, "Main Concepts of Translating," 1596.

42. Translation Frank, "Main Concepts of Translating," 1600.

43. Translation Frank, "Main Concepts of Translating," 1600.

44. Ibid., 1600–1603.

45. Ibid., 1596–97.

46. Apter, "Untranslatables: A World System," 584.

47. Greg Carr, "Translation, Recovery, and 'Ethnic' Archives of Africana: Inscribing Meaning beyond Otherness," *PMLA* 127, no. 2 (March 2012): 360–64, here 361.

48. See chapter 3 in this volume.

49. See chapter 4 in this volume.

50. Ibid.

51. Lydia H. Liu as quoted in Rey Chow, "Translator, Traitor; Translator, Mourner (or, Dreaming of Intercultural Equivalence), *New Literary History* 39, no. 3 (Summer 2008): 565–80, here 570.

52. Yasemin Yildiz, *Beyond the Mother Tongue: The Postmonolingual Condition* (New York: Fordham University Press, 2012).

53. See chapter 7 in this volume.

54. See W. J. T. Mitchell, "Space and Time: Lessing's Laocoon and the Politics of Genre," in his *Iconology: Image, Text, Ideology* (Chicago: University of Chicago Press, 1986), 95–115, for a pertinent reading of the hierarchies implied in the apparently complementary structure set up by Lessing.

55. Clemens Brentano, *Godwi oder das steinerne Bild der Mutter*, in *Werke*, vol. 2, ed. Friedhelm Kemp (Munich: Carl Hanser, 1963), 96–97.

Part I

Untranslatable Maps

Chapter 1

Translation in a Globalizing World

Impulses of a Translational Turn in Literary Studies and the Study of Culture

Doris Bachmann-Medick

When Pepsi Cola tried to expand its market into China, it used the same slogan from its American advertising campaign, proclaiming: "Pepsi brings you back to life!"[1] But the Chinese translation came out differently. It read: "Pepsi brings your ancestors back from the dead!" No wonder Pepsi's market success in China at first was low to nil—with such a blundering intrusion of commercial thinking into the area of cultural traditions that also involved ancestor worship.

What do we learn from this example, so widely used to illustrate possible traps in cross-cultural translation? It teaches us, first, that translations in the context of a globalizing society can have a massive impact in the sphere of manufactured goods and consumption. Even globally known products must adjust to the local conditions if they are to find acceptance, and they must be tailored according to the prevailing cultural contexts. It teaches us, second, that global processes of cultural translation in the sense of localizations become questionable as a result of their one-sidedly Western control. When translation in a worldwide context (and even the translation of global icons) occurs between dissimilar societies and cultural traditions, and with a disregard for the differences and inequalities involved, gaps and misunderstandings become unavoidable. Beyond that: these breakdowns reveal important potentials of such cultural differences—for translations between cultures can challenge us not only to be aware of those differences but also to accept and acknowledge them and even to make them productive. For cross-cultural marketing and comparative management this has long been a well-known insight.[2] But it can also give rise to a critical mode of interculturality that could serve the criticism of such strategies of commercialization and marketing—and it is precisely on this point that the past and current discourse on interculturality reveals its narrow, blinkered focus.

"Translation" is an activity that, as *Über-setzung* suggests, involves a process akin to "transporting" one culture's "goods," as if by bridge or ferry boat, across a divide to another country or culture. But it is rather not in this specific sense that the perspective on "translation" in globalizing contexts which I am offering here is meant. Instead, I try to look beyond the boundaries of the current discourse on interculturality. It is precisely not the metaphor of "bridge building" between cultures, still much in vogue, which is addressed here. This fosters a tendency to cover up, conceal, or jump all too easily over those gaps, barriers, differences, and misunderstandings that have an effect on cultural encounter. This harmonizing notion simply equates *cultural translation* with *cultural understanding*. Nevertheless it appears to be a basic principle in the area of cultural and educational policy—from the UN proclamation of 2001 as a "Year of Dialogue among Civilizations," to the Global Agenda on the Dialogue among Civilizations (UN 2001), to the 2nd World Forum on Intercultural Dialogue in Baku in 2013.

Yet we are living in today's evolving world society with its increasing ethnic and religious conflicts, its separatist secessions, and its bellicose assertions of independence—and this compels us to focus our attention not primarily on cultural diversity or common universal values, but precisely on what separates and divides us. In any case, the traditional understanding of translation as a bridge between cultures, as a medium of cultural understanding and cultural communication, has long since ceased to serve its purpose. This is the opening thesis for my argument. For do we not require a conception of translation that is much more focused on differences, on ruptures and frictions, not least in the field of interreligious conflicts and tensions of social integration? It is true, differences have been a point of explicit emphasis in the analyses by political scientist Samuel Huntington, who claimed that a "clash of civilizations" is unavoidable in current and future world politics.[3] Yet Huntington's understanding of culture is patently not *translative*. Rather, he conceived of cultures as cages in which, for example, the essence of Islam is rigidly defined, codified, and bound to immutable traditions.

By contrast, understanding culture as translation could put forward a translational concept of cultural differences. This could motivate us to seek out and consider the overlapping within and between cultures; it could dissuade us from focusing on differences as essentialized defining characteristics and encourage us instead to see them as negotiable and translatable. Yet that too raises questions: (1) On what understanding of translation is this conception of culture based? (2) What body of workable concepts do we need in order to develop a critical concept of translation in today's world society?

Since the 1980s, translation studies has undergone a "cultural turn"[4] that today is finding an amazing degree of resonance in the social sciences and the study of culture. Thus translation has long since ceased to be confined to the conversion of languages and texts, and instead is being expanded and extended to deal with questions of cultural translation as a social practice in the context of the "cultural encounter."[5] Of course, this "shift" in focus from text relations to connections of life requires from the outset that well-known categories of literary translation—such as "original" and "representation," "equivalence" between texts and "fidelity" to the text—have to be augmented or even replaced through new guiding principles and categories of cultural translation—such as cultural representation and transformation, foreignness and alterity, displacement, cultural differences, and power. Translation is ever more emphatically becoming an indispensable practice or cultural technique in a globalizing society, as well as a far-reaching analytical category of the humanities and the social sciences.

Yet is this translation perspective not thwarted by the immense worldwide inequality and hierarchy of languages? Translation alone clearly reveals that, a far cry from situations of egalitarian communication, hierarchical relationships of languages prevail here—and the resulting marginalization of many languages creates situations of interaction and transference that are characterized by asymmetries of far-reaching impact. The basic operation of translation in world society should take precisely this inequality of languages into account. It has to confront the global hierarchy that prevails between speech and writing, between orality and literacy—and with it the power gap that exists between the first and the third worlds. The more than 6,000 languages listed in UNESCO's "Index Translationum," its register of books translated in the world, all have more or less, but usually less, a chance of gaining any recognition on the translation market, even though their existence is guaranteed by the "Universal Declaration of Linguistic Rights."

To this translation market's hegemonic structure, then, something in the way of a supporting and perpetuating impetus is imparted simply by the tendency of commodity markets to expand and dominate. Thus in the consumer sector in particular everything always appears to have been already translated, since it has been distributed and integrated everywhere the world over (for example, brand names like McDonalds, Coca Cola, Adidas). Even simply the recurrence, interconnection, and circulation of symbols and meanings, even their dissemination through the media, give rise to the production of predominantly linear and, in principle, infinite chains of translation: translation without an original or, as sociologist Armin Nassehi called it, "perennial translation."[6]

In addition, the globalization of economic connections is producing a flourishing translation industry—as we know it, for example, in mostly miserable but massively widespread Internet-translation programs. Here, translation software is supposed to enable the smooth translation of global products: their unimpeded adaptation to conditions guaranteeing local acceptance throughout the world. Yet such a language transfer in the global digital information sphere more often tends to function merely to serve and to facilitate the sale and distribution of goods. And, as the fate of Pepsi-Cola in China demonstrates, such language transfer often ends stranded between the two "poles" or "towers" of the so-called translation "bridge." This ineffectual interpolar position I find to be a characteristic result of the globalization-oriented type of translation prevalent in world society today. But translation as a multipolar process negotiating and mediating critically between cultural positions with the goal of mutual cultural transformations and interventions I see as quite a different matter.

The study of culture in an increasingly transnational context fosters a concept of translation as a multipolar and many-voiced process of dealing with differences. Such a concept focuses our attention more acutely on cultural factors that resist global translation and being translated at all—factors that reside in culture-specific practices and local reluctance to accept change from outside. Homi Bhabha puts it as follows: "Any transnational cultural study must 'translate,' each time locally and specifically, what decenters and subverts this transnational globality, so that it does not become enthralled by the new global technologies of ideological transmission and cultural consumption."[7] Thus translation could provide a more subtle approach to the distribution of "global "commodities and "universal" concepts or theories, even to the phenomenon of "globalization" itself. Michael Cronin's formula "globalization as translation"[8] refers to the decentering of global processes, since globalization is not experienced everywhere in the world in the same way at the same time; rather, individual elements of the global economy are in each case translated into a variety of local contexts and governing factors. The process by which they are adopted is expanded to include, in addition to languages and texts, the broad spectrum of diverse cultural practices, institutions, and judicial and political systems as objects, units, and agents of translating culture. This would provide a possible point of departure for countering the threat of regional decision-making and responsibility that is the other side of the globalization coin.

Cross-cultural translation is thus more than a mere bridging of cultural differences. This insight is visualized in a painting by the Philippine artist Alfredo Esquillo, which is of special interest for this article as it reflects in an artistic way on the question of "Identities versus Globalization?"[9] (see figure 1.1). Global entanglements are illustrated here in the form of a translation bridge that is inflexible to the point of paralysis—an asymmetrical bridge with a main axis reflecting and expressing the worldwide imbalance of power. And above all, individual cultures and societies are no longer able to steer their own course; they are trapped and held fast in the network. So while all the various cultures and societies are in the same boat, each is trapped in half a boat. The hope that translation bridges might create a community of equals proves to be an illusion; the attempt at it was doomed to end in half-measures, mutual obstruction and cross-purposes, paralysis, and loss. Esquillo's inspiration for this painting, entitled *Modus Operandi*, was a statement regarding alternatives to economic globalization, namely "Would it be better to be interconnected but halved, or unconnected but whole?"[10] Yet we must ask if this is really a constructive alternative. Even in the face of

Figure 1.1. Alfredo Esquillo, *Modus Operandi*. 2003. Oil on canvas, 122 × 183 cm. Courtesy of Heinrich-Böll-Stiftung.

global networks it could be more beneficial to abandon the obsession with the model of bridging (and thus eliminating) local and regional differences altogether in favor of translations that would foster dynamic processes of negotiation—thus enabling individual societies, even though they are caught up in global networks, to experience, rather than just losses and limitations in developing a culture of their own, an increase in local possibilities of adoption and even intervention.

In any case, translation is becoming a decisive category for a globalizing world and its analysis—not only by encouraging cultural independence and resistance. Besides that, translation can offer a counter-model to a cultural principle that is widespread today, namely that of the predominance of "immediacy"—a concept clearly evident in new communication technologies such as cellular telephones, which, by minimizing transmission time and with their universal access and availability, aim to avoid any delaying "interim" phase. According to sociologist John Tomlinson, the central idea of such "immediacy" is that it renders redundant any mediating steps and thus, in turn, renders translation invisible, bypassing it with this notion of immediacy without mediators, implicitly eliding it with promises of immediate access to information and consumer goods.[11]

Thus in the transnational, global context, "translation" must first of all be made visible again by making it as a specific cultural practice, like a thorn in the side, into the all too facile and efficient networking trends of worldwide communication. For ultimately translation does not involve only simple "transfers," but rather mutual "transformations" that are highly complex. These transformations have not just two poles, the original and the translation. Rather, they evolve as a multipolar process in an "in-between" zone beyond mere dichotomies. The category of translation is bound up with a conceptual incentive that far transcends sweeping general notions of translating culture: mediacy, mediating activity, situations of transition, determining frames of reference, and, above all, *power* in intercultural communication. These are all concepts that require closer consideration—not to mention as well nonverbal elements such as gestures, gazes, and odors as components of the cultural encounter that might either foster or block contact.

How does this all affect cultural theory? As we know, recent cultural theory has become caught up in a positive reevaluation of all possible contexts and aspects of "interstitial spaces," and in doing so it is turning away from the notion of immutable boundaries and rigidly defined and essentialized identities—turning against binary modes of perception and dichotomous divisions ("we versus the others," for example, or "the own versus the foreign"). Yet such positive reassessment of the interstitial, of the "in-between," should not be devoted entirely merely to finding new, consciousness-raising positions. For in fact, "in-between" spaces should also be made concrete and relevant to interactions by being seen as "translation spaces": spaces for the shaping of relations, for the elaboration of situations and interactions through actual, concrete translation processes.

Making translation visible would amount to an attempt to reassess what has remained until now only a conceptual understanding of culture. With his metaphorical conception of "culture as translation" Homi Bhabha blazed a distinct trail by imparting a dynamic thrust to the exceptionally durable holistic concept of culture in the tradition of Clifford Geertz, making culture appear more than ever as an expression or product of translation processes. His phrase "Culture . . . is both transnational and translational"[12] is more than just a play on words. It makes culture a relationship born of multilayered phenomena of overlapping and transmitting where culture is no longer considered as an "original" and special sphere of life, but rather as a "hybrid," impure, mixed layering of experiences and meanings.

Conflicts and tensions in the area of migration and exile initiated these doubts and critical questionings of the notion of culture as a closed and authoritative meaningful system of fixed traditions and identities. But the phrase "culture as translation" is doomed to remain merely an anti-essentialist metaphor unless we can show more precisely how culture functions indeed as an expression or product of concrete translation processes—the study of culture and the social sciences are only now starting to investigate these specific translational activities. Of course, research in the sociology of worldwide migration processes has undertaken initial steps towards a redefinition of migration, namely as an ongoing process of transformation that conceives of the identity formation of migrants as the result of repeatedly recurring acts of self-translation. In *The Turbulence of Migration*, Nikos Papastergiadis applies the category of translation in the context of the social sciences in order to describe processes of migration more accurately—and this not merely with reference to the integration structures prevailing in so-called multicultural societies but with reference to processes of self-translation.[13] He asks, "How do concepts like deterritorialization, translation, recognition and hybridity expand our understanding of identity and culture in plural societies?"[14]

From such a perspective we are able to extend the category of translation beyond the realm of linguistic representation and into the realm of practical, social hermeneutics. Here translation is understood "as itself a constitutive element of social action or praxis (instead of translation as representation and metadiscourse)."[15] In fact, it takes place not between texts and languages, but between individuals, thoughts, practices, and ways of life. In this sense, the sociologist and anthropologist Martin Fuchs has used the example of India to show how in that country's multicultural society it is possible to mark out translation spaces that are filled with social translation conflicts and interreligious tensions. He thus has examined the self-articulation of "untouchables" as translation procedures: the discourse of resistance of the "Dalit movement" relies, as Fuchs sees it, upon attempts to translate. The social concerns and demands of the "untouchables" must be translated by the Dalits themselves into a kind of "third idiom": into the socio-ethical offerings of universalist religions and above all into the secular language of the law. For only in that context can their demands for social equality and rights find recognition and acknowledgment, only there do those demands become negotiable. It is this translation into a "third idiom" or a "frame of reference" (in this case Buddhism), which has the power "to replace the prevalent dominant language or ideology, using as an alternative platform not one's own local idiom but an idiom that transcends the two conflicted sides or discourses."[16] A sociological study like this one attuned to acts of translation does not merely assert "from above" and from an analytical perspective the existence of counter-discourses within a culture. Instead, through precise investigative analysis of relational social processes, it provides access to pivots for self-organized intervention and negotiation between the differing—and in this case also religiously divergent—group discourses, movements, and individuals.

This example is revealing for a central insight of cultural anthropology and postcolonialism: translations enrich the cultural dynamic only when they address differences, struggles about meaning, misunderstandings, and elements that even resist translation instead of falling back from the start on (harmonizing) bridges of cultural understanding. This insight ultimately lays the groundwork for whole new areas of application for the category of translation—for topics such as "war and translation,"[17] "violence and translation,"[18] "translation and conflict,"[19] "gay in translation,"[20] "global news in translation,"[21] "translating revolution,"[22] and so on.

The conventional success-model of translation ends in a cul de sac when dealing with such (political, conflict-laden) areas of translation. What is needed instead is a model for translating that makes a point of dealing with gaps, barriers, and erroneous translations—if only because global intercourse and interaction have developed multi-branched and multifaceted translation complexes that shift back and forth in a multilayered fashion between practice, text, and representation. Such translation complexes militate against the widespread misunderstanding of "hybridity" as a "mixing" of cultures—for clearly if everything were indeed "mixed," then nothing would need translating. Instead, hybridity should be understood as a sphere of interaction in which shifts or even ruptures between different contexts and therefore translation processes are occurring and ongoing, rather than as a sphere in which mixing and blending have already been achieved. Processes of mediation, alienation, and the formation of differences, likewise areas of interpretation and translation—these are factors whose impact, though all too easily overlooked or suppressed, should be integrated into the equation in the analysis of intercultural relations.

The widespread currency today of a translational perspective on culture is especially evident in the area of aesthetic representations. In particular in the new World Literature, in non-European literatures of the world as well as in contemporary postcolonial writing, cultural contacts are presented specifically as scenarios of interactive translation. Salman Rushdie is one of several "postcolonial" authors who in their literary work take up and reflect on contemporary categories of cultural theory such as hybridity, globalization, translation, and migration. Novels like Rushdie's *The Ground Beneath Her Feet* are revelatory as to the way translation is experienced by its subjects as an intensely existential process. In this, "our migrant century," says the narrator in Rushdie's novel, we have "entered a transit zone: the condition of transformation."[23] In the novel, the rock singers Ormus Cama and Vina Aspara experience their migration as a complex process of translation, as a continuous and ongoing transformation fraught with leeways of liminality, stages of transition, and irritating frustrations. Both figures leave India and emigrate, by way of Britain, to America. During the flight from Bombay to the United States, Ormus, Vina and the other migrants are passing "through the membrane"[24] of air resistance, through "a stretchy translucent membrane across the sky, an ectoplasmic barrier, a Wall"[25] or an "unseen frontier"[26] between cultures, knowing that the "person who arrives won't be the one who left"[27]—a telling image of translation as a resistance-laden, transformatory act. No talk of "cultural understanding" here; instead it is shock, displacement, and transformation through a process of overlayering and juxtaposition that is pointed out as a characteristic of migration. In these "transition zones" of transformation, translating becomes an essential part of a fight for survival within the conflict of cultural allegiances, meanings, and demands. "Translated men," as Rushdie calls them,[28] these men or women transported from one culture into another are translated but nevertheless develop their own active modes of "translating themselves."

In this way, the novel fosters a cultural anthropology of translation, precisely by emphasizing the multipolarity of translation processes. The singer Ormus embodies the ambivalent transformations born of "displacement," and this is also expressed in his music. In this way, the tradition of oriental music is translated into worldwide American pop music—and vice versa—which leads to the astonishing insight "that the West was in Bombay from the beginning, impure old Bombay where West, East, North and South had always been scrambled like codes, like eggs, and so Westernness was a legitimate part of Ormus, a Bombay part, inseparable from the rest of him."[29] This multipolarity of translation emerges here as a potentially divisive multiplicity of interpretations and versions, resulting in the insight that "America is no longer the sole owner of rock 'n' roll"[30] and that American music should open itself up for such "un-American sounds."[31] Whether as a result of cultural displacement or of the experience of fragmented spheres of life, the polyphony of translating back and forth in no way produces a harmonious hybridity, but rather faults in personality or identity resulting from migration. In the novel they are given explicitly *seismographic* expression by the metaphor and reality of an earthquake—thus triggering an irritating but stimulating "shock" rather than a cumulative process of "cultural understanding." And still this entails not so much destruction as it gives a creative, transforming impulse—thus not loss (as in the "bridge" painting), but more a gain born of translation.

Critical translation in a world society is often prefigured in literature, especially in contemporary postcolonial literature. It often involves a rewriting of European classics such as those by Shakespeare and Defoe from a postcolonial perspective and a repositioning with regard to its colonialist complexities. But there also exist visual examples of rewriting, which can be analyzed as translations, as visual translations or visual deconstructions and transformations. This applies for example to a significant rewriting of a European national image by the Nigerian-English installation artist Yinka Shonibare, to his translation of an English painting of 1750 into a hybrid installation in 1998 (see figure 1.3). In it, Shonibare recasts Thomas Gainsborough's painting of an aristocratic couple in an idyllic setting of a noble country estate (figure 1.2) as *Mr. and Mrs. Andrews without their Heads*. The allusions to the French Revolution's guillotine are impossible to ignore here, the postcolonial author thus beheading the symbolic protagonists of British colonialism, tearing them out of their pastoral context, displacing them in African garments, and through such translation highlighting the colonial inscriptions of the intertwined history of Europe and Africa—his rewriting thus functions as a redressing, as a literally refashioning of the European cultural tradition that uses subversive translation to reveal that tradition's deep structures of colonialist violence.[32]

Figure 1.2. Thomas Gainsborough, *Mr and Mrs Andrews*. About 1750. Oil on canvas, 69.8 × 119.4 cm. The National Gallery, London.

Should we call a rewriting like this "hybrid"? Or should we rather bring complex steps of translation to the fore? Certainly, the African garb is by no means an identity-making material of an "authentic" African counter-identity. On the contrary: these materials are mass-produced in African cities and, in a sense, already "translated." For in colonial times they were developed and distributed by the Dutch as South Asian batik materials, then imported to Africa by the British, and then adopted again in recent times: in the process of a redressing and refashioning of African cultures. Thus, culture as translation—but also in another respect: Mr. and Mrs. Andrews, beheaded and depersonalized, displaced from their national countryside. A picture like this has become a symbolic image for the critical possibility to isolate cultural signs from their roots in the traditions of a national culture. A similar critical detachment from the national landscape occurs, when the Nigerian author Chinua Achebe "back-translated" the River Thames to the prehistoric Congo River, which in Joseph Conrad's *Heart of Darkness* was contrasted as a historically significant and evocative river. Achebe's new translation of the Thames into an African landscape occurs as a displacement of this imperial river—by ironically referring to it, as if it were a "Professor Emeritus," as the "River Emeritus"[33] in which British culture and knowledge, along with its colonial tradition, have been sedimented.

With all this I have mentioned only a few examples for translation challenges in a globalizing world. But we must also ask: do these problem fields also entail what we might consider as significant impulses towards a new,

Figure 1.3. Yinka Shonibare, *Mr. and Mrs. Andrews without Their Heads*. 1998. Wax-print cotton costumes on mannequins, dog mannequin, painted metal bench, rifle, 165 × 635 × 254 cm with plinth. National Gallery of Canada, Ottawa, and VG Bild-Kunst, Bonn.

translation-oriented position of research in the study of culture? Is it possible with the category of translation to initiate a move towards a more comprehensive, embracing "translational turn" in the humanities and social sciences?[34] Can this reorientation towards the category of translation be constructively and effectively linked with the other current "turns" throughout various disciplines—with the interpretive, performative, and postcolonial turn, the spatial or iconic turn?[35] And at what point does the translation perspective actually become a "turn"?

In disciplines concerned with the study of culture, theory does not advance via the massive ruptures of "paradigms," but rather via eclectically coexisting "turns." Given this academic landscape, an expanded translation concept can only result in a "translational turn" if it moves through three stages which seem to characterize "turns" in general: (1) *Expansion* of the object or thematic field (in the case of translation: departing from its traditional areas of language and text and developing translation as a category reflecting a social and cultural practice); (2) *Metaphorization* (i.e., the formula "culture as translation"); and (3) *Methodological refinement,* provoking a conceptual and epistemological leap (developing translation—beyond a mere thematic field—as a new category of analysis that pervades all disciplines of the humanities in a way that alters the focus of research).

Only if "translation" is no longer restricted to a particular object of investigation but moves across disciplines as a methodologically reflected analytical category can we really speak of a "translational turn."[36] Of course, mere epistemological conditions are not enough. Rather, it is the indispensability of translation processes in contemporary globalizing world society that provides the springboard for a comprehensive "translational turn." Above all, if a more purposefully concentrated use is made of the methodological potential of the category of translation, then the awareness of the translational character of cultural-studies matters per se will grow—awareness of their non-holistic structure, of their hybrid and multilayered character. This will make it possible to approach complex universal phenomena such as modernization, industrialization, globalization, identity, culture, and interculturality with an eye especially for their translational structures and thus for their multilayered and intrinsically contradictory character. This kind of an operative "translational thinking" makes clear how dubious the supposed "purity" terms and concepts such as culture, identity, tradition, and religion have become.

Beyond this, "translational thinking" on this level of a breakup of established (generalizing or even universalizing) concepts is linked to the level of social practice; it is now bound up with the resolve to approach contacts, transitions, mixtures, transmissions, and so on with an eye to finding the factors and elements involving translations. It aims at using them to disrupt any all too smooth-looking processes of transmission and in that way it is breaking through to the level of cultural differences. This gives rise to an intensified awareness of gaps, barriers, or even instances of untranslatabililty[37]—to the point of acknowledging the heterogeneity of areas of discourse that exists even within one society, an increased awareness of initiatives of resistance, of subcultures, of parallel worlds, and the like. For this purpose, terms of translational investigation such as threshold, transition, boundary, and difference are certainly more revealing than concepts of wholeness such as identity, essence, and tradition.

One stimulating methodological impulse in this direction is already evident in the suggestion of cultural anthropologist James Clifford to consider the concepts of diaspora, migration, tourism, exile, and above all "travel" as comparative "translation terms"[38]—on the grounds, Clifford suggests, that cultural meanings and differences of meaning are not simply transposed or compared. Much as is the case with "traveling concepts,"[39] already it could be possible instead to break with a restricted application of a history of concepts within the European tradition (one example of this being the transformation—rather than mere adoption—of Western concepts in the modernization process of non-European societies).[40] Practices of "displacement," of mediation and dislocation would appear as central for such concept translations.

Intensified attention to "traveling concepts" in the study of culture reveals how the translation perspective also entails a redefinition of interdisciplinarity. But in contrast to the more "leveling" category of interdisciplinarity, the translation category makes it possible to focus more directly on differences, tensions, conflicts as points of departure—including those between different disciplines and research approaches. This enables a deeper and more exact grasp of the "contact zones" (Mary Louise Pratt) between disciplines and approaches.[41] Ultimately these contact zones are especially fruitful for a "trans-lation"—that is, to take up again the German term, "Über-Setzung" in its more literal sense as "transporting" or "carrying across a gap or divide": this kind of cross-disciplinary trans-lation is far-reaching as it envisages transformations of scientific concepts, their reformulation in other genres, in other systems of concepts, and in other contexts—as, for example, in the elaboration of scientific ideas in literature, or in the analysis of emotions in neurobiology. The current debate between neurological researchers and humanities specialists about concepts like "consciousness" and "free will" is an important field for the attempt to translate between disciplines and their separate idioms and systems of concepts.

In addition to interdisciplinarity, intercultural and transnational approaches too could be essentially redefined by using the category of translation. A "translational turn" broadens the horizon to enable a transnational conception of the study of culture and the humanities—not least by illuminating the active role of translation, or rather untranslatabilities, between different knowledge cultures and research systems. In any case, it might be considered to what extent a transcultural and culture-comparative approach benefits from the potential of the translation category.[42] Here I am thinking in particular of the most recent initiatives of a transnational approach to historical studies that turns away from the notion of "the West and the rest" in order to direct attention instead to the "entangled histories" and "connected histories" between Europe and the non-European world.[43] Of course, this kind of historical research that is no longer dominated only by a European or Western perspective requires a more emphatic questioning of its own categories of analysis and an explicit translational approach.[44] In this context a foundational question has been posed: "Which language and which concepts do we need for writing transnational, and even more so, transcultural history?"[45] Thus the impulses towards a "translational turn" could foster the insight that one's own categories of investigation are not neutral and universal (though they are claimed to be), but rather shaped from the outset by the specific cognitive approaches and conceptual standards of Western science.

On this point, Dipesh Chakrabarty's book *Provincializing Europe* proves to be extremely challenging.[46] Translation—says Chakrabarty—should operate not only cross-culturally but also "cross-categorically."[47] What does this mean? As a rule, the comparison of cultures uses reference points (*a tertium comparationis*), that, while universal, nevertheless remain Euro-centered. For example, we tend to compare categories such as religion, work, democracy, and so on and by doing so we inadvertently are still using universalizing Eurocentric terms of comparison. To find a way out of this dilemma, Chakrabarty suggests that we remain open for non-European categories of comparison: "The Hindi *pani* may be translated into the English 'water' without having to go through the superior positivity of H_2O."[48] We would have to suspend the concept of H_2O as a superior category of the Western knowledge system. For only a comparison that does not precipitously turn to universal "middle terms" (*tertium comparationis*) can sound out a common ground for a mutually balanced translation of culture. An example for this also is the concept of "power" and its use in the Japanese context: in Japan there are several expressions for power, depending on whether a quality, ability, or practice of action is involved.[49] Concerning the comparative study of a concept like democracy, a critical translational perspective could "enable us to compare the meanings that underlie 'democracy' and its rough equivalents around the world."[50] A translational approach here brings to the fore that "the cultural premises that infuse American practices and institutions may not be universal."[51]

Thus by working with the analytical category of translation, transcultural studies in the humanities could reach beyond accustomed comparative approaches: the translation perspective directs attention to deep structures of cultural comparisons in a way that can better come to terms with the complex interweaving of relations in an emerging world society. For in contrast to merely comparing cultures, the translation perspective fosters a much more direct access to the actual history of connections and the interactive processes, steps, and phases of intercultural contacts. It could even be developed still further so as to shed light on the active role of translation itself: on interaction, exchange, and reciprocity, as well as on resistances to translation or even untranslatabilities—not least on the active and indispensable role of translators and cultural brokers.

Yet the analysis of complex translation processes in a globalizing world would benefit from this only when translation perspectives in the social sciences and in the study of culture also come to terms with their own Western-oriented categories of analysis. Only then could it be revealed critically how highly questionable the claim of those categories to universal validity is.

Notes

1. I am grateful to Raleigh Whitinger for the translation of this chapter.

2. See Marieke de Mooij, *Global Marketing and Advertising: Understanding Cultural Paradoxes*, 3rd ed. (Thousand Oaks, Calif.: Sage, 2010).

3. Samuel P. Huntington, *The Clash of Civilizations and the Remaking of World Order*, rev. ed. (New York: Simon and Schuster, 2011).

4. See—among others such as Susan Bassnett and Lawrence Venuti—Mary Snell-Hornby, *The Turns of Translation Studies: New Paradigms or Shifting Viewpoints?* (Amsterdam: John Benjamins, 2006).

5. This expansion started to take place already within translation studies; see Lawrence Venuti, ed., *The Translation Studies Reader*, 3rd ed. (London: Routledge, 2012); Susan Bassnett and André Lefevere, eds., *Translation, History and Culture* (London: Pinter, 1990); Susan Bassnett, "The Translation Turn in Cultural Studies," in *Constructing Cultures: Essays on Literary Translation,* eds. Susan Bassnett and André Lefevere (Clevedon: Multilingual Matters, 1998), 123–40.

6. See Armin Nassehi, "Die 'Welt'-Fremdheit der Globalisierungsdebatte: Ein phänomenologischer Versuch," *Soziale Welt* 49 (1998): 151–66, here 159.

7. Homi K. Bhabha, *The Location of Culture* (London: Routledge, 1994), 241.

8. Michael Cronin, *Translation and Globalization* (London: Routledge, 2003), 34.

9. Compare the catalog of the exhibition by Jörg Löschmann, ed., *Identities versus Globalisation?* (Chiang Mai: Heinrich Böll Stiftung/Chotana Print, 2004), 24–27.

10. Alfredo Esquillo: *Modus Operandi*, in Löschmann, ed., *Identities versus Globalisation?*, 24.

11. See John Tomlinson, *The Culture of Speed: The Coming of Immediacy* (London: Sage, 2007).

12. Bhabha, *Location of Culture*, 172.

13. Nikos Papastergiadis, *The Turbulence of Migration: Globalization, Deterritorialization and Hybridity* (Cambridge: Polity, 2000); see also the debate on "Translation and Migration" in the forum of the journal *Translation Studies* 5, no. 3 (2012), 6, no. 1 (2013), 6, no. 3 (2013).

14. Papastergiadis, *Turbulence*, 4.

15. Martin Fuchs, "Reaching Out; or, Nobody Exists in One Context Only: Society as Translation," *Translation Studies* 2, no. 1 (2009): 21–40, here 25.

16. Ibid., 31.

17. On translation "as a matter of war and peace" and of "mistranslation in war," see Emily Apter, *The Translation Zone: A New Comparative Literature* (Princeton, N.J.: Princeton University Press, 2006), 3.

18. Compare Esperança Bielsa and Christopher W. Hughes, eds., *Globalization, Political Violence and Translation* (Basingstoke, Eng.: Palgrave Macmillan, 2009); Veena Das, "Violence and Translation," *Anthropological Quarterly* 75, no. 1 (2002): 105–12; see also Susan Bassnett, "Translating Terror," *Third World Quarterly* 26, no. 3 (2005): 393–403.

19. Mona Baker, *Translation and Conflict: A Narrative Account* (London: Routledge, 2006).

20. Keith Harvey, *Intercultural Movements: American Gay in French Translation* (Manchester: St. Jerome, 2003).

21. See Christina Schäffner and Susan Bassnett, eds., *Political Discourse, Media and Translation* (Newcastle: Cambridge Scholars Publishing, 2010); Esperança Bielsa and Susan Bassnett, *Translation in Global News* (London: Routledge, 2009).

22. Samia Mehrez, ed., *Translating Egypt's Revolution: The Language of Tahrir* (Cairo: American University in Cairo Press, 2012).

23. Salman Rushdie, *The Ground Beneath Her Feet: A Novel* (New York: Henry Holt, 1999), 461.

24. Ibid., 255.

25. Ibid., 253.

26. Ibid., 253.

27. Ibid., 253.

28. Compare Salman Rushdie, "Imaginary Homelands," in Rushdie, *Imaginary Homelands: Essays and Criticism 1981–91* (London: Granta, 1991), 9–21: "Having been borne across the world, we are translated men. It is normally supposed that something always gets lost in translation; I cling, obstinately, to the notion that something can also be gained" (17).

29. Rushdie, *Ground Beneath Her Feet*, 95–96.

30. Ibid., 378.

31. Ibid., 379.

32. Compare Nancy J. Hynes, "Yinka Shonibare: Re-dressing History," *African Arts* 34, no. 3 (2001): 60–65; John Picton, "Undressing Ethnicity—Yinka Shonibare," *African Arts* 34, no. 3 (2001): 65–73.

33. See Chinua Achebe, "An Image of Africa: Racism in Conrad's *Heart of Darkness*," in Joseph Conrad, *Heart of Darkness: An Authoritative Text, Backgrounds and Sources*, ed. Robert Kimbrough, 3rd ed. (New York: Norton, 1988), 251–62, here 252.

34. Compare Doris Bachmann-Medick, "The Translational Turn," *Translation Studies* (special issue: *The Translational Turn*, ed. Doris Bachmann-Medick) 2, no. 1 (2009): 2–16.

35. See Doris Bachmann-Medick, *Cultural Turns: Neuorientierungen in den Kulturwissenschaften*, 5th ed. (Reinbek: Rowohlt, 2014). Translated by Adam Blauhut as *Cultural Turns: New Orientations in the Study of Culture* (Berlin/Boston: De Gruyter, 2016); on the "translational turn," see 175–209.

36. See Doris Bachmann-Medick, "Translation—A Concept and Model for the Study of Culture," in *Travelling Concepts for the Study of Culture*, eds. Birgit Neumann and Ansgar Nünning (Berlin/Boston: De Gruyter, 2012), 23–43.

37. See Emily Apter, *Against World Literature: On the Politics of Untranslatability* (New York: Verso, 2013).

38. James Clifford, "Traveling Cultures," in his *Routes: Travel and Translation in the Late Twentieth Century* (Cambridge, Mass.: Harvard University Press, 1997), 17–46, esp. 39–40.

39. Concerning "traveling concepts" in general see Mieke Bal, *Travelling Concepts in the Humanities: A Rough Guide* (Toronto: University of Toronto Press, 2002); Edward W. Said, "Traveling Theory," in Said, *The World, the Text, and the Critic* (Cambridge, Mass.: Harvard University Press, 1983), 226–47; see also Clifford, Neumann and Nünning, cited in nn36 and 38 in this chapter.

40. See, for example, Douglas R. Howland, *Translating the West: Language and Political Reason in Nineteenth-Century Japan* (Honolulu: University of Hawai'i Press, 2002).

41. Concerning the practice of translation across disciplines and translation as a fruitful analytical category for a reconsideration of interdisciplinarity, see Gurminder K. Bhambra, ed., "Translations and the Challenge of Interdisciplinarity" (special issue of the *Journal of Historical Sociology*) 24, no. 1 (March 2011): 1–8.

42. See Doris Bachmann-Medick, ed., *The Trans/National Study of Culture: A Translational Perspective* (Berlin/Boston: De Gruyter, 2014).

43. See, among others, Shalini Randeria, "Entangled Histories of Uneven Modernities: Civil Society, Caste Councils, and Legal Pluralism in Postcolonial India," in *Comparative and Transnational History: Central European Approaches and New Perspectives,* eds. Heinz-Gerhard Haupt and Jürgen Kocka (New York: Berghahn Books, 2009), 77–104.

44. Compare Monica Juneja and Margrit Pernau, "Lost in Translation? Transcending Boundaries in Comparative History," in Haupt and Kocka, eds., *Comparative and Transnational History*, 105–29 (esp. the chapter "Translation and Representation," 112–15); see also Margrit Pernau, "Transnationale Geschichte und das Problem der universalen Begriffe: Muslimische Bürger im Delhi des 19. Jahrhunderts," in *Area Studies und die Welt: Weltregionen und neue Globalgeschichte,* ed. Birgit Schäbler (Vienna: Mandelbaum, 2007), 117–50.

45. See Juneja and Pernau, "Lost in Translation?," 106.

46. Dipesh Chakrabarty, *Provincializing Europe: Postcolonial Thought and Historical Difference* (Princeton, N.J.: Princeton University Press, 2000).

47. Dipesh Chakrabarty, "Two Models of Translation," in Chakrabarty, *Provincializing Europe*, 83–86, here 85.

48. Ibid., 83.

49. See Linus Hagström, "Ubiquity of 'Power' and the Advantage of Terminological Pluralism: Japan's Foreign Policy Discourse," in *Japanese Journal of Political Science* 6, no. 2 (2005): 145–64.

50. Frederic C. Schaffer, *Democracy in Translation: Understanding Politics in an Unfamiliar Culture* (Ithaca, N.Y.: Cornell University Press, 1998), 13.

51. Ibid., 14.

Chapter 2

Genealogies of Translation Theory

Schleiermacher and the Hermeneutic Model

Lawrence Venuti

The Structures of Translation Theory

Theoretical statements about the nature of translation from antiquity to the present display a basic structure that allows for a precise articulation of their assumptions and the implications of those assumptions, both conceptual and practical. This structure typically consists of one or more theoretical concepts linked to one or more linguistic strategies, so that the strategy is seen as a practical realization of the concept. The concepts fall into three broad categories which are interconnected and mutually defining: (1) the relative *autonomy* of the translated text, that is to say, whatever features or procedures distinguish it from the source text that it translates or from original compositions in general; (2) *equivalence*, or the relation of correspondence established between the source and translated texts; and (3) the *function* performed by the translation, which can range from the communication of information or the production of a particular response in the reader to an institutional or social impact with diverse consequences, cultural, economic, or political, among others.

Eugene Nida's concept of "dynamic equivalence," for instance, emphasizes the relation between the source and translated texts, but it construes that relation in functional terms, as producing a particular reader response. Thus dynamic equivalence is based on what Nida calls the "principle of equivalent effect," the notion that "the relationship between receptor and message should be substantially the same as that which existed between the original receptors and the message."[1] For Nida, dynamic equivalence is obtained through two linguistic strategies. It "aims at complete naturalness of expression," a homogeneity which the translator cultivates by avoiding nonstandard forms such as colloquialisms, archaisms, and jargon in favor of the current standard dialect, the most widely used and therefore the most familiar and seemingly "natural" form of the translating language.[2] Dynamic equivalence also involves cultural assimilation, in which the translator "tries to relate the receptor to modes of behavior relevant within the context of his own culture" by replacing "the cultural patterns of the source-language context" with those of the translating-language context.[3] Nida's example is J. B. Phillips's use of the phrase "with a hearty handshake all around" to render a greeting that St. Paul describes in his letter to the Romans with the phrase "Φιλήματι ἁγίῳ [*philemati agioi*]," or in a close version "with a holy kiss."[4]

Here we can see that the strategy through which dynamic equivalence is practically realized might more precisely be called discursive instead of simply linguistic insofar as it inscribes the source text with a specific discourse in the sense of a fairly coherent body of concepts. The cultural assimilation that produces dynamic equivalence rewrites the source text according to values, beliefs, and representations that are specific to the receiving culture. Phillips's choice replaced a greeting typical of an ancient Mediterranean culture, a kiss, with a greeting typical of the 1940s British culture in which he translated, a handshake. In the process he inscribed St. Paul's Greek text with a distinctively modern separation of sexuality from religious observance, as well as with a conservative sexual morality, if not mere prudery. Early Christian culture not only distinguished between "holy" and profane kisses, but made kissing part of Christian ritual.[5] Phillips replaced this distinction with a merely secular handshake described as "hearty," which could mean heartfelt but possibly robust as well, so that the greeting might be gendered masculine in view of the translator's historical moment. As the vehicle of a rather dense inscription, the discursive strategy makes the translation a text in its own right, relatively autonomous from the source text that it translates. But Nida does not consider or even recognize this autonomy. On the contrary, he mystifies it by means of a concept of equivalence that collapses the translation into the source text on the basis of an effect that they are said to share, an effect that is virtually identical, "substantially the same."

In a translation theory, as Nida's work suggests, the connections among the constitutive concepts and between those concepts and discursive strategies can be complicated because so often the theoretical statement is incompletely formulated or unevenly developed. It may not include or give equal emphasis to each of the three categories that delimit a translation theory. It may also concentrate on a concept to the exclusion of any link to a discursive strategy or, conversely, on a strategy without any formulation of the concept that might provide an explanation or justification. Nida emphasizes the functional aspect of dynamic equivalence but does not acknowledge the resulting autonomy of the translation, particularly its assimilation of the source text to the receiving culture to such an extent that the equivalent effect appears to be the broadest of analogies, shorn of significant cultural and social differences. This telling omission at once puts into question the explanatory power of his theory and points to an underlying conceptual paradigm or model that structures his thinking at a deeper level. The concept of dynamic equivalence rests on an instrumental model in which translation is seen as the reproduction or transfer of an invariant that is contained in or caused by the source text, whether its form, its meaning, or its effect. Nida's concept is instrumental because it assumes not only that a textual effect is an invariant, available to any readership whatsoever, but that an effect of a source text can be reproduced unaltered by a translation, made available for a readership in a different language and culture. In a translation theory, the underlying model is not only paradigmatic but generative: although it may never be formulated explicitly, it can project theoretical concepts or discursive strategies or both, in cases such as Nida's, that is to say concepts linked to strategies.

The instrumental model has dominated theoretical reflection on translation for more than two millennia in the West. In classical antiquity, among Roman and early Christian commentators such as Cicero and Quintilian, Augustine and Jerome, it led to an emphasis on thinking about equivalence and gave rise to the now commonplace distinction between "word-for-word" and "sense-for-sense" strategies.[6] This distinction is instrumental because it assumes the existence of formal and semantic invariants in the source text while downplaying the autonomy of the translation—even when the commentator was an orator or poet who recommended translation as a means of producing a new speech or poem in the translating language. During the early modern period, this model recurrently appears in a clothing metaphor for translation. In John Dryden's *Preface to Ovid's Epistles* (1680), for instance, the translator of poetry is cautioned "to vary but the dress, not to alter or destroy the substance" because "the sence of an Authour, generally speaking, is to be Sacred and inviolable."[7] In Dryden, as in his classical predecessors, meaning is a metaphysical essence inherent in the individual words of the source text, and it is not just immediately perceptible to the translator, but reproducible or transferable intact through words in the translating language which are transparent and therefore interchangeable with source-language words. Hence the instrumental model of translation is itself based on a more fundamental assumption, a theory of language, which can be called empiricist insofar as it conceives of language use as direct expression or reference.

The history of translation theory reveals another model, however, which seeks to avoid essentialism and instead foregrounds the cultural variability and historical contingency of the translation process. Emerging during the late eighteenth century in German romanticism, recurring throughout the nineteenth and twentieth centuries in the tradition of philosophical hermeneutics, and developed in various ways under the influence of such discourses as semiotics, Russian formalism, and post-structuralism, this model can be called hermeneutic: it understands translation as an interpretation of the source text, one among different and potentially conflicting interpretations, each of which varies the form, meaning, and effect of that text according to what is intelligible and interesting in the receiving culture. The hermeneutic model assumes a theory of language that can be called materialist, conceiving of language use as a creative act thickly mediated by linguistic and cultural determinants so that it does not transparently express ideas or represent reality but rather constructs them. Textual features and effects are subject to variation because they are no more than provisionally fixed by contexts that are linguistic and cultural, institutional and social, and those features and effects are radically recontextualized by interpretive acts like translation, which inscribe them with different forms and meanings and enable them to release different effects. As a result, the theoretical statements generated by the hermeneutic model tend to emphasize the relative autonomy of the translated text, how it mediates and transforms its source.

Thus Gideon Toury regards a translation as a "representation" that inevitably involves "shifts" or deviations from the source text caused in the first instance by receiving cultural "norms."[8] In Toury's view, "it is norms that determine the (type and extent of) equivalence manifested by actual translations," whereby equivalence becomes a category that can change historically, between different periods, but also socially, among different cultural constituencies in a specific period.[9] Toury calls equivalence a "*functional-relational* concept": it is ultimately defined by the position and status of translation in the receiving culture, whether central or peripheral, whether prestigious or negligible.[10] In cultures where translation is assigned a centrality, Toury suggests, the translator is likely to adhere more closely to the source text to the point of violating receiving cultural norms, whereas in cultures where translation occupies a peripheral position, the translator is likely to render with latitude so as to preserve norms.[11] He gives a similarly functional account of the discursive strategies that establish equivalence: "the retention of one or another aspect of a source text invariant under transformation is indeed considered a necessary condition for a translation to fulfill the function allotted to it; in the *target* system, to be sure."[12]

Toury's reference to a "source text invariant" is unexpected. His theory of translation as a norm-governed practice would seem to entail variation decisively determined by the receiving culture; he even uses the phrase "under transformation" to describe the work of translation on the source text. He asserts that "equivalence as it is used here is not one target-source relationship at all, establishable on the basis of a particular type of invariant."[13] Yet when he explains how to analyze the relation between the translated and source texts, he claims that "the focal concept is that of *invariance*," that what "concrete coupled pairs *actually* share" must be examined, and he draws a distinction between "what was kept invariant and what was transformed."[14] This inconsistency points to an underlying instrumentalism that limits the impact of the hermeneutic model on Toury's thinking. His notion of a translation shift reveals the same limitation: it conceives of the source text as a container of formal and semantic invariants which become the means of finding deviations in the translation, whereas the very process of locating a shift requires the analyst to apply a third category, a standard of comparison, usually an analytical concept drawn from systemic-functional linguistics or discourse analysis, so as to fix the features of the source text and detect where the translation corresponds to or deviates from them.[15] The notion of a translation shift assumes that textual features are inherent and stable, and that they are available without mediation or processing, without any interpretive act.

I have imagined translation theory as resting on an implicit paradigm or model that, on the one hand, presupposes a theory of language and, on the other, generates concepts concerning the translated text (namely its relative autonomy, its equivalence to the source text, and its function) as well as the discursive strategies by which those concepts are realized in practice. Only two models recur in centuries of theoretical statements, one instrumental, the other hermeneutic, although as models they are ideal constructs which never appear in the abstract formulations I have given them and must be inferred from the concepts and strategies to which they give rise. Each model can generate multiple concepts and strategies which may also be informed by various traditions and discourses, including philosophical speculation, literary theory and criticism, and translation theory and practice. The models, furthermore, are logically opposed, one stressing invariance, the other variability, one essentialist, the other contingent. In the history of translation theory, this binary opposition has been structured as a hierarchy: the millennia-long domination of the instrumental model deferred and then marginalized the articulation and development of its hermeneutic counterpart, repressing the kind of thinking that would question the notion of a source invariant and open the source text to variable interpretation. Yet the opposition is in fact not a strict binary. As Toury's work suggests, both models have sometimes underpinned accounts of theoretical concepts and discursive strategies, resulting in omissions and inconsistencies, regardless of whether the model most effective in shaping the commentary was instrumental or hermeneutic.

In what follows I deploy this account of the structures of translation theory in discussing Friedrich Schleiermacher's lecture "On the Different Methods of Translating" (1813). Schleiermacher assumes the hermeneutic model, posing the problem of cultural difference which subsequently became central to thinking about language and translation—although without appreciably weakening the ascendancy of instrumentalism among translators, translation theorists and commentators, and readers of translated texts, whether professional or popular. My discussion of his lecture is critical: I explore its omissions and inconsistencies so as to expose the limitations of the concepts and strategies that Schleiermacher sets forth. Any such critique can be mounted only from a particular theoretical position that differs from that of its object, and mine is rigorously hermeneutic, although it departs from the German tradition of hermeneutics which Schleiermacher initiated.[16] My aim is to argue that translation research and practice cannot advance until instrumentalism is not simply abandoned but replaced by an understanding of translation that is based on a more sophisticated version of the hermeneutic model.

Schleiermacher between Instrumentalism and Hermeneutics

Schleiermacher sees translating "methods" ("Methoden") as producing a specific "understanding" ("Verständnis") of the source text.[17] He argues that only two methods exist: in Susan Bernofsky's English version, "Either the translator leaves the writer in peace as much as possible and moves the reader toward him; or he leaves the reader in peace as much as possible and moves the writer toward him."[18] Translation makes possible an act of cognition that is figured as movement in space, like travel. It is not synonymy or the transposition of words with like or identical meanings, but rather a means of fostering an intersubjective understanding in which a reader comes to comprehend the linguistic and cultural differences that a foreign-language writer has signified in the source text. Moreover, the understanding is never complete, but only approximate, a matter of "as much as possible" ("möglichst") so that equivalence is viewed as a variable concept that the translator must define anew with each foreign culture, language, and text to be translated.[19]

This point becomes clearer when Schleiermacher describes more specifically the kind of translating that sends the reader abroad, toward the foreign writer. In this case, the translator must take it as his goal to furnish his reader with just such an image and just such enjoyment as reading the work in the original language would have provided the well-educated man whom we are in the habit of calling, in the best sense of the word, an amateur and connoisseur, a man who is well acquainted with the foreign language, yet to whom it remains nonetheless foreign, who must no longer think each detail through in his mother tongue like a schoolboy before he is able to grasp the whole, yet who, even where he can take pleasure unhindered in the beauty of a work, remains ever conscious of the differences between this language and his mother tongue.[20]

Schleiermacher does *not* assert that a translation can provide a reader with unmediated access to the meaning of a foreign word or text. Instead a translation is treated as an "image" ("Bild"), a representation that is relatively autonomous from the foreign text. The image, furthermore, reflects not native proficiency in the foreign language but only a familiarity with it ("geläufig"),[21] so that the foreignness of the foreign language remains perceptible to the translator who therefore produces a translation that somehow registers or signals the linguistic and cultural differences that he or she experiences upon reading the foreign text.

With Schleiermacher, the idea of mediation enters translation theory decisively for the first time and with it the hermeneutic model. Here translation is seen as communicating not the foreign text, but an interpretation of it, one among different possibilities that can be formulated apart from the translation process, and that are inscribed with different linguistic strategies. A translation stands at two removes from the source text: it is said to "imitate" ("nachahmen") an "understanding of the original language" ("Verstehen der Ursprache").[22]

Schleiermacher's thinking about translation is closely allied to his hermeneutics, where the unit of interpretation is the text and every text must be interpreted in terms of linguistic patterns and cultural traditions as well as an individual writer's selection and deployment of those patterns and traditions. "Everything in a given utterance which requires a more precise determination," Schleiermacher states in his manuscripts on hermeneutics, "may only be determined from the language area which is common to the author and his original audience."[23] Schleiermacher recognizes the need to situate a text in its originary context in order to understand it, but he finds useless any attempt to reduce the unit of interpretation to the word. "If one analyses an utterance into its individual parts," he observes, "every part is indeterminate," implying that the same text can support multiple, possibly conflicting interpretations, and that a particular interpretation can only be excluded by philological and historical research applied to the text as a whole, that is to say, by the interpreter's creation of a context which is linguistic, cultural, and social, "common to the author and his original audience."[24] The interpretations inscribed by the translator, furthermore, show that different, competing contexts can be created for the same foreign text by the same method of translation. Schleiermacher acknowledges that his preferred method of signaling the foreignness of the foreign text can give rise to divergent "schools," so that "even though it is the same method that forms the basis of each school, different translations of the same work made from different points of view will be able to coexist" because they may apply different concepts of equivalence, one "approximating the original language, while the other insists that no violence be done to its own."[25]

Schleiermacher has been described as straddling Enlightenment and romantic thinking.[26] Certainly, the rational precision he sought to bring to interpretation and translation seems akin to John Locke's empiricist project of grounding knowledge on a rational basis derived from sense perception. For Schleiermacher, "the more strict practice" of interpretation "assumes that misunderstanding results as a matter of course," and the interpreter proceeds through the elimination of error similar to the scientific method.[27] Yet unlike Locke, Schleiermacher harbors a notion of unknowability, of approximate understanding constrained by the interpreter's or translator's own linguistic and cultural determinations. He shares this notion with other early German romantics. As Manfred Frank shows, they believed that "all of our attempts to explain remain within the realm of the conditioned. For to know 'mediately' means to know by means of a concept or another piece of knowledge, but not from the object of knowledge itself."[28]

In line with this notion of mediated knowledge, Schleiermacher's hermeneutic approach to translation rests on a materialism in which the subject and language are reciprocally determining. "Every human being," he asserts, "is, on the one hand, in the power of the language he speaks," but "on the other hand, every free-thinking, intellectually independent individual shapes the language in his turn."[29] I regard Schleiermacher's concept of individuality as linguistically determined, not a pre-linguistic essence, not a personality or a psychological state standing apart from language, but rather "a unique combination of shared linguistic resources and individual application."[30] Thus he defines "style" as "composition and treatment of language," a selection and arrangement of preexisting items, and he characterizes language use, literary texts, and translations according to genres, discourses, and social functions, distinguishing between "the areas of art and science" and "business transactions."[31] In the lecture on translation, his materialist theory of language leads to an emphasis on the cultural specificity of linguistic communities as mediating individual language use:

> One understands speech both as a work of language and as an expression of its spirit only if, while feeling that only a Hellene, for instance, can have thought and spoken thus, one at the same time feels that only thus can *this man* have thought and spoken in a Hellenic manner, only thus can he have seized and worked to shape this language, and what is here manifested is only his living grasp on the richness of the language, his keen sense of rhythm and euphony, and his capacity to think and to fashion.[32]

The "Hellenic" or Greek language is characterized by a distinctive "spirit" or set of structural differences, and a Greek speaker "works" in a distinctive way to deploy those differences. That work is focused on linguistic features—for example, "rhythm and euphony"—but it is not given a psychologistic treatment.

When Schleiermacher turns to translation, however, this sort of linguistic and cultural mediation becomes a fraught issue. He privileges the kind of translating that inscribes the interpretation of the "well-educated man," as if this interpretation were more adequate to the foreign text regardless of "the differences between [the foreign] language and his mother tongue." Such a translator is not only "well acquainted with the foreign language" but possesses an interpretive mastery that permits aesthetic appreciation, able to "grasp the whole" of the foreign text and to "take pleasure unhindered in [its] beauty."[33] Yet is not the translator's work determined by the translating language and culture according to the very tenets of Schleiermacher's concepts of language and hermeneutics? Are not these determinations at once enabling and constraining, resulting in a particular interpretation and therefore a particular translation of the foreign text? Does not Schleiermacher's thinking lead us to expect that a Greek translator will produce a translation that bears the marks of its production in contemporary Greek culture, that it will somehow present a Greek understanding of the foreign text?

Instead of addressing or even formulating such questions, Schleiermacher offers an inconsistent account of the foreignness signaled by his preferred kind of translating. He refers to "the difficult task of representing the foreign in one's own mother tongue," where "representing" renders the German "darstellen," a Kantian term that refers to the construction of concepts and therefore indicates the relative autonomy of the translation from the foreign text.[34] He argues that signaling the differences of any foreign text requires a huge volume of translations, "a large-scale operation" that facilitates comparisons among them, because "if only individual masterpieces in individual genres are translated," then "even the most educated readers will acquire in this way only a highly imperfect knowledge of the foreign through translation."[35] Hence we should regard the differences perceptible in a translation not as direct access to the foreign text but rather as a foreign*ism*, an image of that text constructed from linguistic patterns and cultural traditions in the receiving situation, a foreignness shaped from and in some relation to receiving cultural values, beliefs, and representations, including representations of the culture where the text originated.

As the lecture unfolds, however, the notion of translation as mediation vanishes. Schleiermacher describes what he calls "the true goal of all translation" as "the fullest possible unadulterated enjoyment of foreign works," where the translator is engaged in "supplying this knowledge of the foreign world by the swiftest, most efficacious means, while allowing the greater lightness and naturalness of the original to shine through everywhere."[36] He similarly speaks of the "aim" of translation as "facilitating the most direct enjoyment of the [foreign] works," where "direct" renders the German "genau," a word that might also be translated as "true," "accurate," "exact," or "careful."[37] Such passages rest on a concept of equivalence not as variable approximation, but as adequacy to the foreign text. The sense of foreignness is assumed to be an invariant that the translator must reproduce or transfer in the translation, and so Schleiermacher's thinking has seamlessly come to depend on an instrumental model, assuming an empiricist concept of language as transparent representation.

A similar inconsistency occurs in the passage where he considers the linguistic strategies that might most effectively signal the differences of the foreign text. "The more precisely the translation adheres to the turns and figures of the original," he asserts, "the more foreign it will seem to its reader."[38] Here Bernofsky has chosen two words, "turns and figures," to translate the German "Wendungen," an expansive rendering that I take as clarifying or explanatory, referring to syntactical turns or turns of phrase and figures of speech, rhetorical or literary figures.[39] Schleiermacher once again recommends a strategy that assumes a concept of equivalence as adequacy, syntax and figure are taken as invariants, and the transparent language of the translation must adhere to them closely so as to reproduce them and thereby to signal the foreignness of the foreign text.

But his account of linguistic strategies does not stop here. "One must admit," he proceeds to suggest, "that an indispensable requirement for this method of translating is a disposition of the language that not only departs from the quotidian but lets one perceive that it was not left to develop freely but rather was bent to a foreign likeness."[40] The English word "quotidian" renders the German "alltäglich," which might also be Englished as "everyday," "ordinary," "workaday," implying a routine, familiar, or conversational use of language, what I shall understand as the current standard dialect, the most widely used form of the translating language.[41] Schleiermacher imagines the language of foreignizing translations as simultaneously adhering closely to the foreign text and departing from current usage, as a hybrid of foreign and receiving linguistic forms as well as calques or literalisms, not so much translationese as "occasionally harsh and stiff," a heterogeneity that undoubtedly resists normative usage to such an extent as to result in "mongrels" whereas the foreign text may not itself be heterogeneous or display exactly the same kind of heterogeneity.[42]

This view is taken up again in his conclusion where he asserts that in the translation culture he advocates for German-speaking regions, "there must be an area of the language reserved for translations, and to them certain concessions will be made that would not be tolerated elsewhere."[43] Departures from the current standard dialect look toward a translation experimentalism that can only deviate as well from the language of the foreign text which may not itself contain such departures at all or not at those points where the translator chooses to make them in the translating language. Schleiermacher calls such verbal choices "deviations and innovations" ("Abweichungen und Neuerungen") which "may, in the end, combine to produce a new characteristic mode of expression."[44] His assumption of the hermeneutic model would seem to give the translator the right to interpret by applying a range of formal interpretants, such as a concept of variable equivalence or a concept of style fitted to a genre or discourse, yet without abandoning the responsibility to signal through these indirect means the differences of the foreign text. It is important to realize, once again, that although foreignizing translation requires innovative language use, the foreign text may not itself contain identical or even similar innovations. Hence it would be transformed when translated in this way, and equivalence would be redefined not only as approximation but as encompassing the sense of foreignness that the translator aims to convey. The models of translation underpinning Schleiermacher's account of linguistic strategies shift uneasily between instrumentalism and hermeneutics, projecting different ideas of autonomy, equivalence, and function for the translated text, assuming now empiricist, now materialist concepts of language.

Interpreting the Translator's Interpretation

In seeking to advance a hermeneutic approach to translation, in arguing that we must recognize the cultural variability and historical contingency of the translation process and the relative autonomy of the translated text, I am far from denying that translation is communicative. It does communicate, but no more than an interpretation, not some invariant form, meaning, or effect believed to be inherent in the source text. In inscribing an interpretation, a translation is inevitably a transformation, whereby the source text is rewritten according to the intelligibilities and interests of a different language and culture. Schleiermacher shows an awareness of this point, even if that awareness is not expressed without contradiction. It is overlooked, however, by his most recent commentator, Michael Forster, who argues that Schleiermacher's description of foreignizing translation as "bent to a foreign likeness" indicates his assumption that the translator's goal is "faithful reproduction of meaning."[45] Forster ignores not only the passage where Schleiermacher links the foreignizing translation to one interpretation or point of view, that of the "well-educated man," but also the passage where he anticipates "different translations of the same work made from different points of view"—passages, in other words, that put into question the instrumentalism implicit in any assumption of "faithful reproduction of meaning." If foreignizing translation is "bent to a foreign likeness," its meaning and syntax, among other features, may in fact resemble those of the source text, but Schleiermacher does not see any such resemblances as reproducing source invariants or preempting variation in the translation.

A translation, more precisely, establishes various relations to the source text, which can start with a correspondence to its meaning and include an approximation of the lexical and syntactical features that comprise its style. Yet these relations cannot stop the transformation. And neither a semantic correspondence nor a stylistic approximation, although admitting of plot summaries and character analyses, summaries of philosophical arguments and explications of conceptual terms, descriptions of a lexicon and syntax and their textual effects—none of the relations established by a translation can be understood as giving back the source text unaltered or as enabling a reader to respond to the translation in the same way that the source-language reader responds to the source text. For a text, especially in humanistic fields like literature and philosophy, is a complex artifact that supports meanings, values, and functions specific to its originary language and culture, and when translated this complexity is displaced by the creation of another text in a different language and culture. As an interpretive act, furthermore, a translation potentially engages in a critical dialectic with the source text, in which each interrogates the other, exposing conditions that are unacknowledged and of which the source-text author as well as the translator is likely to be unconscious.[46]

Consider Susan Bernofsky's English version of Schleiermacher's lecture. She applied a set of formal interpretants: first, a concept of equivalence in which she maintained a semantic correspondence according to dictionary definitions, a lexicographical equivalence, but also a rather close adherence to the syntactical constructions of the German text, as far as the structural differences between English and German would allow, so that her sentences match Schleiermacher's in sheer length and intricacy. She also cultivated a lexicon that draws predominantly on the current standard dialect of English. But her prose contains departures in the form of archaisms or poeticisms, words and phrases that suggest the historical remoteness of the German text, such as "Yea," "we must needs employ," "for the nonce," "an organ of apperception," "folly," "tarried," "wantonness," and "the translator's travails."[47] Her translation can be labelled Schleiermacherian: it brings the reader close to the German text, but the image it creates is decidedly not that text. No, it is primarily by deviating from current standard English, from the style of contemporary anglophone philosophical discourses, and from the linguistic strategies applied in translating foreign philosophical texts where current standard usage prevails, that her translation registers the foreignness of Schleiermacher's text in English.

But Bernofsky's translation does more: it introduces an odd inconsistency between some of her lexical choices and a recurrent theme in Schleiermacher's lecture, German nationalism. His lecture concludes with a rousing call to German-speaking people to produce foreignizing translations so as to develop the German language and culture, practicing translation as *Fortbildung*, culture in the most basic sense of education.[48] He sees no contradiction in yoking the cosmopolitan impulse of foreignizing translation to this essentially nationalistic project: "we cannot accept as true cosmopolitanism," he asserts, "one that at critical moments supplants a man's love of his fatherland."[49] He is delivering his lecture in Berlin during June 1813, not long after Napoleon's armies invaded Prussia and twice defeated coalition forces. He criticizes Frederick II, the eighteenth-century Prussian monarch, for succumbing to French cultural domination: "All the noblest and finest thoughts of our great king came to him in a foreign language," Schleiermacher laments. "He could not possibly have written in German the philosophy and poetry he set down in French."[50] Schleiermacher subsequently dismisses the entire French translation tradition as grossly assimilationist or domesticating. "Who would claim," he declares, "that anything has ever been translated, whether from an ancient or a Germanic tongue, into French!"[51] Bernofsky, however, used French-derived words to render Schleiermacher's account of the foreignizing translator as "an amateur and connoisseur."

Schleiermacher's choice of "Liebhaber" can certainly be translated as "amateur," although "admirer," "enthusiast," "fan," and even "aficionado" are possibilities that maintain a semantic correspondence despite the other resonances they may release. His choice of "Kenner" can likewise be translated as "connoisseur," but "specialist," "authority," "master," and even "*conoscente*" are equally acceptable possibilities. Bernofsky uses "connoisseur" five times in her translation, four to render "Kenner" and once inserted in a passage where no counterpart appears in the German text.[52] The Belgian translation scholar André Lefevere avoids French-derived words in his version of Schleiermacher's lecture, using "lover and expert" for "Liebhaber und Kenner."[53]

Bernofsky also chooses "quotidian," another French-derived word, to render "alltäglich," Schleiermacher's term for the everyday language from which the foreignizing translation should depart. She relies on the same word in another reference to language use, "in both quotidian and nobler contexts," where "quotidian" renders "lebendigen" in the phrase, "für lebendigen und höheren Gebrauch" (in a very close version, "for living and higher use").[54] At the end of the lecture, Schleiermacher himself uses a Gallicism, the phrase "in Masse," identified as such in the Grimm brothers' *Das Deutsche Wörterbuch* (1854–1961), and Bernofsky translates it with the French expression, "en masse," set in italics that indicate its foreignness.[55] Lefevere's choices are "colloquial" and "on a large scale."[56]

Bernofsky's use of French and French-derived words should not be dismissed as careless or erroneous. Such judgments would assume that the German text is a container of lexical invariants which must be reproduced in the English version—in other words, an instrumental model of translation would come into play. I rather want to argue that in the context of Schleiermacher's lecture, in the terms of his linguistic and cultural situation as represented therein, against the backdrop of his German nationalism and his anti-French sentiments, the French and French-derived words constitute a peculiar but intriguing interpretation that, along with such other textual features as the archaisms, establishes the relative autonomy of Bernofsky's translation from the German text. Schleiermacher himself points out in the manuscripts on hermeneutics that interpretation can lead the interpreter to "understand the author better than he does himself" because the author's linguistic and cultural situation can remain "unconscious."[57] Bernofsky's translation exposes a French unconscious in Schleiermacher, inviting us to perceive that the unacknowledged conditions of his discourse are actually French.

Central assumptions in Schleiermacher's translation theory—namely the ideas that thought is dependent on language, and that meaning derives from language use—were articulated first by German philosophers in the late seventeenth and early eighteenth centuries, Leibniz and Christian Wolff, but they were later developed by French thinkers, notably Rousseau and Condillac.[58] The existence of these dual traditions has complicated historical accounts of Johann Gottfried Herder's thinking, which in turn influenced Schleiermacher. Hans Aarsleff describes Herder's "so-called principle of linguistic relativity with its associate doctrines of the ultimate subjectivity of speech and its social nature" as French in origin, whereas Michael Forster, judging Aarsleff's view as "provocative but rather eccentric," argues that their "single ulterior source" is "the Leibniz-Wolff tradition."[59] The fact remains, however, that the two philosophical traditions intersected, and both were received by Herder and subsequently by Schleiermacher, so that any attempt to affiliate the key ideas solely with one or the other culture risks a charge of reductive chauvinism. The cultural conditions of Schleiermacher's translation theory can only be described as Franco-German.

His restatement of the ideas echoes passages in Condillac's *Essay on the Origin of Human Knowledge* (1746). Schleiermacher's conception of language strongly resembles Condillac's, and although the French philosopher singles out "eminent men" in his formulation, they seem comparable to Schleiermacher's notion of the "well-educated man" as the ideal translator:

> Though eminent men in some respect share the character of their nation, they always have something that sets them apart from it. They see and feel in their own particular way, and to express their manner of seeing and feeling they are obliged to imagine new expressions within the rules of analogy or with as little deviation from those rules as possible. Thus they conform to the genius of the language while at the same time adding their own.[60]

The most startling resemblance appears when Condillac asserts that "everything confirms that the language of each nation expresses the character of the people who speak it," although he excepts "cold and phlegmatic people, who are more difficult to size up, since they readily conform to the way other people speak."[61] Schleiermacher closes his lecture by referring to the "Nordic lassitude" of German speakers, which "prevents us from exercising [our language] sufficiently," yet it is this people, "because of its esteem for the foreign and its own mediating nature," that is best suited to the foreignizing translation that seeks to conform to linguistic and cultural differences.[62] The similarity in the passages is uncanny.

Although the German romantics initiated a translation tradition that aggressively opposed the French tendency toward domesticating paraphrase, the tradition of *les belles infidèles*, the conception of language that sowed the seeds of foreignizing translation was articulated by French as well as German thinkers.[63] Indeed, this very conception of translation also appeared in the French tradition. In an essay that appeared in a mid-eighteenth-century miscellany, Jean le Rond d'Alembert asserts that "good translations are the best calculated for enriching the language," where "good" is defined as possessing "that easy and natural air, which is imprinted by the genius of the original, and, at the same time, that taste of the soil which a foreign tincture must give it."[64] Yet the reference to "that easy and natural air" deviates sharply from Schleiermacher's notion that foreignizing translation is "occasionally harsh and stiff," displaying d'Alembert's ultimate allegiance to *les belles infidèles*. His preference for domestication becomes explicit when he argues that "it ought not to be laid down as a rule to translate literally, even in passages where the genius of the languages corresponds, if the translation would be dry, harsh, and inharmonious."[65]

The interpretation I have located in Bernofsky's translation is obviously not deferential toward Schleiermacher's text, but rather differential, distinctly interrogative, enacting what Paul Ricoeur has called a "hermeneutics of suspicion" such as practiced by thinkers from Marx, Nietzsche, and Freud to Louis Althusser and Jacques Derrida.[66] In 2009, when I shared this reading with Bernofsky, she was clearly unaware of any peculiarity in her verbal choices. As far as she could recall a project she had completed in 2003, she was intent on maintaining a semantic correspondence, perhaps assuming the instrumental model that most translators and readers of translation, scholarly as well as popular, continue to assume today. Yet her translation belies any instrumental notion of a source invariant. Her Gallicisms do maintain a semantic correspondence, but they simultaneously allow for an interrogation of Schleiermacher's nationalist thinking which in turn comes back to worry the consistency of her concept of equivalence.

Bernofsky's interrogative choices, I suggest, reveal a desire to challenge the authority that the German author's work has achieved in translation studies as well as in German philosophical traditions, while implementing the very concepts and strategies that he proposed for translation. This desire, partly repressed and clearly conflicted, is at once personal and collective. Her father, a biochemist who like many scientists of his generation learned German to support his scientific research, had "pressed her" to study the language in which she would later conduct her own research for a doctorate in comparative literature, ultimately embarking on a career as a professional translator of German.[67] In a weblog she has maintained since 2010, however, Bernofsky announced that she is the descendant of Polish Jews whose native village of Nowy Targ was the site of a mass execution by the Nazis in 1942; although her maternal grandmother had emigrated to the United States several decades before, Bernofsky assumes that some members of her extended family did not escape the Holocaust.[68] This horrific consequence of German nationalism, at odds with the libidinal investment in the German language initiated by the father's educational guidance, might be included among the historical and biographical conditions that underlie the translator's questioning of Schleiermacher's nationalistic thinking as well as her admiration of his translation theory. They establish the basis for an unconscious motivation that is linguistic and textual, that came into being during the translation process and was expressed indirectly through verbal choices that run counter to an important theme in the source text.[69]

Instrumentalism cannot account for Bernofsky's work with any incisiveness or comprehensiveness. To make sense of what she has done, we must rather apply a different sort of interpretant, a hermeneutic approach that is open-ended enough to account not only for the translator's complicated interpretive act, but also for its unacknowledged conditions and its unanticipated consequences. To advance the study and practice of translation, we must abandon instrumentalism and work to conceptualize and to implement a hermeneutic model.

Notes

1. Eugene Nida, *Towards a Science of Translation, with Special Reference to Principles and Procedures Involved in Bible Translating* (Leiden: Brill, 1964), 159.
2. Ibid., 166–71.
3. Ibid., 159.
4. Ibid., 160.
5. Michael Philip Penn, *Kissing Christians: Ritual and Community in the Late Ancient Church* (Philadelphia: University of Pennsylvania Press, 2005).
6. See Lawrence Venuti, "Genealogies of Translation Theory: Jerome," *Boundary 2* 37, no. 3 (2010): 5–28.
7. John Dryden, *The Works of John Dryden*, ed. E. N. Hooker and H. T. Swedenberg, Jr. (Berkeley: University of California Press, 1956), 1:118.
8. Gideon Toury, *Descriptive Translation Studies and Beyond* (Amsterdam: Benjamins, 1995), 56–57.
9. Ibid., 61.
10. Ibid., 86. Toury's emphasis
11. Ibid., 271–72, citing Itamar Even-Zohar, "The Position of Translated Literature within the Literary Polysystem," *Poetics Today* 11 (1990): 45–51.
12. Toury, *Descriptive Translation Studies*, 12, his emphasis.
13. Ibid., 86.
14. Ibid., 85, 86, his emphasis.
15. See also the critique of Toury's earlier work in Edwin Gentzler, *Contemporary Translation Theories* (London and New York: Routledge, 1993), 131–33.
16. See Lawrence Venuti, *Translation Changes Everything: Theory and Practice* (Abingdon, Eng.: Routledge, 2013), 3–4, 186–87.
17. Friedrich Schleiermacher, "Ueber die verschiedenen Methoden des Uebersetzens," in *Schriften und Entwürfe: Akademievorträge*, ed. Martin Rössler with Lars Emersleben, vol. 11 of *Kritische Gesamtausgabe*, ed. Hermann Fischer, Ulrich Barth, Konrad Cramer, Günter Meckenstock, and Kurt-Victor Selge (Berlin: Walter de Gruyter, 2002), 67–93, here 74. Also see Schleiermacher, "On the Different Methods of Translating," trans. Susan Bernofsky, in *The Translation Studies Reader*, ed. Lawrence Venuti, 3rd ed. (Abingdon, Eng.: Routledge, 2012), 43–63, here 49.
18. Schleiermacher, trans. Bernofsky, 49.
19. Schleiermacher, 74.
20. Schleiermacher, trans. Bernofsky, 51.
21. Schleiermacher, "Ueber die verschiedenen Methoden," 78.

22. Ibid., 76; Schleiermacher, trans. Bernofsky, 50.

23. Schleiermacher, *Hermeneutics and Criticism and Other Writings*, ed. and trans. Andrew Bowie (Cambridge: Cambridge University Press, 1998), 30.

24. Ibid., 31.

25. Schleiermacher, "Über die verschiedenen Methoden," trans. Bernofsky, 55.

26. Richard Crouter, *Friedrich Schleiermacher: Between Enlightenment and Romanticism* (Cambridge: Cambridge University Press, 2005).

27. Schleiermacher, *Hermeneutics and Criticism*, 22.

28. Manfred Frank, *The Philosophical Foundations of Early German Romanticism*, trans. Elizabeth Millán-Zaibert (Albany: State University of New York Press, 2004), 72.

29. Schleiermacher, trans. Bernofsky, 46.

30. Kristen Gjesdal, *Gadamer and the Legacy of German Idealism* (Cambridge: Cambridge University Press, 2009), 189. See also 166–67.

31. Schleiermacher, *Hermeneutics and Criticism*, 97. Schleiermacher, "Über die verschiedenen Methoden," trans. Bernofsky, 44.

32. Schleiermacher, trans. Bernofsky, 47.

33. Ibid., 51.

34. Ibid., 54; Schleiermacher, "Ueber die verschiedenen Methoden," 82; see also Howard Caygill, *A Kant Dictionary* (Malden, Mass.: Blackwell, 1995), 332.

35. Schleiermacher, trans. Bernofsky, 55.

36. Ibid., 60, 61.

37. Ibid., 61; Schleiermacher, "Ueber die verschiedenen Methoden," 91.

38. Schleiermacher, trans. Bernofsky, 53.

39. Schleiermacher, "Ueber die verschiedenen Methoden," 81.

40. Schleiermacher, trans. Bernofsky, 53.

41. Schleiermacher, "Ueber die verschiedenen Methoden," 81.

42. Schleiermacher, trans. Bernofsky, 53.

43. Ibid., 62.

44. Ibid., 54; Schleiermacher, "Ueber die verschiedenen Methoden," 82.

45. Michael N. Forster, *After Herder: Philosophy of Language in the German Tradition* (Oxford: Oxford University Press, 2010), 415. See also 392–93.

46. For an account of this approach to translation analysis, see Lawrence Venuti, "Translation, Intertextuality, Interpretation," *Romance Studies* 27, no. 3 (2009): 218–34.

47. Schleiermacher, trans. Bernofsky, 43, 44, 51, 59, 61, 63.

48. Schleiermacher, "Ueber die verschiedenen Methoden," 93.

49. Schleiermacher, trans. Bernofsky, 58.

50. Ibid., 57.

51. Ibid., 62.

52. Ibid., 49, 51, 53, 47.

53. André Lefevere, *Translation/History/Culture: A Sourcebook* (London: Routledge, 1992), 152.

54. Schleiermacher, trans. Bernofsky, 58; Schleiermacher, "Ueber die verschiedenen Methoden," 87.

55. Schleiermacher, "Ueber die verschiedenen Methoden," 92; Schleiermacher, trans. Bernofsky, 62.

56. Lefevere, *Translation/History/Culture*, 155, 164.

57. Schleiermacher, *Hermeneutics and Criticism*, 33.

58. Forster, *After Herder*, 60–61.

59. Hans Aarsleff, *From Locke to Saussure: Essays in the Study of Language and Intellectual History* (Minneapolis: University of Minnesota Press, 1982), 335; Forster, *After Herder*, 61, 79 n. 39.

60. Étienne Bonnot de Condillac, *Essay on the Origin of Human Knowledge*, trans. Hans Aarsleff (Cambridge: Cambridge University Press, 2001), 190.

61. Ibid., 185.

62. Schleiermacher, "Über die verschiedenen Methoden," trans. Bernofsky, 62.

63. Roger Zuber, *Les "Belles Infidèles" et la formation du goût classique: Perrot d'Ablancourt et Guez de Balzac* (1968; repr. Paris: Colin, 1995).

64. Jean le Rond d'Alembert, "Remarks on Translation," in *Miscellanies concerning Literature, History, Philosophy, and Other Subjects of the Belles Lettres* (Glasgow: Robert Ure, 1765), 5–22, here 15. No translator credited.

65. Ibid., 6.

66. Paul Ricoeur, *Freud and Philosophy: An Essay in Interpretation*, trans. Denis Savage (New Haven, Conn.: Yale University Press, 1970), chapter 1.

67. E-mail interview, November 27, 2011.

68. Susan Bernofsky, "From a Square to a Cemetery," *Translationista: Dispatches from the World of Literary Translation*, November 19, 2011. Available at http://translationista.blogspot.com/2011_11_01_archive.html. E-mail interview, November 27, 2011.

69. For this psychoanalytic approach, see Venuti, *Translation Changes Everything*, chapter 2.

Chapter 3

Translation and the Text's Alterity

Spinoza to Derrida

Willi Goetschel

There is no translation without the untranslatable. There could be none and there would not be any needed. Recasting or transposing any form of expression—linguistic, visual, musical, artistic, or otherwise—into another form or register without any difference or remainder, if it were possible at all, would simply mean an exchange of equivalences. But translation, if it is not to be mere repetition of the same—which even mechanical reproduction can never achieve—means to transfer, transpose, exchange one for another (always a quid pro quo) where it remains clear that the operation is based on difference. Substitution of one for another is just that, a transaction that is always a displacement, a transfer and transference, and it is the play of transference that makes meaning possible.

The untranslatable thus makes translation possible in the first place. Without it the process of signification would be impossible. For meaning is constituted in and through the process of translation, where the moment of expressing the nonidentical makes it possible to signal the unsaid, the new, the particular, the singular that points beyond: in other words, the singular that signifies.

Meaning cannot be found in a word, in a sentence, but as we know since at least Baruch de Spinoza, in their use. But on closer examination, "use" means translation into ever new and changing contents. Another way to express this is that a text is only opening itself to meaning through context. The process of this transaction is translation. In the trajectory that leads from Spinoza to Moses Mendelssohn, this idea is developed in conjunction with a principal reflection on the terms of philosophy itself. In this essay, I want to trace some of the central motives of this critical movement, which assumes sharper contours if examined in the context of the larger project that connects Spinoza and Mendelssohn with other modern Jewish philosophers in reflecting the terms of the modern Jewish experience.[1]

"Passage into Philosophy"

Philosophy is often perceived as a project whose universal scope is in no need of translation, being the blueprint of the universal identity of the language of reason, as it were; or, to express the point in a different register, philosophy claims its own translatability, that is, the idea that "the transfer of a meaning or a truth from one language to another" is possible "without any essential harm being done," as Derrida describes what is often taken to be philosophy's *conditio sine qua non*.[2] If this can be called, as Derrida did, the "problem of the very passage into philosophy," the question of translation opens the door to approaching translation as a site for rethinking the problem of philosophy in principal terms. The engagement of modern Jewish philosophers with the challenge of translation provides an instructive case of the way in which translation, viewed as more than just a problem, can assume an important role in rethinking the terms of philosophy. Their projects accentuate the crucial link between philosophy and translation. If translation is the "passage into philosophy," as Derrida has argued, the work of Jewish philosophers from Spinoza and Mendelssohn to Martin Buber, Franz Rosenzweig, Walter Benjamin, and Jacques Derrida suggests that rethinking translation as a critical project offers a liberating opening of the question of philosophy.

As Jewish philosophers engage critically with philosophy, they share a vigilant concern for philosophy's blindness with regard to the particular and the singular that the philosophic drive to abstract thought tends to ignore, distort, and mute—if not entirely erase. For Jewish philosophers, however, philosophy's universalist drive indicates a limiting condition that calls for critical examination, an examination that in their view represents the foremost purpose of philosophy itself. The issue of rethinking the conditions of the universal that philosophy takes for granted, or—more in line with the thrust of the projects of Jewish philosophers—may hold out as a promise, comes home for Jewish philosophers in the pointed question of whether or not they qualify for a universalism whose particularity hampers the criteria of admission to which philosophy subjects its acolytes. Upping the ante, Jewish philosophers return the question as one of philosophy itself, its conditions and hidden assumptions. They do so not as an academic pastime but out of existential concerns. These concerns express themselves in terms of in- and exclusion fundamental to, but so often tacitly taken as given in, the construction of the framework of first principles and distinctions that philosophy seeks to establish.

If for the European Christian culture in which modernity emerges, Jewish particularity represents the problem of "the Jewish Question," Jewish philosophers respond by rethinking the status of the Bible in philosophical terms as the question of translation. Spinoza, Mendelssohn, Buber, Rosenzweig, and Benjamin all developed a critical approach to the question of translating and interpreting the Bible and the question of translation in general.

These approaches were intimately linked to rethinking philosophy and the question of what it means to read and translate. For these philosophers, reading and translating the Bible or, for that matter, any other text is not just a linguistic—technical problem but an issue that cuts to the core of the project of philosophy itself; and not simply by making translation an integral part of the agenda of philosophy but more challengingly by addressing philosophy itself as a project of translation and self-translation that defies any prescriptive expectations. While a significant number of Jewish philosophers from Spinoza to Derrida reflected their philosophical trajectories as projects of translation and self-translation, they at the same time highlighted the critical significance to theorize philosophy as a work of translation. The ambition of a continually failed universalism whose ultimate failure might be its best feature, philosophy remains critically contingent on the philosopher's recognition of translation as the very moment that secures the condition of the possibility for its critical force.

Spinoza, Mendelssohn, Buber, Rosenzweig, Benjamin, and Derrida, along with other modern Jewish philosophers, thus develop approaches to translation that position them as translators occasionally of the Bible but also at the same time as self-conscious translators of themselves as they critically transpose the terms of philosophy. The translator's agency as double agent, whose mediating efforts run in both directions between "source" and "target" language or culture, represents a crucially empowering moment that situates Jewish philosophers in between rather than on one or the other side of the nonequation that their translating signals.[3] As a result, they understand the text as necessarily open, as its message is constructed only through the practice of reading, that is, interpretative emplotment or translation, whose process they understand as intrinsically dynamic. On their analysis, translation is the rewriting of the text that renders it legible, highlighting an openness that informs the text as text, that is, the text's alterity, its identity in difference. In other words, it is only through the act of translation as a form of rewriting that texts open themselves to reading beyond self-identical repetition of the content they claim. In other words, texts are legible only insofar as readers reflect their perspectives in the readings of the texts they simultaneously produce. This idea plays itself out in the trajectory of the philosophical projects of modern Jewish philosophers from Spinoza to Derrida. Spinoza and Mendelssohn articulate the initial theoretical moves that provide the stepping-stone for theorizing translation as intrinsic to the philosophic movement.

Moses Mendelssohn

Let us begin with a brief look at Mendelssohn, who in a few and telling remarks fleshes out a concern shared by the group of philosophers under discussion. Mendelssohn's project of the translation and commentary of the five books of Moses, the Psalms, and other Biblical writings represents a crucial part of his work. That those literary projects were more than a sideline of Mendelssohn's activity becomes clear once we connect the ideas brought out in his practical work with his theoretical deliberations. Read together, these comments amount to a theoretically consistent position that sheds a suggestive light on the family resemblance among the group of Jewish philosophers grappling with the question of translation.

A central passage in Mendelssohn's *Jerusalem, or On Religious Power and Judaism*,[4] the trailblazing call for Jewish emancipation he published at the height of the German Enlightenment in 1783, captures the idea that the production of meaning depends on the open-ended dynamic of interpretative practice as it creates meaning through the translation of words into actions. Mendelssohn's description of the Biblical *mitzvoth*, or commandments, as "living script" responds in a critical way to Paul's theological—or, more precisely, theological-political—claims. Reclaiming the spirit as what informs and thus defines the content of the letter, Mendelssohn formulates a challenge that places the issue of translation at the heart of the theological-political but also philosophical problem that haunts the Pauline argument: the distinction between spirit and the letter is one that not only is already derived from the Jewish tradition, and, as such, does not refute the challenge of the letter, but inscribes the spirit more deeply in the dialectic that defines the distinction that Jewish tradition already critically reflects, a tradition that calls for both the letter's and the spirit's direct translation into actions, that is, the function it ascribes to *mitzvoth*. Translation, in other words, already takes place at the site of the letter, not just the spirit. To follow the letter is always already a form of translation; and one that Mendelssohn goes to great lengths to explicate in *Jerusalem* as a performative act of practice.

Mendelssohn's argument can be read as a strong interpretation of the central tenet of Spinoza's *Theological-Political Treatise*, to which we will turn. But Mendelssohn's argument assumes richer contours if addressed along with his dense but compact discussion of translation in the introduction to his translation of the Pentateuch, which he oversaw as a project of the Haskalah, or Jewish Enlightenment. To be more precise: this translation represents a practical reflection of the problem of translation in terms of the creative tension between the (capital "E") Enlightenment and the Haskalah and its particular and complicated relationship to and vis-à-vis the Enlightenment.[5]

If Mendelssohn uses the notion of the "living script" as shorthand for a series of complex issues that define the problem of translation, let us now turn to some less well-known and studied passages that highlight Mendelssohn's point on the level of his own practice of translation.[6] In the introduction to his translation of Genesis (1780), Mendelssohn notes that language resists easy fixation of an easily transferable "content":

> Und so unterscheiden sich alle Sprachen in den Wegen des Ausdruckes, und jede von ihnen hat besondere Eigenschaften, die eine andere nicht hat. Deshalb, wenn man einen Text wörtlich, ein Wort nach dem anderen überträgt, versteht ihn der Sprecher jener Sprache überhaupt nicht. Selbst wenn er vielleicht die Hauptabsicht erfaßt, wird er darin nicht die Angenehmheit des Ausdrucks und die Anmut der Anordnung der ursprünglichen Sprache fühlen, aus der sie übersetzt war.[7]

> And in this way all languages are distinguished by their ways of expression, and each of them possesses special qualities that another does not have. Consequently, if one translates a text literally, and does so word for word, a speaker of that language won't understand the text at all. Even if he might grasp the gist he won't experience the pleasantness of the expression and the elegance of the original language from which it has been translated.[8]

Reflecting critically on the task of the translator as the difficult business of substitutive exchange and reconstruction, Mendelssohn notes

> daß der wahre Übersetzer oft ändern, zufügen, weglassen und die Ordnung des Textes vertauschen muß, um die Absicht des ursprünglichen Sprechers wiederzugeben. Niemand verdirbt die Bedeutung mehr und stiftet mehr Schaden, als einer der Wörter bewahrt, der wörtlich Wort für Wort übersetzt, auch wenn er auf den ersten Blick, scheinbar, der getreueste und eifrigste Arbeiter ist. (*Jub A* 9.1, 39)

> that the true translator often has to adjust, add, omit, and change the order of the text in order to render the intention of the original speaker. No one distorts the meaning more, and causes more damage, than he who preserves the words, who translates word for word, even though, at a first glance, this is seemingly the most loyal and most eager laborer.

For Mendelssohn, the paradox "traduttore, traditore" reflects a problem intrinsic to language itself. To ignore or underestimate its theoretical implications would mean to fall back into conceptual realism and its assumption that concepts exist entirely independently from words; a view that, after Condillac and Mendelssohn's early observations on language, is no longer an option.[9] As he continues on the "most loyal and most eager" translator:

> Einen solchen rügten unsere Weisen, ihr Andenken sei zum Segen, an vielen Stellen [nämlichen] einen, der den Vers [genau] nach seiner Form auslegt, womit sie jemanden meinen, der die Wörter bewahrt

> und Wort für Wort übersetzt oder erklärt, ohne irgendeine Veränderung oder Vertauschung, selbst an Stellen, wo die Wege der Sprache ihn zwingen, die Akzente zu bewahren und die Wörter zu verlassen. Und ein Übersetzer dieser Art wird ein Lügner genannt, denn er gibt den Anschein eines getreuen Übersetzers, er läßt kein Wort aus, im Sinne, daß er es nicht übersetzt, doch lügt er, denn hierdurch geht der Inhalt verloren und die Absicht ist verwirrt. So sagen denn auch unsere Rabbinen [. . .] im Kapitel "der Mann heiligt [heiratet]" (Kidduschin 49a), und am Ende von Tosefta Megillah: "Wer einen Vers nach seiner Form [d.h. mechanisch Wort für Wort] übersetzt, ist ein Betrüger." (*Jub A* 9.1, 39)
>
> Our sages, blessed be their memory, chided such a man in many places as one who reads a verse exactly according to its form, by which they meant somebody who preserves the words and translates or explains word for word, without any change or rearrangement, even in places where the ways of the language [die Wege der Sprache] force him to preserve the accents and to abandon the words. A translator of this kind is called a liar for he gives the appearance of a loyal translator, he does not leave out any word in the sense of not translating, but is seen as lying because this way the content is lost and the intention confounded. Consequently, our rabbis say [. . .] in the chapter "the Man Sanctifies [marries]" (Kiddushin 49a), and at the end of Tosefta Megillah: "He who translates a verse according to its form [i.e., mechanically word for word] is an impostor.

For Mendelssohn, then, the linguistic and literary aspects of writing play a crucial role. Translation is not posited as the third element between the original and the translated text via the assumption of a universal or metalanguage; rather, it presents a moment already internal to language.

Mendelssohn hence already considers a notion of the text's alterity whose fuller implications can be better understood when put in the context of Spinoza's theory of language, of which Mendelssohn makes creative use. If we keep Derrida as well as Buber, Rosenzweig, and Benjamin in mind, Mendelssohn's remarks become legible as a decisive moment in a larger conversation on the nature of translation, tradition, and the production of meaning that informs the modern Jewish experience.

This does not come as a surprise. Mendelssohn was not only an accomplished translator of Hebrew but also of Greek and modern European sources such as French and English. Given his extensive practice of translation from both ancient and modern languages, it seems only fair to recognize him as one of the first and paramount comparatists of the eighteenth century. His contribution to the comparative study of literature is at one with his philosophical approach as a whole: attending to the irreducible singularity of the artistic and linguistic moment in literature, Mendelssohn recognizes translation as the work that preserves the text's singularity precisely through the act of translation, which constitutes the source text as such: meaning requires rewriting, that is, a continual hermeneutic effort at understanding through performative realization. The comparatist's task is to introduce readers to those texts and contexts outside the reader's reach by making them accessible by way of enabling a comprehension of the text's uniqueness rather than assimilating it to the reader's "horizon."

Spinoza

Spinoza has not only articulated an illuminating theory of language, interpretation, translation, and their profound nexus with knowledge, but his *Theological-Political Treatise* presents a theory of translation and hermeneutics that has been seminal for Mendelssohn, Friedrich Schlegel, and modern hermeneutics, as well as for the rise of modern Biblical scholarship. His approach highlights the constitutive connection between knowledge and translation. Right at the beginning of the *Treatise*, Spinoza directs our attention to the act of translation, which he defines in terms of prophecy. The meaning of the Hebrew word "prophet," he highlights in the very first paragraph of chapter one, denotes an individual who transmits as he translates and interprets the word of God:

> Propheta enim apud Hebraeos vocatur נביא *nabi*, id est orator et interpres [. . .].[10]

> The Hebrew word for "prophet" is *nabi*, which means "orator" or "interpreter" [. . .][11]

In Latin, *interpretatio* means both translation and interpretation.[12] In other words, they are terminologically not yet fully distinguished. Locating the moment of translation or interpretation in prophecy and revelation—for Spinoza, other names for the moment of cognition—Spinoza theorizes the act of translation as a constitutive moment in the production of knowledge. At the interface between the divine and nature on the one hand, and, on the other, the human intellect, Spinoza casts translation as the defining feature of knowledge. As such, translation assumes a central role in the epistemological process. Furthermore, Spinoza's critical approach marks translation as an issue irreducibly tangled up with the problem of the theological-political complex. For Spinoza, translation is no longer a technical problem of language but comes to the fore as a key issue of principal philosophical significance.

One of Spinoza's bold and challenging claims is his point

> eam autem, ut hic paucis complectar, dico methodum interpretandi Scripturam haud differre a methodo interpretandi naturam, sed cum ea prorsus convenire.[13]

> that the method of interpreting Scripture does not differ from the [correct] method of the interpreting nature, but rather is wholly consonant with it.[14]

Spinoza goes on to explain that just as the correct method of interpreting nature consists mainly in "constructing a natural history," so the method of the interpretation of Scripture requires a truthful history (*sincera historia*) of Scripture. With regard to nature this means that its history yields, as Spinoza puts it, "certain data" (*certis data*): "The [correct] method of interpreting nature consists above all in constructing a natural history, from which we derive the definitions of natural things (*rerum naturalium defintiones concludimus*), as from certain data."[15] This is all Spinoza says explicitly concerning the method of the interpretation of nature in chapter 7 of the *Treatise*, "On the interpretation of Scripture." If we want to find out more we have to follow the other side of the equation and attend to Spinoza's discussion of how to read Scripture.[16] Spinoza's crucial point here is that any kind of knowledge, be it concerning nature or Scripture, relies on an act of "prophecy," that is, translation. For Spinoza, the prophet is simply an interpreter who translates vision into language. Thus, knowledge is a creative linguistic act, namely, a form of rewriting or, more precisely, reading. Knowledge is therefore the result of, and thus presupposes, translation and thus stands always already in a specific context of linguistic exchange that follows one or the other sociopolitical protocol. The critical importance of Spinoza's remark on the prophet as translator and interpreter consists in arguing his point not just for theological-political forms of knowledge, but more systematically and generally for any act of knowledge production. Moreover, he argues this point *expressis verbis* for that type of knowledge otherwise often considered "objective" and free from any interfering act of interpretation: natural science. Religious prophecy and natural science are thus caught in the same act, both predicated on the hermeneutic move of interpretation as transfer and transference.

Spinoza's theory of translation and interpretation in the *Theological-Political Treatise* and his theory of language and signification in the *Treatise of the Improvement of the Intellect* and the *Ethics* are companion pieces. As a consequence, translation emerges in Spinoza as much more than simply a problem of language in a technical sense. Meaning is produced not by an intrinsic operation of language but by the use of it: practice. As Spinoza critically distinguishes truth from meaning, his approach also accentuates the extralinguistic dimension of translation in the constitution and construction of meaning through action. For Spinoza, meaning is the product of the use and practice of words, phrases, and texts. Accordingly, words, phrases, and texts are defined by the creative interface of writing and reading, coding and decoding. These in turn are highly complex processes in which translation emerges as a form of practice that Spinoza reflects on in terms of its enabling openness. Meaning—and thus translation—are constituted not by an infinite loop of regress searching for or identifying any form of intrinsic meaning, but via the opening of the text's alterity that gains meaning through the interpretative practice in which it is engaged.

As Spinoza emphasizes, we only understand a text if we understand the particular uses of language and the locutions of the author in question. Beyond a linguistic grasp, however, interpretation and translation require a deeper historical contextualization that includes an understanding of the particular mind and project that the author in question represents. Interpretation and translation, Spinoza's approach thus suggests, are tasks whose interminable nature remains unquestionable. The embeddedness of language in all human activities makes it impossible to ever arrive at a final, ultimate form of translation. Rather, interpretation and translation remain at best infinitely revisable approximations of the "text," for the simple reason that to understand a text completely would require a complete knowledge and understanding of an author's mind—something Spinoza would be most reluctant to concede as an achievable enterprise for any given reader. Spinoza's approach to the problem can be seen as both: a distinct rejection of any form of exclusive claim to anything but approximative knowledge of a text's meaning on the one hand, and, on the other, the recognition of the fact that meaning is not contained, that one must always deal with the radical openness of the text, and therefore that meaning is not to be found intrinsically within the text but constituted through the creative act of reading, which is to say interpretation. One consequence of this creative openness is that it is part of the reader's protocol to translate texts into their own words. For Spinoza, language is anything but a stable system of signification. As words are products of our imagination rather than the intellect, as he stresses,[17] translation remains a difficult proposition refusing any sort of secure and final closure. For Spinoza's catalog of conditions and criteria for a final translation, as he lays them out in the *Theological-Political Treatise,* remains pointedly infinite and interminable. Furthermore, the status of universals remains for Spinoza profoundly precarious. Spinoza, unlike Descartes and Leibniz, for instance, has no need of presupposing an objective point outside of language that would provide knowledge with any kind of anchor for securing meaning independently from any act of interpretation, that is, translation. Any act of knowledge is thus always already bound to interpretation and translation.

Spinoza thus marks a decisive turning point in modern hermeneutic theory. But Spinoza's outlook was not to remain a unique position. In his wake, the philosophical recognition that translation plays a critical role as a constitutive moment of the very tradition a text can engender gained theoretically profound importance. A critically attentive reader of Spinoza, Jacques Derrida has in a suggestive way highlighted his affinity with some of the sensibilities central to Spinoza. In his lectures "Language and the Discourse on Method," given in 1981–82, Derrida has addressed aspects of Spinoza's view on language that strikingly reverberate with his own approach.[18] Derrida's resonance with Spinoza provides a welcome occasion to explore Spinoza in the wider context of his project's affinity with that of other modern Jewish philosophers such as Mendelssohn, Buber, Rosenzweig, Benjamin, and others. For this group of philosophers, translation is a practice central to their respective projects, which thus become legible as moments of an ongoing conversation on the nature of translation, tradition, and the production of meaning.

With Spinoza's theoretical background in mind, Mendelssohn's view of translation gains sharper precision. At the same time, Mendelssohn allows us to draw out some of the critical implications in Spinoza. Together, they can be seen as the champions of a line of argument that extends to the present and that has, as we will see, direct impact on the way they rethink the project of philosophy. For Mendelssohn, translation is not a process in which a word-for-word transliteration would be adequate for representing a particular thought or concept. Because of the substitutive move that defines the operation of linguistic signs as originally mimetic, but at the same time arbitrary, it is through the process of translation that meaning is produced. Translation has no recourse to any sort of original meaning that would simply need to be recovered. Instead, translation comes into focus as a necessary part in the process of producing meaning.

For both Spinoza and Mendelssohn, translation is a creative process that preserves meaning by creating it, a conscious act of creative substitution whose supplementary aspect is a critical asset rather than a fatality. A tradition is always a transmission that is at the same time both a transfer and a transference, a repetition that spells difference as its condition. At the height of the Enlightenment and the emergence of modernity, when tradition and translation appear as problematic formations and as mere compromises to preserve a heritage and message that otherwise seem lost, Spinoza and Mendelssohn argue against any claim of reason's self-constitution over and against obsolete forms of traditions, instead arguing that knowledge remains contingent on the act of translation. For them, tradition and translation represent anything but rote-like repetition to which the radical strands of the Enlightenment were eager to reduce it. Rather, if the process of the production of knowledge is inseparably inscribed in the process of interpretation as transfer and transference, what is perceived as "old" and established resists the quick and easy removal, either by effacement or replacement, that the more radical champions of the Enlightenment imagined. For this reason, both Spinoza's and Mendelssohn's view of translation enables a more differentiated attitude toward narratives of the past and progress.

For them, a text is always already translation. Translation is not second, but it is also not first. It exposes the question of what is first a false and misleading question. A text, a weave of language, is from the start already translation and is so in decisive manner. What else is language, we could ask, but translation? But, then, a translation from what? And the answer would be: always from a language, another one or the same—but how can we always discern the exact border crossings, the moment of the Shibboleth?—or from what lends itself to the form of language, linguistic or not—or what is the other of language yet lends itself to and calls for translation. One cannot ignore the vicious circle of sorts we find ourselves in at the moment we theorize translation (for what is theorizing but translation, transposition, exposition, and a reflection of the terms in play?). As we ask these types of questions, we might be accused of displacing the issue, moving away from its scope. But then again, what else is language, what else is translation than precisely that: forms of transposition, displacement, carrying-over, that is *trans-latio*?

If we translate, does the precious cargo, which the movement of translation carries, or claims to carry, arrive at its destination? Does it change, transform, transfigure? Was it ever a cargo when it set out to leave for translation? Does it become what it is through translation? Is interpretation just another word for it?

Translation brings out what defines and constitutes the text as text: its alterity, its creative tension to express the difference that makes its identity. The communicative nature of its signifying character does not imply translation and interpretation as its outside, and other than itself, but embraces them as immanent to the text itself, the defining character of textuality. Or, in other words, while some elements of texts are necessarily self-referential, their self-referentiality requires difference in order to make it possible for meaning to constitute itself, at least if it is to be more than tautology and self-identity. This is the opening in the texts that must lend itself to translatability while at the same time resisting complete translation. Translatability, and equally its limits, thus is a defining feature of the text. And this is so for the simple reason that no meaning could possibly be produced by a text that is completely and exclusively self-identical.

Addressing the different projects of Spinoza, Mendelssohn, Buber, Rosenzweig, Benjamin, and Derrida provides a helpful way to understand translation as an issue that is not just a particular topic of theoretical interest to philosophy, but that cuts to the heart of the project of philosophy itself. This group is one that is rarely understood to constitute a group altogether. I would argue, however, that some of the crucial motives of their philosophical trajectories come into sharper focus if understood in the context of a family resemblance regarding their thought on translation as both philosophical problem and project.[19] They all address the problem of singularity and uniqueness as a philosophical problem whose challenge calls for the rethinking of the project of philosophy as a whole, and they all redefine and reimagine this project in their own terms. Resisting a simple switching from the universal to the particular, from the general to the singular, from universality to uniqueness, this group explores the necessity of rethinking the relationship between the particular and the universal as one of mutual reciprocity, a dynamic, and, more precisely, a dialogical interrelationship.

Translation represents, in other words, for this group of philosophers a task that stands at the center of their practice and their need to negotiate their very own situation between philosophy and the Jewish tradition, and also within both: within philosophy and within Judaism. The project of Jewish modernity—the project in which they are engaged, if this form of shorthand may be permitted—brings the meaning of translation to a head and gives it an existential edge that leads to an intensified level of critical rethinking of the very meaning of translation. Translation assumes in this context a significance that points beyond a merely linguistic project to a wider, more comprehensive concern that has profound theological-political implications for philosophy. For these philosophers, the challenge to reflect on the problem of translation stands at the center of their philosophical projects. Translation is the practice they reflect on and engage in as they recognize themselves as translating always already in and through the very process of cognition, reflection, and philosophical practice. Their theories of translation rest on the recognition that their philosophical practice—and any philosophical engagement—is grounded in, or is an epistemic operation of, translation. Their philosophical critique, that is, their critique of philosophy and their philosophy of critique, emphasizes the fundamental role of translation for knowledge: knowledge for them is a form of translation, or, rather, translation is the moment from which knowledge originates.

The moment of displacement, of substitutive exchange, is not one that is exterior to a self-identical construct of the text as a stable system of signification, but what defines the very constitution of the text as a dynamic weave of signification, a weave of dynamic interplay of language that is dependent on the act of translation for the production of meaning. The alterity of the text is thus intrinsic to the text as meaning emerges through the creative tension of the nonidentical rather than through language's claim to self-identity, which, ultimately, would not only rest on tautology but also on the presupposition of closure. To imagine a text as devoid of alterity would mean—to vary Kant—to imagine it as empty. It would be a text whose self-identity would be the dream of the robotic translator and a nightmare to anybody intent on saying anything at all.

Similarly, the text of philosophy, philosophy as a critical engagement with, and production of, texts requires recognition of its own alterity if it is not to submit to arbitrary fixation and closure. But what does this mean in terms of the actual work of the translator? If the purpose of a translation is to open a text and make it accessible to the reader, this also must mean that a translation must reflect the problem of translation by remaining open and resistant to the hermeneutic urge of closure. This does not mean that precision and exactness would be no longer virtues to aim for. On the contrary, hermeneutic openness critically reflected can lead to a more explicit rendering of a text's alterity that does not need to jeopardize but rather calls for the very precision and exactness critical attention makes possible. The implication of course is that precision and exactness are not to be confused with fixation to any one given meaning. Rather, one could argue, the more open the abundance of meaning is, the more a translation approximates those ideals, and the clearer and more accessible it becomes.

The rejection of a metadiscourse, then, means that there is no absolute point of view or perspective from which to judge, construct, or control translation. Translations are inseparable from the specific exigencies of the parameters of so-called source and target culture and inhabit therefore a peculiar in-between whose singularity remains necessarily "untranslatable." Untranslatability represents the very condition for the project of translation. Erasing it would mean to undermine the very condition of the possibility for translation itself. This means that neither philosophy nor any other instance can assume the role or function of ultimate arbiter. Rather, translations pose principal questions with regard to the production of knowledge and meaning that philosophy cannot afford to ignore. If, on the one hand, the translator is no philosopher just because she is a translator, the philosopher, on the other, is not solely in command of the answers to the questions raised by translation. But the philosopher faces the necessity to acknowledge and address them. In practice, this means that while finality is a false criterion for translation, a successful translation is always contextually self-reflective, one that enables critical reflection on the terms of translation itself. If a good translation reflects the untranslatability of what it translates, it nevertheless must do so through translation, very much like Theodor Adorno figures the critical movement of negative dialectics as a movement that preserves what resists conversion into a third. As a result, rather than curbing the call for translations, the issue of untranslatability makes them more necessary, more important, and more rewarding than any normative notion of translation that mistakes untranslatability for an obstacle and limitation rather than recognizing it as the very moment that makes translation not only possible but also so critically decisive and fertile. In other words, a translation is only as good as it reflects its condition as both transfer and transference.

Notes

I thank Oisin Keohane for his critical insight.

1. I use the term "Jewish philosophers" loosely to mean a group whose individual features may differ a great deal but whose family resemblance suggests

nevertheless aspects of a shared critical agenda. For a discussion of the impossibility to pin down anything like a "Jewish philosophy" and the problematic function of the term in the current discussion see Willi Goetschel, *The Discipline of Philosophy and the Invention of Modern Jewish Thought* (New York: Fordham University Press, 2013).

2. Jacques Derrida, "Roundtable on Translation," in *Ear of the Other: Otobiography, Translation, Transference*, ed. Christie McDonald (Lincoln: University of Nebraska Press, 1988), 93–161, 120. For the discussion of the problem of translation as "nothing less than the problem of the very passage into philosophy" to which the discussion in "Roundtable on Translation" returns, see Jacques Derrida, "Plato's Pharmacy," in Derrida, *Dissemination*, trans. Barbara Johnson (Chicago: University of Chicago Press, 1981), 61–171, 72.

3. For the translator as double agent and Jewish translators as sites of untranslatability see Naomi Seidman's excellent introduction "The Translator as Double Agent" to her *Faithful Renderings: Jewish-Christian Difference and the Politics of Translation* (Chicago and London: University of Chicago Press, 2006), 1–35.

4. Moses Mendelssohn, *Jerusalem or On Religious Power and Judaism*, trans. Allan Arkush, ed. Alexander Altmann (Hanover, N.H.: University Press of New England, 1983).

5. For a discussion of how Mendelssohn's position plays itself out critically in relation and dialogue to Kant, see my chapter "'An Experiment of How Coincidence May Produce Unaniminity of Thoughts': Enlightenment Trajectories in Kant and Mendelssohn," in *The Discipline of Philosophy and the Invention of Modern Jewish Thought*, 210–29.

6. For a more comprehensive discussion of Mendelssohn's theory of translation, see Willi Goetschel, *"Lebendige Schrift": Zu Mendelssohns Theorie der Übersetzung als Selbstübersetzung*, Wolfenbütteler Vortragsmanuskripte 20 (Wolfenbüttel: Lessing-Akademie, 2015). For Mendelssohn's concept of the "living script" in the context of his theory of language, see Will Goetschel, *Spinoza's Modernity: Mendelssohn, Lessing, and Heine* (Madison: University of Wisconsin Press, 2004), 161–66.

7. Moses Mendelssohn, *Gesammelte Schriften: Jubiläumsausgabe*, ed. Ismar Elbogen, Julius Guttmann, and Eugen Mittwoch in association with Fritz Bamberger, Haim Borodianksi, Simon Rawidowicz, Bruno Strauß, and Leo Strauß; continued by Alexander Altmann in association with Haim Bar-Dayan, Eva J. Engel, Leo Strauß, and Werner Weinberg (1929–32; Berlin: Akademie Verlag; 1938; Breslau: S. Münzs; Stuttgart-Bad Cannstatt: F. Frommann, 1971–), *Jub A* 9.1, 37. I will refer to this edition as *Jub A*, followed by the volume and page number of the passage in question.

8. All translations from Mendelssohn's introduction to his Bible translation are mine.

9. See also also Willi Goetschel, "Writing, Dialogue, and Marginal Form: Mendelssohn's Style of Intervention," in *Mendelssohn's Metaphysics and Aesthetics*, ed. Reinier Munk (Berlin: Springer, 2011), 21–37.

10. Baruch de Spinoza, *Tractatus Theologico-Politicus*, ed. Günter Gawlick and Friedrich Niewöhner (Darmstadt: Wissenschaftliche Buchgesellschaft, 1979), ch. 1, 30.

11. Benedict de Spinoza, *Theological-Political Treatise*, ed. Jonathan Israel, trans. Michael Silverthorne and Jonathan Israel (Cambridge: Cambridge University Press, 2007), 13.

12. For *traductio* as a later mistranslation of translation, see George Steiner, *After Babel: Aspects of Language and Translation* (Oxford: Oxford University Press, 2nd ed. 1992), 311. In classical Latin *traductio* means metonymy. Metonymy is a suggestive way to think about translation; the verb *tradere* from which it is derived resonates with *transferre*, from which *translation* (past participle: *translatus*) derives.

13. Spinoza, *Tractatus Theologico-Politicus*, 230.

14. Benedict de Spinoza, *Theological-Political Treatise*, 98.

15. Ibid.

16. I have followed this line of examination in the chapter "Spinoza's Smart Worm and the Interplay of Ethics, Politics, and Interpretation," in Goetschel, *Disciplining Philosophy and the Invention of Modern Jewish Thought*, 133–49.

17. Spinoza, *Treatise on the Emendation of the Intellect*, §88f.; compare *Ethics*, E2P49schol, in *The Collected Works of Spinoza*, trans. Edwin Curley (Princeton, NJ: Princeton University Press, 1985), vol. 1, 38 cf. 237.

18. See Jacques Derrida, "Language and the Discourse of Method," in *Bamidbar: Journal for Jewish Thought and Philosophy* 2 (2011): 61–80. For a discussion of Derrida and Spinoza, see Willi Goetschel "Derrida and Spinoza: Rethinking the Theological-Political Problem," in ibid., 9–25.

19. Of course, Ludwig Wittgenstein, who introduced the concept of family resemblance, is also to be seen in the context of this group of philosophers. Wittgenstein suggests that thinking itself is to be understood as a form of translation. See his *Philosophical Investigations*, §597 in Wittgenstein, *Schriften* (Frankfurt am Main: Suhrkamp, 1960), vol. 1, 466. For the term "family resemblance," see §67, in ibid., 324.

Chapter 4

Mapping Geographies of Translation

The Multilingual Imagination in German/European Culture(s)

Azade Seyhan

Whither Translation?

> Imaginons un instant qu'il [Kafka] ait écrit ses livres en tchèque. Aujourd'hui qui les connaîtrait? . . . Même si un éditeur de Prague avait réussi à publier les livres d'un hypothétique Kafka tchèque, aucun de ses compatriotes (c'est-à-dire aucun Tchèque) n'aurait eu l'autorité nécessaire pour faire connaître au monde ces textes extravagants écrits dans la langue d'un pays lointain "*of which we know little.*"
>
> —Milan Kundera[1]

This untranslated quotation that suggests the theme of the present essay, as epigraphs do, brings home the indispensable aid of translation for the non-French speaking reader. This reader may very well be plurilingual, say, a Polish speaker, conversant in Russian, English, and German but not in French. In the countries behind the former Iron Curtain, Russian was mandatory in schools; German was considered the language of learning and of *Wissenschaft* and was also spoken by minority groups in Poland, Hungary, the Czech Republic, Slovakia, Slovenia, and the Banat region of Romania. And English is the modern-day lingua franca. So, this hypothetical multilingual, who may be a Ph.D. in comparative literature, would still read Kundera in translation. A language promises a different weltanschauung, another system of thought, and another semiotic source of meaning. However, we can realize that promise only in a limited number of languages.

In an ideal world, we could and should expand that knowledge. Yet, our everyday reality dictates that we enlist translational aids of various forms for research, writing, keeping up with world news, travel abroad, communicating with the grandmother of our Japanese neighbor, or even with our own grandmother, if as children of migrated parents, we have forgotten our ancestral languages.

Let me now return to the Kundera quotation with a translational aid. "Suppose for a moment he [Kafka] had written his books in Czech," Milan Kundera writes. "Today who would know them? . . . Even if a Prague editor had managed to publish the books of a hypothetical Czech Kafka, none of his compatriots (that is to say, no Czech) would have had the authority needed to familiarize the world with those extravagant texts written in the language of a 'faraway country of which we know little.' "[2] The obscurity of literatures written in the minor or low-status languages of those faraway countries has not diminished since Kafka's day despite the unprecedented movement of populations not only from but also to those faraway countries (currently, there are close to a million citizens of the former Soviet republics working in Istanbul alone). At the same time, in an age of transnational flow of monetary and intellectual capital, high-speed communication, and a singular scale of migratory traffic within and without national borders, the question of "traveling" languages and the growing need for translation have become a focal point of scholarly and political interests. In what follows, I briefly trace the perception, role, and conceptual paths of translation in modernity beginning with the rise of translational activity in romantic-era Germany. In this context, the task of translation in German cultural life is perceived in a continuum, where translation progresses from its status as an enhancement of German language, thereby contributing to the national culture, to a position where a diversity of idioms and cultures in translation inform German and situate it in a transcultural space. In the second part of this chapter, I read the "self-translated" work of two multilingual authors who do not write in a language of their own but in German. This writing represents the experience of exile in translation, which is illustrated here through a symbolic smuggling of cultural goods, censored in their country of origin across borders and as an allegory of a traveling world library, where texts are borrowed, read, translated, and returned into wider worldly circulation.

The Travails and Travels of Translation

As conventional wisdom would see it, translation sets into motion a striving for equivalence between two languages that would ideally yield access to a given culture. However, every translation also initiates a competition between the expressive modalities of original and target languages. This contest between possession and dispossession, reinscription and erasure, and purchase and loss threatens the culture that has less power to preserve its expressive legacy. Since translation issues seismic shifts in the cultural terrain, it becomes the site of global pressures on local cultures. Under what conditions would one culture not dominate another (or a high-status language refrain from exerting power over a low-status one), so as to observe the imperative of cultural translatability? What formal and ideological strategies lead a text from one shared cultural network to another? With the steadily growing interest in translation studies in the contemporary academic context, well-known theories of translation are amply referenced and new conceptual frameworks are developed and debated. In order to test the critical sway of existing and emergent translation theories, I would like to situate the discussion in a *geschichtsphilosophisch* continuum and briefly revisit the late eighteenth-century moment of early German or Jena romanticism (*die Frühromantik*), where the twin fields of modern hermeneutics and translation posed the question of un/translatability at several theoretical registers. In his comprehensive study of the culture of translation in German romanticism, Antoine Berman correctly observes that in our age "the reflection on translation has become an internal *necessity* of translation itself, as was in part the case in classical and romantic Germany. . . . This reflection does not quite take the form of a 'theory.' . . . But in any case, it indicates the will of translation to become an autonomous practice."[3]

During the brief yet electrifying *Frühromantik* renaissance of literary activity the brothers August Wilhelm and Friedrich Schlegel founded the journal *Athenäum* (1798–1800), which was to become the critical voice of some of romanticism's most erudite minds. The editorial collective of the *Athenäum* included, besides the Schlegel brothers, August Wilhelm's wife Caroline, Friedrich's wife Dorothea, the poet philosopher Novalis (Friedrich von Hardenberg), the novelist and playwright Ludwig Tieck, the philosopher F. W. J. Schelling, and the theologian philosopher Friedrich Schleiermacher. While not strictly a school or a movement, Jena romanticism represented a prescient critical consciousness that has resonated with contemporary literary and translation theories. The theoretical imagination of Jena did not vanish with the *Athenäum* but was kept alive by Friedrich Schlegel and Novalis, who envisioned an inherent bond between poetry and translation and regarded translation and criticism—like Benjamin after them[4]—as an enhancement and a re-creation, respectively, of the original text and "translatability" as "the very means of realizing knowledge of the *Encyclopedia*."[5] Thus, Schlegel explains the dialectic of understanding and recreating in the *Athenäum* fragment 393:

> Um aus den Alten ins Moderne vollkommen übersetzen zu können, mußte der Übersetzer desselben so mächtig sein, daß er allenfalls alles Moderne machen könnte; sogleich aber das Antike so verstehn, daß ers nicht bloß nachmachen, sondern allenfalls wiederschaffen könnte.[6]
>
> In order to translate perfectly from the ancient to the modern, the translator had to be so masterful as to be able to render everything

> modern; at the same time, he had to understand antiquity in such manner that he would be able to not only imitate it but also to completely recreate it. (Translation mine)

Schleiermacher's algorithm of hermeneutic understanding draws liberally on Friedrich Schlegel and Novalis's critical insights into questions of poetic language (defined in the *Athenäum* idiom as "potenzierte Sprache" [potentiated language or language to the second power]), translation, and translatability.

Friedrich Schleiermacher ("the veil maker"), who is considered the founder of modern hermeneutics, since he expanded biblical exegesis into an art of interpretation that took into its purview all manner of linguistic analysis, in effect, *unveiled* translation as a cultural and sociopolitical act. Schleiermacher's theory of translation has been unjustly criticized because of its nationalistic bias, a criticism often directed at the German romantic critics, who strove to shape German into a language of world culture and enlighten the German citizenry through its linguistic capital. In fact, Schleiermacher argued that the desire to translate should be understood as a desire of a community to be understood positively, not a desire—by the translating agency—to dominate and domesticate the foreign. Such a desire would be incompatible with Schleiermacher's emphasis on "the interconnectedness of ethics, dialectics, and hermeneutics."[7]

Congruent with Schleiermacher's theory of language which understands each speech (*Rede*) in its historical contingency and with regard to its multireferential nature, is his view of translation as incapable of locating the equivalent in the foreign language, because texts are products of subjectivities within a language network. Such incommensurability stands under the scrutiny of hermeneutic understanding, whose practitioners write metatexts, commentaries, explanations, and editions to facilitate understanding across the lacunae of cultures and histories. However, in Schleiermacher's mind, this external paraphernalia of explication does not establish equivalence between the *Urheber* (the author) and the interpreter. An intersubjective understanding requires a more nuanced approach that includes a "psychologische (technische) Auslegung" (a psychological [technical] interpretation), which, in turn, is performed through a divinatory ("divinatorisch") and a comparative mode of interpretation. In the divinatory mode of interpretation, the interpreter desires to understand directly, without mediation, and merges into the other's (the other language and text or the mind of the author) consciousness: "Die divinatorische ist die, welche indem man sich selbst gleichsam in der andern verwandelt, das Individuelle unmittelbar aufzufassen sucht"[8] (The divinatory is that whereby one transforms oneself into the other, in order to understand the individual directly [translation mine]).

This act of "hineinversetzen," of placing oneself in the other, leads not only to a full understanding of the author by the interpreter but even transcends the author's ownership of meaning, for "die Aufgabe ist auch so auszudrücken, 'die Rede erst ebensogut und dann besser zu verstehen als ihr Urheber'"[9] (the task can also be expressed as such, "to understand the speech first just as well as and then better than its originator/author") [translation mine]). It is important to note that the object of Schleiermacher's analysis is the written text, and his concern is the recovery of the author's or the originator's language and meaning not only in an intact but also an enhanced form. The concept of the divinatory, which has been a source of misinterpretation in Schleiermacher reception, emerges as an indirect allusion in Benjamin's über-referenced essay on *Übersetzung*, "Die Aufgabe des Übersetzers" ("The Task of the Translator), which maintains that in translation a text reveals something not given in the original.

Competing Imperatives of Translation

In what we now call a globalized world, we are increasingly called upon to understand, and in fact, to enter the consciousness of the other to maintain some sense of peace and order in chaotic times. We need to summon, in Cynthia Ozick's words, "multiple histories, multiple libraries, multiple metaphysics and intuitions"[10] to make good on the promise of non-exclusionary conversations to facilitate some understanding of different or unknown cultural worlds. The concept of the global is not universal, since that Enlightenment ideal has proven to be culturally specific; nor does it signify a normative parity of cultures. It does, however, require the accessibility of translational passages. The ongoing traffic of economic and cultural capital has thrown the need for increased translational activity into sharp relief. In addition to the basic necessity of translation in the everyday dealings of transplanted peoples, translations of their social practices, modes of thought and belief, and value systems need to be addressed in order to ensure not only their integration into the life of the host country but also the preservation of their linguistic and cultural heritages.

The writer in diaspora, moving between borders of language, memory, personal and collective identity, and national affiliation needs to plot complex and layered strategies of translating to negotiate competing forms of identification. The writer claims in translation languages that were fractured or lost in traumas of colonialism, political persecution, abjection, and military invasions of sovereign states by imperialist ambitions. The scribes and artists of "postcolonial" diasporas and oppressive regimes become translators of the voices of the dead and the silenced. They are also translators of languages and cultures submerged in the tides of colonialist expansion or else relegated to diminished status in a Europolitan culture whose heirs saw in it, in Paul Michael Lützeler's words, "eine ontologische Tiefenstruktur, ein kulturelles Sediment, eine Traditionsbasis"[11] (an ontological depth structure, a cultural sediment, a foundational tradition [translation mine]).

The actual dictate of political realities—this great divide between the Europolitan and all that falls short of it or between the superpowers and the "small nations" that Milan Kundera sees "secluded behind their inaccessible languages"[12]—constitutes our lived experience. Here Kundera is not referring to a smallness of scale, but of destiny, the destiny of nations that have at some point or another "passed through the antechamber of death; always faced with the arrogant ignorance of large nations."[13] So, why do we have so little access to other imaginations and forms of knowledge? Who declares these languages inaccessible? German was once inaccessible to Yoko Tawada, E. S. Özdamar, Rafik Schami, the Iranian exiled poet Said, and many writers in the German diaspora, before they engaged in their translational endeavors.

Since Walter Benjamin's "Die Aufgabe des Übersetzers" refutes the view of the great divide between languages, I'll briefly refer to it, albeit with the disclaimer that it mystifies rather than clarifies. While the essay is seen *avant la lettre* as a theoretical trailblazer in contemporary debates on the politics of translation, its appeal lies largely in leveling the translational field. Benjamin's idea of a pure, suprasensible or divined language, "die reine Sprache" (which echoes Schleiermacher's hermeneutic category of "divinatorische Auslegung") reveals itself only in translation. This "messianic character of translation," Derrida remarks, referring to Benjamin's essay, is not a result of translation's success, because, "[a] translation never succeeds in the pure and absolute sense of the term. Rather, a translation succeeds in promising reconciliation."[14]

Mediating between languages, translation sets them free from the low-status, high-status duality, for it represents not only the most intimate bond they share ("Ausdruck des innersten Verhältnisses der Sprachen zueinander")[15] but also recognizes both the original and the translation as fragments of a larger language ("Bruchstück einer größeren Sprache").[16] This larger language denotes the translatability of all language.

Yet it is not the act of translation that frees languages from rankings of status among them but rather the desire inherent in this metaphysics of translation, and—if I may be permitted a moment of Derridian ventriloquism—like all desire, it remains desired and never fulfilled in the way desired. Although Benjamin sees the pure language of translation as an arbiter between languages,[17] the tales of today's displaced and exiled come with a more sobering message: that other worlds are not necessarily transparent in translation, that there are spaces of irreducible untranslatability between cultures, that such spaces mark the silences of exile, and that the idea(lity) of a pure language that equalizes languages does not conform to the reality of a world where many are dispossessed of the hospitable environment of their own idiom. It is in the work of writers, whose writing is conceived in and operates between cultural heritages and addresses issues confronting what I call "paranational" communities, that problems of cultural translation are perhaps best articulated.

The crosscurrents of diverse cultures in the contemporary German literary scene, their different ports of entry, and their multiple destinations shape and reshape our notions of critical inquiry and demand appropriate strategies of reading. The upsurge of creative and conceptual wealth that characterizes the recent work of transnational writers poses a continuing challenge to theorizing what one critic calls the "diasporization" of culture.[18] Neither postcolonial theory nor discourses of identity politics can adequately address the diversity and complexity of diasporic narratives that emerge from transit points between languages, cultures, and belief and value systems. Furthermore, the contours of newly emerging maps of translation are very uneven, with "inaccessible" languages still pretty much unmarked and histories of once major languages, which have preserved the intellectual capital of today's high status languages, now forgotten.[19]

With the escalation of movements across borders, sociopolitical and cultural differences across the globe have become more visible, and the role of the translator in negotiating different linguistic and cultural idioms has become increasingly important. Large-scale migrations of our time have intensified the political affiliations of language, which highlight linguistic choices that are permitted and valued or erased and banned in translation. The role of translation in an increasingly globalized world and the political, critical, and academic debates surrounding questions of translation have resulted in an unprecedented semantic expansion of the term "translation." Such expansion has either led to its extensive metaphorical usage or made it simply coterminous with communication. In order to delimit the discussion for purposes of the present topic, I focus here on specific forms of (self-)translation in the literatures of contemporary exilic experience. Recent research on translation studies has highlighted the importance of the work of transnational or exilic writers as a window to understanding cultural differences and convergences not only between geographical sites but also between different temporalities. Since the recent prodigious growth of translation studies as an academic discipline is clearly predicated on the phenomenon of unending migrations within and without national borders, I would like to supplement my overview of the conceptual field by viewing the actual experience of translation, self-translation, and cultural translation in the work of two writers, Emine Sevgi Özdamar and Yusuf Yeşilöz, who, after immigrating, respectively, to Germany and *Deutschschweiz* (German-speaking Switzerland) from Turkey, began writing in and as translation, in other words, in German translation of their native languages. In the case of writers whose work was or may have been banned in their own land and language, a salient feature such self-translation takes is the liberation of the repressed language, a form of anti-cathexis that not only releases the energies of the source language's expression but also enhances the target language, as the romantics envisioned it.

Exile in German Translation

> In der Fremdsprache haben Wörter keine Kindheit. (In the foreign language, words have no childhood [translation mine])
>
> —E. S. Özdamar[20]

> Unsere Hoffnung ist ausgewandert und lebt nun in der Fremde. (Our hope has emigrated and now lives in in a foreign country [translation mine])
>
> —Yusuf Yeşilöz[21]

Both Emine Sevgi Özdamar and Yusuf Yeşilöz, who are first generation Kurdish-Turkish writers/filmmakers, write in German that, as their second and third language, is already a translation. Both writers came to Germany and Switzerland as adults; Özdamar at nineteen as a factory worker and Yesilöz at twenty-three as a political refugee. It is highly probable that their work would have been subjected to censorship, if written in Turkish. Thus, translation reveals something that censorship or fear of persecution holds back or hides. Furthermore, writing in and as translation or through a process of seeking the most appropriate idiom for expressing the original in the target language, the writer can reveal an experience that may have been repressed in the first language.[22] While what is divulged can tell a suppressed history of torture and give voice to what was silenced, it can also offer access to the cultural contexts of another time and place.

The works of Özdamar and Yeşilöz offer a compact archive of censored stories and histories that are smuggled across borders in translation. Both writers belong to the historically persecuted Kurdish minorities of Turkey. While any mention of her ethnic origins is either a veiled or fleeting allusion in Özdamar, Yeşilöz's writing is a self-conscious affirmation of his Kurdish roots. Özdamar, who was born in 1946 in Diyarbakır in the southeastern region of Turkey and studied drama before going to Germany as a guest worker, is one of the best known non-native writers of Germany, the poster girl of women writers of non-German descent. In a career spanning several decades as a novelist, playwright, stage director, and movie actress, she has received numerous awards, including the prestigious Ingeborg Bachmann prize in 1991 for her—at the time—unpublished novel *Das Leben ist eine Karawanserei hat zwei Türen aus einer kam ich rein aus der anderen ging ich raus*.[23] That was the first time that the prize was awarded to a writer whose native language was not German. While at the time, not a few critics raised the question of whether the prize was awarded for reasons of political correctness, Özdamar has since gained considerable critical cachet, especially among American scholars of German literature. Her success as a writer is neither politically enabled, nor is it accidental.

The linguistic innovations Özdamar has introduced into German result, to a great extent, from her ingenious translations of Turkish metaphors into German. While this act of translating what is often not translatable—in these instances, she supplies an annotation of sorts—infuses her German with a picture-like quality, the endurance of her work rests on issues that have a larger appeal beyond the exoticism of a Turkish-German "remix." Her hi/stories preserve and reveal banned chapters of modern Turkish history, put Turkish and German pasts into an open dialogue, and retell suppressed or forgotten tales that help decipher the apparently inscrutable signs of other cultures. These cultures are not always and not necessarily marked by geographical space and national, ethnic, or religious affiliation; they can also refer to historical distance, alternative and counter modes of life in a given place, and "islands" of speech patterns or community memory.

In choosing to translate their hi/stories into the language of their host lands, Özdamar and Yeşilöz hold the censors at bay. Or they restate what was censored, either by censors or through self-censorship, in the protective membrane of translation. Özdamar's experience of political persecution in her country, her witnessing of what practically amounted to a civil war between the Turkish state and the Kurdish insurgency, caused a linguistic amnesia, recovered only in translation. Translation can tell the story of a traumatic past indirectly without necessarily taking away from the effect of the experience. Özdamar has used translation as a self/censoring tool to devastatingly comic effect. In one of the stories in her collection, *Mutterzunge*, the narrator recalls seeing, in the prison where she was held, the brother of a young man tortured to death during a police interrogation. She remembers how many such young men and women were repeatedly arrested and jailed by brutal police forces who "pumped out the milk that their mothers breast fed them through their noses" ("man hat ihnen die Milch, die sie aus ihren Müttern getrunken haben aus ihrer Nase rausgeholt").[24] In the translation of this idiom, the brutality of the event is masked, because the meaning cannot be conveyed in its nakedness and has almost a comical effect, as it suggests a medical procedure—pumping the stomach after food poisoning.

In her self-declaredly favorite novel, *Das Leben ist eine Karawanserei* (and also in the two following books of the trilogy, *Die Brücke vom Goldenen Horn*[25] and *Seltsame Sterne starren zur Erde*),[26] Özdamar tells the translated and simultaneously self-censored history of an earlier regime of repression (1950–60), which she witnessed as a child in fragmented experiences of her immediate world, of her family, and of the many towns where her father found temporary employment. In *Karawanserei*, she reconfigures these shards of memory in a narrative supplanted by contraband and other books in the Turkish and German library/archives. The first translation is from her memory and mother tongue; the second takes the form of a retelling that, in its echoes of *A Thousand and One Nights*, resists the possibility of an external censorial intervention. At the same time, in the German context, her stories gain resonance by her ability to read them against other cultural memories and pasts, where they become one of the "touching tales," to use Leslie Adelson's fitting metaphor for narratives that re/imagine the intersection of German and Turkish confrontations with national pasts and present fears.[27] The tales, we should note, can touch and be touching only through translation. Such translation represents a virtual traveling library that accompanies the peripatetic writer who borrows the primary texts and, in some cases, the hidden documents from the library and the archives; reads, revises, and annotates them; and returns them into circulation in translated form. Özdamar checks out volumes of Heine, Marx, Engels, and Brecht and translates, against the larger narrative of German political history these texts provide, Turkey's trials with modernity and its traumas for the German reader. In Özdamar's novels, short stories, and play, *Karagöz in Alamania*, the metaphor of a mobile world library, where works in many languages are at the writer's disposal as aide-mémoire and translational aid, becomes the operative trope of exile in (self) translation.

Whereas Özdamar is the recipient of numerous awards and her work has been the subject of many critical studies, and continues to enjoy its *Nachleben* in translation into several languages, Yeşilöz remains relatively unknown to critics and to scholars working in bi- and multilingual or transnational literatures of Germany. On the whole, writers of the *Deutschschweiz* diaspora, unlike their counterparts in Germany, have gained little recognition outside German-speaking Switzerland. However, Swiss scholars have been publishing anthologies and critical studies of the many transplanted and translated writers in Swiss exile, among them Serbian-born Melinda Nadj Abonji, whose novel *Tauben fliegen auf* has garnered both the Schweizer Buchpreis and the Deutscher Buchpreis (Swiss and German book prizes) in 2010, Slovakian-born Irma Rakusa, Romanian-born Catalin Dorian Florescu, Croatian-Swiss Dragica Rajcic, and Tunisian Rafik Ben Salah. Like the work of the "hyphenated" German writers, the transnational literary output of the German Swiss diaspora is marked by an emphatic interest in language and translational performance. For writers of non-Swiss heritage, writing in German Switzerland, translation becomes a multidirectional movement in several languages. Most of these writers arrived in Switzerland with eclectic linguistic baggage. Those from the former Yugoslavia and from Eastern Europe had brought with them Slovenian, Serbo-Croatian, Romanian—often accompanied by French[28]—Hungarian, and Russian. Those who arrived in Switzerland as adults not only had to learn High German but also *Schwizerdütsch*, one or more of the Aleman dialects spoken in Swiss Germany. Yeşilöz, fully bilingual in Kurdish and Turkish, came with his contraband books, which by his own account were the reason for his persecution and exile.

Yeşilöz's *Der Gast aus dem Ofenrohr*, like Özdamar's novel trilogy, is a fictionalized account of his exile. However, unlike her *Karawanserei*, which beyond its autobiographical content weaves a tapestry of language games, a magical realistic history tour, and meta-translational acts, *Der Gast* reads, on the surface, like a straightforward account of its author's journey into exile. Nevertheless, Yeşilöz's narrative sustains a certain tension in regard to the fate of the many players of the story that lends the book an edge of suspense. This edge is maintained by several interruptions in the narrative. These intermissions in the drama of exiled lives take on the form of memories, disputed and accepted, reflections on a deterritorialized Kurdish language, sustained and embellished by custom and cultural memory, and information about Kurdish life. As such, these interludes of cultural reference constitute a traveling archive that in German translation remains free of any real or possible censorship. Furthermore, translation itself becomes a trope that forms a continuous thread in the story.

Since most of the story takes place in the *Durchgangsheim*, which is a kind of "holding cell" for refugees who do not speak any German but are subjected to long interrogations to determine their eligibility for asylum, translation literally becomes a matter of life and death. If their appeal is lost in translation or their testimony is falsified in mistranslation, they will be deported and face incarceration and possible death. When the narrator starts learning German, while waiting for a response to his asylum application, he diligently attends German classes and starts translating for his fellow asylum seekers. He acquires a Turkish-German dictionary that becomes his constant and indispensable companion. In fact, he calls the dictionary, which is an unambiguous metonym for translation, his Koran. The irony of this naming should be obvious, since many Muslims hold that the Koran, as the "Word of God" and, therefore, sacred and inimitable, which was revealed to Muhammad in Arabic, cannot be translated into any other language. For Yeşilöz, then, the task of translation becomes a metaphor for an act of divination (in the sense of discerning meaning as in Schleiermacher and Benjamin).

Although Yeşilöz's writing does not offer the interpretive possibilities that have made Özdamar's work the stuff of numerous dissertations and monographs, its translational impulse bears a striking resemblance to Özdamar's. The work of both authors shares in a linguistic imagery that Yesilöz attributes to the metaphorical wealth of Kurdish. Similarly, Özdamar draws liberally on metaphors of the body that abound in Turkish. In many cases, Kurdish and Turkish, which belong to completely different language families, to Indo-European and Turkic, respectively, use the very same metaphors, such as "Mein Blut kocht für dich" (my blood boils for you);[29] "[er] hätte fast seine kleine Zunge verschluckt" (he almost swallowed his little tongue)[30]; or "Stiftfarbe schlecken" (to lick ink).[31] Both authors offer no translational crutches when they place these metaphorical roadblocks on the path of the unsuspecting reader. However, a translation always appears somewhere on the road and gives the reader a chance to look back and recover meaning. Özdamar and Yesilöz often write in a metalanguage which reflects on how self-translation works and makes its structural transformation transparent. In an interview with Bettina Spoerri, Yesilöz explains,

> Ich schreibe in Deutsch, und Kurdisch und Türkisch sind bei mir wie "Nothilfe." Ich möchte etwas in Deutsch schreiben und finde vielleicht gerade nicht . . . dann ersetzt das manchmal ein Bild aus der kurdischen Sprache. . . . Ich erkläre also in einer Bildsprache das, was ich sagen will, damit der Sinn herauskommt.[32]

> I write in German, and Kurdish and Turkish are a kind of "emergency aid" for me. I want to write something in German and perhaps not find the exact word . . . then a picture from the Kurdish language replaces that. . . . Thus, I explain in a picture language that which I want to say, so that the meaning comes out. (Translation mine)

Like Özdamar, Yeşilöz uses *Bildsprache* as a reliable translational aid, and his "translations" both resemble and rival hers.

Although Yeşilöz has a political agenda, to reveal the persecution of Kurds by the Turkish government, he tells his story in an evenhanded and at times "self-censored" way. The Kurdish refugees in the *Durchgangsheim* have all fled the civil war between the Turkish army and the Kurdish insurgent forces that had ravaged the southeastern border areas for years. The narrator remains consistently elusive about his reasons for fleeing Turkey. Neither the Swiss immigration authorities who question him nor the reader gets a clue except that he was persecuted because of the banned books in his possession. On the other hand, another refugee, Melek, who had been tight-lipped about his reasons for seeking asylum for a long time, finally tells his story to the narrator in installments. Melek's account gives the reader a graphic picture of the attacks on Kurdish homes suspected of harboring members of the Kurdish terrorist group PKK.[33] The narrator relates the story of Melek's sister, a feisty and talented teacher who was killed in an ambush by the Turkish army. While the incident is a great tragedy for Melek's family and is the reason for his escape, the narrator does not demonize the killers. The blame is not laid straight on the shoulders of the Turkish government and the army. The story of Melek's sister Ele, as told by her brother to the narrator, is not one of persecution; on the contrary, Ele, the free-spirited star of her family and the village, enjoys the same educational opportunities as all citizens. She is the first one in her village to learn how to drive a tractor. With her father's blessing, she leaves the village to get a higher degree and comes back to serve her people. She is successful in her career and seems content with her lot. However, against her best judgment, she is drawn into the terrorist camp and dies with her warring comrades.

Another asylum seeker, Fate, a young woman with two children, also has a story she does not tell. When questioned by the immigration officials about her husband, she stubbornly remains mum to the bitter end, until denied asylum. While Yeşilöz's story shares many elements of exile stories that form a tapestry of silences, rumor, folklore, memory, and nostalgia, the narrator's gift lies in an effortless unself-conscious presentation of little known cultural information. At the beginning of *Karawanserei*, Özdamar tells a fantastic story of her grandfather traveling in a train and telling the story of the last decades of the Ottoman Empire, and the narrative weaves itself into the grandfather's beard, turning it into a tapestry of a picture story. In *Der Gast*, we get a vivid account from Fate about the actual weaving of carpets using natural dyes, an art that is being replaced by machine weaving with artificial colors. There are many coffee table books on carpet weaving, but I have never seen one written by a weaver herself. The fascinating process of gathering herbs, drying them, collectively deciding on color combinations, washing the sheared wool and boiling wool balls with the dried herbs and plants of different colors (a pot for each color) for the wool to absorb the color, and the final stage of weaving is told by Fate in her native Kurdish and translated into German by the narrator. The translated account becomes an archival record of a priceless and disappearing art. Every connoisseur of carpets knows that they tell a story, but Fate gives the reader the full account:

> In jedem Teppich verbirgt sich eine Geschichte. Ohne Helden- und Trauerlieder beim Weben, ohne das Erzählen abends im Schein der Petrollampe und ohne Gelächter kommen keine schönen Muster zustande. In jedem dieser Muster liegt wieder eine neue Geschichte verborgen.[34]

> In each carpet, hides a story. Without songs of heroes and sorrow while weaving, without telling stories under the light of the gas lamp, and without laughter no beautiful pattern would emerge. In each pattern, a story hides anew. (Translation mine)

The stories of exile form similar frame narratives that circle the globe in translation.

As the network of international and multinational connections expands, the demand for the recognition of diversity in the ways we live, learn, worship, become political, fight, and die becomes increasingly urgent. While the theorization of transnational consciousness has inspired scholars to envision novel modes of cognition and recognition with regard to collective memory and cultural identity formation, critical reflection on the role of translation as a historical and a geographical site of sociopolitical encounters is only poised at the initial station(s) of an unmapped itinerary.

Translation opens up a terrain where critical stakes, concerning the future of an increasingly globalized world with its attendant problems, will be played out. Incorporating critical legacies of translation into the discussion can shed light on contemporary questions of exile and transnationalism. Will the imagined decline of the nation-state render linguistic identity obsolete and make translation the norm? In an ideal or futuristic world, where the nation-state and its sovereignty are no longer the norm and we all live in translation, so to speak, our languages and differences will no longer be sites of competition and conflict. But in the not so ideal world of realpolitik, where millions have been forced out of the comfort zone of their own languages, translation becomes a possible path, however fraught at times, to negotiation of difference. Translation always involves a process of disassembly and reassembly, taking the original language apart and synthesizing its parts with the concepts of the target language; a process that would ideally enhance both expressions in the equation. Ultimately, how we assemble our versions of the self or translate ourselves, lies at the core of our forms of understanding ourselves and others, of being and seeing and facing the brave new world.

Notes

1. Milan Kundera, *Le Rideau: Essai en sept parties* (Paris: Gallimard, 2005), 49.

2. Kundera, "Die Weltliteratur," in his *The Curtain: An Essay in Seven Parts*, trans. Linda Asher (New York: HarperCollins, 1996), 34.

3. Antoine Berman, *The Experience of the Foreign: Culture and Translation in Romantic Germany*, trans. S. Heyvaert (Albany: State University of New York Press, 1992), 1.

4. While Benjamin's work, as it relates to language, translation, and representation is amply referenced, his indebtedness to the critical legacy of the *Frühromantik* is rarely remembered. It is important to remember that Benjamin's doctoral dissertation, *Der Begriff der Kunstkritik in der deutschen Romantik*, is an astute study of the aesthetic philosophy of the *Frühromantiker*. See *Der Begriff*, ed. Hermann Schweppenhäuser (Frankfurt am Main: Suhrkamp, 1973).

5. Berman, *Experience of the Foreign*, 14.

6. Friedrich Schlegel, *Kritische Ausgabe*, 35 vols., ed. Ernst Behler (Paderborn: Schöningh, 1958–), 2:239.

7. Katherine M. Faull, "Introduction," *Translation and Culture*, ed. Katherine M. Faull. Spec. issue of *Bucknell Review* 47.1 (2004): 13–21, here 14.

8. Friedrich Schleiermacher, *Hermeneutik und Kritik: Mit einem Anhang sprachphilosophischer Texte Schleiermachers*, ed. Manfred Frank (Frankfurt am Main: Suhrkamp, 1977), 169.

9. Ibid., 94.

10. Cynthia Ozick, "Literary Entrails: The Boys in the Alley, the Disappearing Readers, and the Novel's Ghostly Twin," *Harpers* (April 2007): 67–75, here 73.

11. Paul Michael Lützeler, *Kontinentaliesierung. Das Europa der Schriftsteller* (Bielefeld: Aisthesis, 2007), 160.

12. Milan Kundera, *Testaments Betrayed. An Essay in Nine Parts*, trans. Linda Asher (New York: HarperPerennial, 1996), 193.

13. Ibid., 192.

14. Jacques Derrida, "Roundtable on Translation," in *The Ear of the Other: Otobiography, Transference, Translation*, trans. Peggy Kamuf and ed. Christie McDonald (Lincoln: University of Nebraska Press, 1985), 93–161, here 123.

15. Walter Benjamin, "Die Aufgabe des Übersetzers," in *Illuminationen* (Frankfurt am Main: Suhrkamp, 1977), 50–62, here 52.

16. Ibid., 59.

17. Ibid.

18. Nikos Papastergiadis, "The Limits of Cultural Translation," in *Over Here: International Perspectives on Art and Culture*, ed. Gerardo Mosquera and Jean Fisher (New York: New Museum of Contemporary Art and Cambridge, Mass.: MIT Press, 2004), 330–47, here 331.

19. See, for example, Roland Barthes, "How remote it seems, that period when the language of Islam was Turkish and not Arabic! This is because the cultural image is always fixed where the political power is." Barthes, "Aziyadé," in his *New Critical Essays*, trans. Richard Howard (New York: Hill and Wang, 1980), 105–21, here 116.

20. Emine Sevgi Özdamar, *Mutterzunge* (Berlin: Rotbuch, 1990), 42.

21. Yusuf Yeşilöz, *Der Gast aus dem Ofenrohr* (Zürich: Rotpunktverlag, 2002), 62.

22. In this context, Antoine Berman supplies an interesting historical reference about a medieval Dutch poet who after the death of his beloved wife wrote a series of epitaphs in his native Dutch, then in Latin and Italian, and some time later again in Dutch. In Berman's words, it is "[a]s if he needed to pass through a whole series of languages and self-translations in order to arrive at the right expression of his grief in his mother tongue" (Berman, *Experience of the Foreign*, 2).

23. Özdamar, *Das Leben ist eine Karawanserei hat zwei Türen au seiner kam ich rein aus der anderen ging ich raus* (Cologne: Kiepenhauer &Witsch, 1991).

24. Özdamar, *Mutterzunge*, 12.

25. Özdamar, *Die Brücke vom Goldenen Horn* (Cologne: Kiepenhauer & Witsch, 1998).

26. Özdamar, *Seltsame Sterne starren zur Erde* (Cologne: Kiepenhauer & Witsch, 2003).

27. See Leslie Adelson, "Touching Tales of Turks, Germans, and Jews: Cultural Alterity, Historical Narrative, and Literary Riddles for the 1990s," *New German Critique* 80 (2000): 93–124.

28. Since Romanian is a Romance language like French, for Romanians it is easier to learn French than it is to learn German. In fact, a number of Romanian-born writers living in German-speaking countries, such as Carmen Francesca Banciu, arrived in Germany fluent in French but with no knowledge of German.

29. Yeşilöz, *Der Gast*, 71.

30. Ibid., 51.

31. Ibid., 111. These metaphors mean, "I like you"; "s/he was really surprised or shocked"; and "to be educated."

32. Bettina Spoerri, "Auszug aus dem Interview mit Michael Guggenheimer und Yusuf Yeşilöz," in *Diskurse in die Weite: Kosmopolitische Räume in den Literaturen der Schweiz*, ed. Martina Kamm (Zürich: Seismo, 2010), 140–46, here 140.

33. The Kurdistan Workers' Party (in Kurdish, Partiya Karkerên Kurdistan, or PKK) is a Kurdish organization which has since 1984 been fighting the Turkish state for an independent Kurdish nation and greater rights (political, social, and cultural, such as broader parliamentary representation, availability of Kurdish language courses, freedom of cultural expression) for the Kurdish minority of Turkey. At the onset, the ideology of the organization, founded in 1978, was based on a combination of revolutionary Marxism and Kurdish nationalism. The PKK is listed as a terrorist organization by a number of nations and international bodies, including the United States and the European Union. Turkey considers the PKK an ethnic secessionist organization that resorts to terrorism and force against both civilians and military targets to achieve its political mission.

34. Yeşilöz, *Der Gast*, 135.

Part II

✦

Cosmopolitanisms

Chapter 5

✦

Early Modern Translation and Transfer

Mixing but (Not) Matching Languages, Johannes Praetorius (1630–1680) and Eberhard Werner Happel (1647–1690)

Gerhild Scholz Williams

There are very few areas of knowledge, superstition, rumor, and prejudice known to his age which Johannes Praetorius (1630–1680) did not gather, reorganize, quote, or otherwise make part of his voluminous body of writings.[1] On the other hand, in his *Geschicht-Romane*, Eberhard Werner Happel (1647–1690) translated and adapted many different textual forms into the fictional context of his multivolumed novels.[2] Their use of media (and here I am including the rapidly expanding news market) confronted Happel and Praetorius with traditional and nontraditional forms of translation and language transfer, of intra- and interlingual contacts with the cultural and linguistic Other. In the following, I will briefly review several instances of translation and transfer found in Praetorius and Happel which make for compelling and amusing reading even today when we are readily involved with languages and cultures way beyond our own borders.

Translation and Code Switching: Johannes Praetorius

To manage the immense assemblage of information and make news palatable to his readers, Praetorius translated and transferred information from and into texts of many differing forms and lengths. He mixed languages such as Latin, German, Greek, and Hebrew, sometimes in the same sentences (*De Coscinomantia, Dulc-Amarus Ancilleriolus*), and he constructed countless lists using acrostics which, in turn, he further structured on the basis of the alphabet (*Rübezahl, Antopodemus Platonic,* tracts about comets) and Roman or Arabic numerals (*Wunder=Chronik*).[3]

Most of Praetorius's tracts are written in German, some in Latin, and, as noted, on occasion in both languages, with Greek and Hebrew words or phrases included for good measure. An example of this early modern form of code switching, as amusing as it is enlightening, can be found in his geo-demonology, *Blockes-Berges Verrichtung* (*Blockes-Berges Report*), in which he discusses the purported ability of witches to make weather. Here, he juxtaposes a discussion of witch lore with a scientific tract on weather phenomena like lightning and thunder, magnetism and meteors written by his contemporary, the Jesuit scientist and indefatigable collector of wonders, Athanasius Kircher. Praetorius quotes Kircher's Latin text alongside his own German translation.[4] By thus confronting his readers simultaneously with the different mentalities inherent in witch beliefs and the new science, Praetorius invites them to make up their own mind about these two dissimilar "ways of knowing" by means of his two very different "ways of telling."

In other texts, Praetorius mixes Latin and German in the same paragraph or even in the same sentence, as he does in his entertaining Latin/German *De Conscinomantia* (1677), a tract about the magical arts. It begins with the acrostic of the title, itself further organized in Roman numerals (I–XIII) to indicate the individual chapters to follow:

I. C/acodaemonis similis aliuas offucias damnandas
II. O/riginem Diabolicam.
III. S/acro-Sancti Verbi abusum
IV. C/reaturae elevationem supra Sphaeram activitatis
V. I/mposturam & malefidam
VI. N/uminis oboediendi improbationem in Pandectis religiosis

This pattern is maintained through the final chapter:

XIII. A/rbitrium infortunii & temeritatem incuriae.

The thirteen chapters undergo additional systematizing: chapter I ("Judicium Primum") is further divided into twenty-two subheadings identified by Arabic numerals. These subheadings present a detailed and carefully arranged list of various magical processes, each supported by appropriate secondary sources. For example, chapter (13.) deals with *Necromantia*. The sources cited are (this is the citation for just one item): Balduin. P. 770. M. Sim. Frid. Frenzellius de preasens. Natur. C.I. §. 6,[5] but essentially anyone who had ever written anything on magic appears in what Praetorius himself calls the Latin/German "Mischmasch" of this tract.

Equally imaginative code switching characterizes Praetorius's cometological tract *Himmlische(r) Comet=Stern*, also of 1677. It begins with a historical reflection on the sighting of a comet in the year 2018 "nach der Erschaffung der Welt," (after the creation of the world) when Abraham was seventy years old.[6] Upon the comet's passing there followed a great "Theuerung in Lande Canaan" (rising prices in Canaan) forcing Abraham, "Hungers halben" (because of great hunger) (n.p.), to flee to Egypt.

Tracking such celestial apparitions through history to his present day, Praetorius employs not only Latin, but also Greek and Hebrew sources, most of which are arranged chronologically. About two-thirds of the way through the text, he stops announcing that he will present "in Synopsi die vollständige Kunst (of astronomy)" (C3v). This is followed by Hebrew words subscribed by the Latin *Andromedae cingulo sub Cometa,* followed by a long quotation from the works of Schickardus,[7] followed by others from Grotius, Cardanus, and many more. Several pages later, again a Hebrew citation underwritten in Latin announces the description of the Jewish exodus at the time of the Roman occupation (D v) followed by a typical neologism of Praetorius, "Anjetzo *mystisire* ich hierüber folgender massen . . ." (Thus I will make up words about this in the following way . . .).[8]

Switching from Latin to German, Praetorius closes the tract with the self-deprecating admission, thereby also linguistically slyly deauthorizing either language: "So wenig Gewißheit du nun aus dergleichen *Mischmasch* zu nehmen hast / so wenig strecket sich ein Naturalist nach daß vorgesteckte Ziel theils der Natur selbst / . . . wann jener die Schwantz- Sterne (comets) seiner *Laßdünckeley* nach / wil aus natürlichen Uhrsachen zusammen kleistern mit *Gehirns=Leim* etwan aus Sonnen=Makeln . . . im vorigen Anno 1676" (italics mine; As little certainty as you can draw from *Mischmasch* like this, so little [certainty] can a naturalist [scientist] draw from nature itself . . . if the latter according to his own thinking and relying on the glue of his own brain wants to blame these comets on natural causes like the sun spots from the year just past, 1676 [E4]).

"Laßdünckeley" seems to mean "each according to his/her liking," an expression which also appears in the pronounced *Mischmasch* of another book, namely in the lengthy *Dulc- amarus Ancillariolus* (1663).[9] Here Praetorius explores the deep divide between women of different social and economic backgrounds implicit in the status of maid and damsel, or *Magd und Jungfrau.* Hiding behind the linguistic acrobatics arranged around the meanings of *Magd* and *Jungfer,* Praetorius offers his urban, literate, and reasonably affluent audience a serious—at times scathing—commentary on early modern issues of class and gender.

In keeping with his wish to convey a serious message in a jocular fashion and contrasting the two modes of telling in code switching which persists throughout the tract, the frontispiece of the *Dulc-amarus* sets forth what emerges as the tract's mock-egalitarian message: "Wiltu die *Mad* nicht; so kehre sie um / daß du eine *Dam* draus machest" (If you reject the maid, turn her around and you can make a damsel [lady] out of her) (emphasis added). It is a challenge to ignore the rather crude sexual innuendo implied in this suggestion.

Starting with the genealogy of the category of "damsel," Praetorius notes that gossipy ladies, *Kakligten Damen,* are grown from the seed planted by language. They issue forth from the *Phy-lo-loch ischen Samen,* that is, they are fashioned in a birthing process guided by their *creatrix,* the patron saint of writerly pursuits, Lady Philology. While clearly meant as a joke—*loch* can mean vagina, *Samen* means seed—Praetorius's concept of *Phy-lo-loch ischen Samen* creates a complex and sophisticated socio-linguistic challenge to the reader. According to Praetorius, language is the seed bringing forth the meaning that is the domain of philology, which in turn produces fruit, namely words, from language. "Maids" and "damsels," chatty women, are all born from the seeds of language. Thus, any difference between them must remain a conceptual illusion: *Mad* and *Dame* are linguistically, physically, and sexually interchangeable.[10]

In keeping with the lengthy message of the frontispiece of the *Dulc-amarus,* maid and damsel, conceived by Philology and created by the language of the author, are delivered at a right and festive time ("hoch-zeitige Geburt").[11] Moreover, the duality of the sweet and the bitter implicit in women's lives and captured in the title's *Dulc-amarus* is echoed in the second line, "der süß-wurtzligte und saur-ampferigte Mägde-Tröster" (the sweet-rooted and sour-herbed comforter of maids). The sweetness of the maid's virtues confronts the bitterness of her life whose praise Praetorius is about to deliver: "Weil nun aber mancher die Mägde nicht lieben will / als Ich gethan habe: so habe ich Ancillariolum Dulc amarum gemacht: Dulcem pro me, amarum pro aliis" (Since many do not want to love the maid, as I have done; I have written the Ancillariolum, which is sweet for me and bitter for them).[12]

Exploring the *Mad—Dam-* dichotomy, Praetorius quotes extensively from many sources, mixing languages, translating, and paraphrasing, all the while holding the reader's attention with his often acerbic, occasionally moving commentary on women's lives. He cites Luther on the virginity of Mary and the Koran on virgins in general: "Userm propo [sic]; da wir erweisen wolten / daβ die Mägde // Liebe kein ungeziemtes Werck sey: Solches will auch weiter haben der Mahomeht im Alcoran, libro 3. cap. 6. Pag. 594 . . . Ihr könnet Mägde zu Weibern nehmen" (Following our proposition in which we wanted to prove that loving maids is not an inappropriate undertaking: this is also confirmed by Mahomet in the Koran: it is fine if you take maids for wives).[13] And following a rather off-color Latin four-liner, he suggests: "Wer dieses verdeutscht haben wil der gebe einem armen Schüler was zum besten / und gedencke seinen Theil" (If anyone wants to translate this into German, he should give small token to a poor student and keep his thoughts to himself).[14] In other words, make a poor student happy by giving him a, presumably paid for, translation assignment.

Finally, lest anyone think equality between maids and damsels translates into equality between man and woman, he pronounces: "Was gehet mich die Gleichheit im Freyen an? *Amicitia aut invenit, aut facit pares:* Oder / daβ ichs rechter bedencke; *Conjuges mihi non sunt in relatione aequiparantiae, sed disquiparatniae: Laudo equitatem, inter equitatem, seu equos:* Wenn da ein paar im Joch zugleich begriffen seyn / und gleiche starck anziehen sollen; die müssen *pares* und *aequi seyn / . . . sed inter conjuges humanos arrider iniquitas, sive non aequitas,* die Ungleichheit: *Viro volo simper superiorem,* Mannes Hand oben . . . der Mann oben / die Frau drunter; so gehet es gut . . . aber mancher lässet das Weib oben geen" (What do I care about equality in courting? Friendship/love makes for equals: or if I really think about it: couples are not in a relationship of equality: If I am praising the equality among equals, I am praising such among horses: if two of them take the yoke together and pull equally strongly then they are a pair, and thus equal . . . but among humans couples there rules pleasing (?) inequality not equality: the man always wants to be superior. If the man has the upper hand, he is up / and the wife is below him (he is on top of her); this is as it should be, but there are many who let their wives be on top).[15]

Mischmasch, indeed, but enjoyable to read, and packing a weighty social commentary in the lightness of the language.

Languages in Contact/Conflict in Happel

From the beginning of his career, Praetorius's contemporary, Happel, emphasized the importance of understanding the culturally Other through the knowledge of languages other than German. Aside from having mastered French well enough to translate challenging documents, Happel had, judging by the many comments on English history and culture offered by his characters, (at least) a reading knowledge of English.[16] In addition, his fluency in Dutch was praised by a writer who borrowed from his news compendium, the *Relationes Curiosae.* As a resident of Hamburg, an international trading metropolis and publishing hub, Happel came into contact not only with the major European languages but also with many of the more exotic discourses from near and far, with new ideas and contested meanings.

References to translating appear already in his first novel, the *Afrikanische Tarnolast* (written in 1666, publ. 1689). The characters speak Coptic, "African," Congolese, and one among them easily projects military sophistication to those around him whose languages he understands without himself being understood: "Sie verzogen aber so lange damit / bis sie auβ allen meinen simulirten Reden sahen / daβ ich ein gutter Soldat seyn müsste . . . und den Spaniern von Hertzen feind" ("They messed around with all this until they surmised by my pretend speech that I must have been a good soldier and a mortal enemy of the Spanish") (*Afrikanische Tarnolast* [Stuttgart, 1689], 2:247). The opposite is, in fact, the case, but for the time being the speaker is safe among his enemies.

A few years later, Happel translated the Koran from French into German. This achievement earned him acerbic criticism from one of his contemporaries, who chided him in the *Monatliche Unterredungen* (January 1689) for making a translation of a translation: "die französische Übersetzung ist ja nicht allenthalben richtig / wie sollte dann diejenige accurate seyn / die nur aus dieser gemacht ist / und deren Arabischer Text wol nicht einmal dabey angesehen worden?" (The [original] French translation is in many places incorrect; how, then, could a translation be correct that was made on the basis of this (incorrect) one, whose Arabic original surely had not even been looked at?). [17]

In another of his earlier novels, the *Insulanische Mandorell* of 1682, Happel presents a review and paraphrase in German of the famously influential discourse on the novel, *Treatise on the Origin of the Novel* (*Traité de l'origine des romans*), by Bishop Huet (1670), who described the novel as a genre of "Fabelhafften/Historischen und Romanischen Schrifften." Prince Mandorell, the novel's protagonist, instructs his friend Prince Covvattiar in the usefulness of speaking languages other than one's own for the specific purpose of reading novels ("ward von Mandorell in vielen Sprachen unterwiesen / also / daß er sich in lesung der Europäischen Bücher / sonderlich der schönen Romane / täglich übete" (Mandorell was taught many languages, so that he daily practiced the reading of beautiful novels).[18] Good novels, Prince Mandorell insists, "teach us to speak and to read in a more effective way than even schools."[19]

In yet another instance of translational dramatics in the *Mandorell*, Dallopo, the protagonist, and his companions reach the safety of an island after being shipwrecked. At the shore, the life-saving power of language skills quickly becomes apparent when they encounter several inhabitants described as being of "Tuckischen Natur" ("mean-spirited") (*Insulanische Mandorell* 2:276). The spokesman of the natives—who is to accompany Daloppo and his castaway friends to the island's royal administrator, Valo—addresses Daloppo in Malaysian, a language the natives do not understand, for the native's mouthpiece is Portuguese by birth. This "very skinny man" introduces himself as widely traveled and fluent in "den meisten Sprachen der Welt" (in most of the world's languages). He warns Daloppo of a trap set for him and his companions by the natives, who are cannibals and regularly feast on the unfortunate people shipwrecked off their shores. The Portuguese explains that the natives spared him because he was too skinny to make a good meal, and because he knew many languages. He had become the translator and intermediary between the natives and their unlucky surviving "guests." It appears that, aside from valuing newcomers as food, the natives were also eager to hear news about foreign peoples and events ("Begierig sind von Außländischen Sachen/ reden zu hören" [they are eager to hear talk about all things foreign]). This meant that the widely traveled skinny Portuguese was their man to deliver such news prior to their grisly feasts (2:279). To be skinny and to speak foreign languages was clearly a winning combination, an opportunity in cultural transfer that saved the novel's characters from a decidedly unheroic fate while foregrounding that even cannibals shared with their unlucky guests a curiosity about the world outside of the island.

Strengthening the verisimilitude of his novels, Happel made abundant use of slave and captive narratives either in the original or in translation. One especially vivid example Happel borrowed from was Emmanuel D'Aranda's autobiographical account of his Algerian captivity (published in French in 1657).[20] In it, D'Aranda described his time as a slave in a place called the "bain/Baing/bagno," a kind of prison or holding pen for slaves, captives, and criminals. It consisted of what appears to have been an enclosed square or street with taverns and shops whose proprietors (*Taverniers:* "unterschiedliche Schenken und Wein Häuser") were often Christian slaves, as were most of the prisoners and customers, Turkish pirates and soldiers ("die Gäste sind Türckische Seeräuber und Soldaten"). According to the author, here Muslims and Christians interacted freely, and, when possible, played tricks on each other. Able-bodied slaves went out to work in the morning and returned at night. Many found themselves conscripted into service on the galleys.

Along with many interesting details, D'Aranda tells of a life of abnormal normalcy in the "baing/bain/bagno," where he was put to work turning a wheel and cursed by the guard when he was too slow at his task. He describes the language spoken among the multinational inhabitants of the "baing" as *lingua franca,* a kind of Creole Praetorius would have called a *Mischmasch,* of Italian, Spanish, French, and Portuguese (*Emmanuel Aranda* 1:59) (Franco, welches die gemeine Sprache unter den Schlaven und Türcken" ["Franco, which is the common language among slaves and Turks]). Considered a language of its own alongside Turkish and Arabic, its mastery was vital for the members of this multinational community, for it established a group consciousness distinguishing insiders from outcasts.[21] If conversant in this Creole, the slave or captive was included in the group; if not, punishment could be merciless, mostly floggings on the soles of one's feet: "Diejenige Sclaven / die erst neue ankommen / und weder die Sprache noch die Sitten diser Barbarn verstehen / werden Wild genannt / und durch Schläge zahm gemacht / wie die unvernünfftigen Bestien" (The slaves who are new and do not understand the language and customs of these barbarians are called beasts and they are tamed with beatings like creatures without reason).[22]

Happel's characters find themselves detained not only in the *bains* of Algiers, but they are also incarcerated in the *bain* of Constantinople, famously called the "Christen=Kercker" and described in detail in the *Ungarische Kriegsroman* (1684) (*Ungarische Kriegsroman* 1:304ff.). Like D'Aranda's autobiography, the portrayal of this prison is based on the authentic account written in 1655 by the father confessor of the imperial ambassador to the Ottoman court, Count Walter Lessle (Leslie) and very reminiscent of D'Aranda's description (309).

In the exceptional situation in the *bain*, mediation between slave owners and slaves, between captives and those who would or could produce ransom money, was provided by Jews. According to Happel, they had "ihre besondere Obrigkeit" (their own system of authority) among the Muslims based on their linguistic dexterity.[23] Like the "skinny Portuguese" the Jewish translators are outsiders, in part, by the diversity of the languages they know and the control over information conferred by this knowledge. Frequently forbidden to own slaves themselves, Jews occupied the position of intermediaries between the motley crew assembled in the *baing* and the outside. They traded slaves and made money by facilitating the ransoming of wealthy captives. They were not only tolerated but indispensable, because they were master-translators who "durch die gantze Welt eine fertige Correspondentz unterhalten . . . Dann die in Europa zerstreute Juden schreiben ihren Glaubens=Genossen zu Algiers über Livorno / alles Haar klein zu" ([the Jews] had corresponded with the whole world . . . because the Jews scattered throughout Europe inform those of their faith in Algiers about everything that goes on in Livorno [a popular slave Mediterranean slave market]).

Conclusion

In this brief chapter, I have shown that, whether we study Praetorius's linguistic "Mischmasch" or Happel's dramatization of life in the *bain*, we encounter, at each turn, a lively interest in translation and cultural transfer on all levels of print production.

As Emily Apter notes, "The task of translation . . . involves working on solutions to linguistic 'untranslatables' while mining the texts' fluctuating mobile status . . . translation as solution seeking."[24] I hope I have shown how two early modern writers approached the search for solutions to the linguistic challenges they faced in the texts I introduced to you, however briefly.

Notes

1. Johannes Praetorius (1630–1680) was born in Zethlingen. He studied first at the Lutheran Gymnasium in Halle and then at the University of Leipzig at the age of twenty-two. In 1659 Praetorius was named imperial poet laureate. In 1680 Praetorius died of the plague in Leipzig. See Gerhild Scholz Williams, *Ways of Knowing in Early Modern Germany: Johannes Praetorius as a Witness to His Time, Literary and Scientific Cultures of Early Modernity* (Aldershot, Eng.: Ashgate, 2006), 6.

2. For a brief review of his life and writings, see Stefanie Stockhorst, ed., *Eberhard Werner Happel: Der Insulanische Mandorell* (1682), vol. 12, Bibliothek seltener Texte in Studienausgaben, ed. Hans-Gert Roloff (Berlin: Weidler, 2007).

3. All discussed in detail in Williams, *Ways of Knowing in Early Modern Germany*.

4. Johannes Praetorius, *Blockes-Berges Verrichtung/Oder Ausführlicher Geographischer Bericht /von den hohen trefflich alt- und berühmten Blockes-Berge: Ingleichen von der Hexenfahrt/und Zauber-Sabbathe* (Leipzig: Johann Scheiben, Frankfurt am Main: Friedrich Arnsten, 1668), 156–89.

5. Johannes Praetorius, *De Cosinomantia; Oder, vom Sieb Laeuffe; Diatribe curiosa indagans ejus exsecrandae superstitionis, vel magiae plutonicae, circa exploratonem futurum praestigiatoriam* (Buchta: Enoch, 1677).

6. Johannes Praetorius, *Himmlischer Comet=Stern, welchen der erzürnete höchste Gesamt=Richter . . . in diesem Vor=Jahre Anno 1677 . . . verhänget hat* (Hall in Sachsen: Melchior Oelschlegel, 1677).

7. *De cingolos Andromedae Hebraeis.* Wilhelm Schickard (1592–1635), known for having built one of the first calculating machines in 1623.

8. Unless otherwise indicated, all translations are by Gerhild Scholz Williams.

9. Johannes Praetorius, *Dulc-amarus ancillariolus: Das ist, Der süß-wurtzligte und saur- ampferigte Mägde-Tröster/erzwingend, Daß die Mägde bessere Thiere seyn, als die so genanten Jungfern: Item, Daß sie einen angenehmlichern Nahmen führen . . . denn eine jedwede Jungfer wil doch gerne eine Magd hinter sich hergezottelt haben* (n.p.1663).

10. "So sehe ich nicht/wie auf irgend einerley Arth / die Mägde schlechter seyn solten / als die Jungfern. . . . Weiters macht die Natur keinen Unterscheid unter Magd und Jungfer" (Therefore, I don't see in any way whatsoever that maids should be inferior to damsels . . . Especially, since it is clear that nature makes no such difference between maid and damsel); ibid., 75–76.

11. "Aus Phy-lo-loch-ischen Samen gezeuget / und an die itzige possierliche Welt gebracht / als ein hoch-zeitige Geburt / oder *foetus posthumus*, von . . ." (frontispiece of Dulc-amarus).

12. Ibid., 440.

13. Ibid., 36.

14. Ibid., 43.

15. Ibid., 220–22.

16. He also published on English history and politics: *Fortuna Brittannica: oder Brittanischer Glücks=Wechsel: Fürstellend Eine kurtzbündige Beschreibung aller Königen von Engelland/und des schier stets unglücklichsten Hauses Stuart* (Hamburg: Thomas von Wiering, 1689).

17. Flemming Schock, *Die Text-Kunstkammer: Populäre Wissenssammlungen des Barock am Beispiel der "Relationes Curiosae" von E.W. Happel*, vol. 68, Beihefte zum Archiv für Kulturgeschichte (Cologne: de Gruyter, 2011), 2.

18. Stockhorst, *Eberhard Werner Huppel*, 432/574.

19. They are "fromme Lehrmeister / welche denen von der Schul folgen / und welche sprechen und lesen lehren auff eine weit lehrsamere und durchdringendere weise / alß die so in den Schulen lehren" (M III: 628), *Mandorell*, 472.

20. Emanuel D'Aranda, *Schauplatz Barbarischer Schlaverey* (Altona: Victor de Löw, 1666).

21. Martin Rheinheimer, "Identität und Kulturkonflikt: Selbstzeugnisse schleswig-holsteinischer Sklaven in den Barbareskenstaaten," *Historische Zeitschrift* 269, no. 2 (1999): 317–69, here 344.

22. Eberhard Werner Happel, *Der Ungarische Kriegs=Roman*, 6 vols. (Ulm: Wagner, 1685–97), (2:472).

23. A case is found in Martin Rheinheimer, "Identität und Kulturkonflikt," 335: "Er habe mit dem Juden gesprochen, so die Schlafen hier löset" (He [a slave from Friesland] had talked with a Jew who arranged for ransom for slaves [to free them]).

24. Emily Apter, "Taskography: Translation as Genre of Literary Labor." *PMLA* 122, no. 5 (2007): 1412.

Chapter 6

✦

On the Semiotics of Cross-Cultural Representation

Cultural Translation in Carl Raswan's *Im Land der schwarzen Zelte*

Nina Berman

In what ways can concepts central to translation studies theory enrich the various analytical frameworks that have been used for the past few decades to interpret fiction and nonfiction cross-cultural representations?[1] I will begin my exploration of this query by meditating upon concepts central to the postcolonial approach to cross-cultural representation, especially since the publication of Edward Said's groundbreaking study *Orientalism* (1978).[2] I will then introduce concepts from translation studies that may serve as alternative tools useful to approaching the issue of textual cross-cultural representation. My examples will be drawn from an analysis of *Im Land der schwarzen Zelte: Mein Leben unter den Beduinen* (1934; *Black Tents of Arabia: My Life among the Bedouins*), Carl Raswan's autobiographical account of his life with Arab Bedouin in the early twentieth century. I will conclude by offering remarks about the benefit of translation studies theory for analyses of cross/bi/multi-cultural writings.

Questions of Representation: Source and Target Cultures

In *The Rhetoric of Empire* David Spurr develops a useful categorization of rhetorical strategies that characterize cross-cultural representations. Idealization, debasement, affirmation, classification, appropriation, aestheticization, and eroticization are among the twelve categories Spurr explores in his study.[3] Spurr's premise is that rhetorical strategies are employed to interpret a specific feature of a colonized country or society, such as a landscape, a social action, or a person, to convey particular messages to the colonizing culture. Essentially, he considers these interpretive messages to emerge *independently* of the actual object of representation. Spurr's approach is typical of those postcolonial literary critics who left the relationship between representations of a culture and the culture itself largely unexplored. Let us briefly reflect on the reasons for this approach. Two terms are crucial in this regard, the notion of "representation" and the notion of "discourse."

The idea that literary and other cultural artifacts are representations of reality and thus need to be interpreted is widely accepted today, but that was not always the case. In *Orientalism*, Edward Said saw the need to point out that "what is commonly circulated by [cultural discourse and exchange within a culture] is not 'truth' but representations." He further insisted: "The things to look at are style, figures of speech, setting, narrative devices, historical and social circumstances, *not* the correctness of the representation nor its fidelity to some great original."[4] What that meant for critics is that in evaluating representations of the Orient (or other cultures, for that matter), a critic did not need to know anything about the represented culture. The task of critics was to describe the rhetorical and aesthetic dimensions of these representations in detail; the aside about "historical and social circumstances" seems to refer to the circumstances of production, and did not imply a mandate to understand the representation in its relation to what Said calls "some great original."

The second term that is central to Said and postcolonial literary criticism is the notion of discourse. Understood here in Foucauldian terms, literary representations were considered part of Orientalist discourse (to stay with the Saidian example), and that discourse was understood to be complicit in political action, namely in the colonization of the Orient. Said asked humanists to challenge "the general liberal consensus that 'true' knowledge is fundamentally non-political (and conversely, that overtly political knowledge is not 'true' knowledge)."[5] So we were presented with what I want to identify as a paradox or a dilemma. Namely, representations of the Orient, in this case, were to be understood as constructions that had no correlation to reality, while the resulting discourse on the Orient had very concrete repercussions in the real world. Critics were asked to analyze representations of historical political, social, and economic events, but only with regard to the function of the representations, *not* with regard to understanding the relationship between the signifier and the signified. That is, critics were not challenged to counter the construction of the Orient by offering an account of why this account was actually a misrepresentation. Rather, if the representation included images that were *widely understood* to be stereotypes, then critics, by and large, would designate it as a misrepresentation.

I have shown elsewhere that this critical practice led to generalizations that perpetuated a widespread ignorance about Middle Eastern political, economic, social, intellectual, and cultural issues.[6] For example, while the sophisticated cultural (and other) achievements of twelfth and thirteenth-century Middle Eastern cultures explain the emergence of the image of the

Noble Heathen during that period; while the actual violent military tactics of the Ottomans were responsible for the image of the violent Turk; and while the military and political cooperation between Prussians, Austrians, and Ottomans does not fit in with Manichean oppositions about a presumed relentless hostility between Europe and the Middle East, the representational model of *Orientalism* did not challenge critics to engage with the political, economic, and cultural dimensions of the Middle East. Some of the images that were/are widely assumed to be clichéd misrepresentations of the Middle East, however, are in fact grounded in historically verifiable political, military, economic, and cultural phenomena. In a gesture that, paradoxically, could itself be considered to be Orientalist, critics assumed that Europe not only had always *thought* itself superior over but had *actually been* more powerful than the Middle East, while the *longue durée* of this intercultural story is certainly more complex. Surely, the clichéd use of certain images over the centuries led to misrepresentations, but only a deeper engagement with the material would allow a critic to evaluate images that are in circulation in literary and other writings in their historical context.

Said himself became increasingly frustrated with the lack of attention critics paid to specific historical contexts and the complexity of power relations; in spite of his own responsibility for having contributed to setting up discussions of European representations of the Middle East in this distinct way, his critique of postcolonial literary criticism was pronounced.[7] Whereas the political thrust of Orientalist critiques was mostly relevant to the imperialist period that began with Napoleon's invasion of Egypt, it was not adequate to explain the role of the Ottoman Empire during this period; various cross-cultural political and economic alliances to this day; and the role of Christianity in the longer history of the region. One could summarize this reductive approach to European representations of the Middle East as at heart a Saussurean understanding of Orientalist semiotics which assumes that the signifier is arbitrary and which impedes an engagement with the ultimately unknowable signified (the Orient), but makes very explicit claims about the function and effect of Orientalist discourse.

In *German Literature on the Middle East*, I argued that we need to liberate ourselves from the restrictions of the linguistic turn (in its Saussurean form) and understand textual discourses as one type of practice among others, all of which need to be interpreted.[8] At this point, let me simply invoke the practice-based method of cultural interpretation, and ask: what would an approach that engages with the signified look like? And how might translation studies offer new tools for the interpretation of textual cross-cultural representation, in particular for instances of cultural translation?

One of the fundamental differences between the approach pursued by many postcolonial literary critics and translation studies critics is that knowledge of the two or more involved cultural and linguistic contexts is critical to the latter group of critics. Umberto Eco suggests "that studying translation is like studying bilingualism," and we can extend this analogy to the study of cross-cultural representation: studying cross-cultural representation is like studying biculturalism in that it requires the critic to be familiar with both cultures that are at play.[9] Two terms from the field of translation studies allow for useful distinctions: *target* and *source* texts and cultures. Postcolonial criticism contends that cross-cultural representations ultimately tell us more about the *target* culture than the source culture. While this assumption, to some extent, is also relevant to translation studies (historical, cultural, geopolitical, and many other factors structure the aesthetics and content of translations), translation studies makes the tension between source and target cultures and languages *the object of study*, by evaluating the shifts that occur in the process of transferring a source language text into a target language text. Most translation studies critics, such as Susan Bassnett, Umberto Eco, and the late André Lefevere, agree that all translation is, in one form or another, interpretation—though not all interpretation is translation.[10] That is, translation studies critics do not operate with a naive notion of the "true" meaning of a text, an expression, or a word, but rather acknowledge that meaning is always contextual and a moving target. What distinguishes the analysis of *interlingual* translation (Jakobson) from the analysis of *cross-cultural representation* is the differential way critics treat the status of the source language and culture.[11] In order to evaluate translations, the ground rules of translation studies require critics to be bilingually competent—knowledgeable of both the source and the target language. Critics agree that the quality of a translation is dependent on the translator's competency in both languages, including their cultural and historical contexts, and, of course, on the theoretical approach taken by the translator.

However, when it comes to cross-cultural representation in fiction and nonfiction writings, understood here as the representation of a source culture in the language of a target culture, we do not have an original source text readily available to which we can compare the target language textual representation. The original cultural text can only emerge through background research and analysis, carried out on the basis of linguistic competence: only by contextualizing and probing the presentation of historical and cultural information, which requires bicultural literacy and linguistic competence of the critic, would we be able to evaluate fully the relationship between source culture and its representation in a target text. This is not to argue for a naive belief in some sort of easily accessible "reality" that exists beyond "representation." What I am suggesting is a parallel between, first, a linguistic (and always also cultural, historical, geopolitical) translation of a source text into a target language text, and, second, the translation ("representation") of a source culture, through the medium of writing, for a target audience. In both cases, the analysis of the translation depends on the critic's familiarity with both target and source culture.

Im Land der schwarzen Zelte

Let me illustrate the merits of a translation studies approach for the study of cross-cultural representation by turning to Carl Raswan's autobiographical account of his life with Rwala Bedouin in the early twentieth century, *Im Land der schwarzen Zelte*. Carl Reinhard Raswan was a flamboyant figure who spent his life exploring, crossing, and transcending cultural boundaries. He was born in Dresden in 1893, and, after studying Greek and Latin at a humanist gymnasium, traveled through Greece and the Ottoman Empire in 1911. Later in 1911 he embarked on his first trip to Egypt, and during several excursions into the desert made first contact with Bedouin nomads in 1912. Over the next few decades, Raswan served in what he describes as the "German-Turkish army," migrated to California, and continued to return to Arabia to spend extensive periods living with Bedouin.[12] He became an expert in Arabian horse breeding, and wrote several books on the subject, including the famous Raswan Index, an extensive catalog of Arabian horses.[13] He also composed autobiographical accounts of his time with the Bedouin, and it is to one of these accounts that I turn here.[14]

In *Im Land der schwarzen Zelte*, Raswan clearly *intends* to contribute to a specific form of intercultural understanding (*Verstehen* in the Gadamerian sense). This notion of *intent*, which I borrow from Paul Grice, is central to my suggested reading of Raswan's text.[15] Seen as a communicative act, the utterances that make up Raswan's text convey a specific meaning. As will become evident, Raswan communicates this intended meaning by drawing on specific rhetorical and conceptual strategies to translate his experience among the Bedouin to the German readership of the 1930s. One of the key concepts in translation studies is the idea of "equivalence."[16] With regard to interlingual translation, issues of equivalence may occur on various levels, such as grammatical, syntactic, lexical, semantic, phonetic, rhetorical, textual, and stylistic levels. Finding equivalence is one of the key challenges a translator faces, and in evaluating the choices made by translators, translation studies employs, among others, the concepts of "domestication" and "foreignization," concepts that were first introduced by Lawrence Venuti in the 1990s.[17] Over the centuries translators and critics, from Jerome on, have disagreed over which one of these two approaches is superior. Domesticating translators have often drastically altered aspects of source language texts to appeal to reader expectations. The strongest proponent of foreignization is without a doubt Friedrich Schleiermacher, who argues that a translator should not erase aspects of the source text that may be foreign to his target language readers, but rather strive "den Ton der Sprache fremd zu halten" (to keep the tone of the language foreign).[18] Schleiermacher's stance, groundbreaking at the time, resonates with ideas expressed by postcolonial critics such as Kwame Anthony Appiah and Gayatri Spivak.[19] When foreignization is the preferred strategy, the principle of equivalence is in effect abandoned in favor of an attempt to highlight linguistic and cultural difference.[20]

Raswan, in his attempt to translate Bedouin culture for a German audience, uses both domestication and foreignization strategies, and the result is a text that wavers between emphasizing cultural equivalence on the one hand and cultural difference on the other hand. Before assessing specific instances of Raswan's approach, let us briefly review the content of the autobiography. *Im Land der schwarzen Zelte* is based on eleven visits Raswan paid his Bedouin friends over a 22-year period.[21] The recounting of his often extensive visits includes descriptions of his horseback and camelback rides through the desert; deadly internecine hostilities between different tribes; a battle during which several of his companions are killed; the devastating effects of a drought on the Bedouin; romantic episodes; and passages about food, clothing, and various customs. The account documents the Bedouins' conflicts with the French, British, and Ottomans, including difficulties that arise as new state boundaries prevent the Bedouin from pursuing their traditional lifestyle and from moving to different grazing grounds in times of drought.

Raswan domesticates the Bedouin context by establishing equivalence in five different ways. The first of these representational tools stresses aspects that appeal to notions of a shared humanity and to various values that had currency among Germans, his target audience, at the time. From the beginning, Raswan presents *himself* as a vehicle that allows the reader to enter the cultural context of the Bedouin. As early as the second page, he states that he lived as a Bedouin, that he never had to deny his race or religion among the Arabs, and that he was always treated with respect. He announces that Bedouin are terrifying ("schrecklich") only from the outside (*Im Land*, 6). Raswan sets the tone for the entire account by referring to the Bedouin as his friends.[22] Thus the presumed strangeness of the Bedouin is quickly dissolved in ideas of friendship and a shared humanity. Links to the German context are created when Raswan stresses the strong sense of family and clan relations. Bedouin tribes adopt Raswan (13–15, 121), and he uses the word "lieben," to love, to describe his strong emotional ties to the Bedouin.[23] Raswan mentions Bedouin gift-giving throughout (especially 120, 121, 122) and praises the Bedouin for their generosity (123). Whereas the social and economic meaning of gift-giving in any cultural context is not at all obvious, and gift-giving may have had a different meaning for 1930s Bedouin than for Germans (and also granting considerable differences within those groups), Raswan clearly appeals to some sort of generalizing notion that considers giving and being generous as positive traits.[24]

A Darwinist worldview emerges in several instances and might have had particular appeal in the context of the 1930s: "Über dem häßlichen Sterben der Schwachen und Verlassenen erfüllte sich das ewige Naturgesetz, das weder vor dem einzelnen, noch vor der Masse haltmacht. Das Starke schritt über der Schwache hinweg und gebar auf dem Wege wiederum das

Kraftvolle und Zähe" (The eternal natural law, which does not spare the individual nor the masses, fulfilled itself beyond the ugly dying of the weak and abandoned. Strength strode past the weak and on its way gave birth once more to the strong and enduring; Raswan, *Im Land*, 68). Raswan assesses the harsh conditions of Bedouin life as exemplifying laws of nature: "Denn nur das Schwache stirbt, damit das Starke lebt" (Because the weak dies only so the strong can live; 142). In addition to this biologistic approach to social life, the downplaying of Muslim aspects of Bedouin culture and emphasis on *pre*-Islamic Bedouin traditions may have been appealing to a society that rediscovered Germanic rituals and celebrated features of premodern heroism. But these ideas were popular beyond the German context, and the 1935 translation into English of Raswan's text took its place next to "other best sellers, such as a translation of Hitler's *Mein Kampf* and of Mussolini's autobiography."[25]

A second way in which Raswan domesticates Bedouin difference is by describing aspects of Bedouin life with a vocabulary that insinuates cultural familiarity to the German audience, particularly through sense-for-sense rather than word-for-word translations. For example, he talks about "rehfarbene Kamelherden" (deer-colored herds of camels; *Im Land*, 11) and calls tents "gewebte Häuser" (woven houses; 11). Phrases such as "in die Wiege gelegt hatte" (put into the cradle; 13) draw on imagery that is clearly not part of the Bedouin, but rather the German, cultural experience in order to provide a point of identification for the German reader. Often Raswan explains differences through analogy, for example, when he describes "Nadelschwanzhühner" (a kind of fowl)[26] and writes, "Diese Wüstenvögel—so groß wie unsere Rebhühner" (These birds of the desert—as big as our partridges; 20). A group of Bedouin is compared to gypsies (45), and a foreign type of meat rendered as something familiar: "[Es] schmeckte wie fettes Trappenfleisch" (It tasted like fatty meat of cranes; 48). When he is given a present, alien elements (such as Koranic verses on blankets) are mitigated by other aspects that suggest familiarity.[27]

The vocabulary used to describe landscapes, in particular, creates a sense of familiarity for the German audience. Words and phrases such as meadows, fields, sheep, shepherds, migratory birds, wolf, foxes, owl, chamomile, hills, the gentle wind, the silver moon, the quiet moon, and the mild moon (Wiesen, Felder, Schafe, Hirten, Zugvögel, Wolf, Füchse, Eule, Kamille, Hügel, lauer Wind, der silberne Mond, der stille Mond, and der milde Mond) are bound to evoke in German readers associations with *Heimatliteratur* (literature about the homeland) and other romantic portrayals of nature. These terms are juxtaposed with vocabulary that depicts unfamiliar aspects of the environment, such as sandstorm, steppe, desert, and wild lavender (Sandsturm, Steppe, Wüste, wilder Lavendel). In effect, the vocabulary establishing familiarity domesticates or mediates the unfamiliar. "Rührei zum Frühstück" (scrambled eggs for breakfast; 68) compensates for another scene in which Raswan and his friends eat locusts (59). A good example of this type of cultural sense-for-sense translation is provided in the description of one particular breakfast scene: scrambled eggs are made from the tiny eggs of "Nadelschwanzhühnern," honey is wild honey, butter and milk are made from sheep milk, and bread is flat bread. It seems as if part of German everyday life exists in Bedouin culture, albeit with slight differences.

Thirdly, Raswan domesticates Bedouin difference through a form of linguistic appropriation carried out, especially, in his use of possessive pronouns: "Ich war zurückgekehrt! Ich lebte wieder bei meinen Beduinen" (I had returned! Once more I lived with my Bedouin; 30). A fourth element of familiarity that leads to an effective domestication of Bedouin culture is the link Raswan establishes to topoi familiar from German fiction and nonfiction texts on nomadic cultures. Since the middle of the nineteenth century, German readers had been flooded with popular culture texts on Arabic culture, as conveyed in, among others, travel accounts and autobiographies by Fürst Hermann Ludwig Heinrich von Pückler-Muskau, Friedrich Martin von Bodenstedt, Ida Hahn-Hahn, and Max Eyth; the highly popular novels by Karl May; and translations of English-language *Sheikh* literature.

Because of audience expectations in this regard, references to certain aspects of Bedouin culture may have been read as signs of familiarity by the 1930s audience. For instance, terms such as "chief" and "blood brother" would be recognized by German readers as features expected in accounts about Bedouin and other nomads (13, 15, 30). Raswan's dialogues even echo the drama of Karl May's diction, as exemplified in expressions such as "Weit ist es in der Finsternis zu deinem Vater" (Far is the way in the darkness to your father; 24) and "Gesegneter Laut, der uns Weide verheißt!" (Blessed the sound that heralds the meadows; 53). Core values that Raswan associates with Bedouin, such as pride, courage, and honesty, also play a central role in May's and other German representations of Native Americans. Clearly, the setting and lifestyle bear resemblance to those of Native Americans: as nomads, the Bedouin live in tents, hunt for sustenance, are seen to be in tune with nature, and enjoy the freedom of the desert (the plains). Aspects of Bedouin difference are thus domesticated via a familiar vocabulary and frame of reference. In *Kindred by Choice,* Glenn Penny has elaborated on the "striking sense of affinity for American Indians that has permeated German cultures for two centuries, and which stems directly from German polycentrism, notions of tribalism, a devotion to resistance, a longing for freedom, and a melancholy sense of shared fate."[28] Clearly, key aspects that define this German affinity with American Indians according to Penny's interpretation also appear in Raswan's account of the Bedouin, especially an interest in tribalism, a fascination with resistance, and the longing for freedom. Bedouin are thus domesticated for the German reader via this shared framework of values associated with idealized nomadic peoples. Similarities are also evident in German representations of the nomadic Masai and Samburu of Kenya.[29]

Finally, Raswan domesticates Bedouin society by referring to a presumably familiar historical and political context. He describes Bedouins as a people caught up in state-border issues, a nation subjected to the ploys of colonial powers. Tactics employed, for example, by Ibn Sa'ud "um endlich zu jenem beinahe unumschränkten Diktator Arabiens zu warden, dem die Welt heute ihre aufrichtige Bewunderung zollt" (In order to finally become the almost absolute dictator of Arabia to whom today's world pays its honest admiration;12) are evaluated positively. Raswan's descriptions of political strife are rendered by drawing on concepts familiar to a German reading audience, such as the struggle over political leadership, succession issues, and fighting between factions.

But Raswan not only domesticates, he also uses foreignizing strategies in his account. One of the most pronounced instances occurs early in the narrative, when Raswan repeats stereotyped and clichéd images in his description of blood feuds, slavery, and leadership struggles (11). The third part of the book, entitled "Wie die Beduinen leben" (How the Bedouin Live, 143–54), provides even more examples as Raswan shifts, in this section, from a more autobiographical mode of writing to ethnographic writing. He describes the social, political, and economic distinctness of Bedouin society, and comments on, for example, the organization of Bedouin society into free and unfree individuals; forms of slavery; concepts of leadership; forms of superstition; funeral rites; hunting customs; camel, horse, and sheep breeding; and the status and life of women. He explains how the traditional lifestyle has been eroded through the impact of colonialism, modern technology, and encroaching state borders, and he chastises attempts at sedentarization both for being implemented without the necessary sustainable models of peasant culture and for ultimately killing Bedouin culture. Raswan suggests that Bedouin attacks and robberies are integral to their economic survival, but that the use of cars for scouting and raids increased internecine warfare and led to a high number of casualties. He also addresses ecological issues in his comments on climate and its effects on the Bedouin.

In this third section, Raswan, for the most part, does not domesticate aspects of Bedouin culture that are unfamiliar to the German reading audience but rather acknowledges their distinctness. As a result these instances function as elements of foreignization, although Raswan continues to mediate Bedouin difference through various explanations. In one instance, he describes an episode of unfamiliar behavioral codes and then writes "und doch durfte man ihm nicht böse sein. War doch sein ganzes Denken anders als das europäische" (but one couldn't be mad at him, as his entire thinking was different from that of a European," 14). Overall, Raswan balances the foreignizing elements with this type of mediating discourse, as well as with the various forms of domestication present throughout his narrative.

Analyzing Raswan's autobiography by drawing on a translation model developed by Jean-Paul Vinay and Jean Darbelnet in the 1950s further elucidates the author's representational strategies.[30] The scholars' translation model identifies four categories of domestication that they call "oblique translation," among which the categories of "equivalence" and "adaptation" are clearly present in Raswan's text, while instances of "transposition" and "modulation" occur less often.[31] Their three categories of "direct translation" are particularly useful to the analysis of Raswan's foreignizing strategies. The first of these three is "borrowing." Examples occur when Raswan borrows directly from the Arabic and provides no translation: "Aziz" (*Im Land,* 30); "El–Hamdu l'illah" (30); Zaraghrit" (66). In some instances the terms are explained later in the text. For example, the caption to one photograph reads "Opfer eines 'Ghazu' " (88); later in the text, the Arabic word is explained as "raid" (149).[32] The second category from Vinay and Darbelnet's model is the "calque," and I would like to suggest that all place names (Rub el-Khali, Scheded Umm-Kur; Nusud; Jabal Tawil, Jabal Druz, Haara, Abu Rijmeyn, Wadi Sirhan, Aleppo, Beyruth), personal names (Amir Fuaz, Tuëma, Faris, Maha, Mnahi, Dhadan, Mawia, Attala, Farhan, Tra'd Ibn Sattam, Abd el-Karim, Sleyman, Hajem-Pascha, Ali Ibn Achmed Hafiz, Muhamad Abd-er-Rachman-at-Tai, Mischal ibn Faris), and names of tribes (Rueyli, Hamad, Saba', Muwali, Tai, Schammar, Fid'an) function as orthographic calques. In all cases, calques are clearly foreignizing the text, as in the following example: "Tarfa, eine Schwester von Amir Fuaz, die Mijhem Ibn Meheyd, den Häuptling der Fid'an geheiratet hatte, war plötzlich gestorben" (Tarfa, a sister of Amir Fuaz, who had married Mijhem Ibn Meheyd, the chief of the Fid'an, had died suddenly; 67).

The third category identified by Vinay and Darbelnet is word-for-word translation. This occurs in Raswan's text whenever he translates from the Arabic, as in "Rafiq (Begleiter)" (companion, 105) and "Dira (Weidegebiet)" (grazing area, 15).[33] Variations of this feature occur when Raswan translates by paraphrasing: " 'Weltliche Wissenschaften' (wie die Araber Lesen und Schreiben nennen)" ('Worldly sciences' (as the Arabs call reading and writing; 13). When he does this he first translates an Arabic term and then presents us with an example of intralinguistic translation by rewording the term (in this case incorrectly, as the rewording does not correspond to the Arabic understanding of "weltliche Wissenschaften").[34]

These three strategies occur on the linguistic level and, clearly, in order to evaluate them, knowledge of Arabic is paramount. In this regard, the cultural critic, just like the translator, needs to have sufficient knowledge of both target and source languages to evaluate Raswan's representational strategies. But beyond the linguistic knowledge, the analysis of strategies such as domestication, foreignization, and finding equivalence, all of which Raswan uses in his representation of Bedouin life, also requires knowledge of both German and Arab Bedouin culture. We can only state that Raswan domesticates or foreignizes a particular aspect of Bedouin culture if we have a general sense for the cultural distinctness of Bedouin and German life (at a particular moment in time). We will only be able to evaluate how Raswan renders a historical event or cultural practice if we can draw on additional knowledge about social, economic, and political practices and about material dimensions that put Raswan's representation in perspective.[35]

Translation Studies and Cross-Cultural Representation

Raswan uses his intimate knowledge of both Bedouin and German culture to mediate his cross- cultural experience among the Rwala Bedouin. His knowledge of the Arabic language is excellent, and he performs the bilingual competence required of a successful translator. His portrayal of cultural and political detail betrays his own perspective and preferences, as the balancing of both domestication and foreignization strategies culminates in a predominantly positive view of the Bedouin. This positive view is communicated to a specific audience, the German readership of the 1930s, which is able to decode connotations and references that are *implicated*—to use another central concept developed by Paul Grice—because of the referential framework shared by Raswan and his readers.[36] The communicative intent, the larger meaning of Raswan's text—namely to convey a positive view of Bedouin society—is generated by way of these various strategies of domestication and foreignization. The photographs included in the autobiography also contain domesticating and familiarizing messages, and function similarly to the textual strategies—a subject for further exploration of cultural translation through visual forms of representation. Domestication here facilitates the acceptance and appropriation of cultural difference, and cultural difference is preserved and stressed via foreignization methods. The resulting—in this case—positive portrayal and, in effect, identification with nomadic cultures, from Native Americans to Arab Bedouin and East African Masai, is a remarkable phenomenon in German society.

On the theoretical level, the link to translation studies raises the issue of the status of the source culture. Ultimately, we cannot avoid engaging with the source language and culture. Any discussion of the representation of the source culture needs to draw also on knowledge about the source language and culture (some of which was undertaken here, for example with regard to his use of the Arabic language and several cultural references), otherwise the critic ends up mystifying the "culture of the other" by rendering it as unknowable or irrelevant. While my analysis considered the effect of Raswan's translation of select aspects of the source culture and language on the target audience, future explorations might explore additional aspects relating to the represented culture. In order to evaluate whether, for instance, Raswan's foreignizing representations are actually *mis*representations we would have to research the particular practice or feature he describes, as they appear in self-representations, anthropological accounts, or any other form of, among others, nonfiction, scholarly, documentary, and fictional representations in various media. We may not come up with anything conclusive, depending on the kinds of sources available, but we can certainly shed light on Raswan's rendering of his experience through comparative analysis. The framework of comparative literature, and comparative cultural studies more broadly, has much guidance to offer in this regard.

On a methodological level the analysis of Raswan's text shows that translation studies does indeed provide valuable tools for analyzing cross-cultural representations. Raswan's use of domestication and foreignization strategies, his attempts to find equivalence but also assert difference, and his use of various forms of oblique translation create an ambivalent text that performs gestures of distancing and appropriation simultaneously. Based on this analysis of Raswan's text, it is safe to suggest that the theoretical framework and methodological tools of translation studies improve our understanding of the semiotics of cross-cultural and transnational interactions, as represented in autobiographical and other writings.

Notes

1. This essay is dedicated to my late uncle Gottfried Müller, who gave me an original copy of Carl Raswan's autobiography (and countless other books throughout my life). Gottfried Müller, flamboyant and from Saxony as was Raswan, managed to maintain a bookstore, a rare books section, and a publishing house in private ownership throughout the period of the German Democratic Republic. Unable to keep up with the resources of West German chain-store booksellers, he had to face bankruptcy of the business owned by the family for almost one hundred years. As Gottfried said, "I survived two dictatorships, the Nazis and the Communists. But I did not survive the dictatorship of capitalism."

2. I focus here on postcolonial literary criticism; other approaches, such as *Interkulturelle Germanistik,* postcolonial area studies, and transnational studies take distinct stances regarding the questions explored here.

3. David Spurr, *The Rhetoric of Empire: Colonial Discourse in Journalism, Travel Writing, and Imperial Administration* (Durham, N.C.: Duke University Press, 1993).

4. Edward Said, *Orientalism* (New York: Vintage Books, 1978), 21.

5. Ibid., 10.

6. Nina Berman, *German Literature on the Middle East: Discourses and Practices, 1000–1989* (Ann Arbor: University of Michigan Press, 2011).

7. See, for example,, Edward Said, "In Conversation with Neeldari Bhattacharya, Suvir Kaul, and Ania Loomba." For an edited version of the interview, see *Relocating Postcolonialism*, ed. David Theo Goldberg and Ato Quayson (Oxford: Blackwell, 2002), 1–14.

8. This practice-oriented approach draws on an understanding of *language* and *culture* as defined by, among others, Ludwig Wittgenstein, Paul Grice, Max Weber, Clifford Geertz, William Sewell, Sherry Ortner, and Andreas Reckwitz.

See the introduction to *German Literature on the Middle East*, especially 2–9. See also Andreas Reckwitz, "Toward a Theory of Social Practices: A Development in Culturalist Theorizing," *European Journal of Social Theory* 5, no. 2 (2002): 243–63.

9. Umberto Eco, *Experiences in Translation*, trans. Alastair McEwen (Toronto: University of Toronto Press, 2001), 5.

10. André Lefevere and Susan Bassnett write that "translation is, of course, a rewriting of an original text." "General Editors' Preface," in André Lefevere, *Translation, Rewriting, and the Manipulation of Literary Fame* (London: Routledge, 1992), vii-viii, here page vii. But interpretation is not always a form of translation; as Umberto Eco states, "there are forms of interpretation that are not wholly comparable to translation between natural languages." *Experiences in Translation*, 73; see also 67–74.

11. Roman Jakobson explains the terms "intralingual," "interlingual," and "intersemiotic" in "On Linguistic Aspects of Translation," in *On Translation*, ed. Reuben A. Brower (Cambridge, Mass.: Harvard University Press, 1959), 232–39.

12. Carl R. Raswan, *Im Land der schwarzen Zelte: Mein Leben unter den Beduinen* (Berlin: Ullstein, 1934), 17. All translations from the German are mine. His comment about the "German-Turkish army" refers to the military alliance between Germany and the Ottoman Empire during World War I.

13. See *Raswan Index and Handbook for Arabian Breeders*, 3 vols. (Ames, Iowa: I-Tex, 1969); the first edition was published in seven volumes (Mexico: Editorial Anthony, 1957–67). Other publications include Carl R. Raswan, *Der Araber und sein Pferd* (Stuttgart: Schickhardt & Ebner, 1930), and several articles focusing on specific topics.

14. *Im Land der schwarzen Zelte* was translated twice into English, as *The Black Tents of Arabia: (My Life Amongst the Bedouins)* (London: Kegan Paul, 1935) and as *Black Tents of Arabia: My Life Among the Bedouins* (New York: Creative Age, 1935; also Boston: Little, Brown, 1935); in both versions, the names of the translators are missing. The same year, it was also translated into French by George Montandon as *Au pays des tentes noires: Mœurs et coutumes des Bédouins* (Paris: Payot, 1936). Translations into Danish, Swedish, Arabic, and Chinese of this and other texts also exist. Other autobiographical texts include *Escape from Baghdad* (London: Hutchinson, 1938) and *Trinker der Lüfte: Auf der Suche nach Ismaels Pferden zwischen Euphrat und Nil* (Rüschlikon-Zürich: A. Müller, 1942), a translation, by Ursula von Wiese, of *Drinkers of the Wind* (London: Hutchinson, 1940).

15. See, for example, H. P. Grice, "Utterer's Meaning and Intentions," *The Philosophical Review* 68 (1969): 147–77; and "Intention and Uncertainty," *Proceedings of the British Academy* 57 (1971): 263–79.

16. On discussions of "equivalence," see Susan Bassnett, *Translation Studies* (New York: Routledge, 2007 [1980]), 30–36; Eco, *Experiences in Translation*, 9–12.

17. Lawrence Venuti, *The Translator's Invisibility: A History of Translation* (New York: Routledge, 1995). On these concepts, see also Eco, *Experiences in Translation*, 22–25.

18. Friedrich Daniel Ernst Schleiermacher, "Ueber die verschiedenen Methoden des Uebersetzens," in *Kritische Gesamtausgabe,* ed. Günter Meckenstock et

al., vol. 11: *Akademievorträge*, ed. Martin Rössler (Berlin: de Gruyter, 2002), 67–93, here 81. See also the brilliant translation by Susan Bernofsky, "On the Different Methods of Translating," in *The Translation Studies Reader*, ed. Lawrence Venuti (New York: Routledge, 2000), 43–63.

19. See, for instance, Kwame Anthony Appiah, "Thick Translation," *Callaloo* 16, no. 4. (1993): 808–19; Gayatri Chakravorty Spivak, "The Politics of Translation," in *Outside in the Teaching Machine* (New York: Routledge, 1993), 179–200.

20. While "foreignization" displays some similarities with the notion of exoticization, I choose to use this pair of terms coined by Venuti to highlight the connection between these key concepts of translation studies.

21. Raswan, *Im Land*, 13. All further references to the text will be noted parenthetically.

22. The first part of the autobiography is entitled "Bei meinen Freunden, den Rauala-Beduinen." Ibid., 9; also 19.

23. "Dass sie mich liebten, wie ich sie liebte" (ibid.,, 13).

24. In his seminal study on gift-giving, *Essai sur le don: Forme et raison de l'échange dans les sociétés archaïques*, Marcel Mauss argues that gifts are never devoid of expectations about reciprocity. His study inspires scholarly discussion to this day. *L'Année sociologique, Nouvelle série,* v.1 (1923/1924): 30-186.

25. John Ure, *In Search of Nomads: An Anglo-American Obsession from Hester Stanhope to Bruce Chatwin* (New York: Carroll and Graf, 2003), 109.

26. I was unable to find the equivalent English term.

27. For example: "Dafür legte er aber in meine Arme einen uralten aus Holz geschnitzen Kaffeemörser" (ibid.,120).

28. H. Glenn Penny, *Kindred by Choice: Germans and American Indians since 1800* (Chapel Hill: University of North Carolina Press, 2013), xi.

29. Nina Berman, "Autobiographical Accounts of Kenyan-German Marriages: Reception and Context," in *Germany's Colonial Pasts*, ed. Eric Ames, Marcia Klotz, and Lora Wildenthal (Lincoln: University of Nebraska Press, 2005), 205–26.

30. Jean-Paul Vinay and Jean Darbelnet, *Comparative Stylistics of French and English: A Methodology for Translation*, trans. and ed. Juan C. Sager and M.-J. Hamel (Amsterdam: Johns Benjamins, 1995 [1958]), 30–42.

31. Instances of changing perspective (modulation) occur when Raswan describes how he acts according to Bedouin codes. Exemplary are passages in which he does not erase cultural difference, but in effect signals to his readers that one can learn to live according to unfamiliar cultural codes (e.g., *Im Land*, 14).

32. Similarly, "Jesira" (*Im Land*, 105) is explained later as "Mesopotamien" (109).

33. See also "Mejlis, die Versammlung der Häuptlinge" (ibid., 32–33); "Ghada, eine Tamariskenart" (49); "samh, eine feinblättrige niedrige Krautpflanze" (40); "Dhalul, einem Milchkamel" (54); "Ya ummi—meine Mutter!"; "Ya hayat—o Leben!" (80); "Wukil (Vertreter)" (105); "Iblis (dem Teufel)" (109); "Dakhil (unverletzlich)" (125); "Kuhl (Antimonium)" (123).

34. Roman Jakobson defines intralingual translation or "rewording" as "an interpretation of verbal signs by means of other signs from the same language." Jakobson, "On Linguistic Aspects of Translation," 233.

35. A more detailed evaluation of the cultural dimensions of Raswan's account would benefit from drawing on scholarship by, for example, William Lancaster, Clinton Bailey, Dawn Chatty, Lila Abu-Lughod, and Talal Asad and on autobiographies and travel accounts by, among others, Claude Scudamore Jarvis and Wilfred Thesiger.

36. H. P. Grice, "Logic and Conversation," in *Syntax and Semantics*, vol. 3, *Speech Acts*, ed. Peter Cole and Jerry L. Morgan (New York: Academic Press, 1975), 41–58.

Chapter 7

✦

Feng Zhi's 1949 *Entsagung*

Translating Rilke and Goethe across the Cold War Divide in China

Xiaojue Wang

In his acceptance speech at the ceremony of the Inter-Nationes Kunstpreis (Inter-Nations Art Prize) in 1987, Feng Zhi (1905–1993), the eminent Chinese poet and German literature scholar, talked about the influences he had received from Goethe and Rilke and noted that every time he read Rilke's *Duineser Elegien* and *Die Sonette an Orpheus*, what came to his mind were the last lines in Goethe's *Faust II*, the "chorus mysticus":[1]

> Alles Vergängliche / Ist nur ein Gleichnis;
> Das Unzulängliche / Hier wird's Ereignis;
> Das Unbeschreibliche, / Hier ist's getan;
> Das Ewig-Weibliche / Zieht uns hinan.

Feng translated the chorus into Chinese:

> 一切無常的/只是一個比喻;
> 不能企及的/這裡成為事跡;
> 不能描述的/這裡已經完成;
> 引渡我們的/是永恆的女性。(5: 204)[2]

How to understand the verb "hinanziehen" in relation to the eternal feminine complicates the concluding verses of Goethe's play. The Bayard Taylor version (1870–71), for instance, renders it as "lead upward and on," although an upward ("hinauf" or "aufwärts") movement is not indicated in the original word. The chorus was first translated into Chinese in 1921 by Guo Moruo, who used it as the epigraph for his own poetry collection *Nü Shen* (*The Goddesses*, 1921).[3] Guo chose the verb "lingdao" ("lead") to translate "hinanziehen," with no specific reference to the direction of movement. The term "yindu" selected by Feng Zhi, however, not only elicits a lateral trajectory of crossing a river but also carries strong Buddhist connotations. *Yindu* suggests ferrying over the sea of mortal life to the other shore, to complete the process of transformation to attain the supreme state of spiritual rebirth. For Feng Zhi, this marks the moment of *Vollendung*, perfection, in both poets. *Yindu*, a trope that Feng Zhi evoked constantly in his writings of the 1940s, best conveys his idea of transferring from one state to another through the mediation of spiritual forces. Transmutation or translation plays a crucial role in the process of transformation and self-fulfillment, which stands at the core of Feng's poetic world.

For Feng Zhi, translation means transformation. It is not that transformations happen as a result of the translation practice. Rather, translation is transformation in that translation constitutes a process of transmutation and production. In this light, translation is more than a transfer between two languages, or, a trope for cultural interchangeability. Translation concerns not merely interchange or exchange, but more importantly, change. As a force of change, translation bears transformative and generative powers. In Feng's poetic meditations, this process of production involves at least two forms of transformation: the re-formation of the poetic subject; and the revelation of the essential principle that enacts the cosmology of life: change, or spiritual renewal.

In conceptualizing the concept of transformation, Feng drew key inspirations from both Chinese and German traditions. In Chinese, *yi* 譯 (translation) and *yi* 易 (change) are homophonous words. In the ancient ritual classic *Zhou Li* (*The Rites of Zhou*), *yi* (translation) means *yi* (change): translation denotes a change between two languages in order to elucidate each other. The word *yi* (change) has rich connotations. In the esoteric Chinese classic *Yi Jing* 易經 (*The Book of Change*), which deeply influenced Feng's work, change is considered the essential form of cosmic life. Change constitutes a generative momentum that facilitates and furthers the process of production and reproduction. According to *Yi Jing*, "production and reproduction is what is called change."[4]

The German tradition provides another significant intellectual resource for Feng Zhi. In his reading and translation of Rilke and Goethe from the 1920s across the 1949 Cold War divide in China, Feng found not only a new lyric inspiration that allowed him to express a reinforced sense of autonomous poetic subjectivity but also crucial ideas about analogy, change, and spiritual rebirth. At the core of Feng's reflections on transformation and rejuvenation are Rilke's notion "Einsamkeit und Geduld" (loneliness and endurance) and the Orpheus figure, as well as Goethe's notion "stirb und werde" (death and transformation), which Feng regarded as "the supreme maxim" through all his life.[5] While his reading of Rilke helped form a unique concept of relational solitude in the unitary wholeness, it was through his study of Goethe that Feng effectively bridged the inward and outward life, the aesthetic and the social. Through a Goethean *Entsagung* (disavowal), this transformed and re-formed poetic subject relates to the universe, the social, and the national, and eventually completes a transition to the ideology of socialist collectivism.

By examining his concepts of poetic solitude, analogy, and transformation, this chapter takes issue with Feng Zhi's controversial political and aesthetic transformations across the 1949 Chinese division. In that year, with the Cold War bamboo curtain sealed along the Taiwan Strait, China was ideologically and territorially severed into various entities. This division pressed upon every single Chinese writer with utmost urgency. Some writers terminated their literary careers either by force or by will; some were forced into exile, within or outside the Chinese mainland; and some sacrificed their lives to defend their ideals. Feng Zhi, the "greatest Chinese lyricist"[6] of the 1920s and the modernist poet par excellence of the 1940s, however, seemed to be effortlessly assimilated into Chinese socialism and exchanged the aura of poet for the license and medallion of Maoist literary worker. It has often been noted that Feng's unexpected conversion reflected the schizophrenic mentality of Chinese intellectuals of the mid-twentieth century, and the conversion has usually been attributed to external political contingencies. Friedrich Engels observed in 1847 that Goethe had a double nature: "Thus Goethe is at one time colossal, at another petty; sometimes a defiant, scornful genius full of contempt for the world, other times a cautious, contented, narrow Philistine."[7] Citing Engels's comments on Goethe, Feng Zhi's critics, for instance He Guimei, pointed out that Feng revealed the same duality as his most revered cultural hero. Rather than accusing him of betraying his aesthetic ideals, however, this chapter suggests that Feng's 1949 conversion is in various ways a consequence of his poetic crisis amid the historical and political changes of mid-century China. Feng's ideas of *Entsagen*, change, and spiritual rebirth significantly informed his mid-twentieth-century transition from poetry to politics in socialist China.

The formation of modern Chinese literature has been from the very start entangled with the influences of Western literature and philosophy, among which the impact of German aesthetics has been crucial. German intellectual dynamics of enlightenment, romanticism, and modernism have been significant resources in China's quest for modernity. Feng Zhi followed a long line of Chinese intellectuals immersed in German culture. Feng studied German literature at Beijing University between 1921 and 1927 before he went to Germany to pursue his doctoral research. From 1930 to 1935, he studied at Heidelberg University and the University of Berlin. In 1933 he returned from Berlin to Heidelberg to attend Karl Jaspers's lectures and to complete his dissertation, "Die Analogie von Natur und Geist als Stilprinzip in Novalis' Dichtung" ("The Analogy of Nature and Spirit as the Principle of Style in Novalis's Work") under the guidance of Ewald A. Boucke. On June 26, 1935, he passed his dissertation defense, whose committee also included Jaspers. After returning to China, Feng taught German and German literature at various universities while continuing his poetic work.

Critics have duly noted Rainer Maria Rilke's influence on Feng Zhi. Without Feng's introduction and translation of Rilke and his own poetic experimentation, the constellation of Chinese modernist poetry would have been quite different. While Rilke's notion of solitude helped Feng overcome his early aesthetic crisis, it also suggested a dangerous tendency toward a mysterious and nihilistic attitude that could not effectively address the relationship between the poetic subject and the social reality. The recognition and contestation of this very dilemma characterize Feng Zhi's poetry of the 1940s in its most modernist form.

In 1924, when he was still an undergraduate student at Beijing University, Feng Zhi first read Rilke's *Die Weise von Liebe und Tod des Cornets Christoph Rilke*. However, it was not until 1931, when Feng Zhi read the first published volume of Rilke's correspondence, that the Austrian poet truly struck him with force. In a letter to his friend Yang Hui dated April 10, 1931, Feng noted, "In these six books [i.e., the six volumes of the first complete works of Rainer Maria Rilke (Leipzig: Insel, 1927)], I saw my ideal poetry, ideal prose" (*Feng Zhi quanji*, 12: 118). In the next few years, in addition to his dissertation research on *Die Aufzeichnungen des Malte Laurids Brigge* (*The Notebooks of Malte Laurids Brigge*, 1910), he translated a number of Rilke's writings into Chinese, including a slim collection of poems,[8] *Briefe an einen jungen Dichter* (*Letters to a Young Poet*, *Gei yige qingnian shiren de shifengxin*, 1903), a small section of the *Notebooks*, and Rilke's article "Von der Landschaft" ("On Landscape," 1902). A close reading of Feng's writings of the time reveals that his interest in Rilke lay not just in his poetic style but more in his meditations on the existential condition of human beings and the status of the aesthetic subject.

Poetic solitude is one of the defining themes of Feng Zhi's early poetry. In the 1930s, like Rilke, Feng experienced a decade of writer's block before he finally broke through with his most mature works in early 1940s, *Shisihang shi* (*Sonnets*, 1941) and *Wu Zixu* (*Wu Zixu*, 1943). Through his reading of Rilke, Feng conceptualized a notion of solitude as an autonomous, complete status of the "selbständig," or aesthetic self. This aesthetic solitude is only complete in its faculty to build an analogical relationship with the others in the world, thus forming a whole. The Rilkean notions of solitude and analogy have their fullest representations in Feng's writings of the 1940s, in particular *Sonnets*. The 1941 sonnet collection was written during wartime when Feng worked as a German literature professor at the exiled Beijing University in Kunming. This collection has often been regarded as his greatest contribution to modern Chinese poetry. It is innovative both structurally and thematically, a successful combination of the essences of the Western sonnet and classical Chinese poetry.

In *Sonnets* Feng sought to create a new notion of aesthetic solitude, which is complete in its analogical relationship with all other beings in the universe. In the preface to his translation of Rilke's *Briefe an einen jungen Dichter*, he noted, "But Rilke told us that the human being who was born into this world is lonely. Every human being in the world is like those trees standing side by side in the garden. There may be some connections among their branches and leaves, but their roots, which extend deep into the ground in order to obtain nutrition, are separated from each other. They are silent and solitary" (*Feng Zhi quanji*, 11: 282). In this distinctive concept of solitude, every individual is fundamentally lonely yet complete. The state of solitude is essential, the prerequisite for the formation of an analogical "living republic" (4: 85).

This autonomy of solitude not only leads to one's inner self but also envisions a new relationship with the outside world. Indeed, it is both inward and outward. Among Feng's translations of Rilke, there is an interesting small piece entitled "Von der Landschaft" ("On Landscape"), originally written by Rilke in 1902 as the preface to his book *Worpswede*.[9] In this article, as he maps out the development of landscape painting in Western art history, Rilke in effect attempts to conceptualize the relationship between humans and nature. Rilke observes,

> Landschaft so zu schauen als ein Fernes und Fremdes, als ein Entlegenes und Liebloses, dass sich ganz in sich vollzieht, war notwendig, wenn sie je einer selbständigen Kunst Mittel und Anlass sein sollte; denn sie musste fern sein und sehr anders als wir, um ein erlösendes Gleichnis werden zu können unserem Schicksal. Fast feindlich musste sie sein in erhabener Gleichgültigkeit, um unserem Dasein eine neue Deutung zu geben mit ihren Dingen.[10]
>
> If landscape is to become the medium and motive of an independent art, it has to be looked at as something distant and foreign, as something isolated and impassive, as something that progresses in itself; because it has to be distant and totally different from us, in order to become a redemptive equivalent of our fate. It has to be almost hostile in its lofty nonchalance, in order to provide, with its things, a new explanation for our existence.

An independent landscape painting in "erhabener Gleichgültigkeit" (lofty nonchalance) is created on the basis of detachment between the human and the natural worlds. Here, Rilke proposed a new way to observe and depict nature: to distance first the artist from his object in order to see it as it is in and of itself. Feng Zhi described such an artwork as "wuwo de" (without the poetic subject), and composed a set of landscape essays to illustrate this ideal relationship between the artist and his object. He entitled his prose collection *Shan shui* (*The Landscape*, 1943). In the epilogue, Feng remarked,

> What I described in this slim volume are not the so-called well-known sceneries . . . the real wonder of Nature is in an ordinary plain: the figure of a tree, the growth of a blade of grass, the flight of a bird, all contains an infinite, eternal form of beauty . . .
>
> We should restore the original shape of landscape and stop mingling it with human traces . . . only so will Nature erect in front of us; at the same time, we will feel how we should develop (*Feng Zhi quanji*, 3: 72–73).

Landscape painting and literature are the primary category of Chinese cultural tradition. Whereas metaphor, allegory, personification, and symbolism constitute the main approaches to convey nature, Feng asserts a notion of nature that has not been mediated and intervened in by human civilizations. Here, Rilke's influence is evident. One needs to look at the world of things as something "distant and foreign" to grasp its true meaning as well as its implication for one's own existence.

It is pertinent to note that Rilke, in the same passage in "Von der Landschaft," also emphasized the notion of *Gleichnis*, an analogical relationship between the self and the landscape. This principle of analogy marks the foundation of a *Weltinneraum*. If the initial stage is to establish a mutual independence of the poet and the natural world, it is then crucial to create a new connection between them. In one of his letters to the young poet Franz Xaver Krappus, translated by Feng into Chinese as early as 1931, Rilke observed, "Denn der Schaffende muß eine Welt für sich sein und alles in sich finden und in der Natur, an die er sich angeschlossen hat" (1903) (For the creator must be a world for himself and must find everything in himself and in Nature, with whom his whole life is connected).[11] This correlation between the artist and nature is what Feng described as the state of "communication between the poet and *wanwu* [all things]." To illustrate this relationship, Feng further observed, "One the one hand, the poet regrets—allow me to quote two lines from Tao Yuanming (365–427)—'all the myriad creatures have their refuge, / the lonely cloud alone has no support.' On the other hand, he feels that everything real in this world should be admired, be it with a name or not, be it capable of enduring and taking responsibilities" (*Feng Zhi quanji*, 5: 201). The embrace of a solitary yet complete subjectivity allows one to experience the expansiveness that leads to the overcoming of one's finitude and to the union between the self and nature.

In her *Flesh of My Flesh*, Kaja Silverman outlines a lineage of a different modernity that emphasizes resemblance, kinship, and analogies among various categories of things, among disparate times and spaces.[12] Unlike Descartes who claimed a unique, exclusive, and heterogeneous individual, intellectuals including Leonardo Da Vinci, Darwin, Fourier, Baudelaire, Freud, Rilke, Whitman, and so on, looking back at Ovid, asserted that all beings derive from the same flesh. Analogy is the principle of our world.

Rilke's *Die Sonette an Orpheus* speaks to this very connection: "Ohne unsern wahren Platz zu kennen, / handeln wir aus wirklichem Bezug. / Die Antennen fühlen die Antennen, / und die leere Ferne trug . . . / Reine Spannung" (pt. 1, XII) (Without knowing our proper place, / we act as if from true relations. / The antennae feel their sister-stations, / and the emptiness of space / bore . . . pure tension).[13] Feng Zhi's writings elucidate similar ideas of an analogical relationship between the poetic subject and other beings in the world. "Sonnet No. 16" makes a good example in this context:

我們站立在高高的山巅
化身為一望無邊的遠景,
化成面前的廣漠的平原,
化成平原上交錯的蹊徑。

哪條路、哪道水, 沒有關聯,
哪陣風、哪片雲, 沒有呼應:
我們走過的城市、山川,
都化成了我們的生命。

我們的生長、我們的憂愁
是某某山坡的一棵松樹,
是某某城上的一片濃霧;

我們隨著風吹, 隨著水流,
化成平原上交錯的蹊徑,
化成蹊徑上行人的生命。(*Feng Zhi quanji*, 1: 231)

We stand on the top of the mountain
And are transformed into the boundless panorama,
Into the vast plain in front of us,
Into the criss-crossing paths on the plain.

Which road, which river, doesn't have correlation,
Which wind, which cloud, doesn't have correspondence:
The cities, mountains, and rivers we have been through,
Have all been transformed into our lives.

Our growth, our sorrow
Are a pine tree on a certain hill,
A thick fog over a certain town;

We blow with the wind, flow with the water,
And are transformed into the criss-crossing roads on the plain,
Into the lives of the travelers on the paths.[14]

This poem constructs an analogical network among humans, plants, and places, and yields an ideal fusion of men and the natural world through bidirectional transformations and disseminations. While things and places we have experienced turn into part of our lives, our experiences also pass into animate and inanimate beings. This interconnected relationship is also displayed in lines such as "Thousands of years ago / there seemed to exist everywhere / our lives" (Sonnet No. 24, 1: 239) and "How many times have we been / projected onto a remote sky, / providing boatmen or travelers in the desert / with fresh nutrition for their dreams" (Sonnet No. 20, 1: 235). Such correspondences precipitate change, interaction, and communication. The transformative force works against stasis and generates poetry, or spiritual renewal.

In his article "Rilke: For the Tenth Anniversary of His Death," Feng Zhi wrote, "Rilke realized that each object has its own world, and all of the objects together constitute a real, serious, and living republic" (*Feng Zhi quanji*, 4: 85). This living republic is exactly what Feng describes as "the ideal world," the "collection of thousands of loneliness." While Rilke's notion of the living republic on the basis of analogy helped Feng confront his acute aesthetic crisis, it paradoxically suggested a mysterious and nihilistic tendency that could hardly reconcile the relationship between the poetic subject and the social reality. Although the aesthetic self finds a secure position in a world where every solitary object is interconnected according to an immanent order, it is accompanied by a deep skepticism toward this very ideal republic. How to avoid sliding into a void, a utopian empty space? This dilemma significantly informed Feng's composition of *Sonnets*, which was finished at a time of massive Japanese air raids. With his wartime exile into the vast interior of China, Feng's doubt became all the more intense. Indeed, Feng's poetic thinking is marked by the ambivalence between the world of interconnectedness and its paradoxical form of infertility and isolation, between artistic renewal and a total separation between the poetic and the social. In this sense, *Sonnets* is rather a reflection on the crisis than its poetic overcoming.

It is exactly this impasse that prompted Feng's 1949 transition both aesthetically and politically. The transition is first anticipated in his historical fiction *Wu Zixu* (1943), which brings up the concept of endurance as a way of social engagement and Goethe's *Naturdenken* of metamorphosis, the notion of *Stirb und werde* in particular, as a way of subject re-formation and rebirth. At the wartime university, Feng Zhi taught courses on German literary history, German lyric tradition, Nietzsche, Goethe, and special topics on Faust. Feng Zhi read Goethe's *Die Leiden des jungen Werthers* in the early 1920s, but the Sturm und Drang passion struck him only temporarily. It was during the anti-Japanese war of the late 1930s and 1940s that he came to Goethe again. Interestingly, it was the late Goethe, the author of *West-östlicher Divan* (1819), *Wilhelm Meisters Wanderjahre oder die Entsagenden* (1820s), and the last version of *Faust* (1832), that fascinated Feng Zhi and helped him forge a viable intersection between the aesthetic and the political to resolve his poetic crisis of the time.

The overcoming of one's finitude through aesthetic creativity is not sufficient to build an effective relationship with society. The introspective cultivation of the subject is not fertile. Feng resorted to Goethe's notion of a life of fullness, a life inward and outward, in order to expand and enrich the aesthetic experience and develop a positive relation between the aesthetic and the social. Like Leibniz and Schelling, Goethe thought that inner and outer experiences were comparable and inseparable. The particular reflects the whole, what is inward is also outward: "Müsset im Naturbetrachten / Immer eins wie alles achten; / Nichts ist drinnen, nichts ist draußen: / Denn was innen, das ist außen. / So ergreifet ohne Säumnis / Heilig öffentlich Geheimnis" (You must, when contemplating nature, / Attend to this, / in each and every feature: / There's nought outside and nought within, / For she is inside out and outside in. / Thus will you grasp, with no delay, / The holy secret, clear as day).[15] In Feng's Goethe study, he particularly highlighted Goethe's notion of a dynamic unity of inward and outward forces in one's life, following the natural rhythm of the living organism, that of the eternal breathing in and out (*Ein- und Ausatmen*). He saw Goethe as a full human being, who was able to balance an outward life, in which he served as a privy councilor in Weimar and observed nature, and an inward life, which "required him to disavow external business and return to an inner world." Feng then asserted, "an outward pursuit and an inward homecoming to the self—these two forces alternate and exert mutual impacts, which gradually uplift and deepen Goethe's feelings and thoughts" (*Feng Zhi quanji*, 8: 7). He quoted from *Wilhelm Meisters Wanderjahre* to further illustrate Goethe's efforts to fuse an inward and outward life: "Denken und Tun, Tun und Denken, das ist die Summe aller Weisheit, von jeher anerkannt, von jeher geübt, nicht eingesehen von einem jeden. Beides muss wie Aus- und Einatmen sich im Leben ewig fort hin und wieder bewegen; wie Frage und Antwort sollte eins ohne das andere nicht stattefinden" (Thinking and doing, doing and thinking—that is the sum of all wisdom, recognized and practiced from of old, yet not understood by everyone. Like breathing in and out, both should occupy life in a ceaseless alternating flux; like question and answer, neither should occur without the supporting of the other).[16]

Feng often reflected that at the heart of his Goethe reception and interpretation are three notions: the affirmative spirit; the *Metamorphosenlehre*, a process of transformation through death and rebirth; and the unity of an outward and an inward life.[17] He regarded *Faust* as a work of a contestation between the affirmative, positive and the passive, negative forces, which enabled him to resist the nihilistic and pessimistic atmosphere pervasive in wartime China. In his article "Fushide li de mo" ("The Demon in *Faust*," 1943), Feng argued that the spirit in *Faust* can be conveyed by a line in the *Book of Change*: "Heaven moves vigorously; the gentleman in the same spirit strives to strengthen himself without cease" (天行健，君子以自強不息).[18] Feng Zhi was particularly fascinated by Goethe's idea of metamorphosis ("Gestaltung-Umgestaltung") and by such images of transformation as the chrysalis and the snake repeatedly shedding its skin. Similar images often appear in Feng's 1940s writings: for instance, in Sonnet No. 2, lines 7–9 read "we arrange ourselves / In nature, as cicadas and moths / Cast all old skins into the mud"; (*Feng Zhi quanji*, 1: 217). The third stanza of Sonnet No. 3 starts with "You are shedding your shell all the time, / and grow in the moment of withering" (1: 218). In life's enduring mutability, he saw its force of renewal and eternity. In Feng's reading, the conception of metamorphosis is best illustrated in Goethe's poem "Selige Sehnsucht" ("Spiritual Yearning"), which praises the dynamics of the life force and its perfection as unfolded in an upward spiral of deaths and rebirths.

Feng Zhi quoted Goethe's maxim "Stirb und werde" in the last line of his sonnet dedicated to Goethe.

你生長在平凡的市民的家庭，
你為過許多平凡的事物感嘆，
你卻寫出許多不平凡的詩篇；
你八十年的歲月是那樣平靜，

好象宇宙在那兒寂寞地運行，
但是不曾有一分一秒的停息，
隨時隨處都演化出新的生機，
不管風風雨雨或是日朗天晴。

從沉重的病中換來新的健康，
從絕望的愛里換來新的營養，
你知道飛蛾為甚麼投向火焰，

蛇為甚麼脫去舊皮才能生長；
萬物都在享用你的那句名言，
它道破一切生的意義："死和變。"

The last two tercets read as follows: "From serious illness comes new health, / from desperate love comes new nutrition, / you know why the moth flies into the flame, / why the snake grows by shedding its old skin; / everything in the universe benefits from your maxim, / which reveals the meaning of life: "Stirb und werde." In his Chinese rendition of "Stirb und werde," Feng chose the characters 死和變 "si he bian," literally meaning "death and transformation."

Later in his 1947 essay "Gede de xidong heji" ("Goethe's *West-Eastern Divan*"), he translated the entire poem into Chinese and further considered the significance of self-sacrifice and spiritual rebirth. Scholars such as Marian

Galik have pointed out that Feng Zhi's translation and interpretation of *stirb und werde* as "dying and transforming" were actually not accurate.[19] Feng himself was not unaware of it. In a 1982 study of Goethe's poems entitled "Qianshi Gedeshi shisan shou" ("Interpretations of Thirteen Poems by Goethe"), Feng clarified his decision to translate the German imperative "werde" as "bian" (metamorphosis or change). He explicated that a faithful rendition of the original word "werde" is "wancheng" (self-fulfillment, perfection). However, he could not find a better monosyllable word in Chinese than "bian" to render "werde," and thus remained firm on his original word choice (*Feng Zhi quanji*, 8: 149).

Given Feng's conceptualization of change and subject re-formation, it is evidently not a translation failure to select "bian" rather than "wancheng" for "werde." It concerns not so much the issue of the infidelity of the translator to the original language, semantic or stylistic, but more a strategic moving away from it and changing it. The connotative differences of "bian" (metamorphosis) and "wancheng" (self-fulfillment) indicates that Feng interpreted Goethe's *Metamorphosenlehre* as an everlasting process of transformation through death and spiritual rebirth of the poetic subject. In this light, as Emily Apter argues, translation serves as "a significant medium of subject reformation and political change."[20] Furthermore, for Feng Zhi, the process of change itself, rather than the consequence of "self-fulfillment," is significantly valued. Feng's sense of historicity brings him close to his German contemporary, Walter Benjamin, in his reflections on translation, transformation, and the historicity of language. In his 1916 article "Über die Sprache überhaupt und über die Sprache des Menschen" ("On Language as Such and on the Language of Man"), Benjamin observes, "Die Übersetzung ist die Überführung der einen Sprache in die andere durch ein Kontinuum von Verwandlungen. Kontinua der Verwandlung, nicht abstrakte Gleichheits- und Ähnlichkeitsbezirke durchmisst die Übersetzung" (Translation is removal from one language into another through a continuum of transformations. Translation passes through continua of transformation, not abstract ideas of identity and similarity).[21] What Benjamin stressed is not so much a movement between languages as the space and time that this movement involves.

The principle of transformation applies not only to the development of plants and insects but also to that of human beings and society. Accordingly, Feng found in Goethe's *Entwicklungsroman* (development novel) the best novelization of the theory of metamorphosis in the human world: "The growth of the protagonist of the novel *Wilhelm Meister* also goes through the development from one stage to the next, until he eventually understands the meaning of life, which therefore contributes the notion of 'Entwicklungsroman' to German literary history. However, the advance from one phase to the next is not easy. One has to experience an arduous death of the previous phase in order to fulfill a happy rebirth of the next one" (*Feng Zhi quanji*, 8: 7). While the *Entwicklungsroman* is better known as the *Bildungsroman*, in

Feng Zhi's Goethe studies, he preferred using the former term, which bears a distinct reference to *Entwicklung* (development), deeply consonant with Feng's contemplations on the process of transformation for the subject.

In his interpretation of "Stirb und werde," Feng Zhi stays close to scholars such as Konrad Burdach, who in his introduction to the Cotta edition of Goethe's *West-östlicher Divan* understands the formula "Stirb und werde" to reflect Goethe's natural philosophy.[22] What intrigues Feng Zhi is not the moth's surrender to the two primal forces: eros and the death instinct, but rather, its desire for light, a higher form of self-fulfillment. In his reading, it is through the self-annulment or self-absorption into the light that the moth is able to overcome the lower form of consummation of carnal love to accomplish ultimate spiritual enlightenment and perfection. In this light, Feng is a scholar of the Enlightenment par excellence, much like his spiritual mentor Goethe. In a 1980s elucidation of "Selige Sehnsucht," Feng quoted two lines from a poem by King Wu of the Liang dynasty, which used the same image of a moth incinerating itself in a flame to illustrate the idea of obtaining artistic perfection through self-sacrifice, and argued that Goethe's moth imagery contains a deeper dialectic meaning of "sacrifice and completion, death and rebirth" (*Feng Zhi quanji,* 8: 149). For Feng, the earlier titles of "Selige Sehnsucht," "Selbstopfer" or "Vollendung," are probably more incisive.

Feng Zhi's work *Wu Zixu* best illustrates his reflections on the Goethean concept of death and becoming. It is written in the form of poetic prose based on a famous historical tale about the politician Wu Zixu (559?–484 B.C.) of the Spring-Autumn period around 500 B.C. Zixu, the junior son of an ex-Chu official, fled the state of Chu to seek revenge for his father's death. Exiled, he passed through a number of different states and finally sought asylum in the state of Wu and helped it become one of the strongest states of the time. With the help of the Wu army, Zixu eventually conquered his home country, the state of Chu, and lynched the dead body of the former Chu king who was responsible for his father's death. While other historical or fictional accounts mainly focus on the dramatic experiences of war, revenge, and betrayal, Feng takes only Zixu's exile as the subject matter. What emerges is a story about *Entwicklung* rather than retaliation.

Interestingly, Feng Zhi first came up with the idea to write about Wu Zixu after he read Rilke's prose poem *Die Weise von Liebe und Tod des Cornets Christoph Rilke* (*The Lay of Love and Death of Cornet Christopher Rilke*) in 1924. He later recalled that he was immediately touched by its "rich color, fine tone, and a haunting melancholic and mysterious atmosphere."[23] Although it was one of Rilke's few works that enjoyed popular success even during his lifetime, scholarship on *The Cornet* has been surprisingly sparse. Judith Ryan has pointed to the tension between "neo-Romantic sensibilities and modernist understandings of the psyche" in this work and thus regards it as an important transitional piece in Rilke's literary trajectory.[24] This text's musicality, explorations of interiority, and highly stylish combination of aestheticism and historicism must be among the main features that inspired Feng Zhi to write about the legendary historical character Wu Zixu in the same manner. However, it was not until sixteen years after his first reading of Rilke's *Cornet* that Feng started to write his own version. The final form is totally different from the initial idea of a romantic retelling of a historical story. As Feng observed, "comparing [it] with that prose poem by Rilke, there is nothing the same or even similar. It lacks musical elements, as well as a certain kind of innocence. There are many mundane events, which reflect the calamity experienced by modern men, especially by Chinese people in recent years" (*Feng Zhi quanji*, 3: 427).

Wu Zixu is not just an aesthetic success but also a work with an incisive concern for social realities in a transitional historical time. The poetic subject does not indulge in the divine beauty of nature symbolized in the scene of "Linze" ("The Woods"), "while he is aware that there would come the day when there would be no innocent place left uncorrupted anymore" (*Feng Zhi quanji*, 3: 375–82). He "cherishes his own harsh destiny," and disavows the preservation of pure interiority and noble personality represented in the figure of Jizha in "Yanling" ("The Town of Yanling," 3: 413–17), who refuses to ascend the throne to avoid contamination of his integrity by political and social engagements. Even the loss of the mother that pervades Feng's early poems is transformed into the scene of the laundry woman who offers Zixu rice—an allegorical image of the mother of life and the goddess of order, thus sublimated into the mythology of genesis ("Lishui," 3: 408–13). In this way, Zixu bids farewell to the innocent dreams and ideals of his past and marches arduously yet firmly toward the "ugly society," to confront the site "full of spider webs, which stick to the body with every step" (3: 401). The poetic subject, or *der Entsagende*, eventually disavows the divine beauty of nature as well as introspective self-cultivation in order to embrace the idea of social and political commitment as the highest form of self-fulfillment through a series of transformations and self-sacrifice, through the unification of the inward and outward aspects of life. Notably, while Rilke's poetic musicality and form shape the poetic world of Wu Zixu, it is Goethe's conception of metamorphosis and death and spiritual rebirth that informs its thematic structure.

The central theme of *Wu Zixu* is "a parabolic trajectory" of transformation. Feng illuminates that "a piece of beautiful life, be it for love or hatred, for life or death, is like tracing an arch: there is persistence in the standstill, overcoming in the descending" (3: 425). For Zixu, "stirb und werde" means the abandonment of freedom but the simultaneous confinement of moral perfection and self-preservation, and the unreserved self-submergence in a higher unity, in social responsibility as analogized by revenge. After completing *Wu Zixu*, Feng bid farewell to reclusive academic life and participated affirmatively in various social and political gatherings and demonstrations.

With this critical transformation, when confronted with the crucial 1949 division in China, Feng Zhi chose to remain on the mainland and merged seemingly unproblematically into the new socialist state. He was a member of the Chinese delegation to Hungary, Czechoslovakia, East Germany, and the Soviet Union, representing liberated new Chinese writers and scholars. In the 1950s, Feng was successively assigned as editor of the literary column of the leading party newspaper *Renmin ribao* (*People's Daily*), associate editor-in-chief of the People's Literature Publishing House, chair of the Department of Western European Languages and Literatures at Beijing University, and member of the Chinese Academy of Social Sciences, among other positions. In June 1956 he joined the Chinese Communist Party. His political engagement expanded.

What appears perplexing is not just that Feng became a successful public figure in the post- 1949 Communist regime, but more intriguingly, he did it effortlessly, without a strenuous process of assimilation. I suggest that Feng's 1949 transition must be viewed in the larger context of his conceptualization of the poetic subject, transformation, and rebirth formulated in his study and translation of Rilke and Goethe in the 1930s and 1940s. The shock of the infinite solitude of aesthetic beauty forced him to seek a more dynamic relationship with the external world. In Chinese socialism he envisioned a new collectivity, a living republic, and a higher stage of the life force. In the socialist totality, Feng imagined an opening to a substantially capacious relationality and a possible situation of the aesthetic subject within a larger Whole. The reformation and redemption of the aesthetic subject can only be achieved by its total absorption into the national collectivity. The socialist totality would set the normative framework for, and yet simultaneously free, the aesthetic and the political subject. Only in the socialist society would the bourgeois humanist ideal of the unity of "freedom and law, the individual and the collective" be realized, which is manifested in the closing lines in Goethe's sonnet "Natur und Kunst": "In der Beschränkung zeigt sich erst der Meister, / Und das Gesetz nur kann uns Freiheit geben." (Only in limitation is mastery revealed, / and law alone can give us freedom).[25] In 1957, during the Anti-Rightist campaign with accelerating radical ideological control by the Chinese Communist Party, Feng utilized a newly adopted aesthetic discourse of "Marxist historical materialism," highlighting a heroic sublime figure of the people as a collective subject of history in a teleological trajectory of progress to reinterpret Faust's verses before his death as conveying a socialist utopia: "Solch ein Gewimmel möcht ich sehn, / Auf freiem Grund mit freiem Volke stehn!" ("Such a swarming of people I would like to see, / to stand on free ground with free people!").[26] Feng contended that in Goethe's time, "when the proletariat just began to form a class," it was never possible to actualize such a utopian vision. In the twentieth century, however, this ultimate goal had been "achieved in socialist countries led by the party of the working class" (*Feng Zhi quanji*, 6: 19–20). Therefore, in Goethe's time, the final scene could be nothing more than a Catholic transcendental illusion.

In proposing this statement, Feng Zhi went even further than Georg Lukács in the latter's speech titled "Unser Goethe" at the celebration of Goethe's 200th birthday in East Germany in 1949, in which Lukács asserted that Faust's final vision of "a free people on free land" could only be composed by Goethe when he saw "contemporary capitalism penetrated into the corrupt world of the Holy Roman Empire." According to Lukács's point of view, Goethe's work reflected in a realistic manner the emergence of capitalism in a splintered Germany. In his work *Goethe und seine Zeit*, which laid the cornerstone for the East German interpretation of the classical Goethe, Lukács discussed Goethe and his work against the backdrop of the political and cultural history of Goethe's time, in particular, that of the desperate combat of the growing bourgeoisie against the oppressive feudal conditions in Germany.[27] In the 1950s, when he had to reevaluate Goethe according to the dominant socialist ideology in the People's Republic of China, Feng may or may not have been aware of Lukács's Goethe studies. After all, Lukács was also denounced in socialist China after the 1956 Hungary Revolution as in other socialist countries, including East Germany.[28] However, Feng was well acquainted with the official cultural policy in East Germany, especially that regarding Goethe. According to his later recollections, when he taught Goethe at Beijing University during the 1950s, he followed the major thesis of Goethe assessment advocated in East Germany: Goethe held a positive attitude toward the French Revolution; Goethe maintained a socialist vista for the human being as evidenced in Faust's final lines; and Goethe was a classical realist as he expressed in one of his conversations with Eckermann that "klassisch ist das Gesunde, romantisch das Kranke" ("classicism is healthy, romanticism is diseased") (*Feng Zhi quanji*, 8: 9–10).[29] Although Feng knew all too well the party policy behind these partial or distorted opinions, he remained convinced that a re- or /misinterpretation of Goethe was necessary to help forge a national culture and collectivity in socialist Germany as well as socialist China.

The need of people, a "new collectivity as anticipated in Goethe's *Wilhelm Meisters Wanderjahre*," is the ultimate call for Feng Zhi across the Cold War division, which was addressed in his "Gede yu ren de jiaoyu" ("Goethe and the Education of Human Beings") (*Feng Zhi quanji*, 8: 85–86). In "Xieyu wendaihui kaihui qian" ("Before the Conference of Chinese Literature and Art Workers Takes Place"), the first article he published in socialist China, he described his mental metamorphosis as follows: "I have to wash off all the narrow characteristics of intellectuals in front of the people. At this moment I hear a forceful call that I have never heard before: 'The need of the people!' If more fire is needed, make yourself a piece of wood and throw yourself into the fire; if more water is needed, make yourself a drop of water and throw yourself into the water" (5: 341). Ironically, Feng might not have expected that his idea about fulfilling the mission of the poetic subject through social engagement and through intersection with a larger collectivity could only be realized by the total annihilation of that very subject. Death would not lead to rebirth. He had to denounce his previous poetry that foregounds spiritual autonomy. When the first German literary history was composed "collectively" in socialist China, Feng Zhi, the director of the writing collectivity, had to categorize his intellectual guide Rilke into the "decadent groups of imperialism" and define Goethe as a writer of capitalism with limited *Weltanschauungen*.[30] Once committed to Rilke's idea that poetry was based not on emotion but on experiences, Feng Zhi now threw himself into the revolutionary romanticism mandated by none other than Mao Zedong.

Notes

1. This chapter is adapted with revisions from "Fashioning Socialist Affinity: Feng Zhi and the Legacy of European Humanism in Modern Chinese Poetry," in Xiaojue Wang, *Modernity with a Cold War Face: Reimagining the Nation in Chinese Literature Across the 1949 Divide* (Cambridge, Mass.: Harvard University Asia Center, 2013), 202–54.

2. Johann Wolfgang von Goethe, *Faust: A Tragedy. The Second Part*, trans. Bayard Taylor (Boston: Houghton Mifflin, 1871), 314. Feng's speech later appeared in his article, "Zai lianbang deguo guoji jiaoliu zhongxin 'wenxue yishu jiang' banfa yishi shang de daci" ("Speech at the Ceremony of the Endowment of 'Inter-Nationes Kunstpreis' of the Federal Republic of Germany"), collected in his twelve-volume *Feng Zhi quanji* (*Complete Works of Feng Zhi*) (Shijiashuang: Hebei jiaoyu chubanshe, 1999).

3. Guo was the key figure during the May Fourth New Culture Movement in China, who translated and introduced Goethe's work. In 1921 Guo translated Goethe's *Die Leiden des jungen Werthers* into Chinese, an instant bestseller that went through over fifty editions before the Sino-Japanese War broke out in 1937. All translations from the Chinese are my own unless otherwise noted.

4. For the elucidation of the concept "yi" (change), see for instance, Cheng Zhongying, *Yixue benti lun* (*The Ontology of Changes*) (Beijing: Peking University Press, 2006), 3–34.

5. Feng Zhi described Rilke's ideas of "Einsamkeit und Geduld" in a letter to his friend Yang Hui (*Feng Zhi quanji*, 12: 123); for Feng's response to Goethe's "stirb und werde," see his 1934 letter to his friend Willy Bauer (12: 188).

6. Highly praising Feng Zhi's first poetry collection *Songs from Yesterday*, Lu Xun called the young poet "the greatest modern Chinese lyricist" in his preface to the second volume of *Zhongguo xinwenxue daxi* (*Anthology of New Chinese Literature*) (Shanghai: Liangyou, 1935), reprinted in *Lu Xun quanji* (Beijing: Renmin wenxue chubanshe, 1981, 6: 243).

7. Quoted from Peter Demetz, in *Reflections: Essays, Aphorisms, Autobiographical Writings*, ed. Peter Demetz (New York: Harcourt, Brace, Jovanovich, 1979), 169. Feng Zhi first read Engels's review of Karl Grün's *Über Goethe vom*

menschlichen Standpunkte in 1948, but did not discuss it at length until the end of the Cultural Revolution, when he picked up his study of Goethe study again, which he stopped after the foundation of socialist China in 1949.

8. Feng Zhi's translations of Rilke's six poems were published in the special edition marking the tenth anniversary of Rilke's death in *Xinshi* (*New Poetry*) in 1936: 豹 ("Panther"); "Pietà"; 一個婦女的命運; 啊，朋友們，這並不是新鮮 ("Du, mein Freund, bist einsam, weil"); 奥爾弗斯 ("Nur wer die Leier schon hob"); 縱使這世界轉變 ("Wandelt sich rasch auch die Welt"), *Feng Zhi quanji*, 9: 431–77. *Letters to a Young Poet* was first serialized in the feuilleton of *Huangbei ribao* (*North China Daily*) in 1931, and was later published as a monograph by Shangwu Press. The selected translation of *The Notebooks of Malte Laurids Brigge* was first published together with "On Landscape" in the journal *Chenzhong* (*Die versunkene Glocke*), and was later collected as an appendix in the monograph of *Letters to a Young Poet* (11: 277–342).

9. However, it was eventually not included in the book and published posthumously in 1932. This article had a tremendous influence on Feng Zhi. Later, he used the same title for his own prose collection "Shan shui" ("The Landscape," *Feng Zhi quanji*, 3 :3–76).

10. Rainer Maria Rilke, "Von der Landschaft," in *Rainer Maria Rilke: Sämtliche Werke* (Wiesbaden/Frankfurt am Main: Insel Verlag, 1955–66), 5: 516–23.

11. Rainer Maria Rilke, *Briefe an einen jungen Dichter* (Leipzig: Insel, 1929), 12.

12. Kaja Silverman, *Flesh of My Flesh* (Stanford, Calif.: Stanford University Press, 2009).

13. Rainer Maria Rilke, *Die Sonette an Orpheus. Sonnets to Orpheus*, trans. C. F. McIntyre (Berkeley and Los Angeles: University of California Press, 1967), 25.

14. Dominic Cheung translated all twenty-seven sonnets by Feng Zhi in appendix 1, 77–89, in his book *Feng Chih* (Boston: Twayne, 1979). English translations here are based on Cheung's renditions with minor revisions.

15. Johann Wolfgang Goethe, "Epirrhema," in *Johann Wolfgang Goethe: Sämtliche Werke nach Epochen seines Schaffens*, ed. Karl Richter (Munich: Hanser Verlag, 1997), 12: 92; *The Essential Goethe*, ed. Matthew Bell (Princeton, N.J.: Princeton University Press, 2016), 29.

16. Münchner Ausgabe, 17: 493. The English translation comes from *Wilhelm Meister's Travels*, book 2, chapter 9, in *Goethe's Works*, vol. 9, edited and translated by Edward Bell (London: George Bell and Sons, 1885), 264.

17. See Feng Zhi, "Gede de wannian" ("Late Goethe"), *Feng Zhi quanji*, 8: 72–80; his speech at the ceremony of the endowment of the Friedrich Gundolf Preis by the Deutsche Akademie für Sprache und Dichtung in 1988, 5: 219–21.

18. Feng Zhi, "Fushide li de mo" ("The Demon in *Faust*," 1943), *Feng Zhi quanji*, 8: 25–45. For the illustration of the line in *Book of Change*, see Li Xueqin, ed., *Zhouyi zhengyi* (*Annotated Zhouyi*) (Beijing: Beijing daxue chubanshe, 1999), 10.

19. Marian Galik, "Feng Zhi and His Goethean Sonnet," in *Crosscurrents in the Literatures of Asia and the West: Essays in Honor of A. Owen Aldridge*, ed. Masayuki Akiyama and Yiu-nam Leung (Newark, Del.: University of Delaware Press, 1997), 123–34, here 124–25.

20. Emily Apter, *The Translation Zone: A New Comparative Literature* (Princeton, N.J.: Princeton University Press, 2006), 6.

21. Walter Benjamin, "Über die Sprache überhaupt und über die Sprache des Menschen," in *Gesammelte Schriften*, ed. Rolf Tiedemann and Hermann Schweppenhäuser (Frankfurt am Main, 1974), 4: 151. The English translation is from *Reflections: Essays, Aphorisms, Autobiographical Writings*, ed. Peter Demetz (New York: Harcourt, Brace, Jovanovich, 1979), 325.

22. Goethe, *Sämtliche Werke Jubiläums-Ausgabe*, vol. 5, *West-östlicher Divan*, ed. Konrad Burdach (Stuttgart: Cotta, 1902–12), xxxiii.

23. Feng Zhi, "Rilke: For the Tenth Anniversary of His Death," 5: 83. Rilke's prose poem *The Lay of Love and Death of Cornet Christopher Rilke* has several Chinese renditions and is still very popular among Chinese readers. The favorite translations are 軍旗手的愛與死之歌 by Liang Zongdai (1903–1983) and 旗手克里斯托夫・里爾克的愛與死之歌 by Bian Zhilin (1910–2000), both of whom were prominent modern poets in the 1930s and '40s.

24. Judith Ryan, *Modernism and Poetic Tradition* (Cambridge, Eng.: Cambridge University Press, 1999), 41.

25. Münchner Ausgabe, 16.1: 780. Feng Zhi, "Lüelun ouzhou zichan jieji wenxue li de rendao zhuyi he geren zhuyi" ("On Humanism and Individualism in European Bourgeois Literature"), *Feng Zhi quanji*, 6: 270–88. This article was first published in *Beijing daxue xuebao* (*Journal of Beijing University*, no. 1, 1958: 19), and was later included in the collection *Shi yu yichan* (*Poetry and Legacy*) in 1963. It is the only anthology of Feng Zhi's scholarly articles between the establishment of the People's Republic of China in 1949 and the outbreak of the Cultural Revolution in 1966, which revealed his ideological and cultural accommodations and his determination to acquire Marxist Maoist discourse in the fledgling socialist state. When *Poetry and Legacy* was republished in *Feng Zhi's Complete Work* in 1999, the editor noted that few changes had been made to the highly politicized terms and languages used in the original articles, in order to remain faithful to the specific historical situations of high socialism. However, in the aforementioned article "On Humanism and Individualism in European Bourgeois Literature," the passages on Goethe and Feng's socialist criticism of *Faust* and *Wilhelm Meister* were deleted. Here, the quotation comes from the article first published in the *Journal of Beijing University*.

26. Goethe, *Faust II*, Münchner Ausgabe, 18.1: 335.

27. Georg Lukács, "Unser Goethe," address, August 31, 1949, in Berlin, in "Kulturbund zur demokratischen Erneuerung Deutschlands," in *Goethe und seine Zeit* (Berlin: Aufbau Verlag, 1950), 330–65 (my translation). Since Lukács tended to stay remote from the actual literary texts in his Goethe analysis, Herbert Marcuse in his review of *Goethe und seine Zeit* in 1950 criticized that Lukács's methods failed to connect the social analysis with that of the literary style and content of Goethe's work. See Marcuse, "Review of Georg Lukács, Goethe und Seine Zeit," in *Philosophy and Phenomenological Research* 11, no. 1 (September 1950): 142–44.

28. In the 1960s, after the Soviet Union started to reevaluate Lukács and his work, socialist China paid more attention to Lukács and began to introduce his work systematically. Feng Zhi was a member of the group that worked on a selection and translation of Lukács's work from German into Chinese in the 1960s, shortly before the outbreak of the Cultural Revolution. However, the selected works by Lukács were not published until 1980.

29. Also in the *Wanderjahre*; Münchner Ausgabe (1905), 17: 893. For a study of Goethe's reception in East Germany, see, for instance, Daniel J. Farrelly, *Goethe in East Germany, 1949–1989: Toward a History of Goethe Reception in the GDR* (Rochester, N.Y.: Camden House, 1998). For a discussion of the reception of Weimarer Klassik in East Germany with regard to the Bauerbach case, see Ingeborg Cleve, "Subverted Heritage and Subversive Memory: Weimarer Klassik in the GDR and the Bauerbach Case," in *German Literature, History and the Nation: Papers from the Conference "The Fragile Tradition," Cambridge 2002*, vol. 2, ed. Christian Emden and David Midgley (New York: Peter Lang, 2004), 355–81. I would like to thank Catriona MacLeod for bringing it to my attention.

30. See "Di si bian: Diguo zhuyi shiqi de wenxue" ("Part Four: Literature of the Imperialist Period"), in *Deguo wenxue jianshi* (*A Brief History of German Literature*) (Beijing: Renmin wenxue, 1958), 331–35. In the 1950s, no work was sanctioned as the original authoritative creation of any individuals; as a result, almost all scholarly works were composed by a group of people, usually professors and their young college students. In this context, the first Chinese book on the history of German literature was written by Feng Zhi and a group of his students at Beijing University, including Tian Dewang, Zhang Yushu, Sun Fengcheng, Li Shu, and Du Wentang, who later all became professors in the German Department at Beijing University. This book was actually based primarily on Feng's manuscript prepared for German literary history lectures at Beijing University.

Part III

✦

Mobile Peripheries

Chapter 8

China in Two Yiddish Translations

Ethnographic and Modernist Appropriations

Kathryn Hellerstein

How can Chinese be translated into Yiddish? This unlikely question was addressed in the early decades of the twentieth century by various Yiddish writers in Warsaw and New York engaged in the project of creating a modern literature in the Jewish vernacular language of eastern Europe. Chinese texts and culture presented a challenge to the assumptions of Jewish tradition, and the attempts of Yiddish writers to translate such works were driven by a sense that knowledge of the many cultures beyond the circumference of Jewish life would transform Yiddish writing into a world-class, modern literature.

The history of the Jews in China (both modern and medieval) has attracted considerable scholarly attention, but the history of Yiddish in China remains, with the exception of the work of one established scholar, an untold story.[1] Jewish traders first found their way from the Middle East to Kaifeng, in northern China, in the thirteenth century, where they established a community that lasted until the eighteenth century. In the mid-nineteenth century, Jewish merchants, mainly from Iraq, often via India, arrived in China and played a major role in the building of modern Shanghai. After 1898 Jews from Russia settled in the northern Chinese city of Harbin, first as traders and later as refugees from the Bolshevik Revolution and Russian Civil War. In the first decades of the twentieth century, a very few Jews from Poland and Russia visited China as tourists, drawn by a combination of curiosity about the cultural exoticism of a truly foreign culture and an affinity that Polish Jewish socialists and communists felt as these political movements began to emerge in China. During World War II, Shanghai served as a port of refuge for European Jews, including many Yiddish-speakers.

From the start, China fascinated the Eastern European Jews, and among them, Yiddish writers. For these writers, China represented the ultimate "Other," and in their writings, they began to translate that otherness for readers of the Yiddish press from the cities to the remote *shtetlekh* (towns) of Poland, and throughout the United States. Such acts of translation consisted of actual Yiddish renderings of Chinese poems and other texts, but they also included travelogues, ethnographic reports, journalism, memoirs, stories, and original poems that made China comprehensible to Jewish readers. These acts of literary, cultural, and existential translation brought something new to Yiddish writing, which was at that time transforming itself into a modern literature. As they began to conceive of Yiddish as the language for a world-class literature, Yiddish writers in Europe and America struggled to determine what of their traditions to keep and what to leave behind as well as what of the other cultures in the world, including China's, to bring into Yiddish. It is important to note, too, that the cultural dialogue was reciprocated. The sinologist Irene Eber has observed "that the Chinese were reading Yiddish literature in the 1920s and the Yiddish writers were reading Chinese at the same time. Yet the two peoples met only through translation and did not actually encounter one another."[2]

In this essay, I will look at two examples of cultural translation, through which Jewish writers conveyed aspects of China to audiences, in Warsaw and New York, the two centers of interwar Yiddish publication. Different as they are, these two cases—one ethnographic and the other literary—provide occasion to consider the limits and possibilities of communicating cultural differences and commonalities. The first case is a book published in Warsaw in 1918, called *Khine* (*China*), from a series, *Lender un felker* (*Countries and Peoples.*).[3] (See figure 8.1) This book is a compilation of writings by major European authors such as Carlyle, Schlegel, and Humboldt on "China and Manchuria, Mongolia, Tibet, Korea, and others," selected and translated into Yiddish by Menakhem Birnboym,[4] an illustrator, and David Kassel, a Bundist poet and translator of world literature.[5] It is illustrated with drawings, photos, and calligraphy and was assembled to teach a popular Warsaw readership about China as an example of an "exotic" people and place. The eclectic nature of this volume, comprised of Yiddish translations of high culture nineteenth-century literary figures reflecting in English and German on China and surrounding regions, raises many issues about the layering of cultural transmission. Yet perhaps the most striking example of how this book "translated" Chinese culture through a European lens for Yiddish readers can be found on its cover.

The cover image of a woman, in what appears to be traditional garb, seated in an elegant setting, with bound feet, dressed in a stiff silk Chinese gown, and holding a fan, her face placid and inscrutable, evinces Western clichés about the East. The Yiddish letters stating the title, כינא *Khine* (*China*) run vertically down the left-hand side of the cover. These Hebraic letters are stylized to resemble the brushstrokes of Chinese characters, and their vertical layout, the columns of traditional Chinese writing. In contrast, at the top of the panel, two neoclassical male figures, muscle-bound and almost nude,

Figure 8.1. Book cover, *Khine un Mantsurian, Mongolian, Tibet, Korea, un andere* (*China and Manchuria, Mongolia, Tibet, Korea, and Others*), ed. M. Birnboym and D. Kassel (Warsaw: Farlag Yudish, 1918). Courtesy of the National Library of Israel.

open a globe depicting Africa and Europe on the left and Asia and Australia on the right. In the middle of this split image of the Earth, a streamlined, modernist font proclaims in Yiddish, "Countries and Peoples." The photograph of the Chinese woman and the drawing of the male nudes depict an explicit non-Jewishness, mediated for the Yiddish reader by the stylized lettering, which brings the world—East and West—home to Polish Jews. One can read in this book cover a cultural mission of exploration, apprehension, acquisition, and revelation that will break open the traditionalism of Yiddish by importing the traditions of China and indeed peoples and nations world over, and thus expand the Jews' known world.

This process of expansion was complicated by the limitations most Yiddish writers had in their ability to apprehend Chinese culture. Things were not always what they may have seemed. Take, for example, the cover photograph for this 1918 volume. According to scholar Xiaojue Wang, photography studios were introduced in China in the early twentieth century. Most were located in Shanghai, where their most frequent customers were courtesans, photos of whom, dressed in traditional garb, "were exhibited in show windows of photo studios and published in newspapers."[6] Given this historical context, it is very likely that the woman depicted in this photograph was a courtesan, and yet it seems unlikely that the Yiddish authors or the press editors were aware of this fact. On the cover of the 1918 Yiddish book, then, this photograph of a Shanghai courtesan, intended to represent the Western perception of traditional Chinese culture, interjects an erotic and illicit subtext into a Warsaw Yiddish reader's expectations of what the book would reveal about Chinese culture. Moreover, this implicit, costumed eroticism, whether or not recognized by the Yiddish audience, would counterbalance the Grecian nudity of the male figures holding up the globe at the top of the cover. The foreignness of both images—female and male, clothed and nude, Eastern and Western—may well have conveyed to the Polish Yiddish reader the message of how extensively the Jewish world had expanded. The title page of this volume, which prints "*Khine*" (*China*) in red ink, bears the stamps of the various libraries and archives that have owned it, and resembles a world traveler's passport (see figure 8.2).

The 1918 example of the importation of the outside world into Yiddish is balanced by the contemporaneous movements that described Yiddish culture with the eye of an outsider. Such Yiddish depictions of China occur within the context of several earlier ethnographic expeditions among Jews living in the Pale of Settlement and Poland, by I. L. Peretz, S. Anski, and Noah Prylucki. As modernization, migration, urbanization, and war threatened to erase traditional Jewish life, these Yiddish cultural leaders organized expeditions to collect and study oral, written, and material artifacts from their own Jewish folk culture.[7] It worth noting that in order to become modern writers and to gain an ethnographic perspective, Peretz, Anski, Prylucki, and others had themselves earlier rejected that same shtetl religious and folk culture that they recorded. In fact, the ethnographic impulse of these Jewish figures to preserve the expressions of traditional Jewish folk culture made ephemeral by the modern world gave impetus to the writers who translated other cultures, such as China's, into Yiddish literature. In the attempt to transform Yiddish literature by introducing the foreignness of China, these writers implicitly reiterated in a complementary form the same urge as that driving the Jewish ethnographers' attempts to preserve and reconstruct Jewish tradition.

To further consider the ways that the old becomes new and that the exotic illuminates the familiar, I will turn to the second, literary case, that of the Yiddish modernist poets and writers in New York in the first decades of the twentieth century. The final issue of a New York modernist miscellany, *Shriftn* (1925–26), included a section called "*Fun alte kvaln*" ("From

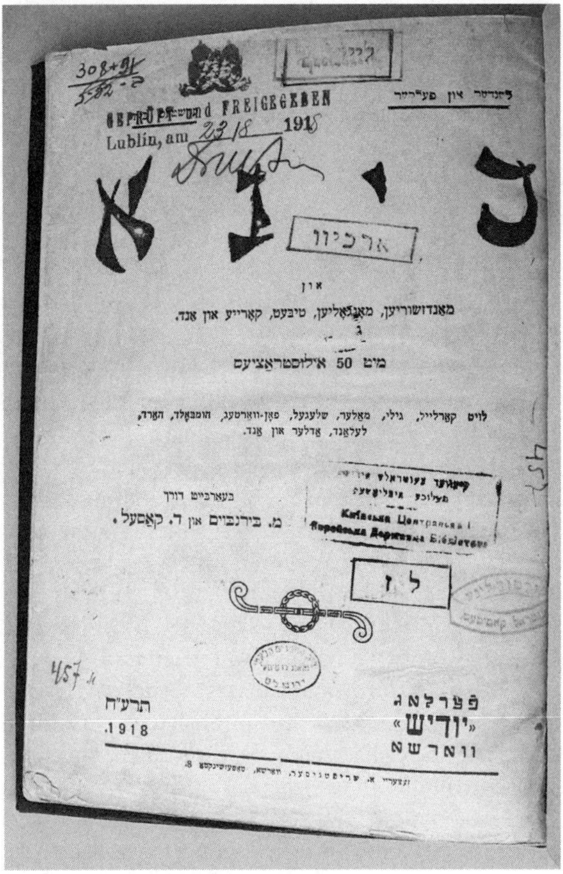

Figure 8.2. Title page to *Khine un Mantsurian, Mongolian, Tibet, Korea, un andere.* Courtesy of the National Library of Israel.

Old Wellsprings"), which featured translations into Yiddish of the Chinese poet Li Tai Po (Li Bai), published alongside Yiddish versions of Japanese haiku, Egyptian, Arabic, and American Indian poems, as well as an excerpt from the Finnish *Kalevala* and "The Birth of Buddha."[8] This eclectic group of translated works was characteristic of this publication. Earlier issues of *Shriftn* had included translations of Greek and Latin classics, as well as of nineteenth-century Americans like Whitman and Longfellow. The act of translation broke down the perceived provincialism of the Jewish language and opened it up to the world's traditions.

The 1925/1926 translators—David Ignatov, Meyer Shtiker, Hersh Rosenfeld, and A. Almi (pen name for Elihu-Khayim Sheps)[9]—selected and translated these works in the context of American modernism. These East Asian translations were not the first to appear in American Yiddish. Yehoash (pseudonym of S. Bloomgarden, 1872–1927), best known for his literary translation of the Hebrew Bible into Yiddish, had published Chinese-themed poems and translations of Chinese stories in the first decade of the twentieth century. And they were not the last: A. Almi published a book-length collection of Chinese philosophy and poetry in 1925 and, in 1930, Bernard Witt translated Lafcadio Hearn's 1887 *Some Chinese Ghosts* into Yiddish as *Khinezishe legenden.*[10] These Yiddish writers were part of a wider Jewish interest in China, exemplified by Martin Buber's converging interests in Hasidism and Chinese philosophy in 1910 and 1911.[11]

Shriftn was a modernist Yiddish miscellany published in New York between 1912 and 1926. The novelist and poet David Ignatov established this serialized anthology to present the works of the immigrant avant-garde poets who, after the publication of their collection *Yugnt* in 1908, had been derisively labeled *Di Yunge* (Youth) by the mainstream Yiddish press. The journal was published in 1912, 1913, and 1914. From 1915 through 1918, the editors suspended publication of *Shriftn,* and resumed it in summer 1919. Issues appeared in fall 1919 and spring 1921. Publication again ceased from 1922 to 1925, and the final issue appeared in winter 1925/1926. The journal featured poets who became the major figures in Yiddish modernist literature and thought, such as Moyshe-Leyb Halpern, Mani Leyb, Zishe Landau, Reuven Iceland, and I. J. Schwartz; fiction writers David Ignatov, Joseph Opatoshu, and Lamed Shapiro; and essayists, such as Khayim Zhitlovski. In the name of modernism, *Shriftn* also published a very limited number of poems by women, such as Celia Dropkin, Malka Lee, and Rashel Veprinski.

In the 1925/1926 volume of *Shriftn*, the Yiddish translations of six poems by the Tang Dynasty poet "Li Tai Po" (known today as "Li Bai," 701–762 A.D.), considered one of China's greatest classical poets,[12] included: "*Vaynlid*" ("Wine Song"); "*A briv fun tshang'kan*" ("A Letter from Tshang'Kan"); "*Tsu zayne kinder*" ("To His Children"); "*Di froy redt*" ("His Wife Speaks"); "*Er gezegnt zikh mit ir*" ("He Takes Leave of Her"); and "*Kroen farnakht*" ("Crows at Dusk"). The translator, Meyer Shtiker (1905–1983), a Galitsianer who had studied in a German-language school and lived in Vienna, came to New York in 1920, where he worked as a news editor for the Yiddish press into the 1970s. Starting at age nineteen, in 1924, Shtiker published poetry, short stories, and many literary translations, including T. S. Eliot, Rimbaud, Rilke, Julian Tuavim, Mandelshtam, and Ernest Hemingway, as well as his "exotic" translations. We can see the significance of Shtiker's translations of Chinese in terms of his participation in the larger enterprise in American Yiddish. The translations are a means of expanding the Yiddish cultural repertoire and vocabulary: by dipping into "Old Wellsprings" of other traditions, Shtiker creates an analogue to the modernist effort of inventing a literary tradition for Yiddish. This process of invention is at work in the first of Shtiker's Yiddish translations of Li Bai, "*A briv fun Tshang'Kan*" ("A Letter from Tshang' Kan"):[13]

A BRIV FUN TSHANG"KAN

Ikh hob zikh geshpilt mit blimelekh baym toyer.
Mayne hor hobn koym dergreykht mayn shtern.
Du bist ongekumen raytndik af dayn bamboo-shtekn
Un farveylt zikh bay der bank
Mit grine floymen anshtot shpilekhlekh.Ot azoy hobn mir gevoynt in shtot Tshang-kan,
Kinder tsvey vos hobn zikh af gornisht nit gerikht.

Tsu fertsn yor hostu mikh far dayn vayb genumen.
Ikh bin bevezn shemevdik, un nit gekent mayn ponem trogn fray
Hob nokh gelozt mayn kop,Un oysgedreyt im tsu der shvartser vant.
Du host mikh efsher toyznt mol gerufn—
Ikh hob geshvign, un zikh nit umgekukt afile . . .

Bay fuftsn hob ikh shoyn gekent farikhtn zikh di bremen
Un betn zolst mikh hobn lib—Biz mir veln vern shtoyb un ash.

Du host gegloybt in gloybn fun Vei-Sheng,
Vos hot gevart unter der brik—
Dos harts akegn toyt.
Un ikh hob keynmol nit gevustAz ikh vel darfn ven aroyfkletern
Dem barg Vang-Fu,
Aroyskukn af dir azoyfil teg.

Ven ikh bin alt gevorn zekhtsn yor
Bistu avek fun mir.
Avek tsum beyzn Klin Kiu-Tang
Vu riznshteyner shteln zikh akegn impetikn taykh,

Un di shliuzem ken men nit adurkhgeyn zumer tsayt.
Host khotsh gevert di malpes klogn
In di hoykhe felzn?
Un veystu, az di tseykhns fun dayne
fustrit Bay unzer toyer zaynen alt,
Un az yeder tseykhn iz badekt mit grinem mokh?

Der mokh iz tif un ayngevoksn,
]Men ken im nit avek-kern shoyn mer,Un di bleter faln shoyn in osyenvint.
Di gele shmeterlingen fun oktober
Flatern pornvayz ibern groz fun vyanedikn gortn
Mayn harts tut vey—ven ikh kuk af zey.

Ikh zits un troyer eyn aleyn un—o—
Di roytkayt fun mayn ponem vyanet.

Oyb du vest zikh umkern amol aheym—
Un oyb du vest mir onshraybn a briv foroys—
Vel ikh kumen dikh bagegeenn (der veg iz azoy kurts!)
Tsum "Taykh fun Langen Vint."[14]

In order to discuss Shtiker's work, I bring his Yiddish translation into English:

A LETTER FROM TSHANG"KAN

I played with blossoms by the gate.
My hair barely reached my forehead.
You arrived, riding on your bamboo stick
And amused yourself by the bench
With green plums instead of toys.That's how we lived in the city of
  Tshang-Kan,
Two children who had nothing to contend.

At fourteen years, you took me as your wife.
I was bashful, and could not show my face freely
I bent my head
And turned it to the black wall.
You called me perhaps a thousand times—
I stayed silent, and didn't even look around . . .

At fifteen, I could smooth my brows
And ask you to love me—
Until we become dust and ash.

You professed the faith of Wei-Sheng, Who waited under the bridge—
His heart against death.

And I never knew
That, climbing up
The mountain Wang-Fu, I would need
To watch for you so many days.

When I was sixteen years old
You left me.
Went off to the sinister Klin Kiu-Tang
Where giant stones stand opposite the racing river,
And one cannot pass through the sluices in the summertime.

Did you at least hear the monkeys complaining
In the high cliffs?
And do you know that the traces of your footprints
By our gate are old,
And that every trace is covered with green moss?

The moss is deep and overgrown,
It can no longer be swept away,
And the leaves are falling in the autumn wind.
The yellow butterflies of October
Flutter in pairs over the grass of fading gardens
My heart hurts—when I look at them.
I sit and sorrow all alone and—oh—
The flush of my face fades.

If you will return home sometime—
And if you write me a letter beforehand—
I will come to meet you (the way is so short!)
At the "River of the Long Wind."[15]

Although I will not discuss the Chinese poem on its own terms, I will briefly outline what Shtiker's translation of Li Bai's "Letter from Tshang'Kan" brings into Yiddish poetry and put it into the context of modern Yiddish poetry.[16] In the form of a letter, spoken by a dramatic persona, a young Chinese wife poignantly recounts her lifelong relationship to her husband, whom she addresses in his absence. She reminds him how she met him when they were both very young children, how they married at age fourteen, and how she overcame her initial shyness and silence to ask him to love her forever at age fifteen, at a time when he began to "profess the faith of Wei-Sheng." A year later, when she was sixteen, he left her, traveling down the river to "the sinister Klin Kiu-Tang," an impassable, treacherous place. When she asks if he could "hear the monkeys complaining / In the high cliffs," she expresses, within her fantasy of his experience, a worry that he might not have survived the journey. The speaker turns, then, to describe what is left of him at home—"the traces of your footprints / By our gate," which have been there so long now "that every trace is covered with green moss," that cannot be swept away. As she contemplates her situation at home, waiting for him, she invokes the changing season, as leaves fall "in the autumn wind," and yellow butterflies "of October" / "Flutter in pairs over the grass of fading gardens." The image of the mating butterflies and the progression of time from summer into fall makes her "heart hurt," and she mourns his absence as she grows older and "The flush of my face fades." The poem ends with her hope that he will return home, in anticipation of which, she offers to walk out to greet him, stating that the distance is short, or would seem short to her in her desire, should he write her in advance.

Contrary to what one might expect, Shtiker's translation of Li Bai's poem brings into Yiddish only two distinctly "exotic" elements:

> 1. The Chinese names of places and people Tshang'Kan, Wei-Sheng, Wang-Fu, Klin Kiu-Tang, which are hard even to transliterate into the Hebraic Yiddish alphabet—lend the translation an apparent authenticity. In fact, because there are only two Hebraic words in Shtiker's translation (*ponem*—face, and *afile*—even) and few Slavic words in the predominantly Germanic diction of this poem, the Chinese names stand out and mark it as foreign.
>
> 2. The imagery of blossoms, bamboo, plums, racing river, monkeys, moss, and butterflies, which recur in many of Li Bai's poems, taken together, are not native to Shtiker's Galicia or New York. Such specificity and concreteness further emphasize the foreignness of the poem.

In contrast to these features of "otherness," though, the poem's form and tropes speak in a familiar way to the sophisticated Yiddish reader of 1925/1926. First, the form of a poem spoken by a dramatic persona to reveal character, situation, and narrative was of great interest to many modernist Yiddish poets in the 1920s, who were experimenting with genres and language to expand the repertoire of poetry beyond what Zishe Landau, another *Shriftn* writer, called "the rhyming department of the Labor movement." Poets such as Mani Leyb, Moyshe-Leyb Halpern, and Anna Margolin in New York, as well as Moyshe Broderzon and Roza Yakubovitsh in Poland, adapted the persona poem to ironic or other effect at this time. Secondly, the choice of a female persona in a poem written by a man (or the reverse) was also familiar to a mid-1920s Yiddish reader, as were the questions of gender and imagination that such gender-crossing raises, as in poems by Halpern, Margolin, and Zishe Landau, who published a sequence called "Meydlishe-lider" ("Girl Songs") in an earlier volume of *Shriftn*. Finally, the story of a girl married off very young who comes to love her husband is also not an alien subject for this revolutionary generation of Yiddish writers who themselves (or whose older siblings) had rebelled outright against the long-standing Old World custom of arranged marriages, along with most other features of traditional Judaism. To make such an old-fashioned wife deeply sympathetic, as the poem does, requires a leap of the cultural imagination and calls up a reconsideration of tradition. Such invocation of archaic practices posed aesthetic and ideological challenges that a number of modernist poets embraced.

This reconsideration of tradition, all and any traditions, especially those as far from Jewish religious tradition as possible, strikes me as the primary motivation for these translations "From Old Wellsprings." By seeking commonality in the traditional poetry of the ancient or medieval cultures of places and peoples virtually unknown to Yiddish-speaking Jews, the *Shriftn* writers bolstered their effort to create a new context for modern Yiddish literature. The fact that Shtiker translated this poem in particular, ten years after Ezra Pound had made it famous in English as "The River Merchant's Wife: A Letter" in *Cathay* (1915), links Yiddish modernism with American modernism.

As well as exemplifying the ethnographic and literary aspects of modern Yiddish translations, what the 1918 *Khine* book cover shares with Shtiker's 1925/1926 rendition of Li Bai's *"A Briv Fun Tshang'Kan"* is the centrality of a Chinese woman. The photograph of a Shanghai courtesan and the lament of an eighth-century abandoned wife are, respectively, an objectification and an empathetic portrait of the other "other" in traditional Jewish culture—the female. These two examples of the translation of China into Yiddish, then, tap the deepest issues and concerns of Jewish culture as it transforms itself into a modern entity.

Notes

1. Irene Eber, *Voices from Shanghai: Jewish Exiles in Wartime China* (Chicago: University of Chicago Press, 2008); Irene Eber, "Translation Literature in Modern China: The Yiddish Author and His Tale," in *China and Jews: Encounters Between Cultures*, ed. Irene Eber (London: Vallentine Mitchell, 2008), 123–47.

2. Irene Eber, personal correspondence via email to Kathryn Hellerstein. Eber first stated this idea in print in Irene Eber, "Yiddish Literature and the Literary Revolution in Modern China," *Judaism* 16 (1967): 42–59. This article was translated into Yiddish in *Yiddishe Kultur* 29 (June-July 1967): 21–30. Eber developed the idea further in a later article, in *Asian and African Studies* (Jerusalem), 8, no. 3 (1972): 291–314.

3. *Khine un Mantshurien, Mongolien, Tibet, Korey, un andere, loyt Carlyle, Gili, Mahler, Schlegel, Von Varteg, Humboldt, Hardt, Leland, un andere* (*China and Manchuia, Mongolia, Tibet, Korea, and others, according to Carlyle, Gili, Mahler, Schlegel, Von Warteg, Humboldt, Hardt, Leland, and Others*), assembled by M. [Menakhem] Birnboym and D. [David] Kassel, for the series, *Lender un felker* (Warsaw: Farlag Yudish, 1918), illustrated.

4. Adina Bar-El, 2011, "Children's Literature: Yiddish Literature," *YIVO Encyclopedia of Jews in Eastern Europe,* http://www.yivoencyclopedia.org/article.aspx/Childrens_Literature/Yiddish_Literature.

5. Mikhail Krutikov, 2011, "Yiddish Literature: Yiddish Literature after 1800," *YIVO Encyclopedia of Jews in Eastern Europe*, http://www.yivoencyclopedia.org/article.aspx/Yiddish_Literature/Yiddish_Literature_after_1800.

6. Xiaojue Wang, "Concession, Courtesan House and Contestation of the 'Modern': Han Bangqing, *Haishanghua liezhuan*" (unpublished English article), 13, expanded from her article in Chinese, "Concession, Courtesan House and Contestation of the 'Modern': Han Bangqing, *Haishanghua liezhuan*," in *From the Late Ming to the Late Qing: Historical Dynamics and Cultural Innovations*, ed. Chen Pingyuan, David Der-Wei Wang, and Wei Shang (Wuhan: Hubei Jiaoyu,

2002), 232–332. I thank Xiaojue Wang for her generosity in showing me her work in progress. Also, see Catherine Vance Yeh, *Shanghai Love: Courtesans, Intellectuals, and Entertainment Culture, 1850–1910* (Seattle: University of Washington Press, 2006).

7. On the Jewish ethnographic expeditions, see Itzik Gottesman, *Defining the Yiddish Nation: The Jewish Folklorists of Interwar Poland* (Detroit: Wayne State University Press, 2003); and Kalman Weiser, *Jewish People, Yiddish Nation: Noah Prylucki and the Folkists in Poland* (Toronto: University of Toronto Press, 2011).

8. Rachel Rubinstein, *Members of the Tribe: Native America in the Jewish Imagination* (Detroit: Wayne State University Press, 2010), 76.

9. Irene Eber, "Chinese and Jews: Mutual Perceptions in Literary and Related Sources," *East-West Dialogue, Special Issue, "Chinese and European Literature: Mutual Influence and Perspectives"* 4, no. 2–5, no. 1 (June 2000): 209–27, here 222.

10. Ibid., 223, note 31.

11. For an excellent discussion of Buber's concurrent interest in Hasidism and Chinese religious philosophy, see Irene Eber, "Martin Buber and Chinese Thought," in *Wege und Kreuzungen der China-Kunde an der J. W. Goethe Universität, Frankfurt am Main* (Frankfurt am Main: IKO—Verlag für Interkulturelle Kommunikation, 2007), 23–49. See also Irene Eber, introduction to Buber, *Chinese Tales: Zhuangzi: Sayings and Parables and Chinese Ghost and Love Stories*, trans. Alex Page (New Jersey: Humanities, 1991), ix–xxiii.

12. "Li Bai," *Encyclopaedia Britannica*, Encyclopædia Britannica Online, 2011, http://proxy.library.upenn.edu:7116/EBchecked/topic/338660/Li-Bai.

13. The Chinese text of Li Bai's poem can be found on http://www.ccview.net/htm/tang/shi/lb009.htm. Thank you to Jin Jiang. A variant text and "literal" translation can be found on http://www.chinese-poems.com/lb1t.html. According to this website, the Chinese poem is 30 lines long, each line composed of 5 characters.

14. Meyer Shtiker, trans., "A briv fun Tshang'Kan" ("A Letter from Tshang'Kan"), *Shriftn: A Zamlbukh* 8–9 (1925/1926): section 9, 11–12.

15. Kathryn Hellerstein, English trans., Meyer Shtiker, Yiddish trans., "A briv fun Tshang'Kan" ("A Letter from Tshang'Kan"), *Shriftn: A Zamlbukh* 8–9 (1925/1926): section 9, 11–12.

16. For a discussion of the forms of Tang era poetry, see Kiang Kang-hu, "Chinese Poetry," in *The Jade Mountain: A Chinese Anthology, Being Three Hundred Poems of the T'ang Dynasty 618–906* (New York: Alfred A. Knopf, 1929), xxi–xxxvii. Based on Kang-hu's essay, and without direct access to the Chinese text, I believe that Li Bai's poem, "Chang-Kan," is in the genre of "Ancient poems of five-character lines" (xxvii), as described by Kang-hu.

Chapter 9

✦

Translations from German in Yiddish Literary History

Ken Frieden

At the start of the nineteenth century, when modern Yiddish and Hebrew narrative were just finding their literary voices, translations contributed new forms and inspired fresh trends.[1] Outstanding translations produced important literary works, adding meaning to the oft-mocked phrase *fartaytsht un farbesert* (translated and improved). We may laugh at pretentious Yiddish theaters, writers, or their publishers who—according to a popular belief or myth—claimed to have bettered Shakespeare and other classics. In extraordinary instances, however, it was true that groundbreaking Yiddish translations were even more influential in Yiddish literary history than were their sources in German literary history. In context, these translations possessed a freshness and originality that exceeded that of the originals.

Recent scholarship on translation theory has emphasized the creativity of the translator,[2] pointing to the potential creation of a "second original."[3] Fidelity to the original is less decisive than the independent strengths of the new work. In some instances, at least viewed retrospectively, "the task of the translator" may be understood to have influenced literary history.[4] Scholars know this already with regard to the King James Version and Luther's German translation of the Bible, the Schlegel/Tieck translation of Shakespeare, and some of Baudelaire's French versions of Edgar Allan Poe's stories. The time is ripe to recognize the full significance of the turning point in Jewish literary history that has been called "between Haskalah and Hasidism."[5]

Two of the primary contributions of the Yiddish texts I will discuss are the use of colloquial language and hard-edged realism (which I also call "referentialism"). As the spoken vernacular, Yiddish was capable of representing everyday language, and yet before 1800 Yiddish writing had seldom tapped into this potential. Moreover, the realism that was already common in English novels had not entered Yiddish.

It is difficult to comprehend the nascent Jewish literary field in Eastern Galicia and Ukraine around 1800. Khone Shmeruk and Sara Tsfatman have detailed the complex scene of premodern Yiddish literature; more should be done to pinpoint narrative precursors of the classic authors who wrote in the second half of the nineteenth century.[6] Extraordinary forerunners hailed from Berlin, Satanov, Mikolayev, Tarnopol, Uman, Kremenetz, Kamenetz-Podolsk, and Zhitomir. A definite lineage ran from Mendel Lefin and Khaikl Hurwitz—by way of Joseph Perl, I. B. Levinsohn, A. B. Gotlober, and Mordechai Suchostover—to S. Y. Abramovitsh. The "Grandfather" (as Sholem Aleichem dubbed Mendele/Abramovitsh) also had nineteenth-century grandfathers, even if he coyly refused to name them as sources of his much praised Hebrew *nusah*.[7]

Mendel Lefin was a remarkable Hebrew author who also played a seminal role in the rise of modern Yiddish prose. Lefin was born in 1749 in Satanov, Russia, and died in 1826 in Tarnopol, then in Austria. He was deeply influenced by Moses Mendelssohn and his circle during the early 1780s, when he lived in Berlin, though he rejected their antitraditional and assimilationist leanings. At Mendelssohn's suggestion and using his knowledge of French, Lefin first translated S. A. Tissot's medical work *Avis au peuple sur sa santé* (also relying heavily on the German edition). When Lefin published his Hebrew adaptation under the title *Refu'at ha-`am* (*Healing* [*for*] *the People*, 1789/1794), with an approbation by Mendelssohn (written shortly before his death), it was a popular success. Not until 1808 did Lefin publish his next major work, *Heshbon ha-nefesh* (*Moral Accounting*), which achieved wide popularity after Israel Salanter reissued it for use by the Musar movement in 1844. Despite his connections to the Berlin Enlightenment, Lefin's teachings were acceptable to Salanter, whose movement emphasized ethics. In scholarly opinion, the importance of this book has been somewhat eclipsed by its association with Musar, by the fact that only one copy of the first edition is extant, and by recognition of its direct borrowing from the method of self-improvement in Benjamin Franklin's *Autobiography*, which Lefin read in French.[8] Based on its fresh Hebrew style and clarity of thought, *Heshbon ha-nefesh* merits a fuller study. The present chapter, however, focuses on Lefin's contribution to Yiddish narrative literature.

Raised in Satanov, Lefin was no doubt influenced by the example of his elder townsman Isaac Satanov.[9] After Lefin left Berlin, he lived in Mikolayev; sometime after his wife died, he moved to Brody and then to Tarnopol, where he was in intimate contact with Joseph Perl until his death. Between 1809 and 1815 the region was in transition, because Tarnopol was temporarily under Russian rule until it was returned to Austria. During this period, Perl consulted with Lefin while setting up his school based on the Berlin model.[10] Perl is now remembered for his epistolary novel *Megale temirin* (*Revealer of Secrets*), which parodies the Hebrew style of Hasidic authors.[11]

Meanwhile, back in the Ukraine, two pivotal Hasidic books were published: *Shivhei ha- Besht* (*In Praise of the Baal Shem Tov*, 1814–15) and Nahman's *Sippurei ma`asiyot* (*Tales*, 1815), including an account of Nahman's journey to the Holy Land ("Seder ha-nesi`a shelo le- Eretz Israel"). The

Hebrew version of *Shivhei ha-Besht* was soon followed by popular Yiddish translations, while Nahman's *Tales* appeared in a bilingual Hebrew/Yiddish edition. Enlightened authors saw the widespread popularity of Hasidic writing as a threat to the spread of modern education and as an obstacle to the dissemination of their own books. In 1816, Joseph Perl commented on the many editions of *Shivhei ha-Besht* in his unpublished polemic against "the sect of the Hasidim."[12] When his masterwork *Megale temirin* was published in 1819, Perl expressed his resentment of the seminal Hasidic book *Shivhei ha-Besht,* noting that it had sold 6,000 copies in two years.[13] Decades later, when he printed his second epistolary novel *Bohen tzaddik* (*Test of the Righteous*), Perl again vented his anger while adjusting the sales figures higher—writing that 10,000 copies were sold in the first two years.[14] *Shivhei ha-Besht* soon appeared in several Yiddish editions, while Nahman's tales was a bilingual Hebrew/Yiddish edition from the start.

Although Mendel Lefin was more renowned as a Hebraist, Yiddishists have rightly claimed him as an important figure in early modern Yiddish writing. Since the 1930s, several scholars have referred to his innovative translations of biblical Hebrew into Yiddish. Following in the footsteps of Zalman Reyzn,[15] Simkhe Katz,[16] Israel Zinberg,[17] Israel Weinlös,[18] Khone Shmeruk,[19] and Nancy Sinkoff,[20] Roland Gruschka recently analyzed Lefin's published Yiddish translation of Proverbs and his unpublished drafts of Ecclesiastes, Psalms, and Job.[21]

My goal is to extend the study of Lefin's Yiddish to a bilingual Hebrew/Yiddish adaptation of one of J. H. Campe's travel narratives (*Reisebeschreibungen*, vol. 5, 1788) under the title *Oniya so`ara* (*Raging Ship*).[22] In the past I thought that Lefin was the translator of *Oniya so`ara,* but stylistic and statistical analysis have changed my mind. Nevertheless, I think it is certain that the translation originated among the circle of enlightened authors in Galicia, who knew Lefin. While this Hebrew/Yiddish adaptation is third-hand (based on the German, which was based on the Dutch original), this does not diminish its originality and significance in Yiddish literary history. Campe adapted this *Reisebeschreibung* from French (1696, 1750) and German (1751) translations of the 1646 Dutch narrative of Bontekoe's sea travels.[23] Campe's work is itself a free translation intended for young adults, supplemented by pedantic, moralistic remarks; the Hebrew/Yiddish translator wisely omitted most of Campe's heavy-handed pedantry.

The authorship of *Oniya so`ara* has not been established, but some scholars have attributed it to Mendel Lefin.[24] In any case, the importance of this text does not depend upon it having been authored by Lefin. The date of the first edition in Hebrew and Yiddish—which is the only known bilingual edition, including the only extant Yiddish version—has been listed by bibliographers as 1815(?) or 1818(?);[25] a Hebrew-only version was published in 1823.[26] In a previous study, I showed that Lefin's Hebrew translations in *Mase`ot ha-yam* (1818) were important, innovative works in the history of

Hebrew narrative.[27] The contribution of *Oniya so`ara* to Yiddish narrative is unprecedented and, at the same time, comprehensible in context.

One way to appreciate the novelty of the new Yiddish style is to compare it to popular contemporary texts and to prior works such as *Toyzend und* [*sic*] *eyne nakht* (*Thousand and One Nights*).[28] This wildly popular translation was reprinted often, from the 1790s to the 1830s and after. Written in Judeo-German (essentially German written in Hebrew characters) mixed with Western Yiddish, that work avoids Hebrew and Slavic components and closely follows its German source. In contrast, *Oniya so`ara* translates Campe into the spoken idiom of the translator's region, using many Hebraisms and Slavicisms that were typical of Ukrainian Yiddish. For this reason, *Oniya so`ara* has little in common with Western Yiddish precursors and instead resembles some Hasidic writing and Khaikl Hurwitz's *Tsofnas pa`neakh* (*Revealer of Secrets*, 1817). This is significant because the translator was clearly influenced by the Haskalah. For ideological and pedagogical reasons, like other *maskilim*, he could have written in German, Western Yiddish, or Judeo-German *(Jüdisch-Deutsch)* rather than in Eastern Yiddish.[29] Instead he chose to write for Ukrainian Jews in their everyday vernacular.

Lefin took a radical step in 1814 with his Yiddish translation of the book of Proverbs. As is well known, Tuvia Feder attacked Lefin's Yiddish translation of Proverbs.[30] In a sense, Feder was right: the oral style of Lefin's highly idiomatic Yiddish was ill-suited to the high register of biblical poetry. And it may be that Feder's satiric attack pushed Lefin and the translator of *Oniya so`ara* in the right direction—toward translating secular prose narratives, as Lefin did with *Mase`ot ha-yam* (Zholkva: Letteris, 1818). It was an especially astute idea for Lefin to translate Campe's German sea narratives into Hebrew, because the originals were written by ship captains in a vernacular style, without literary pretensions.[31] Translating Campe gave Lefin and his contemporaries the chance to show what Hebrew and Yiddish could do. For the most part, Lefin kept close to the details of Campe's German version, while developing a Hebrew that was more flexible than typical Hebrew of the *maskilim*, and the translator of *Oniya so`ara* broke away from the old-fashioned Yiddish style that emulated literary German.

One could call *Oniya so`ara* (*Raging Ship*, 1815?) the Rosetta Stone of modern Jewish literature. As the ancient Rosetta stone, with its translations, helped scholars decipher Egyptian hieroglyphics, the German-Hebrew-Yiddish Rosetta stone gives a key to the possibilities for writing in Hebrew and Yiddish circa 1815, anchored to the source German. Like Mendel Lefin, the translator of *Oniya so`ara* had a genius for creating natural-sounding modern narrative. In Hebrew, as scholars like Joseph Klausner have noted, Lefin (influenced by Isaac Satanov) transcended the mainstream Berlin Haskala tradition by incorporating Mishnaic Hebrew rather than mimicking the biblical prophets.[32] In Yiddish, Lefin avoided Western Yiddish and distanced himself from the tradition of copying a stiff, Germanic style. When he escaped the orbit of German writing, he helped create a new literary Yiddish that was closer to everyday speech.

Lefin's ideological position was striking. For a millennium, the prominent travel narratives in Hebrew had been pilgrimages.[33] Rather than write about pilgrimages to the Holy Land, however, Lefin wanted to broaden the horizons of his readers and move them beyond a traditional, unquestioned yearning for Zion. Leaving aside ideology, the literary position is also clear: in both Hebrew and Yiddish, Lefin deliberately used a popular, folksy style. His Hebrew was adapted from rabbinic, post-biblical Hebrew;[34] in Yiddish, Lefin approximated the spoken Yiddish of the Ukraine. As a result, Lefin's Yiddish somewhat resembles the Yiddish of popular Hasidic writings—such as the Yiddish versions of *Shivhei ha-Besht* and Nahman's tales. This could explain why the translator of *Oniya so`ara* may not have wanted to acknowledge authorship.[35]

It is easy to appreciate the superiority of the Yiddish in *Oniya so`ara* over the outmoded language of *Toyzend und eyne nakht*.[36] Nights 70–90, for example, contain the well-known accounts of seven trips by Sinbad the Sailor and resemble some Hebrew tales.[37] This rendering of *Toyzend und eyne nakht*—written in a mixture of Judeo-German and Western Yiddish—was published in Frankfurt an der Oder in 1794.[38] Even in the subsequent reprints from Prague (Scholl, 1816) and Warsaw (Lebenssohn, 1835 and 1839), it closely calques the German model.

Two examples, in which I preserve the original orthography and punctuation, show how closely the translator adhered to his German source (in turn based on Antoine Galland's French). First, early in the cycle, the narrator sets the scene:

> אונטר דער רעגירונג דעס **קאליפֿען האַרין אַלראַשיט** וואר צו **באַגדאַד**
> איין ארמר לאסטטרעגר נאמאנס **הינדבאַד**.
> (118)

> Under the rule of the Caliph Harin Alrashid, there was in Baghdad a poor porter named Hinbad.[39]

This follows the German almost word for word: ". . . unter der Regierung des nämlichen Kalifen Harun Alraschid, wovon ich bereits geredet habe, war zu Bagdad ein armer Lastträger, Namens Hindbad."[40] Later, when Hinbad addresses God, he echoes the German:

> אללמעכטיגר שעפֿר דער וועלט, בעטראכטע דען אונטערשיד צווישן
> **זינדבאַנד** אונד מיר . . .

This is taken from the German source: "Allmächtiger Schöpfer der Welt, betrachte den Unterschied zwischen Sindbad und mir . . ." (ibid., 3). Both the

Judeo-German and the German may be translated: "Almighty Creator of the World, observe the difference between Sindbad and me . . ."

As Dov Ber Kerler has shown, "the old literary language was primarily and, until its decline in the late eighteenth century, almost exclusively based on Western Yiddish."[41] Kerler takes a linguistic approach to the shifting literary practices, illustrating how Eastern Yiddish elements were gradually introduced. He notes that "some factions of Hasidism contributed to the changing status of the everyday language, and the movement as a whole played an important role in the adoption of modern Eastern Yiddish as a literary language" (*Origins of Modern Literary Yiddish*, 20). But he adds that "it was the leaders and proponents of the East European Jewish Enlightenment who actually developed it into a written language with an ever expanding range of didactic, educational, ideological and literary functions" (ibid.).

The early Jewish versions of *Thousand and One Nights* exemplify the reliance on German models. Although *Oniya so`ara* sometimes also incorporates German vocabulary from its sources, the translator rewrites the sentences into idiomatic Eastern Yiddish. Lefin, Hurwitz, and some of their Hasidic contemporaries published narratives that were at the vanguard of a new Hebrew and Yiddish style, eschewing the style of literary German.

Literary evidence shows a close connection between the *maskilim* (Enlightenment intellectuals) and the Hasidim, and biographical evidence substantiates the presumption of direct contact. According to Avraham Hazan, Rabbi Nahman and his scribe Rabbi Nosn (whom I prefer to call Nathan Sternharz) knew the Hurwitz family in Uman.[42] Moreover, an 1811 letter from Jacob Samuel Bik shows that Lefin and Perl knew Hirsh Hurwitz (the son of Khaikl); in the same letter, Bik mentions Nahman's teachings in *Likutei Moharan*.[43] While there was competition and probably even direct literary influence, this is perhaps not the main point; their shared inspiration was Yiddish as it was then spoken in the Ukraine.

The publication of popular Hasidic narratives presented a problem for *maskilic* authors who wanted to combat Hasidic influence. As early as 1792, Lefin suggested satirizing the Hasidim in literary works (*Essai*, #79),[44] and apparently he left behind an unpublished manuscript, now lost, called *Der ershter khosed*. Just as interesting as Joseph Perl's satiric *Megale temirin* from 1819 is Lefin's attempt to produce a positive counterexample to the adulatory and fantastic Hasidic narratives.

As a thought experiment, we may compare the bilingual printing of Nahman's *Sippurei mayses* and the bilingual printing of *Oniya so`ara*. Both works are translations from an admired narrative source. Nathan Sternharz translated the oral Yiddish storytelling of his Rebbe into Hebrew and then back into Yiddish. *Oniya so`ara* translated the German narrative for young adults by Campe into colloquial Yiddish and readable Hebrew.

There are obvious similarities between some writings by *maskilim* and by Sternharz, such as *Oniya so`ara* and Nahman's canonical tale 2 about "The

King and the Emperor." Thematically, both involve sea travels; they are also similar linguistically, using the regional vernacular. Stylistically, however, they are quite different, because Nahman's story evokes the vague generality of a fairy tale while *Oniya so`ara* has the hard edges of a chronicled sea journey based on Captain Bontekoe's memoirs. Two passages from Nahman's *Sippurey mayses*, published by Nathan Sternharz in 1815, resonate superficially with other Yiddish sea narratives. In Nahman's tale called "The King and the Emperor," the emperor's daughter and king's son elope and begin a sea journey together:

נאך דעם · האבין זייא איין עצה גיהאלטין · זייא וועלין זיך
אוועק לאזין אויף דעם ים · אונ האבין זיך גידונגין איין שיף ·
אונ האבין זיך אוועק גילאזט · אויף דעם ים · זענין זייא גיגאנגין
אויף דעם ים ·
(7b)

After that, they thought it over, that they would go out to sea. So they rented a ship and went out to sea. They went on the sea.[45]

Another passage from Nahman's Tale 2 further illustrates the vagueness of Nahman's sea descriptions:

ער וויל גיין זיך שפאצירין מיט זיין ווייב אף דעם ים · כדי זיא זאל
גיוואונט ווערין מיט דעם אויר פֿון דעם ים · . . . און האבין זיך גילאזט
אף אשיף אונ זענין דארט זייער פֿריילך גיוועון . . .
(11a)

He wanted to go on an excursion with his wife on the sea, so that she would get used to the sea air. They went out on a boat and were very happy there.

In contrast to Nahman's sketchy and repetitive descriptions, *Oniya so`ara* provides concrete observations:

דר וייל האט (באנטעקוע) גילאזט די שאלופֿע . . . ארויש נעמין אונ
איז מיט עטליכֿה מאן אוף גזעסין · אונ האט גיהיישין דר וייל דעם
שטייער מן [מיט?] דער שוף הין אונ הער צו קרייזי[ן] כדי ער זאל
ניט קענין וייט אוועק ק[ומין] און ער האט גירידרט מיט דר שאלופע
צו דר קוסטע :
(6-7)

Meanwhile, Bontekoe had the *shalupe* [a small boat] . . . lowered and he sat in it with several men. And he commanded that in the meanwhile the helmsman should cross back and forth with the ship

> so that he could not get far away. And he steered with the *shalupe* to the coast.[46]

While Nahman and Sternharz give no graphic details, *Oniya so`ara* follows Campe, describing the scene in depth and explaining nautical terminology along the way. Nahman was looking beyond the tale to its spiritual meanings, while for the translator of *Oniya so`ara* the sea journey seems to be an end in itself.

Maskilim countered Nahman's fantastic tales by offering concrete travel accounts. In place of vague narratives with mystical undertones, their narratives taught about history, geography, and about distant native tribes. When Nahman refers to encounters with non-Jewish nations, as in tale 4 ("The King Who Decreed *Shmad*"), there is often a chauvinistic tone that emphasizes Jewish superiority. In contrast, *Oniya so`ara* and *Tsofnas pa`neakh* show respect for other peoples—while sometimes criticizing the Europeans' treatment of native peoples. The linguistic and literary contributions of Yiddish translations are linked to an ideological component.

Khaikl Hurwitz was born in about 1750, lived in Uman, and traveled widely until his death in 1822. Based on Campe's *Die Entdeckung von Amerika* (*The Discovery of America*), Hurwitz's *Tsofnas pa`neakh* (*Revealer of Secrets*) contributed to the emergence of a modern Yiddish literary style. Hurwitz adapted *Tsofnas pa`neakh* more freely from its source than did the translator of *Oniya so`ara*. Also striking is its criticism of European colonization.[47] Before turning to his linguistic and literary innovations, we should acknowledge his forward-looking ideas. Hurwitz and Lefin, in their descriptions of European encounters with natives, hint at the contemporary Russian treatment of the Jews.[48]

At several points in the narrative, Hurwitz condemns the Europeans' search for gold.[49] He places this critique in the mouths of Native Americans, as when a tribal leader tells others:

> דיא ווייסע מענטשין גייען אום [אויס?] אוף אלע אינדזילין און זוכין זייער גאט, דאס גאלד.

> The White Men are going around to all of the islands and looking for their God, gold. (*Tsofnas pa`neakh*, 54c)

In part 3, a Peruvian tribal leader tells the Spaniards:

> שעהמט אייך, עס איז זייער א גרויסע חרפה און אַ בושה, אז איבער אזו אַ נאר[י]שקייט, זאלט איר אייך קריגין, און אז איר פראגגיט [פראגט] יוא אזו נאך דעם גאלד פאר שטייא איך איצונד אז דאס חשקות וואס איר האט צו דעם גאלד, דאס האט אייך אַ וועק גיטריבין פון אייער היים, און איר זענט גיקומין, אין אזעליכי לענדיר ארײן,

> וויא אלע פעלקיר זיצין במנוחה ושלום ושלוה, און איר שטעהרט זייא
> דיא מנוחה, כדי אז איר זאלט פיהל גאלד ב[אַ]קומין.

> You should be ashamed; it is a great disgrace that you fight over such a foolish thing. Since you ask so much about it, I understand now that the desire for gold is what drove you away from your home. And you have come to such countries where all of the peoples sit in calm, tranquility, and peace, and you disturb their calm in order to get a lot of gold (*Tsofnas pa`neakh,* 129c).

In general, Hurwitz presents the Spaniards as aggressors, as in the description of Barthelmeos's capture of the King of Paraguay (*Tsofnas pa`neakh,* 44c).[50]

Hurwitz also describes Spanish missionary activity, including some conversions to Christianity. He calls the Native American converts to Christianity *meshumodim*—a pejorative term that was usually used to describe Jews who had converted to Christianity—and views them with scorn (54d). This is specific and virulent in the case of an interpreter named Fila Fila (*Tsofnas pa`neakh,* 165b; also 158b).[51]

Hurwitz becomes cautious, however, when he touches on the subject of the Spanish Inquisition. He writes, "In those countries, the Spanish government had already introduced the Holy **Inquisition**," after which he adds a footnote: "**Inquisition** I know a lot that I could write about the Holy Inquisition, but I don't want to write anything bad about a government or about a matter of faith. There is nothing good that one can write about it, and so I write nothing at all about it" (*Tsofnas pa`neakh,* 164d and note; bold in original). This note alludes to the precarious position of Jews in Russia.

The ideological aspect of Hurwitz's translation is as interesting as his linguistic and literary originality. Clearly he was trying to have a modernizing influence by writing about geography and history in the New World. But he also attacked some outmoded features of life in the Old World. For example, he writes vehemently against superstition. When Columbus's ship is one of the few to survive a particularly stormy trip back to Spain, Hurwitz takes a traditional view and comments that "God (*ha-shem yisbarakh)* saved him by His Providence" (*Tsofnas pa`neakh,* 39c). In contrast, he is critical of the superstitious Spaniards, who accuse Columbus of witchcraft.

The literary movement toward historical travel narratives reflects the Enlightenment distrust of fictional narrative. Campe expressed a view that typified some *maskilim.* In a preface to one of his many books, this moralistic pedagogue openly advised against "the reading of novels, as well as generally all books that aim only to arouse fantasy, imagination, and sentiments, out of full conviction of their great harmfulness."[52] To compensate for this prohibition, Campe offers other pleasures that he considers harmless. In his series of travel narratives, then, Campe has "taken as a rule—not only to select the most interesting of this type, but also beyond this—to intersperse, now and then, one or another of those completely extraordinary travel accounts, whose story completely matches the charm and splendor of novels without thereby leading us, as in novels, away from reality into the world of fantasies and whims."[53]

Early Yiddish narratives vary widely in the way they present everyday speech. One of the main successes of *Oniya so`ara*, Hurwitz, and the best Hasidic writers is that they embrace the vernacular. Sometimes this echoes the colloquial language of ship captains like Bontekoe. For instance, Campe quotes Bontekoe's own account of his shipwreck. Following Campe and using Eastern Yiddish, the passage in *Oniya so`ara* is remarkable:

> איך האב מיך דר שראקן זאגט באנטעקו אונ זיינר רייזבעשרייבאנג אונ בין ארפ גילאפֿין: וויא איך בין ארפ גיקימין האב איך דר זעהין אז דר הויפֿין קולין אונ גאנצין איז שוין גאר איין העליש פֿייאר גווארין: אזו באלד האבין מיר גיגעסין [?] און גיגאסין ימים ווייש מיט וואשר, אבֿר צום אומגליק האט זיך ווידר איין נייא בעגעגניש גיטראפֿין, דאש זעהר פֿיל וואסר וואש מן האט אויף דיא קוילן גיגאסין, האט גימאכט איין זעהר דיקין שוועבליגן דאמפף (סמאנד אדר טשאד) וואש עש איז גאר ניט מיגלך גיוועזין און קעליר אוש צו האלטין:
>
> (17)

> I was terrified, Bontekoe says in his travel description, and ran down below. When I reached the lower level I saw that the entire pile of coal had already become a hellish fire. Immediately we poured and poured seas of water, but unfortunately a new situation arose—the great amount of water that had been poured on the coal made a very thick, sulfurous mist (smoke or fumes), which made it impossible to remain in the lower cabin.[54]

The translator succeeds in making the narrative sound like oral storytelling, anticipating the later accomplishments of authors such as Sholem Aleichem.

An example from Hurwitz's *Tsofnas pa`neakh*, when Columbus's men are complaining, illustrates his distinctive use of dialogue:

> מיר האבין גימיינט אז מען פיהרט אונדז אין איין אורט אַריין, וויא מיר וועלין קענין געך עשירות אַן קלויבין, און איצונד מוזין מיר אזו שוועהר ארבאטין, וויא דיא מענטשין וואס מען דינגט, אז זייא זאלין ארבאטין, אוף דעם טאג .
>
> (23d)

> We thought we were being led to a place where we would be able to gather riches quickly, and now we must work as hard as day laborers, who are hired to work.[55]

It is instructive to compare this to Mendelsohn-Frankfurt's earlier Hebrew translation, because it uses such stiff *melitza*—the neo-biblical style of German-Jewish Enlightenment—in contrast to Hurwitz's Yiddish:

> למה זה הבאתנו הנה, ארץ ציה ואוכלת יושביה; הזאת ארץ חמדה וזהב וכל הון יקר אשר אמרת לתת לנו? אם זאת המנוחה והמרגוע אשר הבטחתנו עליה, כי תעבוד בנו בפרך כל היום . . . ?
>
> Why did you bring us here, to this desolate land that devours its inhabitants; is this the land of delight and gold and all precious riches that you said you would give us? Is this the calm and comfort you promised us, where you crush us with hard labor all day . . . ?[56]

It was bold of Hurwitz and his enlightened contemporaries to write vernacular Yiddish prose, because this linked them to contemporary Hasidic authors. Especially the bilingual format gives *Oniya so`ara* a look similar to that of Nahman's *Sippurei ma`asiyot*.

Yiddish and Hebrew narrative took a leap forward around 1815–18, superseding premodern works like *Toyzend und eyne nakht* with *Oniya so`ara*, Hurwitz's *Tsofnas pa`neakh*, and Lefin's *Mase`ot ha-yam*. It is intriguing to find literary echoes between these enlightened authors and their enemies, the Hasidic compilers and translators of *Shivhei ha-Besht* and Nahman's *Sippurei ma`asiyot*. There was stiff competition for readers, as reflected in Joseph Perl's envious comments on the popularity of Hasidic books.

Hurwitz and other *maskilim* were implicitly in competition with Hasidic writers of their time. They strove to expand their readers' horizons, making available gripping travel accounts by British, Dutch, and Spanish sailors. Travel literature is not always accepted into the realm of *belles lettres*, and yet *Oniya so`ara* shows how a sea voyage can be the basis for a turning point in literary history. This Yiddish translation provided a model of realistic description lacking in most Yiddish writing at the time. *Oniya so`ara* and Hurwitz's narratives of travel in translation widened the traditional Hebrew worldview, which centered on the Holy Land, and at the same time exposed Jewish readers to the western European genre of travel narrative. Nahman used his stories as allegories that expressed kabbalistic ideas. *Oniya so`ara* and Lefin's *Mase`ot ha-yam*, in contrast, taught worldly perseverance by holding up the example of sailors who survived extreme adversity. Hurwitz taught the history of the Americas and, at the same time, suggested some critiques of European conquerors and tyrannical governments.

On the basis of comparison with other Yiddish narratives published early in the nineteenth century, I conclude that Hurwitz and the translator of *Oniya so`ara* were as impressive as Yiddish stylists as Lefin was in Hebrew. Far ahead of its time, *Oniya so`ara* is a kind of missing link between the outmoded *taytsh-sforim* of the eighteenth century and modern Yiddish literature from the second half of the nineteenth century. It is even possible to show a lineage from Hurwitz and Lefin, via the pedagogue A. B. Gotlober and his student S. Y. Abramovitsh, to Sholem Aleichem.

It would be useful to explore this moment in Yiddish literary tradition further in terms of the diglossia and polysystem theories discussed by Itamar Even-Zohar.[57] These theories help to describe the literary use of colloquial language as well as the movement between language systems. Even-Zohar writes that "during the nineteenth century, European Romanticism and Realism encouraged the introduction into literature of elements from 'natural language,' that is, which reflect 'authentic' features of the characters' speech." He then points out that, in this respect, "Yiddish possessed some very conspicuous advantages over Hebrew."[58] Elsewhere Even-Zohar points to the influences of Slavic languages on Yiddish and of Yiddish on Hebrew (Even-Zohar, *Polysystem Studies*, 99, 117). We may say that the Yiddish *Thousand and One Nights* relied excessively on the German literary system, while the Yiddish of Nahman's tales is based primarily on spoken Yiddish. *Oniya so`ara* and Hurwitz's *Tsofnas pa`neakh* are remarkable because they follow Campe's German literary model while, at the same time, they draw heavily from colloquial Yiddish. This enabled them to import German literary forms and yet assert the legitimacy of Yiddish writing based on everyday Yiddish speech.

For Jewish literary history, the significance of translation from German has been underestimated, and not only in the cases of Lefin and Hurwitz. Translations from Campe's German works into Hebrew include those by Moses Mendelsohn-Frankfurt (1807), M. A. Günzburg (1823), and David Zamosht (1824). We should also mention S. Y. Abramovitsh's translation of *Sefer toldot ha-tev`a* (1862–72) from Harald Othmar Lenz's works on natural history.

Translation was an essential means by which *maskilim* brought new styles and genres into Hebrew and Yiddish. Thanks to Lefin, Hurwitz, and the translator of *Oniya so`ara,* the German travel narratives by Campe were indeed *fartaytsht un farbesert*. Moreover, their Yiddish narratives introduced a hard-edged realistic style that was foreign to most Hasidic writing. In the ongoing battles between mitnagdim and Hasidim, enlightened authors followed Campe in his skepticism regarding fantasy literature, while translated travel books ushered in a new era of nineteenth-century Yiddish realism.

Notes

This chapter shares some themes and examples with my article "Literary Innovation in Yiddish Sea Travel Narratives, 1815–1824," *Poetics Today* 35 (Fall 2014): 357–382. With a somewhat different focus, in that essay I also discuss the place of sea narratives in the emergence of modern Yiddish prose. For help with proofreading, the author thanks Segev Amossi and Marion Aptroot.

1. There have also been many bad translations and adaptations that added nothing to literary history—or even set back modern Yiddish writing, as Sholem Aleichem complained in *Shomers mishpet* (*The Trial of Shomer,* 1888). For a discussion of the influence of Yiddish on Hebrew writing, see my "Innovation by Translation: Yiddish and Hasidic Hebrew in Literary History," in *Arguing the Modern Jewish Canon: Essays on Literature and Culture in Honor of Ruth R. Wisse*, ed. Justin Cammy, Dara Horn, et al. (Center for Jewish Studies and Harvard University Press, 2008), 417–25.

2. See, for example, Willis Barnstone, *The Poetics of Translation: History, Theory, Practice* (New Haven, Conn.: Yale University Press, 1993).

3. Naomi Seidman, *Faithful Renderings: Jewish-Christian Difference and the Politics of Translation* (Chicago: University of Chicago Press, 2006), chapter 6 on the creative transformations of I. B. Singer's fiction in English.

4. Walter Benjamin's essay "The Task of the Translator: An Introduction to the Translation of Baudelaire's *Tableaux Parisiens*" is one inspiration for this study of Yiddish translations. See Walter Benjamin, *Illuminations*, trans. Harry Zohn, ed. Hannah Arendt (New York: Schocken Books, 1969), 69–82. A new translation by Steven Rendall is included in Lawrence Venuti's *The Translation Studies Reader* (New York: Routledge, 2012), 3rd edition, 75-83. In German, "Die Aufgabe des Übersetzers," in Walter Benjamin, *Gesammelte Schriften* (Frankfurt am Main: Suhrkamp, 1972), vol. 4, part 1 [*Werkausgabe*, vol. 10], 9–21.

5. Khone Shmeruk, *Sifrut Yidish be-Polin: Mekhkarim ve-`iyunim historiim* (Jerusalem: Magnes, 1981), part 2. In the Yiddish Department at the Hebrew University, students were routinely taught that this literary tradition could be divided into three periods: Old Yiddish Literature; Between Haskalah and Hasidism; and Modern Yiddish Literature. One thrust of this chapter is to emphasize that some *maskilic* and Hasidic authors had already initiated modern Yiddish writing.

6. Khone Shmeruk, *Sifrut Yidish: Prakim le-toldoteiha* (Tel Aviv: Porter Institute, 1978); Sara Tsfatman-Biler, "*Ha-siporet be-Yiddish mi-reishita `ad 'Shivhei ha-Besht' (1504–1814)*," vols. 1–2 (Ph.D. diss., Hebrew University of Jerusalem, 1983); Sara Tsfatman, *Ha-siporet be-Yiddish mi-reishita `ad 'Shivhei ha-Besht' (1504–1814): Bibliografiya mu`eret* (Jerusalem: Hebrew University of Jerusalem, 1985).

7. See Abramovitsh's letter to Y. H. Ravnitzky, dated September 11, 1906, contained in *Halifat 'iggrot bein S. Y. Abramovitz u-vein H. N. Bialik ve-Y. H. Ravnitzky ba-shanim 1905–1908,* ed. Khone Shmeruk (Jerusalem: Israeli Academy of Sciences and Humanities, 1976), 67–70. On "*nusah* Mendele," see my essay "Epigonism after Abramovitsh and Bialik," *Studia Rosenthaliana* 40 (Amsterdam, 2007–2008): 159–81.

8. See Nancy Sinkoff, "Benjamin Franklin in Jewish Eastern Europe: Cultural Appropriation in the Age of the Enlightenment," *Journal of the History of Ideas* 61 (2000): 133–52. See also Hillel Levine's "*Menahem Mendel Lefin: A Case Study of Judaism and Modernization*" (Ph.D. diss., Harvard University, 1974). Immanuel Etkes discusses Lefin's influence in *Rabbi Israel Salanter and the Mussar Movement: Seeking the Torah of Truth*, trans. Jonathan Chipman (Philadelphia: Jewish Publication Society, 1993), esp. chap. 9.

9. Satanov moved to Berlin in 1771, published and edited many books in Hebrew, and worked in Mendelssohn's circle. He edited the publishing house connected to the Jüdische Freischule.

10. For a discussion of Perl's creation of the Israelite Free School in Tarnopol—the first modern Jewish school in Galicia—see Nancy Sinkoff, *Out of the Shtetl: Making Jews Modern in the Polish Borderlands* (Providence, R.I.: Brown Judaic Studies, 2004), 225–37.

11. I analyzed this work in "Joseph Perl's Escape from Biblical Epigonism through Parody of Hasidic Writing," *AJS Review: The Journal of the Association for Jewish Studies* 29 (2005): 265–82.

12. Joseph Perl, *`Al mahut kat ha-hasidim,* ed. Avraham Rubinstein (Jerusalem: Israel Academy of Sciences and Humanities, 1977), 77–78. From the first two years following publication, Perl lists three Hebrew printings (Kapust, Berdichev, Laszczow) and two Yiddish editions (Ostroh and Laszczow).

13. Joseph Perl, *Megale temirin* (Vienna: Anton Strauss, 1819), letter 78 (30b). See also the Yiddish edition of *Megale temirin*, contained in Yosef Perl, *Yiddishe ksavim*, ed. Israel Weinlöz and Zalman Kalmanovitsh (Vilna: YIVO, 1937), 123.

14. Joseph Perl, *Bohen tzaddik* (Prague: Landau, 1838), 23–24.

15. See Zalman Reyzn, *Fun Mendelssohn biz Mendele* (Warsaw: Kultur-lige, 1923), 147–62.

16. Simkhe Katz, *Kiryat sefer* 16 (1939–1940): 114–33.

17. Israel Zinberg, *A History of Jewish Literature*, vol. 6 (part 7): *The German-Polish Cultural Center*, trans. and ed. Bernard Martin (Cincinnati, Ohio: Hebrew Union College Press, 1975), 271–81.

18. Israel Weinlöz, "Mendel Lefin-Satanover," *YIVO Bleter* 2 (1931): 334–57.

19. Khone Shmeruk, section on Lefin in *Sifrut Yiddish: Prakim le-toldoteiha* (Tel Aviv: Tel Aviv University, 1978), 181–87; Khone Shmeruk, "`Al `ikronot 'ahadim shel tirgum Mishlei le-Mendel Lefin," in *Sifrut Yidish be-Polin: Mekhkarim ve-`iyunim historiim* (Jerusalem: Magnes, 1981), 165–83.

20. Sinkoff, *Out of the Shtetl*, 176–202.

21. Roland Gruschka, *Übersetzungswissenschaftliche Aspekte von Mendel Lefin Satanowers Bibelübersetzungen* (Hamburg: Buske, 2007). This book originated as a dissertation completed at the Universität Düsseldorf in 2005.

22. See *Oniya so`ara* (Zholkva?: n.p., 1815?); opening pages lacking. The only known copy of this bilingual edition is at the Jewish National and University Library in Jerusalem; I thank the librarians there for providing scans of this rare book. The title appears to be a pun on the biblical phrase *`ania so`ara* (raging or storm-tossed poor woman), from Isaiah 54:11. This title shifts the meaning by changing a poor woman (עניה) into a storm-tossed boat (אניה).

23. See Melchisedec Thévenot, *Relations de divers voyages curieux qui n'ont point esté publiées*, vol. 1 (Paris: Moette, 1696), 1–49; Antoine Prévost, *Histoire générale des voyages, ou Nouvelle collection de toutes les relations de voyages par mer et par terre Qui ont été publiées jusqu'à présent dans les différentes Langues de toutes les Nations connues*, vol. 8 (Paris: Didot, 1750), 417–50; and the German based upon the latter French edition, in *Allgemeine Historie der Reisen zu Wasser und zu Lande; oder Sammlung aller Reisebeschreibungen, welche bis itzo in verschiedenen Sprachen von allen Völkern herausgegeben worden*, vol. 8 (Leipzig: Arkstee and Merkus, 1751), 378–411.

24. See, for example, Sinkoff's *Out of the Shtetl*, 195n–196n. For the purpose of rethinking Yiddish literary history, it probably does not matter whether the author was Lefin or someone else in the *maskilic* circles of Tarnopol and Brody.

25. Yitzhak Yudelov gives the date as 1818? in *Sefer ginzei Yisrael: Sfarim, hovrot ve-`alonim mi-osef Doktor Israel Mehlman asher be-veit ha-sfarim ha-le'umi ve-ha-universitai* (Jerusalem: National and University Library, 1984), 208. Sinkoff cites Samuel Poznanski's unequivocal but unsubstantiated claim that Lefin was the author of *Oniya so`ara*, in "Wiener's 'Bibliotheca Friedlandiana,'" *Jewish Quarterly Review* 9 (1897): 159. The catalog entry for the only known copy of the first edition, at the Jewish National and University Library, lists the work as (Zholkva?: 1815?).

26. *Oniya so`ara* (Vilna: Menahem Mann, 1823); reprinted in Vilna-Horodna: Dfus ha-shutafim, 1825; also Warsaw: Bomberg, 1854, and Warsaw: Unterhendler, 1878. A Yiddish-only version entitled *Historiye, oder geshikhte fun shif brokh* (Vilna: n.p., 1823) was available and was researched by David Roskies at the National Library of Israel in the 1970s; but since then it has been reported lost. See David G. Roskies, "Ayzik-Meyer Dik and the Rise of Yiddish Popular Literature," Ph.D. diss., Brandeis University, 1974, 84–85.

27. Ken Frieden, "Neglected Origins of Modern Hebrew Prose: Hasidic and Maskilic Travel Narratives," *AJS Review* 33 (2009): 3–43.

28. *Toyzend und (!) eyne nakht* (Frankfurt an der Oder, 1794, 1796, 1803; Prague, 1816; Warsaw, 1835; and many more editions). Haim Liberman refers to an earlier version of the first seven nights entitled *Mara'ot ha-tzeva'ot* (Wanzbek, 1718). See his "Targum Yidi bilti yadu`a shel sefer 'Elef leilot ve-laila," in *Ohel Rach"l*, vol. 2 (New York: Empire, 1981), 486–96.

29. Compare Sinkoff, *Out of the Shtetl*, chapter 3, and her article "Benjamin Franklin in Jewish Eastern Europe," 133–52.

30. Many scholars have reviewed the drama of Tuvia Feder's attack on Lefin's translation of Proverbs, the reaction of Lefin's supporters, and the price they paid to coerce Feder to withdraw his book from publication. See nn6–10 in this chapter, as well as Avraham-Ber Gotlover's account, reprinted in *Zikkaronot ve-masa`ot*, ed. Reuven Goldberg (Jerusalem: Mossad Bialik, 1976), 2: 197–208.

31. On the coarse style of Bontekoe's original, see Pieter Geyl's introduction to Willem Ysbrantsz Bontekoe, *Memorable Description of the East Indian Voyage 1618–25*, trans. C. B. Bodde-Hodgkinson and Pieter Geyl (London: Routledge, 1929). Mediated by prior French and German translations, Campe's version uses straightforward language, geared to young adults.

32. See Joseph Klausner, *Historia shel ha-sifrut ha-hadasha*, vol. 1 (Jerusalem: Ahiasaf, 1952), chapter 4 on Mendel Lefin; and Klausner's "Mehkarim be-toldot ha-sifrut ha-`Ivrit ha-hadasha: Le-hishtalsheluto shel signon-ha-Mishna be-sifrut ha-hadasha," in *Kitvei ha-Universita ha-`Ivrit be-Yerushalaim: Mada`ei ha-Yahadut*," vol. 1 (*Yedi`ot ha-makhon le-mada`ei ha-Yahadut*, vol. 3) (Jerusalem: Ha-madpis, 1926), 163–78.

33. For helpful anthologies of this literary tradition, see *Masa`ot Eretz Israel shel `olim yehudim mi-yemei ha-benaim ve-`ad reishit yemei shivat Zion*, ed. Avraham Ya`ari (Tel Aviv: Histadrut ha-Tzionit, 1946) and *Igrot Eretz Israel she-katvu ha-yehudim ha-yoshvim le-aheihem she-ba- golah mi-yemei galut Bavel*

*ve-`ad shivat Zion she-be-yameinu*, ed. Avraham Ya`ari (Ramat-Gan: Massada, 1971). For a study of travel narratives in modern Yiddish literature, see Leah V. Garrett, *Journeys beyond the Pale: Yiddish Travel Writing in the Modern World* (Madison: University of Wisconsin Press, 2003). See also David G. Roskies, "The Genres of Yiddish Popular Literature 1790–1860," in *Working Papers in Yiddish and East European Jewish Studies* (New York: YIVO, 1975), 18–22. Roskies astutely refers to sea adventure as "the main area of maskilic contribution to Yiddish popular literature before Ayzik-Meyer Dik" (18).

34. Post-biblical, rabbinic Hebrew had been evolving continuously for centuries. A landmark precedent was the neo-Mishnaic style of Maimonides in his *Mishne Torah*. It is instructive to contrast Lefin's practice with that of Joseph Perl. When Perl wrote in Hebrew in *Megale temirin*, he parodied the way Hebrew was written by Hasidic authors. Because of the satiric intent, Perl conveyed no positive evaluation of the possibilities for writing in a more popular, post-biblical Hebrew style. Mainly in his earlier writings in *Luhot ha-lev* (ca. 1813–16), for readers' ease, Perl did use a folksier style. In contrast, Lefin embraced a simpler, post-biblical Hebrew throughout much of his life, from *Refu'at ha-`am* (1794) to his sea narratives (1815–23) and his mishnaic retranslation of Maimonides's *Guide to the Perplexed*. Following Lefin's example, Perl translated his own *Megale temirin* and Fielding's *Tom Jones* into Yiddish.

35. This is not entirely clear because we are lacking the title page of the original *Oniya so`ara* (1815?), leaving unknown whether his authorship was indicated there. But since Lefin did not list his name on his 1814 publication of Proverbs, having the title page of *Oniya so`ara* (1815?) may not solve anything. Even on *Mase`ot ha-yam* he listed only his initials, leading some readers to misattribute the book to Meir Letteris. See Letteris's *Zikkaron be-sefer: Ein Beitrag zur Literatur- und Culturgeschichte im XIX. Jahrhundert* (Vienna: Schlossberg, 1869), 39n. The initials ***ל ***מ also led the Austrian National Library to incorrectly attribute *Mase`ot ha-yam* to Meir Letteris. I recently discovered their important copy of this book—the only known complete copy, because the copy in Jerusalem is missing sixteen pages—on Google Books under the title *Sepher mas coth hayam*. See https://play.google.com/books/reader?id=JyZiAAAAcAAJ&printsec=frontcover&output=reader&hl=en&pg=GBS.PA1 (accessed Jan. 18, 2016). The scanned original comes from the Kaiserliche Königliche Hofbibliothek in Vienna, now the Österreichische Nationalbibliothek: http://digital.onb.ac.at/OnbViewer/viewer.faces?doc=ABO_%2BZ204376208 (accessed Jan. 18, 2016).

36. I leave aside earlier Western Yiddish editions of the *Thousand and One Nights*, starting with *Arabishe ertseylunge oys Toyzent und eyn nakht* (Hamburg, 1700?) and *Mara'ot ha-tseva'ot* (Wansbeck, 1718). See Sara Zfatman-Biller, "*Yiddish Narrative Prose from Its Beginnings to 'Shivhei haBesht' (1504–1814)*" (Ph.D. diss., 2 vols., Hebrew University, Jerusalem, 1983). Compare the bibliographic information in Sara Zfatman's *Ha-siporet be-Yiddish: Mi-reishita `ad 'Shivhei ha-Besht (1504–1814): bibliografiya mu`eret* (Jerusalem: Institute for Jewish Studies, Hebrew University, 1985). Compare also Haim Liberman's "Tirgum yidi bilti yadu`a shel sefer 'Elef leylot ve layla,'" in *Ohel Rah"l*, vol. 2 (New York: Empire, 1980), 486–96.

37. See J. Perles, "Rabbinische Agada's in 1001 Nacht: Ein Beitrag zur Geschichte der Wanderung orientalischer Märchen," *Monatsschrift für Geschichte*

und Wissenschaft des Judenthums 22 (1914): 14–34, and other references in the notes to that article.

38. The Yiddish version was reprinted without substantial changes in 1796, 1803, and in part in 1813, published by Itskhak and Nahman at the press of Professor Elsener.

39. *Toyzend und eyne Nakht* (Warsaw: Lebenssohn, 1835), 118. Identical to Prague: Scholl, 1816 and Warsaw: Lebenssohn, 1839

40. "Under the rule of the Caliph Harun Alrashid, of whom I have just spoken, there was in Baghdad a poor porter named Hinbad." *Die Tausend und eine Nacht: Arabische Erzählungen*, trans. Johann Heinrich Voß, vol. 2 (Bremen: Cramer, 1781), 1.

41. Dov Ber Kerler, *Origins of Modern Literary Yiddish* (Oxford: Clarendon, 1999), 21.

42. See my "Neglected Origins," 6, where I discuss Avraham Hazan's *Kokhevei 'or* (first. pub. 1933), ed. Shmuel Ha-Levi Hurvitz (Jerusalem: Hasidei Breslov, 1987), section entitled "Sippurim nifla'im," 8. Cited and discussed by Haim Liberman, Mendel Piekarz, and Shmuel Feiner.

43. The letter from Jacob Bik to Mendel Lefin, on the occasion of Bik's daughter's wedding, attests to the connection between Hurwitz's son and Lefin. Sent from Brod in 1811 to Lefin, who was staying at the house of Joseph Perl in Tarnopol, the letter is in German, written in Hebrew characters. It begins:

איהריביידי ווערטי בריפע ע"י ר' הירש הורוויץ וע"י ר' מרדכי
בערנשטיין האבי איך מיט פרגניגן ריכטיג ערהאלטן.

This could be rendered in German: "Ihre beide werte Briefe *al yedei* Reb Hirsh Hurwitz *ve-al yedei* Reb Mordecai Bernstein habe ich mit Vergnügen richtig erhalten" (I have received with pleasure both of your valued letters, at the hands of Mr. Hirsh Hurwitz and at the hands of Mr. Mordecai Bernstein). That is, Bik received letters from Lefin and Perl that were delivered by Hurwitz and Bernstein. Hirsh Hurwitz, the son of the successful businessman Khaikl Hurwitz of Uman, was presumably traveling for business purposes when he traveled from Uman via Tarnopol to Brody. Contained in Israel Weinlöz, "Mendel Lefin-Satanover," *YIVO Bleter* 2 (1931): 342.

44. Mendel Lefin, "Essai d'un plan de réforme ayant pour objet d'éclairer la nation juive en Pologne et de redresser par là ses mœurs," in *Materiały do dziejów Sejmu Czteroletniego*, vol. 6, ed. Artur Eisenbach et al. (Warsaw: Instytut historii Polskiej akademii Nauk, 1969).

45. 7b. I follow the first edition of 1815, with the original punctuation that was changed in later editions.

46. The German original by Campe reads: "Bonteku ließ indessen die Schaluppe aussetzen; stieg mit einigen Leuten hinein; befahl dem Steuermann in seiner Abwesenheit vor dem Busen hin und her zu kreutzen, um sich nicht zu entfernen; und ließ sich hierauf nach der Küste rudern." See J. H. Campe, *Sammlung interessanter und durchgängig zweckmäßig abgefaßter Reisebeschreibungen für die Jugend*, vol. 5 (Braunschweig: Schulbuchhandlung, 1788), 16.

47. Chaikl Hurwitz, *Tsofnas pa`neakh* (Berdichev: Bak, 1817). Because it is translated from J. H. Campe's *Die Entdeckung von Amerika*, one might wonder whether to attribute the criticism to Campe, to Hurwitz, or both. Close analysis

shows that Hurwitz expresses some criticism in his own voice, and that he sympathizes with the plight of Native Americans from the standpoint of a Jew in Czarist Russia.

48. Compare articles by Moshe Pelli and Nancy Sinkoff, which allude to this analogy between Jews and natives. Sinkoff writes of Lefin that, "in the realm of metaphor, he appears to be comparing the 'noble savages' with east European Jewry and the British and their world with Western, non-Jewish culture." See Nancy Sinkoff, "Strategy and Ruse in the Haskalah of Mendel Lefin of Satanow," 93. Sinkoff cites Moshe Pelli's article on "The Literary Genre of the Travelogue in Hebrew Haskalah Literature: Shmuel Romanelli's Masa Ba`rav," *Modern Judaism* 11 (1991): 241–60.

49. I quote from scans of the only known extant copy of *Tsofnas pa`neakh*, in the library of the YIVO Institute. Zalman Reyzn, Ber Shlosberg, and Israel Zinberg apparently had access to a more complete copy of the three-volume book, before the Second World War. See Zalman Reyzn, "Campes 'Antdekung fun Amerike' in Yiddish," *YIVO bleter* 5 (1933): 29–40; Ber Shlosberg, "Khaikl Hurvitses 'Sefer tsofnas pa`neakh,'" *YIVO bleter* 12 (1937): 546–58; and several passages in Israel Zinberg, *History of Jewish Literature*.

50. The episodic narratives of Pizzaro and the other conquistadores in South America sometimes seem to resemble tales in Nahman's *Sippurei mayses*.

51. Letters written by Khaikl Hurwitz attest that he had open relations with Karaites, who were spurned by some Jews.

52. In Campe's original: "das Lesen der Romane, so wie überhaupt solcher Bücher, welche nur darauf abzwecken, die Phantasie, die Einbildungskraft und die Empfindungen anzuregen, aus voller Ueberzeugung von ihrer großen Schädlichkeit" (7). See "An die jungen Leser," preface to "Wilhelm Isbrand Bonteku's merkwürdige Abentheuer auf einer Reise aus Holland nach Ostindien," in *Sammlung interessanter und durchgängig zweckmäßig abgefaßter Reisebeschreibungen für die Jugend*, vol. 5, 7.

53. In Campe's original: "Deswegen habe ich mir . . . zur Regel gemacht, nicht blos das Interessanteste dieses Fachs für euch auszusuchen, sondern auch noch überdem von Zeit zu Zeit eine und die andere von jenen ganz ausserordentlichen Reisebegebenheiten einzuwenden, deren Geschichte an Annehmichkeit und Wunderbarkeit den Romanen völlig gleichkommt, ohne daß wir dadurch, wie von diesen, aus der wirklichen Welt in die der Phantasien und der Hirngespinnste hinausgeführt werden." The rationalistic rejection of romanticism is as far- reaching as it is excessive and untenable. Campe elsewhere rejects the "Arkadische" vision, and yet he romanticizes the "noble savages" in George Keate's version of Captain Wilson's travel narrative. Keate himself was a poet whose works included *The Monument in Arcadia: A Dramatic Poem in Two Acts* (London: J. Dodsley, 1773).

54. Campe's German original reads: "Ich erschrak, sagt Bonteku in seiner Reisebeschreibung, und lief hinab. So wie ich in den Raum kam, sahe ich, daβ die Kohlen, die der ausgeronnene Branntewein entzündet hatte, in lichten Flammen standen. Alsobald goβen wir Wasser in erstaunlicher Menge darauf; aber nun ereignete sich ein neuer Zufall. Das auf die Kohlen gegossene Wasser verursachte einen so dicken, schwefelichten und erstickenden Dampf, daβ es fast unmöglich war, im Raume auszuhalten" (24–25).

55. Campe's German is quite different: "Sie waren mit den ausschweifendsten Erwartungen hieher gekommen; hatten sich ungeheure Schätze und ein müβiges bequemes Wohlleben versprochen: und nun solten sie Tag vor Tag in brennender Sonnenhize, wie Tagelöhner, arbeiten." See J. H. Campe, *Die Entdekkung [sic] von Amerika, ein angenehmes und nüzliches Lesebuch für Kinder und junge Leute*, 2nd ed., part 1 (Hamburg: Karl Ernst Bohn, 1782), 177.

56. See Moses Mendelsohn-Frankfurt, *Metziat ha-aretz ha-hadasha* (Altona: Ha-mehaber, 1807), 74. Mendelsohn-Frankfurt generally wrote in the style of maskilic Hebrew, using biblical style and *shibbutz*, incorporating biblical phrases such as ארץ . . . אוכלת יושביה from Numbers 13:32.

57. See, for example, "Le-berur mahuta ve-tifkuda shel lashon ha-sifrut ha-yafa be-diglosia," *Ha- Sifrut* 2 (1970): 286–302; and *Polysystem Studies*, a special issue of *Poetics Today* 11 (1990): 1–268.

58. *Polysystem Studies*, 155–56.

Chapter 10

✦

Lost and Found in Translation

The Itinerant Kafka Translations of Edwin and Willa Muir

Catriona MacLeod

Emily Apter's book *The Translation Zone* devotes a chapter to a language she describes as "the language of damaged experience," namely the literary output of a post-1980s generation of working-class Scots (the so-called New Scotologists), writers such as Iain Banks, James Kelman, Duncan McLean, and Irvine Welsh. Her alignment of this scatological, scabrous regional language with Deleuze and Guattari's influential if controversial reading of Kafka's "minor" literature is based on what she sees as a congruence in its resistant quality with the linguistic means by which "Kafka subverted the vehicular [bureaucratic German] by freighting it with unwelcome baggage, from Yiddish inflections to scraps of Czech vernacular."[1] In Apter's reading, the emphasis is, however, on the entrapment and servility of this traumatized, colonized Scottish language, which is able at best to lash out, in Apter's terms "with the slings and arrows of warped speech" (Apter, *The Translation Zone*, 155) untranslatable to the non-Scottish reader of English (and to many native Scots as well, I would qualify). Where the analogy breaks down still further, however, is in the pronounced crudeness and orality of a decisively "unbureaucratic" language. Yet Apter's sense of the affinity between writers on the periphery of languages and her astute recognition about the centrality of (un) translatability in their literary power struggles lead me back in this chapter to an earlier, not only associative, connection between Kafka and a contested Scottish literary language. I want to return us here to the earliest translators of Kafka into English, Edwin (1887–1959) and Willa (1890–1970) Muir, and to their central role in the formation of a Scottish modernism, a modernism that was riven with bitter political debates about the Scottish writer's relationship to English. Poignantly aware of their status as writers of an essentially foreign language—anticipating, as we shall see, Derrida's claim to have "only one language, yet it is not mine"[2]—it is through the very act of translation, and through the very act of translating Kafka's German (and other German modernist works), that the peripheral Muirs circle and powerfully enter the terrain of modernism in English, examples of what Pascale Casanova has called translators as "foreign exchange brokers."[3] Indeed, the Muirs for decades also provided the port of entry for all English readers of Kafka, until the new translations made possible by the editorial work of Malcolm Pasley.

To extend the metaphor of translators as mobile merchants of language, carrying with them their own baggage, this chapter will consider Kafka as a touchstone for Scottish modernism via a brief reading of the Kafka novel which is most deeply about the problems of translation, namely *Amerika* (as the Muirs titled their translation, following Max Brod). Beginning with a consideration of this novel and its resistance to translatability, I will then examine the novel's implications for the area of transnational translation, which has become a substantial focus of the new translation theory.

Amerika, or as Kafka untranslatably titled the novel, *Der Verschollene*, has deservedly been recognized as a traveling text. Carolin Duttlinger goes so far as to call it a "fictional travelogue," while John Zilcosky, with a different angle on travel, emphasizes the profound disorientation experienced by immigrant Karl Rossmann, summing it up as a novel about how to get lost.[4] Getting lost is profoundly interconnected with translation problems. *Translatio,* or the carrying over of meaning, is an act that implies conveyancing and future arrival at a destination. But in Kafka's novel, which the Muirs translated in 1938, the traffic in meaning from Europe to America is a process without foreseeable end point and unmoored from the possibility of return to a linguistic homeland: Karl, perpetually on the move by boat, elevator, car, and train, is, as it were, adrift in translation. This despite what I would suggest is the overemphasized nonchalance with which Karl seems to learn English in the second book: Karl approaches the task as if it were an activity as comparably straightforward as learning to play the American national anthem on the piano, simply learning to play a new tune on a familiar instrument.[5]

Karl even manages to produce, to ingratiate himself at his uncle's dinner party, "eine etwas newyorkisch gefärbte Redeweise" (Kafka, *Der Verschollene*, 650; several characteristic New York expressions),[6] though the witticism that he utters to the general mirth of the guests is in fact completely lost on him. But the narrator's simultaneous affirmation and qualification of the ease of mastering English should raise some doubts in readers: "er war auch *wirklich* seines Englischen schon *ziemlich* sicher" (ibid., 650, emphasis added). On this point, the Muirs capture the linguistic hesitation slightly better than Mark Harman's excellent recent translation: compare "he was now pretty certain of his English" (Muirs, 49) and "he was already quite confident about his English" (Harman).[7] The reality is that Karl Rossmann is getting lost in English, a language that he can at times not even distinguish from others heard around him. Faced with a police interview later in the narrative, Karl, lapsing into silence, lets his aptly named companion Delamarche speak for him, and is overcome by the hotel porters' English swirling around him, which clatters rather than is spoken: "das Durcheinander der Stimmen . . . , die in einem gänzlich unverständlichen vielleicht mit slavischen Worten untermischten Englisch mehr polterten als redeten" (Kafka, *Der Verschollene,* 800). I want to dwell for a moment on one word in the translation that the Muirs give us for this key sentence in the novel relating to untranslatability: "the incessant chatter of these same porters, who babbled rather than spoke in a quite incomprehensible *jargon* which was perhaps broken English interspersed with Slavonic words" (Kafka, *Amerika*, 216, emphasis added). Adding the word "jargon" to the phrase, they place the emphasis on this English as belonging to a hybrid idiolect, rather than on English itself as alien. But they are also taking us to the heart of Kafka's Yiddish-German language politics, to the uncanniness of Kafka's German. As is well established, the word "jargon" has had a complex and contested social history since the Jewish Enlightenment, referring to the language of eastern European Jewry in predominantly negative terms as a hodgepodge of childish or primitive incomprehensible sounds (in contrast to German, the language of assimilation). Kafka in 1912 gave a speech on "Jargon" that recuperated this language's potency for an audience of probably suspicious German speakers, composed as it is only of ceaselessly mobile and hybrid foreign words. As Yasemin Yildiz has recently argued, Kafka demonstrates the uncanniness of Yiddish's apparent transparency to a German speaker, yet unique untranslatability into that tongue: "In this uncertainty, German becomes uncanny, as its boundaries, coherence, and identity are put into question from within."[8] Whether the Muirs could have known Kafka's speech, delivered only months after Kafka's first engagement with Yiddish theater, is improbable, yet their imbuing of Karl Rossmann's English with the terminology of jargon certainly thickens the problem of untranslatability with relevance to Karl's American English, to Kafka's German, and not least to their own English. Here I want to allow for moments of productive friction in the Muirs' language and translation practice, and place the emphasis rather differently than Michelle Woods. In her timely recent book *Kafka Translated* Woods in my view rightly urges contemporary readers before dismissing the Muirs to understand their cultural context and their language politics, while she continues to emphasize what she sees as the Muirs' "domestication" of language, their "repression" of their own identities in order to produce "normalizing" translations.[9] Willa Muir certainly showed a keen awareness of the language politics of Prague in the 1920s, noting the ascent of Czech from its prewar status as a "kitchen language."[10] Her autobiography, ironically entitled *Belonging*, traces the virtually never-ending geographical dislocations of the writing couple beginning with their arrival in Prague in 1921, where, absolutely at sea and "having no clue at all to the Czech language," they are immediately confronted with a linguistic impasse: "As soon as we got out of the train in the large station, a mathematically symmetrical station, we were faced by identical stairways at either end. One stairway was marked Vchod, the other Vychod. 'Now, which of these?' we said to each other, but at once abandoned visual aids."[11]

Before turning to the Muirs and their own hybrid linguistic identities, I want to discuss one more example of how the Muirs approach *Amerika*. Once again, the theoretical and affective kinship between translators and author may help us read anew a translation that has rightly been identified as a problematic mistranslation. It cannot be denied that their translation of the opening sentences of *Der Verschollene*, much like their translation of *Das Schloß* (*The Castle*), steers Kafka's narrative into more unambiguously allegorical religious terms than the original German warrants: where Kafka's "Freiheitsgöttin" (goddess of liberty) raises her sword to the sky, into the "freien Lüfte" (Kafka, *Der Verschollene,* 607), the Muirs emphatically render the final word of the paragraph as "heaven" (Kafka, *Amerika,* 3).[12] And the Muirs also project a harsher view of the agents of the expulsion, Karl's parents, who are now no longer described as "arm" (poor). In general, though both Harman and Hofmann seek to substitute the sunny innocence of the Muirs' view of Kafka with a bleaker overtone (after all, Arthur Holitscher's misspelling of Oklahoma in *Amerika heute und morgen* (*America Today and Tomrrow*), a key source for Kafka, occurs in a photo caption to a lynching titled "Idyll in Oklahama"),[13] I would suggest that the opening scene sets the stage for Karl's (with the Muirs') expulsion from a lost Eden, an expulsion that is profoundly connected with language. Considering the Muirs' own roles in a strained modernist language debate enables us, I think, to go beyond critiques such as those of George Steiner, who noted critically if simplistically that the Muirs had effaced the Jewish religious dimension of Kafka, inserting a gulf between human and divine law, because of Edwin's Kierkegaardian-tinged Scottish Calvinist background as well as Brod's influence.[14] In fact, despite the religious themes of much of his own literary work, and despite the fact that he wrote a book about John Knox, Edwin Muir's relationship with Calvinism was nothing if not critical: his book *Scott and Scotland* goes so far as to charge the Reformation with the utter coarsening of "a high culture of the feelings as well as the mind," and Calvinism with the impoverishment of Scottish poetry *tout court.*[15] Far from invisible translators, the Muirs not only travel with and through Kafka to their own modernist poetic voices, they impart to his narrative a distinctive mystical signature that would also mark Edwin (who had undergone Jungian analysis in 1919), and his later poetry.

Kafka may have described the novel as a point of orientation for himself as a writer, a "block" he clung to as a pedestal (May 9, 1912), but as a narrative it refuses the allegorical fixity of the commemorative statue, and Kafka confesses to Felice (January 2 and 3, 1913) that he is barely able to hold on to the fugitive protagonists by their coattails.[16] In a novel that dispenses with most landmarks or points of orientation, other than the Statue of Liberty with its forbidding greeting in the opening paragraph, the Brooklyn Bridge, in a rare feat of engineering, and crossing the wrong New York river, is a bridge too far, spanning New York and Boston (Kafka, *Der Verschollene,* 704). More pertinently, it immediately strains the credibility of the bridge metaphor commonly used for translation, and as a physical structure it too vibrates in perpetual motion.[17] Yet more extreme, Kafka's chosen title, *Der Verschollene*, connotes an absolute severing of communication ties with the outside world, a man who walks off a bridge to nowhere. Not for nothing does one of Karl's travel companions, the supposedly Irish Robinson, reference Defoe's castaway Crusoe.

Translation, or mistranslation, is what Kafka's novel already performs in its original German. The opening paragraph of the novel, with its representation of a sword-wielding Statue of Liberty barring Karl from the Promised Land rather than welcoming him (Kafka, *Der Verschollene*, 607), of course sets up this disorientation. The very currency of this Amerika is wrong too, British pounds rather than the U.S. dollar (ibid., 708). New York is spelled as one word in the first sentence (ibid., 607) and elsewhere. Karl's final destination is Oklahama (ibid., 873), a misspelling that, like that of Newyork, Kafka inherited from the travel reportage *Amerika heute und morgen* of Budapest author Arthur Holitscher. Max Brod notoriously edited these blockages in the novel, smoothing over factual inconsistencies and orthographic "mistakes" such as the spelling of Oklahoma from the manuscript; following the editorial work of Malcolm Pasley, Kafka's text, in the S. Fischer critical edition, was returned in 1983 to its original form, bearing Kafka's chosen title, restoring the orthography, and reordering several of the chapters with a fragmentary effect. The recent English translations of Michael Hofmann (2002)[18] and Mark Harman (2008), both of which are based on the new edition, go a long way to restoring in English, too, the jarring effect of the so-called mistakes, which highlight the linguistic strain in a migrant's translation of America, though both still stop short at Kafka's "Newyork" and normalize the city name. Kafka's novel, the work of an author who had never visited the United States, also constitutes an imaginary cross-cultural translation project, approaching America via, among other European literary proxies, Charles Dickens, who had famously traveled in America, and his orphan David Copperfield. Bearing in mind that translation, by definition, entails cultural transfer, a carrying-over, Kafka's novel presents itself both as an immense challenge to any translator (beginning but not ending with the geographical "mistakes" contained in the text), but also as a meta-narrative about translation itself. If the translator is a tour guide, bringing us in the first paragraph, along with Karl and his baggage, to an ominous sighting of the Statue of Liberty, how can or should he or she continue to orient the reader in the face of incongruities and unreliable or lost meaning?[19] Such questions about the translator as a transnational broker of language need to be applied, too, to the pioneering work of the Muirs.

Edwin and Willa Muir make apposite first translators, in 1938, of Kafka and his Amerika, via British English, not American English. The Muirs, both Scots, and both successful literary authors in their own right,[20] though they also translated over forty European novels by authors including Heinrich Mann, Hermann Broch, Gerhart Hauptmann, and Scholem Asch, had roots in the remotest insular periphery of the British Isles, the periphery of the periphery: Edwin was born in 1887 in the far-flung Orkney Islands, Willa, in 1890, in Montrose, to parents from the still further-flung island of Unst, in the Shetlands. (Edwin would dub Scotland his "second country" [McCulloch, *Edwin Muir,* ix].) Mark Harman, who wrote the second, and much-praised, English translation of the *The Castle* after the Muirs, is not alone in observing the "smoothness" of their English: noting their "naturalization" of Kafka, he further comments more generally that early translators of modernist prose "sought to smuggle in through the back door the very prose style that the modernists sought to subvert" (Harman, "Digging the Pit of Babel," 292). But the smooth, "standardized" English of the Muirs is unquestionably as complicated, for its own geocultural reasons, as the insouciant English of Karl Rossmann or the German of his creator, which Pascale Casanova has described as a borrowed language, a translation from a Yiddish that he did not and could not write (Casanova, *The World Republic of Letters,* 269). To be sure, the Muirs inherited from the problematic edition of Max Brod the smoothing over or correction of Kafka's "mis"-translations. Monopolists on Kafka they may have been for decades, and authors of many apparent lapses, as several critics have pointed out: however, it does them a disservice to assert, as one recent reviewer, Paul Reitter, has, that they did not feel "wary" enough around English, and may have been, quite simply, writing too fast. (Edwin Muir described their work himself as "a sort of translation factory.")[21] With only a few exceptions (Ritchie Robertson, Michelle Woods), Kafka scholars have tended to overlook the Muirs' own literary productions; conversely, scholars of Scottish literary modernism have not read their writing in the context of the translations. If anything, as I shall argue, it is a wariness about English that propels the Muirs' literary entrance in that arrival via the intense engagement with literary translation into English. Casanova's account of global literary power relations notes, indeed, a "special perceptiveness of contestants on the periphery" that enables them to perceive affinities with others who share their literary 'destitution.' "[22] Ritchie Robertson already in 1984 comprehensively addressed Edwin Muir's responsiveness to Kafka via literary criticism, in the form of the paratexts, the introductions and notes that amplified the translations for an English readership,[23] but I want to turn our attention to the strategic activity of translation itself. Far from being a derivative activity, translating for the Muirs was a creative vehicle that enabled them to launch their own literary careers, careers that straddled languages and nations, and in the case of Edwin, the near-contemporary of Kafka, as he asserted in a diary during the late 1930s, historical epochs:

> I was born before the Industrial Revolution, and am now about two hundred years old. But I have skipped a hundred and fifty of them. I was really born in 1737, and till I was fourteen no time-accidents happened to me. Then in 1751 I set out from Orkney to Glasgow. When I arrived I found that it was not 1751, but 1901, and that a hundred and fifty years had been burned up in my two days' journey. But I myself was still in 1751, and remained there for a long time. All my life since I have been trying to overhaul that invisible leeway.[24]

Edwin Muir was not only a major poet, but also a forceful critical voice in the literary debates of his day, which were bound up with issues of self-assertion and national identity. Most notably, he authored a polemic on the urgent need of Scottish authors, in the vein of Deleuze and Guattari's still influential theory of "minor" writers, to deterritorialize, to make their national mark in what was quite potentially a strange language, standard English. Yet Muir's own English would probably have contained many Norse elements, and he noted in his autobiography that his speech as a child was thoroughly Orcadian, "a mixture of Norse, Scots, and Irish," while the language of island poets was "laboriously learned from the grammar books" (*An Autobiography*, 53). Much of his own poetry—with shades of Karl Rossmann's ejection from home—is preoccupied with re-creating the lost Edenic world of his Orcadian childhood, and indeed a 1956 collection bears the title *One Foot in Eden*. Willa Muir came to English still more circuitously. Her book on ballads reveals that because as a child she spoke Shetland dialect with her parents at home, she learned a second dialect before English, and was excluded by other schoolgirls because of her linguistic outsider status.[25] Introduced to Edwin Muir in Glasgow in 1918 by a literary friend who was impressed by Edwin's recently published *We Moderns*, Willa disappointingly for the hostess immediately found a kindred spirit in language and neglected to speak about the book:

> Listening to Edwin's soft voice I remembered that he was an Orkneyman and I turned to him and told him that my people came from Unst in Shetland. We began to exchange Orkney and Shetland words and phrases and to discuss the habits and temperaments of the Islanders. From Mam's [the hostess's] point of view this must have seemed grossly unfair; she deflected me by asking me to sing some student songs at the piano. . . . Now, instead of roaring the usual student choruses with E., I crooned one or two Gaelic songs . . . (Willa Muir, *Belonging*, 16)

Edwin Muir's on the face of it surprising disputatious remarks about the viability of modern literature written in vernacular Scots, which enraged among others his nemesis, poet Hugh MacDiarmid, for whom the recuperation of the vernacular represented a modernist and deeply ideological literary language choice, are contained in his 1936 book-length study *Scott and Scotland: The Predicament of the Scottish Writer*.[26] That book was written during a period in Scotland of nationalist modernism in which rival poets were consciously turning away from standard English to a literary renewal of the Scots and Gaelic languages,[27] and it coincided as well with Muir and his wife's work translating Kafka. Other contemporaries, including the noted Scots novelist Lewis Grassic Gibbon (James Leslie Mitchell, 1901–35), would foreground the "essential foreignness" always adhering to the Scottish writer of English.[28] In an essay published in 1934, he claims: "For, however the average Scots writer believes himself Anglicized . . . it is not English. The English reader is haunted by a sense of something foreign stumbling and hesitating behind this smooth but arduously acquired façade of adequate technique: it is as thought the writer did not *write* himself, but *translated* himself" (quoted in McCulloch, *Modernism and Nationalism*, 34). Grassic Gibbon nevertheless tellingly writes off a number of Scottish authors—including, notably Willa Muir—writing in "orthodox" English as English themselves (ibid., 36).[29] Edwin Muir would also write in the 1930s of Scotland as a species of undead, "neither really quite alive, nor quite dead," "not yet quite fully digested by England" (quoted in McCulloch, *Modernism and Nationalism,* 241).

The dominant spatial metaphor, however, of Muir's study is that of the blank and stationary center with which every Scottish writer, according to Muir, must necessarily contend. His primary charge against the most successful Scottish author, Walter Scott, concerns Scott's essential "emptiness" (Muir, *Scott and Scotland,* 11). This "nothing in which Scott wrote" encompasses several related issues. First, Scott's derivative, vacuous literary output, which Muir characterizes as "nonsensical trash" (ibid., 144), gathered-up relics from an imagined past, and "second-hand," based on an English tradition with which Scott was intimately familiar yet which was "semi-foreign" (ibid., 12).

Second, and more broadly, there is the spatial emptiness of a "parochial and conglomerate" (Muir, *Scott and Scotland*, 179) country that was "neither a nation nor a province, and had, instead of a centre, a blank, an Edinburgh, in the middle of it" (ibid., 12). To extrapolate from Muir's position, this would explain why the Scots had not been able to recuperate a metropolitan center, as Joyce had done for Dublin, via the adoption and adaptation of English.[30] The radicality of Muir resides in his disavowal of conservative Edinburgh not for a more open, alternative literary capital (the more recent Glasgow of Kelman, for example), as Casanova describes a typical spatial configuration (Casanova, *The World Republic of Letters,* 247), but for the cities that unleashed his and his wife's poetic creativity, Dresden, or Kafka's Prague. Why travel from London to Prague, where the peripheral Muirs knew nothing of the languages or culture? Willa Muir puts it plainly: Europe was entirely "an imaginary region" and "Prague was in the very middle of Europe" (Willa Muir, *Belonging,* 54). (Glasgow, for Edwin Muir, represented his adolescent uprooting from an agrarian island community and a traumatic displacement marked by grinding urban poverty and the deaths of four immediate family members within two years.) There is a poignant and revelatory moment in Muir's *Autobiography* when he describes the liberation he experienced upon first living in Dresden, feeling suddenly that his sight and childhood were being restored in this "resting place." The notion of being able to rewrite and relive one's lost past, and of simultaneously emerging into a new poetic voice, in a foreign city whose language one is still learning, conjures up for Muir a poetic couplet, not of German modernist poetry, or of standard English, but rather, by the Middle Scots poet Robert Henryson (1430–1490): "And with ane blenk it come into his thocht, / That he sumtime hir face befoir had sene" (Muir, *Autobiography,* 187).

The third emptiness for Muir in *Scott and Scotland* arose from an intermittent cultural and literary history, "a temporal Nothing . . . , dotted with a few disconnected figures arranged at abrupt intervals" (Muir, *Scott and Scotland,* 12). These three forms of blankness—lack of original voice, lack of metropolitan center, and lack of historical continuity even in the tongues that authors such as Hugh McDiarmid (Scots) and Sorley MacLean (Gaelic) sought to revive for modernism—all relate back to the central issue at stake in Muir's book, namely the blank spot of estrangement in the Scottish writer's relationship with his or her own tattered language, which he believes is an apt vehicle for feeling (note the emotional appearance of Scots in his own autobiography), but not for abstract thought (Muir, *Scott and Scotland,* 31). Thus Robert Burns, according to Muir, lapses into a confused hybrid language, "a ragtag of phrases" composed of a random mixture of vernacular speech and poetic diction (48). The Scottish writer lacks both a whole language and a whole mind (22), and Scottish literature, put starkly, "has been a literature without a language" (18). The future autonomous success of this language is guaranteed only via the active creation of a homogeneous (English) language offering access to mature diction, and indeed to the world (71).[31] Against the backdrop of an empty center and of a literary culture that manages to be at once static and discordant, English offers the only safeguard against ever smaller regionalisms and schisms. It is striking, in this fiercely argued book about the Scottish writer's alienated condition, that Muir, noting the characteristic poetic stance of that writer as "occupying a half-way-house" recoiling between the prosaic intellect and the fantastic imagination, cites not a Scottish work as an example of such internal conflict, but Kafka's aphorism about a man who is pinned by one shirt collar to the earth, and by the other to the heavens (105). Kafka makes other appearances in Muir's Scottish criticism. An essay by Edwin Muir on Robert Louis Stevenson—himself the author of a travel account about a miserable, alienating journey in 1879 from New York via railroad to the Californian frontier—presents the sickly and fantastic Scottish author as Kafka's twin.[32]

Muir's *Scott and Scotland*, as discussed earlier, trenchantly diagnoses the divided linguistic consciousness of Scots, who, asserts Muir, feel in one language and think in another. The result, he concludes, is a state of perpetual translation through which all words, whether those of thoughts or feelings, must pass: "their emotions turn to the Scottish tongue, with all its associations of local sentiment, and their minds to a standard English which for them is almost bare of associations other than those of the classroom" (21).

Muir's own literary itinerary journey, along with that of his wife, notably took him beyond the Scottish islands and cities, beyond the sparse intellectualism of London's linguistic terrain, to a rootless existence in Europe, via stations in Prague, Dresden, Italy, Salzburg, and Vienna, and to the modernism and polyphonous linguistic identity of Kafka, personifying in the character Karl Rossmann translation without arrival point. In France the Muirs translated Feuchtwanger's *Jud Süss* (*Jew Süss*), followed by *Die hässliche Herzogin* (*The Ugly Duchess*), and the early 1930s saw them embarking on Hermann Broch's *Die Schlafwandler* (*The Sleepwalkers*), Kafka's *Das Schloss* (1930) and *Beim Bau der chinesischen Mauer* (*The Great Wall of China*, 1933). It was when Muir and his wife had returned to Scotland, between 1935 and 1945, that the book on Scotland's linguistic predicament, and Muir's mature poetry and novels, were written. As I have shown, the relationship to English and English literature is, to say the least, a deeply wary and aware one, based on triangulated translational and transnational relationships among it and other (also divided/also suppressed) languages. The liberating boldness that Willa Muir described in confronting the opacity of communication in Prague, necessitating what she called "a wild farrago of French, German, Czech, English, and gesturing" (Willa Muir, *Belonging,* 58), was what enabled the writer-translators to stage their own literary interventions in standard English. The carrying over of German into English, then, is also smuggling in negotiations between outside dominant languages and their fractious, fugitive "others," as crystallized in the power struggles between Czech and German, a language which by the time the Muirs returned to Prague after the war had itself vanished apparently without trace behind what Willa Muir called an "invisible but unyielding barrier"—and leaving not even a ghostly presence of Kafka, whom they would never meet in person (Willa Muir, *Belonging*, 62).[33]

I have viewed Kafka's American novel as a metanarrative about translation, the movement of and between languages and cultures. In closing, let me turn to a famous passage from the first chapter in which Karl, also in motion with the motion of the ship, and peering through the portholes, watches the ceaseless motion of the harbor: "eigentümliche Schwimmkörper, tauchten hie und da selbständig aus dem ruhelosen Wasser, wurden gleich wieder überschwemmt und versanken vor dem erstaunten Blick" (Kafka, *Der Verschollene*, 620; curious objects bobbed independently out of the restless water, were immediately submerged again and sank before his astonished eyes, *Amerika*, 17). While Michael Hofmann opts for the literal nautical "strange floats" (Kafka, *Amerika: The Man Who Disappeared,* 13), Kafka's German leaves the question open as to whether these could be creaturely bodies. What—or who—are these mysterious floaters? Ambiguously untranslatable traces perhaps of those "Verschollene," as Karl himself will soon be, at sea in language. If we look closely enough at the Kafka translations of the Muirs we will also find bobbing up from the supposedly smooth waters of their English, floating residues ("curious objects" [Kafka, trans. Muirs, *Amerika,* 17]) of their troubled and incessant linguistic passages in and through German and its others.

Notes

1. Emily Apter, *The Translation Zone: A New Comparative Literature* (Princeton, N.J.: Princeton University Press, 2005), 155. Apter has continued this work, more recently, in *Against World Literature: On the Politics of Untranslatability* (New York: Verso, 2013). See also Gilles Deleuze and Félix Guattari, *Kafka: Toward a Minor Literature*, trans. Dana Polan (Minneapolis: University of Minnesota Press, 1986). For a useful recent analysis of Kafka's own diary entries on "kleinere Literaturen" (minor literatures), see Lowell Edmunds, "Kafka on Minor Literature," *German Studies Review* 33, no. 2 (2010): 351–74. Edmunds directs our attention to the defensive, self-sufficient role of literature in the "kleinere Literaturen," countering Pascale Casanova's claim that it is characteristic of minor literatures to rise up against and struggle with major literatures. See Casanova, *The World Republic of Letters*, trans. M. B. Debevoise (Cambridge, Mass.: Harvard University Press, 2004), esp. 173–204 for Casanova's revisionary reading of Deleuze and Guattari insisting on the literariness of Kafka's politics, and more recently, Casanova, *Kafka, Angry Poet* (London: Seagull Books, 2015). The literature on Kafka's relationship with German is of course vast: David Suchoff has explored in detail the Jewishness of his language in his excellent *Kafka's Jewish Languages: The Hidden Openness of Tradition* (Philadelphia: University of Pennsylvania Press, 2012).

2. Jacques Derrida, *Monolingualism of the Other; or, The Prosthesis of the Origin*, trans. Patrick Mensah (Stanford, Calif.: Stanford University Press, 1998), 2.

3. Casanova, *The World Republic of Letters*, 21.

4. Carolin Duttlinger, "Visions of the New World: Photography in Kafka's *Der Verschollene*," *German Life & Letters* 59, no. 3 (2006): 423–45, here 423; John Zilcosky, *Kafka's Travels: Exoticism, Colonialism, and the Traffic of Writing* (New York: Palgrave Macmillan, 2003), 41. Edwin Muir viewed "the road," always either receding from or pursuing the protagonist, as the central image in reading Kafka's narratives. See Muir, "A Note on Franz Kafka," *Scottish Periodical* 1.1 (1947): 3–6, here 3–4. Muir concluded that "Kafka's detail is like that of a travel book which recounts minutely the customs, dresses and utensils of some newly discovered tribe; everything is strange" (6).

5. Franz Kafka, *Der Verschollene,* in *Romane* (Düsseldorf: Patmos, 2007), 605–894, here 45. All further German quotations from the novel, unless otherwise indicated, will be to this edition.

6. Franz Kafka, *Amerika*, trans. Willa and Edwin Muir (New York: Schocken Books, 1996), 49.

7. Franz Kafka, *Amerika: The Missing Person*, trans. Mark Harman (New York: Schocken Books, 2008), 45.

8. On Kafka and jargon, see Yasemin Yildiz, *Beyond the Mother Tongue: The Postmonolingual Condition* (New York: Fordham University Press, 2012), 50–66, here 56.

9. Michelle Woods, *Kafka Translated: How Translators Have Shaped Our Reading of Kafka* (New York: Bloomsbury, 2014), 5.

10. See Margery Palmer McCulloch, ed., *Modernism and Nationalism: Literature and Society in Scotland 1918–1939* (Glasgow: Association for Scottish Literary Studies, 2004), 194–95.

11. Willa Muir, *Belonging: A Memoir* (London: Hogarth, 1968), 56. The "belonging" to which Muir is referring is centered on her relationship with her husband rather than on geographical locale. See ibid., 11.

12. Harman's translation of the phrase as "the free winds" is more faithful to Kafka. See Kafka, *Amerika: The Missing Person*, trans. Harman, 3.

13. Arthur Holitscher, *Amerika heute und morgen: Reiseerlebnisse* (Berlin: S. Fischer, 1912), 367.

14. George Steiner, "Introduction," Franz Kafka, *The Trial*, trans. Edwin and Willa Muir with additional material by E. M. Butler (New York: Schocken, 1995), vii–xxi, here xii. Mark Harman has also discussed the religious inflections of the Muirs in an essay about his translation of *The Castle*, proposing that the Muirs represent the castle as a salvific structure akin to the allegory of Bunyan's *The Pilgrim's Progress*. See Harman, "Digging the Pit of Babel: Retranslating Franz Kafka's 'The Castle,'" *New Literary History* 27, no. 2 (1996): 291–311, here 296.

15. Edwin Muir, *Scott and Scotland: The Predicament of the Scottish Writer* (London: George Routledge, 1936), 61, 23–24.

16. Erich Heller and Joachim Beug, eds., *Dichter über ihre Dichtungen: Franz Kafka* (Munich: Ernst Heimeran, 1969), 31, 37.

17. It may be useful to think of the Brooklyn Bridge, as Ashley Lazevnick has suggestively described it in a recent talk on Hart Crane and Walt Whitman, as an "unmanageable object" in the modernist imagination. Designed by engineer John Roebling, a student of Hegel, the suspension bridge was intended to withstand shocks by virtue of its own state of perpetual vibrating movement. Lazevnick, "'Terrific Threshold of the Prophet's Pledge: Representing the Brooklyn Bridge," presentation at Languages of Art: Interactions between Art and Literature, Rutgers University, April 11, 2014. Kafka's geographical "error" was corrected by Max Brod. See also Holitscher, *Amerika heute und morgen*, 55, for a photograph of the Brooklyn Bridge.

18. Franz Kafka, *Amerika: The Man Who Disappeared*, trans. Michael Hofmann (New York: New Directions, 2002).

19. Willa Muir's memoir, recounting the couple's year at Harvard in 1955–56, spends some time on the uncanniness of a language that should have been, unlike Czech, immediately familiar: "some words were indecent as if they were naked." See *Belonging*, 286–87.

20. Tellingly, the title of Margery McCulloch's monograph *Edwin Muir: Poet, Critic and Novelist* (Edinburgh: Edinburgh University Press, 1993), does not

refer to the prodigious output of translation work. Though the Kafka translations are often largely ascribed to Edwin, Willa Muir's collaboration should not be underplayed, as Michelle Woods has demonstrated in her article "Reassessing Willa Muir: Her Role and Influence in the Kafka Translations," *Translation Studies* 4, no. 1 (2011): 58–71. Woods argues that Willa Muir was in fact the dominant partner in the translations, pointing out, in particular, her linguistic skills, including in Scots.

21. Qtd. in J. M. Coetzee, "Kafka: Translators on Trial," *The New York Review of Books*, May 14, 1998, http://www.nybooks.com/articles/archives/1998/may/14/kafka-translators-on-trial/?pagination=false&printpage=true; Coetzee concluded with a reminder that, for all the evident flaws in their translations, Edwin Muir was not an assembly line translator, but a modern master in his own right. See also Paul Reitter, "That Other Metamorphosis," review of Franz Kafka, *Amerika: The Man Who Disappeared*, trans. Michael Hofmann (New York: New Directions, 2002), *The Germanic Review* 81, no. 1 (2006): 87–95. In the late 1920s the Muirs had to maintain their pace of translations in order to be able to write their own books, but as Willa noted in a letter of May 30, 1929, ". . . if life were nothing but translation what a swindle it would be." (National Library of Scotland, Acc. 13266.)

22. Casanova, *The World Republic of Letters*, 247. One might recall here as well Milan Kundera's observations about the precariousness of "small nations" (forming "another Europe") which have all, at one time or another, "passed through the antechambers of death." Kundera continues these reflections by commenting on the familial stresses experienced by the artists who belong to these defensive, secluded nations. See Kundera, *Testaments Betrayed: An Essay in Nine Parts*, trans. Linda Asher (New York: Harper Collins, 1995), 192–94.

23. Ritchie Robertson, "Edwin Muir as Critic of Kafka," *The Modern Language Review* 79, no. 3 (1984): 638–52.

24. Edwin Muir, *An Autobiography* (Edinburgh: Canongate, 1993), 289.

25. See Willa Muir's book on oral poetry *Living With Ballads* (London: Hogarth, 1965), 19. Willa Muir also describes her parents in a notebook as D.P.s (Displaced Persons) in the northeastern Scottish county of Angus, where her parents had moved to from Unst in the Shetland Islands. See ms 38466/5/3, Special Collections, University of St Andrews.

26. A comprehensive overview of the vernacular debate is contained in the collection of primary texts assembled in Margery Palmer McCulloch, ed., *Modernism and Nationalism*, esp. the chapter "Language, Identity and the Vernacular Debate," 11–51; see also McCulloch's study *Scottish Modernism and Its Contexts 1918–1959: Literature, National Identity and Cultural Exchange* (Edinburgh: Edinburgh University Press, 2009). Seamus Heaney, (as McCulloch notes in *Scottish Modernism*), otherwise bemoaning the lack of a native British modernism in a 1986 essay first published in the *Yale Review*, sees Muir as a rare exception to insularity. See Heaney, "The Impact of Translation," in *The Government of the Tongue, Selected Prose 1978-1987* (New York: Farrar, Straus and Giroux, 1989), 36-44, in which Heaney attributes to Edwin Muir, who had characterized himself as out of time with his own age, an "audible . . . note which sounds both elegiac for and posthumous to the European civilization which produced it" (43). See also Alasdair D. F. Macrae, "Edwin Muir: One Foot in Europe," *Miscelánea:*

A Journal of English and American Studies 20 (1999): 103-14. MacRae views Edwin Muir's contributions to British modernism less in his "stationary" poetry and more in his role as a vector for and promoter of Continental literature.

27. Edwin Muir's own first poetic efforts were also aligned with the vernacular tradition of the medieval Orcadian ballad. He would later write about the impossibility of returning to the "unforced and unschooled" genius of that tradition. See McCulloch, *Modernism and Nationalism*, 25.

28. Edwin Muir, with shades of Kafka's descriptions of "Jargon," comments on the synthetic quality of McDiarmid's Scots poetry, with its inclusion of disparate voices ranging from Gaelic bards, to Einstein, to Rilke, to the popular Scottish entertainer Sir Harry Lauder. See McCulloch, *Modernism and Nationalism*, 73, 81.

29. Quoted in McCulloch, *Modernism and Nationalism*, 34, 36. Willa Muir did, however, like her husband, write dialect poetry. Several examples can be found in the Special Collections, St. Andrews University, and the National Library of Scotland. Acc.13226 at the National Library of Scotland contains a notebook of Willa Muir's that, in a sort of literary bricolage, was used to compose a sketch about upper-class Edinburgh church-goers written in an affected "pan loaf" vernacular, as well as a short story in Scots, and notes about translations.

30. Casanova is right to point out that Irish writers had and continue to have available a "polycentric" range of literary spaces, including Dublin, but also Paris, London, and now, New York (Casanova, *The World Republic of Letters*, 318). Indeed, Muir makes the same observation about Scotland in comparison to Ireland in 1934. See McCulloch, *Modernism and Nationalism*, 99.

31. Muir, interestingly, while ruling Scots out as a "complete and homogeneous language," does not exclude the possibility that Gaelic may yet become one in the future (Muir, *Scott and Scotland,* 178).

32. Edwin Muir, "Robert Louis Stevenson," *The Modern Scot* 2, no. 3 (1931): 196–204. Kafka, taking out of his desk drawer a copy of *Treasure Island*, had commented to Gustav Janouch about the tubercular Stevenson's flight to the South Seas and the taking flight of imagination on a tropical island. See Janouch, *Conversations with Kafka*, trans. Goronwy Rees (New York: New Directions, 1971), 42–43.

33. The point I am making is thus different from Emily Apter's argument, concerning contemporary world literatures, that "rather than a major language acting as the general equivalent between two or more minor languages, the translation process is now conceived as occurring within a field of the minor." See "Balkan Babel: Translation Zones, Military Zones," *Public Culture* 13, no. 1 (2001): 65–80, here 65.

Part IV

Intimate Geographies

Chapter 11

✦

Staging Untranslatability

Magnus Hirschfeld Encounters Philadelphia

Heike Bauer

This chapter examines the role of translation in the work of Magnus Hirschfeld (1868–1935) to consider how the relationship between discourse and experience is recorded within the sexological archive. It explores a verbal attack on a homosexual man and the role of translation in critiquing such a negation of queer existence. Hirschfeld, a Jewish physician from the north of Germany, is one of the most influential figures in the history of modern sexuality.[1] He is best known today for his homosexual rights activism, his coinage of the term "transvestism," and his crucial role in the institution of sexology in Germany. His work has been read in terms of the political history of modern Germany, covering the period from the turn of the twentieth century to debates about the abolition of Paragraph 175, which criminalized sex between men, to the Nazi destruction of Hirschfeld's Institut für Sexualwissenschaften (Institute of Sexual Science) in Berlin in 1933.[2] Scholars have also recognized the international scope of his work, the fact that he was "cosmopolitan to the core," as Elena Mancini writes in an examination of Hirschfeld's central role in the "first international sexual freedom movement."[3] He collaborated, for example, with international scholars and activists as copresident of the World League for Sexual Reform, and traveled widely, most famously completing a two-year world lecturing tour that helped him escape from Nazi persecution and that was organized with the help of colleagues from the United States, Japan, China, the Philippines, India, and the Middle East.[4] Unsurprisingly, then, the practice and theory of translation played a significant role in Hirschfeld's writings.

A considerable part of Hirschfeld's work was conducted in translation, through textual and face-to-face encounters with men and women from around the world. This chapter takes Hirschfeld's international links as its prompt for reading more closely for his textual politics of translation. Specifically, it considers evidence of Hirschfeld's use of translation as a narrative device, arguing that he wrote issues of translation into his sexological writings to make visible the textual fault lines that appear when personal experience and social and cultural circumstance are transcribed onto the page. In what follows, I want to explore some of the critical issues at stake, revisiting debates about identity, translation, and location, before considering how and why they are addressed in Hirschfeld's own work. It seems fitting in a chapter inspired by a conference at the University of Pennsylvania to hinge the discussion on examples in Hirschfeld's work that focus on homosexual subcultures in Philadelphia. These passages show, I argue, that he used translation to disrupt the narrative flow in a way that problematizes the relationship between the sexologist and his subjects of study and brings into question the assumptions about scientific objectivity that underpinned sexological discourse formations in the early twentieth century. Even more importantly, perhaps, these examples make clear that Hirschfeld refused to translate phrases that contain overtly homophobic content. These instances, in which German and English words are left side by side, suggest that Hirschfeld deliberately "staged untranslatability" in an attempt to draw attention to the violent effects of normative discourses on the lives they inscribe.

Queer Acts of Translation

Hirschfeld's purposely disruptive narrative method speaks to critical debates about translation and sexuality, debates which focus on the interrelated sociocultural contingencies of knowledge and identity and which consider what is at stake in the way such discussions are formulated. Here untranslatability tends to be associated with a process of localizing difference, the point, as Homi Bhabha has so influentially argued, where cultural difference is staged.[5] According to Bhabha "the act of translation" is fundamentally shaped by the "apprehension of difference," the recognition that when "the 'given' content [of language] becomes alien and estranged" it is "always confronted by its double, the untranslatable."[6] For Bhabha this process is specifically tied to the narration of nation, or what he calls "the complex strategies of cultural identification and discursive address that function in the name of 'the people' or 'the nation' and make them the immanent subjects of a range of social and literary narratives."[7] Bhabha thus usefully turns to translation to conceptualize the shaping of collective identities, specifically the political entity of the state, whose linguistic condition is uneasily forward-looking. But issues of translation also play a role in the identification of the inhabitants of the state. The medical, legal, and cultural discourses of the "sexual subject" that circulated around the formation of Europe's modern nations show how difference was localized within the nation itself. As sexual acts and desires were translated into a language of sexuality, words such as "homosexual" came to demarcate discursively the lived experience and sense of self of those subjects of the state who were thus categorized.

The question of what to make of this process of identification, conceptualized by Foucault in terms of a paradigm of "reverse discourse," has preoccupied critics concerned with the histories and politics of identity and its limits.[8] Some scholars, troubled by the question of where to find the individual within the discursive landscape, have focused on issues of agency to approach the difficult relationship between discourse, experience, and the real.[9] Others have focused on the performative aspects of subjectivation, notably Judith Butler, whose writing has increasingly moved away from the sense of optimism about the subversive potential of reverse discourse "whose future is partially open" found in her early work.[10] In a chapter on "The Fantasy of Norms" published in 2000, Butler cautions against the assumption that "by embracing the subject on grounds of agency, we will have countered the effects of regulatory power," reiterating her suspicions of agency as an analytical tool while introducing a renewed concern for how to stage a critical intervention on behalf of the subject.[11] In her later work, *Undoing Gender*, Butler pays close attention to the fact that even the most careful deconstruction of norms does not undo their immediate impact. Here she productively shifts focus to an exploration of "what it might mean to undo restrictively normative conceptions of sexual and gendered life" specifically by bringing into dialogue her theoretical observations and what she earlier called "the struggles that constitute present life."[12] Butler's renewed attention to the relationship between discourse and the contingencies of life raises fresh critical questions. Specifically, it forces consideration of *how* to conceptualize and locate within texts the meeting points between norms and lives.

Butler's recognition that "theory emerges from location" provides a way to address this problematic, especially for an investigation such as this one, which reaches backward to a point in time when the sexual theorist-cum-homosexual activist Hirschfeld engaged with the discourse of homosexual identity, and its experience, through an examination of localized examples.[13] Hirschfeld's project is a reminder of why, despite the fact that "queer critics have generally understood the concept of identity to be both politically and philosophically bankrupt," we have yet to write, as Heather Love has so forcefully argued, "an account of identity that allows us to think through its contradictions and to trace its effects, [critiquing] identity without dispensing with it as a category of historical experience."[14] Hirschfeld himself was invested in the question of how to account for the experience of homosexuality. Concerned with what Naoki Sakai has called "the problematic of bordering," "the processes of drawing a border, of instituting the terms of distinction in discrimination, and of inscribing a continuous space of the social," he deliberately used translation to embed into his writing a reflection on the relationship between text, discourse, and the experiential reality of the subject.[15]

Hirschfeld's Sexological Translations

With more than fifty publications in German, lectures presented in English, sex education films, and a photographic archive of sexual subcultures and transgressive subjects, Hirschfeld's oeuvre is vast. A considerable amount of this material was destroyed by the Nazis, which, together with the relative dearth of published English translations of his work, helps to explain why Hirschfeld has been relatively marginal in Anglo-American histories of sexuality. During his lifetime, however, he was a hugely influential figure.[16] By the time he began his sexological work, the discipline had become well established internationally in debates about medicine, social health, and hygiene, as well as in the sexual and social reform movements of the early twentieth century. He directed sexology outward, moving beyond the walls of the clinic where early sexology had been practiced and into the realm of the social. Drawing on sociological and anthropological approaches, he employed a range of methods of observation and writing, with the aim of gaining a better understanding of what he called the "Quelle des Lebens" (Source of Life), which for him lends meaning to sexuality.[17] Most famously, this included his development of a "psychobiologischen Fragebogen" (psychobiological questionnaire), which comprised 127 questions ranging from issues of home life to the description of sexual fantasies and desires.[18] The questionnaire, answered by around 10,000 women and men, is considered the first large-scale sex survey of its kind, predating the postwar efforts of Alfred Kinsey in the United States or the Mass Observation's sex surveys in the United Kingdom.[19] But unlike Kinsey, Hirschfeld did not aim to establish distance between himself and his subjects of study.[20] He actively sought contact with men and women from around the world, recording in his writings encounters with international visitors to his institute as well as extensive correspondence with lay people and experts on sexual matters.

Hirschfeld moved freely through urban gay sexual subcultures both in Berlin, where he frequented gay bars with his lovers, sometimes as a cross-dresser, and in the cities he visited around the world where he deliberately sought out the meeting points of men who love men as well as related spaces of sexual transgression such as brothels, parks, bars, and nightclubs. These trips were not infrequently organized by the physicians and scientists who hosted his visits. They subsequently made their way into Hirschfeld's sexological textbooks in the form of anecdotes used to illustrate particular concerns about the shape of homosexual subculture and its regulation. This work underpinned Hirschfeld's theory that sexuality manifests as what he called "sexuelle Zwischenstufen" (sexual intermediaries): an infinite number of variations in sexual instinct and its psychic and physical manifestations.[21] While he never wrote his own sexual encounters into the sexological narrative, Hirschfeld's writings nevertheless show that he deliberately turned to particular locations to discuss the lives of men who loved and had sex with other men, bringing their experience into proximity with his own as a traveler and scientist of sex.

Hirschfeld Encounters Philadelphia

Two observations on Philadelphia indicate how Hirschfeld used location and translation together to write experience into his work. He first traveled to the city as a young man in 1893, returning in 1930 during the early stages of his world lecturing tour. A record of his earlier visit appears in his most significant study of *Die Homosexualität des Mannes und des Weibes* (1914; *The Homosexuality of Man and Woman*), a tome of more than one thousand pages. Combining Hirschfeld's comments on his own travels to Philadelphia and his correspondence with men from the city, these passages illustrate the powerful interventions made possible by Hirschfeld's method of bringing together expert and anecdotal data on homosexuality.

Hirschfeld first mentions Philadelphia in a chapter on "Die Homosexualität in den germanischen und angelsächsischen Ländern und deren Kolonien" (Homosexuality in German and Anglo-Saxon Nations and Their Colonies).[22] Here he cites his own visit to the city to question stories about Philadelphia's allegedly thriving homosexual scene. Hirschfeld describes how in advance of his own visit he had been told by a correspondent from Colorado that "in Philadelphia existiert ein [türkisches] Bad, in welchem man Sonnabend Nacht c. 60 Homosexuelle treffen kann, unter einem homosexuellen Bademeister, der die Aufsicht mit gebührender Rücksicht gegen die Klientel der Anstalt führt" (in Philadelphia there exists a Turkish bath where one can find around 60 homosexuals on Saturday nights, supervised by a homosexual bath attendant who acts with due regard to the visitors of the institution).[23] Hirschfeld does not directly challenge the veracity of this claim but suggests that during his own visit he could "kaum etwas von Homosexualität wahrnehmen" (barely notice homosexuality), despite the fact that "Besucher" (visitors) from Philadelphia and Boston "[mir] später versicherten, daß in diesen Zentren der Quäker und Puritaner in intimen Kreisen 'kolossal viel' los sei" (later told him that in these centers of Quakers and Puritans in intimate circles a "colossal amount" [of homosexual activity] happens).[24] If Hirschfeld does not comment further on the disjunction between the stories and his own experience, the fact that he renders in inverted commas the idea of "a colossal amount" of homosexual activity in Philadelphia ensures that his own voice is demarcated from that of the unreliable narrator whose story Hirschfeld is unable to translate into experience, yet whose words he nevertheless allows to stand next to his own.

This fairly lighthearted anecdote provides an example of the characteristic insertion of Hirschfeld's own authorial voice alongside the voices of others, a method he uses regularly to disrupt the flow of scientific discourse. It shows that while he might question other accounts, he does not deny them, hence allowing into the text a connection between textual practice and experiential context that deliberately undermines the notion of scientific distance by which objectivity is commonly established.

The importance of letting nonscientific voices speak is reinforced in an altogether more serious turn to translation, in a passage where Hirschfeld directly offsets different languages against each other to illustrate the very real and dangerous impact words can have on individual lives. Philadelphia appears again in a chapter on the "Folgen der Verfolgung" (Consequences of Persecution), which critiques the impact of antihomosexual legislation on the lives of men who love men.[25] Focusing on the issue of blackmail, Hirschfeld points out that the law is responsible for numerous deaths because many men commit suicide rather than risk being publicly tried, shamed, and punished. He turns particular attention to the extralegal enforcement of homosexual persecution by those institutions of the state—the church, the medical profession—which for many homosexual men were ports of call when looking for guidance on their own conduct.

Hirschfeld recounts an encounter with an American patient who told him that

> der Arzt, den er in Philadelphia seiner homosexuellen Leiden halber um Rat gefragt habe, ihm geantwortet hätte: "es gäbe für ihn nur drei Möglichkeiten: Selbstbefriedigung (use his right hand), freiwilligen Aufenthalt in einer Irrenanstalt (place himself in a madhouse) oder Selbstmord (or better commit suicide).[26]

This passage roughly translates as follows: the Philadelphia-based doctor, when asked for advice about homosexuality, had responded by suggesting that the patient had three possible ways to deal with his homosexuality—masturbation, voluntary commitment to an asylum, or suicide. My choice of words for translating the three options—masturbation, voluntary commitment to an asylum, and suicide—aims to provide a fairly literal rendering of Hirschfeld's German words, employing English terms that would have been in circulation in early twentieth-century North America.

However, Hirschfeld includes in parentheses the English expressions used by the Philadelphia-based physician, which tell their own story of the doctor's negative stance towards homosexuality. According to this information, the doctor had advised his patient to "use his right hand," employing a slang term for masturbation, a practice that at the time was still largely a social taboo.[27] Next, the patient is offered the option "to place himself in a madhouse," a choice of words that reinforces the derogatory tone of the doctor's advice. For it is worth noting that while in the early twentieth century mental health issues were still understood in terms of "mental deficiency" and "mental hygiene" debates, the clinical terminology of the "asylum" and, increasingly, "psychiatry" had replaced the term "madhouse."[28] Philadelphia itself was a place in which the advancement of psychiatry was taken seriously, as the founding in 1844 of the Ivy League Private Psychiatric Hospital Group in the city indicates. These contextual particularities reinforce that the doctor's use of the explicitly negative terminology of the "madhouse" deliberately denigrated his patient. Most chillingly, the physician makes clear that the preferred cause of action for his homosexual patient would be to "better commit suicide." It is not clear why Hirschfeld does not translate the emphatic "better." However, his decision to include the doctor's English words in the German text ensures that their devastating implications are not missed. From contextual evidence we know that Hirschfeld wrote for an educated audience which would have been able to read both German and English. Leaving alongside each other the original and Hirschfeld's translation ensures that the deadly climax of the Philadelphian doctor's words is not lost in translation. It powerfully enables Hirschfeld to undermine the notion of the doctor's professional objectivity, critiquing the pathologization of homosexuality and drawing attention to the complicity between medical and legal discourse in violence against homosexuals.

Violent Conclusions

If "the act of translation" is inevitably tied to what Bhabha calls the "apprehension of difference," then Hirschfeld's refusal to translate homophobic content constitutes a particular kind of discursive intervention, one that turns to location to allow the untranslated to speak on its own behalf.[29] The first Philadelphia example shows that Hirschfeld deliberately inserted his own experience into the sexological text to disrupt assumptions about the possibility of neutral scientific observation, suggesting instead that sexual discourse, like all transcriptions of lived experience, are constructed by more or less reliable narrators. The second Philadelphia example in turn emphasizes the very real connection between texts and lives, as it critiques the fact that a suggestion of homosexual suicide is presented as medical advice. The particulars of Hirschfeld's bilingual turns—where they occur within the narrative and why—suggest that he deliberately maintained a practice of untranslatability at particular points in his writings to indicate some of the connotations and generic conventions by which words transmit violence.

For Hirschfeld, then, issues of translation were central to understanding the different currencies of "homosexuality" within expert discourses and the personal accounts of men who have sex with other men; but he crucially also considered the relationship between discourse and lived reality. Gayatri Spivak, in her observations on the "politics of translation," has argued that "language is [in effect] not everything. It is only a vital clue to where the self loses its boundaries."[30] Hirschfeld's work shows, however, that for an investigation of the discursive and lived realities of subjects in the past, it is more productive to turn around the emphasis of Spivak's words and argue that while language is indeed not everything, it *is* a vital clue to where the boundaries of self are made and undone across time. Hirschfeld interrogated the processes by which the homosexual subject encounters homophobic violence, for instance through medical discourses that become valorized as truths. His project, then, deliberately stages untranslatability to render visible the "process of bordering" by which homophobic discrimination is perpetuated and encountered.

Notes

1. The Magnus Hirschfeld Society has published an excellent online exhibition on his work at http://www.hirschfeld.in-berlin.de/.

2. For example, Charlotte Wolff, *Magnus Hirschfeld: A Portrait of a Pioneer in Sexology* (London: Quartet, 1986); Ralf Dose, *Magnus Hirschfeld: The Origins of the Gay Liberation Movement* (New York: Monthly Review Press, 2014); Elke-Vera Kotowski and Julius H. Schoeps, eds., *Der Sexualreformer Magnus Hirschfeld: Ein Leben im Spannungsfeld von Wissenschaft, Politik und Gesellschaft* (Berlin: Bebra, 2004); Elena Mancini, *Magnus Hirschfeld and the Quest for Sexual Freedom: A History of the First Sexual Freedom Movement* (New York: Palgrave, 2010).

3. Mancini, *Magnus Hirschfeld and the Quest for Sexual Freedom*, 3.

4. Ralf Dose, "The World League for Sexual Reform: Some Possible Approaches," *Journal for the History of Sexuality*, 12, no. 3 (2003): 1–15; Magnus Hirschfeld, "Presidential Address to the Third International Congress for Sexual Reform on a Scientific Basis," in *Sexual Reform Congress (London, September 8–14, 1929)*, ed. Norman Haire (London: Kegan Paul, 1930), xii–xv; Magnus Hirschfeld, *Die Weltreise eines Sexualforschers* (Brugg: Bötzberg, 1933). The American edition of the *Weltreise* was entitled *Men and Women: The World Journey of a Sexologist*, trans. Oliver Green (New York: G.P. Putman's Sons, 1935). The title of the British edition shifted the focus to *Women East and West: Impressions of a Sex Expert*, trans. Oliver Green (London: Heinemann, 1935).

5. Homi Bhabha, *The Location of Culture* (New York: Routledge, 1994), 325.

6. Ibid., 201.

7. Ibid. See also his "Introduction: Narrating the Nation," in *Nation and Narration,* ed. Homi Bhabha (New York: Routledge, 1990), 2–7.

8. Michel Foucault, *History of Sexuality*, vol. 1: *An Introduction*, trans. Robert Hurley (London: Penguin Books, 1990), 101.

9. Seyla Benhabib, Judith Butler, and Drucilla Cornell, eds., *Feminist Contentions: Philosophical Exchange* (New York: Routledge, 1995); and Benhabib's account of her critical disagreements with Judith Butler in "Sexual Difference and Collective Identities: The New Global Constellation," *Signs*, 24, no. 2 (1999): 335–61.

10. Judith Butler, *Excitable Speech: A Politics of the Performative* (New York: Routledge, 1997), 38.

11. Judith Butler, Ernesto Laclau, and Slavoj Žižek, *Contingency, Hegemony, Universality: Contemporary Dialogues on the Left* (London: Verso, 2000), 151.

12. Judith Butler, *Undoing Gender* (New York: Routledge, 2004), 1; and Butler, *Contingency, Hegemony, Universality*, 151.

13. Butler, *Undoing Gender*, 201.

14. Heather Love, *Feeling Backward: Loss and the Politics of Queer History* (Cambridge, Mass.: Harvard University Press, 2007), 44.

15. Naoki Sakai, "Translation and the Figure of the Border: Toward the Apprehension of Translation as a Social Action," *Profession* (2010): 25–34, here 25.

16. Heike Bauer, *English Literary Sexology: Translations of Inversion, 1860–1930* (Basingstoke, Eng.: Palgrave Macmillan, 2009), 1–50; Anna Katharina Schaffner, *Modernism and Perversion: Sexual Deviance in Sexology and Literature, 1850–1930* (Basingstoke, Eng.: Palgrave Macmillan, 2011).

17. Magnus Hirschfeld, *Die Homosexualität des Mannes und des Weibes, Nachdruck der Erstauflage von 1914 mit einer kommentierten Einleitung von E.J. Haeberle* (Berlin: de Gruyter, 1984), iv.

18. Ibid.,, 240–62.

19. See Miriam G. Reumann, *Sexual Character: Sex, Gender, and National Identity in the Kinsey Reports* (Berkeley: University of California Press, 2005); Liz Stanley, *Sex Surveyed, 1949–1994: From Mass Observation's "Little Kinsey" to the National Survey and the Hite Reports* (London: Taylor and Francis, 1995).

20. For a discussion of Hirschfeld's influence on Kinsey see Heike Bauer, "Sexology Backward: Hirschfeld, Kinsey and the Reshaping of Sex Research in the 1950s," in *Queer 1950s: Rethinking Sexuality in the Postwar Years*, ed. Heike Bauer and Matt Cook (Basingstoke, Eng.: Palgrave Macmillan, 2012), 133–49.

21. Hirschfeld, *Die Homosexualität des Mannes und des Weibes*, 348–69. The theory also gave name to a scientific journal, the *Jahrbuch für sexuelle Zwischenstufen* (*Yearbook for Sexual Intermediaries*), which was published under Hirschfeld's editorship by the "Wissenschaftlich-Humanitäres Comitée" (Scientific-Humanitarian Committee) between 1899 and 1923.

22. Hirschfeld, *Homosexualität des Mannes und des Weibes*, 526.

23. Ibid., 551.

24. Ibid., 550.

25. Ibid., 899.

26. Ibid., 909.

27. Paula Bennett and Vernon Rosario, eds., *Solitary Pleasures: The Historical, Literary and Artistic Discourses of Autoeroticism* (New York: Routledge, 1995), 1–19.

28. Andrew Scull, *Social Order/Mental Disorder: Anglo-American Psychiatry in Historical Perspective* (Berkeley: University of California Press, 1989), 96–118.

29. Bhabha, *The Location of Culture*, 325.

30. Gayatri Chakravorty Spivak, "The Politics of Translation," in her *Outside in the Teaching Machine* (New York: Routledge, 1993), 179–200.

Chapter 12

Trans(fel)latio

Gerard Reve, Jürgen Hillner, Paul Verhoeven, and *De vierde man*

Simon Richter

Language has a body in at least two respects. For one thing, we might talk about its material qualities, such as the sound and grit of its phonemes or the lines and curves of its written letters, both essential to the communicability of meaning but not, in most instances, because of the inherent corporeality of any specific elocution. As Ferdinand de Saussure taught us in *The Course in General Linguistics*, the relation between the word's physical manifestation and its meaning is arbitrary. But there is a second way of thinking about language's body which allows for a greater degree of specificity and is more in line with the concerns of this chapter. The point would be to pay attention to the phantom body that inhabits the imaginary of a given language or a text in a given language, paying particular attention to the scatological, obscene, and vulgar words that have shown an irrepressible tendency to extend into other domains of linguistic and communicative life. Take the words *prick* and *cunt*, for example, which metonymize across English, or the time-honored verb *fuck*, which, along with *shit*, may be one of the English language's most successful exports, a triumph of linguistic globalism. To put the matter in other terms, what we are talking about is what Mikhail Bakhtin called the grotesque body.

> The body that figures in all the expressions of the unofficial speech of the people is the body that fecundates and is fecundated, that gives birth and is born, devours and is devoured, drinks, defecates, is sick and dying. In all languages there is a great number of expressions related to the genital organs, the anus and buttocks, the belly, the mouth and nose.[1]

Bakhtin was convinced that "wherever men laugh and curse, particularly in a familiar environment, their speech is filled with bodily images."[2] A corollary of this observation is that the grotesque body of any given language, the sum of its vividly imagined and embodied figurality, is unique.

Acknowledging the existence of the grotesque body of language raises important questions for translation. What happens to the body of a given language when it is translated into another? How may we describe the work of the translator in addressing the body of language? Is it a matter of dutifully inserting the linguistic equivalents, *lul* and *trut* for *prick* and *cunt* or vice versa, assuming the languages in question are Dutch and English? Obviously not, insofar as the sexualized phantom bodies of the respective languages differ greatly. A specific and corporeally attuned hermeneutic will be required. Thanks to Walter Benjamin, we are inclined to think of the translator and his or her daunting task. But in Friedrich Schleiermacher's discussion of the various methods of translation, a potentially different model of translation comes into view. According to Schleiermacher, the translator is positioned between the original text and the reader in such a way as to facilitate the reader's *Genuss* (pleasure).[3] Readers have not been inclined to make much of this word in its Schleiermachian setting and most English translators, most recently Susan Bernofsky, offer "enjoyment" in its stead.[4] But what happens if we tug *Genuss* in the direction of pleasure? And what if we take note not of the translator's task, but of his or her particular pleasure in serving the text (and the reader) in a particular way? To what extent is the untranslatable linked to pleasure and to be found in a space beyond terms such as fidelity and liberty, the moralizing binary of translational Manichaeism? The title of my chapter mischievously imagines translation as a matter of taking the body of the other language into one's mouth and bringing it to orgasmic release with one's tongue—mouth and tongue being, of course, two prevalent metonymies for language. As you no doubt suspect, the phantom and foreign body of one language does not necessarily map onto the body of another. This is what makes trans(fel)lation intriguing and it is this difference and how translation approaches it—"hinübergebogen" (bent over), as Schleiermacher says (93)—that will be my particular focus: not the task, but the pleasure of the translator.

One doesn't have to be a Lacanian to acknowledge that the penis seems to stand in a special relationship to language. The archeological world is strewn with phallic statues, myths, and mysteries, even if our Christian age has insisted on keeping a veil over the phallus. That is certainly how Lacan saw things: "the phallus is a signifier"[5] and it "can only play its role as veiled."[6] If we look around our cultural landscape, we may detect the veiled phallus in many places, but the exposed phallus rarely and only in specialized locations often marked by an X. Of course, Lacan categorically denied that the phallus and the penis were one and the same thing—and they're not—categorically—but in other ways, of course, they are.

From my earlier remarks, it follows that the penis inhabits the imaginary of every language somewhat differently. We may find cognate terms or ideas such as the Latinate word *penis* itself, which cuts across numerous languages and is etymologically derived from the Latin word for "tail." Other terms may be unique to a language and lead a life of their own. This is certainly the case with the Dutch, where the word *lul* has colonized considerable linguistic terrain in surprising ways. Let's start with the word itself: it would seem to contradict observations from the field of phonosemantics according to which words flavored with the lilting phoneme /L/ are linked with affective qualities such as pleasantness, tenderness, and passivity.[7] It's no accident that the comforting song parents sing to their children is called a lullaby. That *lul* would be the Dutch counterpart to *prick* seems counterintuitive. But it is, nonetheless. And like *prick*, *dick*, or *pecker*, *lul* can signify a disagreeable or contemptible person. But that is not where *lul* stops. It also functions as a verb: "ik lul maar" in the sense of speaking nonsense. "Dat is allemaal gelul"—it's all nonsense.[8] Here we see a distinct difference between the bodies of language. Where Dutch imagines the production of nonsense in relation to a penis, English envisions bullshit. Both grotesque, but decidedly different.

Lul is but one example of the linguistic life of the penis in Dutch. In Dutch literature, we find two major twentieth-century authors who glory in the penis in ways that test the limits of trans(fel)lation: Jan Wolkers and Gerard Reve.[9] They couldn't be more opposite.[10] Wolkers came from the predominant Protestant (Calvinist) milieu in the Netherlands. His graphic depictions of straight sex in his 1969 novel *Turks Fruit* (*Turkish Delight*) scandalized the literary establishment.[11] Reve, by contrast, converted to Catholicism in the mid-1960s and simultaneously outed himself as a queer writer. *De Avonden* (1947; *The Evenings*), his first major novel, is considered a classic of Dutch literature. From the early 1960s on, the epistolary novel with all its confessional improprieties was his genre of choice. Reve is particularly esteemed as a Dutch literary stylist. In 1966 he was prosecuted for blasphemy in connection with his epistolary novel *Nader tot U* (*Nearer to Thee*).[12] Church and state took offense at the depiction of queer sex between the author and God. It would doubtless be useful to investigate the untranslatable in both writers, but for present purposes I will limit myself to Reve.

The timing of Reve's conversion and public avowal of his sexuality was no accident: Reve's faith and sexuality are inextricably linked, together with his devotion to alcohol and his focus on death. In *Nader tot U*, Reve gives his rendering of a famous Pauline verse: "Seks, drank en Dood, deze drie; maar de meeste van deze is de Dood" (Sex, alcohol and Death, these three; but the most of these is Death).[13] In a letter from 1966, Reve seeks to describe how his conception of God differs from the mainstream: "[De God] van mij lijdt, [heeft] met mij seks, [is] niet altijd zondevrij, en verkwijnt als ik Hem niet liefheb. Mijn God is wel een schat van een God, vind ikzelf. Ik houd machtig veel van hem. Hij is veel rommeliger & kitscheriger dan die van jullie [. . .]. Ook drinkt Hij erg veel" (My God suffers, has sex with me, is not always free of sin and sulks when I don't love him. He is much messier and kitschier than your god. He also drinks a lot).[14] If wine is the blood of Christ, whisky (and Reve was very fond of whisky) is God's sperm.[15] What he calls the "oeroude symbolenwereld van Rome" (ancient Roman [Catholic] world of symbols) is a "volstrekt eroties kanal" (thoroughly erotic channel) that he requires in order to translate (*vertolk*) himself, that is, his "seksuele agressie, tederheid, haat, veroveringszucht en behoefte aan onderwerping" (sexual aggression, tenderness, hatred, addiction to domination and need to submit).[16] At the same time, God is "diepste, wezentlijkste & verborgenste waarheid in de mens, & in zoverre is Hij even onveranderlijk & onuitsprekelijk als altijd. Hij zal, om vertolkt te kunnen worden, geprojekteerd moeten worden door het hart" (*Brieven aan Josine M*, 211) (deepest, most essential and most hidden truth in mankind, and to that extent he is immutable and ineffable as ever. In order to be translated, he will have to be projected by the heart). For Reve the apprehension of God himself is already an act of trans(fel)lation.

Reve is a challenge to any translator. He is sovereign in his mastery of the Dutch language, specializing in creating an inimitable frisson through the precise and creative use of archaic language to articulate jarring content. To translate his writing into English, he says, would not be too difficult, simply a matter of rendering his Dutch into the English of, say, a Samuel Johnson. He knows a thing or two about translating and shifting between languages. In the 1960s he translated plays by Edward Albee and Harold Pinter, and in the 1950s he published original stories written in English, later translated into Dutch by his estranged wife.[17] While English translation of his works has been haphazard and scant, in the late 1960s he became acquainted with Jürgen Hillner, who would become his friend, occasional neighbor, and devoted, collaborative translator.[18] Born to German parents in the Dutch East Indies, Hillner was bilingual and was, at the time of their meeting, starting to do yeoman's work on behalf of Dutch literature.[19] Reve held Hillner's ambitious efforts to mainstream translations of Dutch literature in the German book market in high esteem.[20] The results, however, were more modest. As Herbert van Uffelen points out, major German presses and reviewers were nonplussed by the erotic and occasionally pornographic content of the authors Hillner chose to translate.[21] For his part, Hillner sees Reve in a tradition that includes Novalis, Eichendorff, Flaubert, and Baudelaire. "Hij heeft de Nederlandse romantiek, en wel in haar decadente fase, op Europees peil gebracht" (He brought Dutch romanticism, and that in its decadent phase, up to European standards).[22]

While Hillner, in consultation with Reve, continued to work on projects of literary translation in an effort to secure his deserved place in a European canon from a German perspective, Reve also saw pragmatic and pecuniary opportunities in film adaptation of his works, even if he was skeptical about film's ability to adequately "translate" them. A first attempt to adapt *Lieve Jongens* (1973; *Sweet Boys*) in 1980 by Paul de Lussanet was a disappointment: "alles zeer grof en letterlijk vertolkt" (everything very coarse and literally translated).[23] More satisfactory would be the production of another work undertaken by Paul Verhoeven in 1982 at the point when Verhoeven was preparing to leave the Netherlands for Hollywood, where he would go on to make *RoboCop* (1987), *Total Recall* (1990), and *Basic Instinct* (1992). In Reve's estimation, Verhoeven is "een eersteklas vakman maar tevens iemand met buitengewoon vulgaire opvattingen over het menselijk bestaan en de liefde" (a first-class professional, but also someone with exceptionally vulgar opinions about human existence and love).[24] Reve knew that Verhoeven had adapted Wolkers's *Turks Fruit* in 1973. What he probably did not and could not know was that Verhoeven had an abiding scholarly interest in the life of Jesus and that he would become a member of the Jesus Seminar in the mid-1980s, eventually publishing *Jesus of Nazareth* in Dutch, German, and English in 2007.[25] This coincidence, as we will see, goes a long way toward explaining Verhoeven's success in trans(fel)lating Reve to the screen.

The work that Verhoeven adapted and Hillner later translated is *De vierde man* (*The Fourth Man*).[26] Seen in the context of Reve's oeuvre, this novella is an outlier. Commissioned by the Stichting Collectieve Propaganda van het Nederlandse Boek (Foundation for Collective Promotion of the Dutch Book) for its annual Book Week (involving a free book written for the nationwide event by a prominent author commissioned with the task), Reve took some pains to shift his protagonist (a novelist by the name of "Gerard Reve") from his usual gay milieu into a heterosexual setting and to de-archaize his language, intentionally making his language and himself more available for mass consumption. Of the four sex scenes, as Reve points out, three involve a young woman and only one involves a man. All for naught—when the manuscript was complete, the foundation still rejected it by a vote of 4 to 3. With a framing tale that explicitly discusses the aptness of the event in the writer's life as a story, *De vierde man* comes across as a queer and contemporary version of a German romantic work, Joseph von Eichendorff's *Marmorbild*, a potentially fatal detour into the precincts of the *Venusberg*.[27] At the same time, the narrator periodically challenges an anonymous film director to realize a film adaptation of the novella in progress and introduces Hitchcock's *Dial M for Murder* as an intertext. Verhoeven rose to the bait and Reve certainly savored the check for 100,000 guilders, which he received for selling the film rights. The result was a splendidly lush film that depicts the hallucinated descent of a gay writer into a frightening heterosexual world, where ambiguity and violence prevail. Think of Verhoeven's *The Fourth Man* as the queer and superior counterpart to *Basic Instinct*.[28]

Allow me to set up the situation so we can zero in on a single instance of untrans(fel)latability. The narrator "Gerard Reve" has been invited by a book club to give a reading in a small Dutch town. Contrary to his custom, he spends the night after the reading at the home of the young woman who is the club's treasurer. Although plainly out of his element and disturbed by uncanny feelings and dreams, he believes he can play the heterosexual and master the situation. He declares that "Christine" has the body of a boy and when he spies a letter and a picture of her current lover he is smitten by the latter. He'll access Herman's body (that's the name of her lover) through hers or, to put it in Catholic terms, as "Reve" does as he comes: "Door Maria tot Jezus" (Through Mary to Jesus).[29]

Our quotation comes from the moment when he looks at "Herman's" photograph.

> Die mond . . . het haar over zijn voorhoofd . . . het spijkerpak, het jek open, het witte openstaande werkhemd, de riemgesp boven zijn nog net zichtbare, argeloze kruis . . . "Jij . . . jij . . . ," fluisterde ik . . . "al zul je mijn dood zijn . . .
>
> That mouth . . . the hair over his forehead . . . the denim suit, the jacket open, the white work shirt with the collar open, the belt buckle above his just barely visible, unsuspecting crotch . . . "You . . . you . . . ," I whispered . . . "and if you are the death of me . . .".[30]

Here is Hillner's translation.

> Dieser Mund . . . das Haar über der Stirn . . . der Jeansanzug, die Jacke offen, das weiße offene Arbeitshemd, die Gürtelschnalle über dem gerade noch sichtbaren, nichtsahnenden Schritt . . . "Du . . . du," flüsterte ich . . . , "auch wenn du mein Tod sein wirst . . ."[31]

As we can see, this is not a particularly difficult passage to translate. Much of it consists of "Reve" listing parts of his phantom lover's body and items of clothing, separated by ellipses, and modified by adjectives that alternate between visibility and hiddenness. But then we come to the word *kruis*. Hillner is not wrong in opting for *Schritt*. Both are terms from the domain of tailoring and designate what the English calls *crotch*. As metonymies, *crotch* and *kruis* can signify the genitals, and *Schritt* can too, in principle, although it is uncommon. The modifiers "just barely visible" and "unsuspecting" bring the *kruis* and even the *Schritt* to unaccustomed erotic life. But that is where the German stops and the Dutch opens onto a dimension of meaning that coincides with Reve's eroto-Catholic preoccupations. For *kruis* also means "cross" and this meaning almost certainly conditioned its selection. As such, *kruis* becomes untrans(fel)latable in German. Had Hillner opted for the German word *Kreuz*—not that it's really an option—he would not only have forfeited the sartorial meaning of crotch, but also the specific association with the male genitals. *Kreuz* does refer to the body in German, but it's the wrong part of the body, the posterior, something that interested Winckelmann and certainly Reve, too, but not in this passage.[32] Where *Schritt* stops, *kruis* comes.

To be honest, I suspect that most Dutch readers miss the connotation, and some may dispute its relevance. In other words, the *kruis* (cross) in *kruis* (crotch) is "just barely visible" and "unsuspecting," unaware of the load it may come to bear. Could this be what "Reve" was thinking about as he returns to the frame of the novella and debates with his current lover the viability of his account as literature, as "verhaal" (story)? "Het is net of het in het midden leeg is . . . Het heeft geen . . . *body* bij wijze van spreken . . . In het midden gebeurt niks, eigenlijk . . ." (It is as if it were empty in the middle . . . It has no *body* as it were . . . Nothing really happens in the middle . . .).[33]

If Hillner's *Schritt* necessarily fails to trans(fel)late, Paul Verhoeven, by contrast, seems to have a limitless visual vocabulary at his disposal.[34] If Reve's narrator is spooked by the possibility that Christine has already killed three husbands and flees before she returns with the longed-for Herman, Verhoeven brings Herman into view, gives us the body that "Reve" suspected was missing and then some.

In the filmic counterpart to the scene involving the photograph of Herman, the screenplay dispenses with the word *kruis*. "Wat een lijf, wat een stuk, die moet ik hebben, al wordt het mijn dood" (What a body, what a piece, I have to have him, even if it is the death of me). In lieu of the word, Verhoeven translates *kruis* into an elaborate visual network of *kruis*-related images. As the credits roll in the film's opening sequence we see a black widow spider dispatching three flies—her web spans a *crucifix*. Picking up on the fact that Reve named Christine's beauty salon *Sphinx*, Verhoeven envisions a neon sign on which only the letters *S*, *P*, *I* and *N* are illuminated, that is, the Dutch word for spider, *de spin in de sphinx*. The image of the crucifix with the spider is part of the Sternbergian disarray of "Reve's" bedroom in the opening scenes, a haphazard jumble of Marian and crucifix knickknacks, with Reve (and his *kruis*—Jeroen Krabbé, the actor playing Reve, is naked from the waist down) moving among them. Much later, after seeing the photograph of Herman, Reve enters a church with the intention of praying to Mary. He is distracted by a human-size crucifix within hands' reach on which he hallucinates Herman's body, thus repeating the progression "door Maria tot Jezus" (through Mary to Jesus). He approaches the cross, kisses the bleeding feet, and raises his head and hands to focus on the *kruis* (crotch) on the *kruis* (cross). Tugging on the red Speedo, he prepares to take the word of the cross of the Word on the cross into his mouth. But Verhoeven cuts in this crucial moment and this signature act of transfellation is cut short.[35]

The cut, key component of film composition, could be read in line with a scissor/castration motif that Verhoeven gets from Hitchcock's *Dial M for Murder* (according to the novella, the movie is playing in the town where Christine lives) and plays up in a dream sequence. I think, however, that it makes more sense to read this cut as a peculiar and characteristic instance of filmic untrans(fel)latability, as a paradoxical limit of cinema. The ease and facility with which cinema trans(fel)lates is unveiled as a moment of untrans(fel)latabilty, whether the cut is required to appease an audience rating system, to stop short of the line marked by *XXX*, or, more likely, because the cinematic act of trans(fel)lation becomes something else (i.e., flat pornography) the moment it is fully indulged. The crucifix reverts to its objective appearance. Reve does a double take: still a cross, but not a *kruis*.

Where does this leave us? Back at the source text and its fundamental untrans(fel)latability? Hardly. Even if the projects of Hillner and Verhoeven are stopped short by opposite moments of untrans(fel)latability, of semantic dearth and visual abundance respectively, this moment of suspension itself—of being utterly stymied in finding the right locution, of throwing the veil over the act of trans(fel)lation—may well contribute to the pleasure of the translator and the refined enjoyment of the reader. And even if Reve would not again be tempted to repeat his detour into heterosexual space, he persisted in his transgressive and joyful attendance on the body of Christ in the prose of his world. Each act of Catholic (ir)reverence, each sip of whisky, each moment of ecstatic sex, each act of writing—all of these should be understood as Reve's fundamental dedication to a project of trans(fel)lation. It is, paradoxically, in encountering the untrans(fel)latibility of Reve's transgressions, that translators become most acutely aware of the erotic body of language and the cultural-linguistic possibilities and limits of their pleasure.

Notes

1. Mikhail Bakhtin, *Rabelais and His World*, trans. Hélène Iswolsky (Bloomington: Indiana University Press, 1984), 319.

2. Ibid.

3. Friedrich Schleiermacher, "Über die verschiedenen Methoden des Übersetzens," in *Kritische Gesamtausgabe*, vol. 11.1, ed. Martin Rössler (Berlin: Walter de Gruyter, 2002), 67–93.

4. Friedrich Schleiermacher, "On the Different Methods of Translating," trans. Susan Bernofsky, in *The Translation Studies Reader*, ed. Lawrence Venuti, 2nd ed. (New York: Routledge, 2004), 43–63.

5. Jacques Lacan, "The Signification of the Phallus," in *Feminine Sexuality and the école freudienne*, ed. Juliet Mitchell and Jacqueline Rose (New York: W. W. Norton, 1985), 79.

6. Ibid., 82.

7. Cynthia Whissell, "Phonosymbolism and the Emotional Nature of Sounds: Evidence of the Preferential Use of Particular Phonemes in Texts of Differing Emotional Tone," *Perceptual and Motor Skills* 89 (1999): 19–48.

8. The etymology of *lul* is somewhat confusing. It may be a figurative adaptation from an early modern object also known as a "pijpkan," a container with a tube from which sick people or infants could suck liquid nourishment. Through analogy of form to the "pijpkan" it may be related to the "doedelzak," also known as a "lullepijpe." Through association with the music produced by the "lullepijpe," it forges a connection with cognates in English and German formed on the phoneme *L* (*lullen, lollen*) that refer to the quiet singing of nonsense syllables and or chatter and gossip. Indeed, it is likely that we are dealing with two distinct etymological origins that have, over time (since the

sixteenth century?), become indistinguishable within the Dutch linguistic imaginary. "lul," *Het Woordenboek der Nederlansche Taal op internet*, http://gtb.inl.nl/iWNTLINKS/DATADIR/paginazy.html?EWN+/iWDB/search?actie=article_content&wdb=EWN&id=ewn007973.

9. It is common to regard Reve and Wolkers as two of the four most significant Dutch authors. The others are Harry Mulisch and Willem Frederik Hermans.

10. Reve speaks about their oppositeness in an interview: "Een groot deel van het werk van Wolkers is ook erg mooi. . . . Literair is hij heel anders dan ik. Er is vrijwel geen verwantschap tussen ons. Misschien alleen dat ons beider werk nergens over gaat dan over de dood. . . . Hij wordt dan ook wel de ´pornograaf van de dood´ genoemd. Ook in zijn beschrijving van seksualiteit is hij vaak te plastisch, waardoor hij zijn doel voobijschiet (A great deal of Wolkers's work is quite beautiful. In terms of literature, he and I are very different. There is practically no relation between us. Perhaps only in that our respective work is about nothing other than death. . . . He is also called the "pornographer of death." Also in his depiction of sexuality, he is often too plastic and thus shoots past the goal). Gerard Reve, *In Gesprek. Interviews* (Baarn, Neth.: de Prom, 1983), 77.

11. Jan Wolkers, *Turks Fruit* (Amsterdam: Meulenhoff, 1969). *Turks Fruit* was translated into ten languages.

12. Gerard Kornelis van het Reve, *Nader tot U* (Amsterdam: van Oorschot, 1966). For Reve's statements before the court in response to the charges brought against him for blasphemy, see Gerard Kornelis van het Reve, *Vier Pleidooien* (Amsterdam: Athenaeum, 1971).

13. Reve, *Nader*, 44. See 1 Corinthians 13:13 for the original Pauline verse.

14. Gerard Reve, *Brieven aan Josine M. 1959–1975* (Amsterdam: G. A. van Oorschot, 1981), 170.

15. "Ik konsakreer thuis . . . in een soort zelfbediening, rode wijn en wiskie tot respektievelijk het Bloed en het Zaad van de Eeuwige en Enige God" (*Klein Gebrek Geen Bezwaar,* 43) (At home, I consecrate, as a sort of self-service, red wine and whisky to be, respectively, the Blood and the Sperm of the Eternal and Only God).

16. Gerard Reve, *Brieven aan Wimie, 1959–1963* (Utrecht: Veen, 1980), 118–19.

17. Gerard-Kornelis van het Reve, *The Acrobat and Other Stories* (Amsterdam: G. A. van Oorschot, 1956).

18. Nop Maas describes their working relationship at some length in *Gerard Reve: Kroniek van een schuldig leven*, vol. 2: *De "rampjaren" 1962–1975* (Amsterdam: G. A. van Oorschot, 2010): "Reve controleerde en becommentarieerde de vertaling" (451; Reve oversaw the translation and provided comments).

19. Hillner jump-started the German reception of modern Dutch literature in 1969 with his anthology of translated short stories, *Niederländer erzählen* (Frankfurt am Main: Fischer, 1969).

20. On Reve's relationship to Hillner, see Maas, *Reve*, 2: 450–52.

21. Herbert van Uffelen, *Moderne niederländische Literatur im deutschen Sprachraum 1830–1990* (Münster: Lit, 1993), 43–49.

22. Jürgen Hillner, "Gerard Kornelis van het Reve: 'Ik ben een romantisch decadent auteur,'" in *Tussen chaos en orde: Essays over het werk van Gerard Reve*, ed. Sjaak Hubregtse (Amsterdam: Loeb, 1981), 240.

23. Reve, *Brieven aan Josine M*, 470.

24. Ibid., 504.

25. The Jesus Seminar was a collective of 150 scholars and laypeople, notably including John Dominic Crossan, founded in 1985. The Jesus Seminar applied contemporary methods from a variety of disciplines (including anthropology) in order to bring the historical Jesus into view.

26. Gerard Reve, *De vierde man* (Amsterdam: Elsevier Mantheau, 1981); Gerard Kornelis van het Reve, *Der vierte Mann: Roman*, trans. Jürgen Hillner (Frankfurt am Main: Suhrkamp, 1993).

27. For a reading of Eichendorff's *Marmorbild* that picks up on its latent queerness, see Simon Jan Richter, "Under the Sign of Venus: *Eichendorff's Marmorbild* and the Erotics of Allegory," *South Atlantic Review* 56 (1991): 59–71.

28. For more on Verhoeven's negotiations with Reve, see Rob van Scheers, *Paul Verhoeven: De geautoriseerde biografie* (Utrecht: Bijleveld, 1996).

29. Reve, *De vierde man*, 79.

30. Ibid., 52.

31. *Der vierte Mann*, 57.

32. On the eighteenth-century German art historian Winckelmann's interest in the *Kreuz* of ancient classical statues, see Simon Richter, *Laocoon's Body and the Aesthetics of Pain* (Detroit: Wayne State University Press, 1992), 48–59, especially 57.

33. Reve, *De vierde man*, 120.

34. Reve regards this as a weakness. "Alles is mogelijk: flashbacks, het tonen van gedachten van iemand tijdens een handeling, álles kan. Dat is zo eindeloos, dat iemand verzuipt die zich daarin niet beperkt" (Everything is possible: flashbacks, presentation of someone's thought during an action, everything goes. It is so boundless that one drowns if one does not set limits). Tom Rooduijn, *Revelaties: Gerard Reve over zijn werk en leven* (Schoorl: Conserve, 2002), 55.

35. Reve scholars may well recognize the figure of "de Meedogenlozen Jongen" (the merciless boy), an abiding Revian fantasy, in Herman and by extension Jesus. In *Nader to U* there is a passage that extends a version of the basic fantasy beyond the cut: "dat ik eens . . . zijn hemd zou mogen aanraken en zijn rug en lendenen zou mogen aanraken en zijn donzen borst strelen . . . om dan, als in een duizeling, mijn hand te laten afdalen, onder zijn broekriem door, tot ik zijn kloppende, van bloed verzadigde dolk en levensboom zou voelen, die ik niet meer zou loslaten voordat hij mij zou zegenen en ik zijn Heilig Vocht, in een weldadige, verzengende gloeiing, in mijn handpalm zou voelen spuiten" (47; that I would once . . . be allowed to touch his shirt and his back and loins and stroke his downy breast . . . in order then, as if in a dizzy state, to let my hand descend, under the belt of his pants, until I should feel his beating, blood-thickened dagger and tree of life, which I would not let go until he bless me with his Holy Moisture, which, in its beneficial, burning glow, I would feel spurting into the palm of my hand).

Part V

✦

Intermedial Itineraries

Chapter 13

Material Meanings

What a Medieval Badge Can Tell Us about Translation in the Middle Ages

Ann Marie Rasmussen

Medieval badges are small brooch-like objects featuring a vivid image and manufactured to be worn, most commonly to be sewn or pinned on clothing.[1] Cheap to make and to buy, badges intended for both secular and profane purposes were mass-produced in casts using tin-lead alloy. The oldest badges date from the last decades of the twelfth century. Their number and use increased steadily throughout the high and late Middle Ages, reaching a high point in the fifteenth century and then declining precipitously in the decades of the sixteenth century following the Reformation, after which they largely disappeared. Some 15,000 badges survive. They represent, however, only the tiniest fraction of the badges once manufactured, a number historian Carina Brumme and other experts now estimate to have been in the millions.[2]

What do badges have to do with translation? At first glance they might appear to have nothing in common with this volume's intellectual project, because badges are anonymous, mass-produced, image-using, material objects, and not written texts (though some of them sport inscriptions or pseudo-texts). Yet as I hope to show in this chapter, looking sideways at these seemingly irrelevant objects brings into focus a historical meaning and understanding of translation, now largely lost to us, that was widely shared in the late Middle Ages all across Europe. Recovering meanings of translation lost to modernity can do many kinds of intellectual work. It can inform readers about the sophistication and complexity of language and translation in the Middle Ages, pushing back on progressive models of historical change, so dear to the self-understanding of modern world, that equate the past with simplicity and the present with complexity. It can also make visible surprising parallels between medieval and postmodern notions of translation, providing provocative yet trenchant comparative frameworks that can expand and make more complex the intellectual dialogues

Figure 13.1. Lead-tin alloy badge from Wilsnack, Germany, showing three hosts attached to one another as a trefoil, with images from Christ's crucifixion. 15th century. 3.6 × 3.1 cm. Found in Nieuwlande, The Netherlands. With permission from the Van Beuningen Family Collection, Langbroek, The Netherlands, inventory number 1709.

informing postmodernity's drive for new theorizations of materiality and of translation.

The Holy Wafers of Wilsnack

For this chapter, one religious badge will serve as an exemplar for all religious badges (in actuality, about 40 percent of the surviving badges feature secular themes). This paper's badge originates from one of the most popular and controversial holy or charismatic sites in continental Europe north of the Alps, the town of Wilsnack in Brandenburg, Germany (figure 13.1).

Like all the surviving Wilsnack badges, ours is tiny, about 1.25" by 1" (36 mm by 31 mm), and at 2.9 grams it weighs almost nothing. Surviving images showing this badge on the hats of people in religious paintings confirm that it was sewn onto clothing and worn so that it was visible to others. The Wilsnack badge consists of three small circles, each the same size, arranged on a triangle pointing upwards and touching at the center. Each circle is impressed with an image referring to a key episode in the Passion of Christ. Read clockwise from the bottom, the images narrate this Christ's crucifixion and resurrection. The bottom image depicts Christ bound to a whipping post, being tortured; the left-hand image depicts the next episode in the story, Christ's crucifixion; the right-hand image shows the final episode, Christ's resurrection, and depicts Christ emerging triumphant from a tomb or grave, a banner in his hand. The two uppermost circles are topped by tiny crosses, usually missing from the surviving badges because of their extreme fragility. Originally, all or parts of the badge would have been painted red, but the paint is missing here (as it is from most surviving examples) because it has worn off.

The three circles represent three communion hosts that are bleeding. Religious badges were designed to correspond in visually indelible ways to the veneration they served. In 1383 the Wilsnack village priest Johannes Kabuz supposedly discovered "in the charred remains of the altar several days after the village was torched by a marauding knight" three miraculous hosts, "dry and intact, and in the center of each was a drop of blood."[3] As Bynum eloquently and succinctly puts it in her masterful study of the late medieval theology of blood, "both pilgrimage and criticism of it flourished at once."[4] From the 1380s until into the sixteenth century, Wilsnack was one of the most popular pilgrimage site in northern Europe, after Aachen and Cologne, and its visitor numbers rivaled even the ancient and venerable pilgrimage sites of Compostella, Rome, and Jerusalem.[5] The Wilsnack badge, then, is in the shape of the holy objects celebrated there, and intimately tied to the devotional trends that flourished in late medieval Catholicism, especially Corpus Christi and the newly flourishing mysticism of the Eucharist, with its devotional practices associated with Christ's Passion and with the late medieval religious veneration of holy blood.

Translation in the Multilingual Middle Ages

Having introduced the object, let me turn now to this volume's topic: translation. To write about the problem of translation in the Middle Ages is to open a perspective on the issue of globalization and language change that is at once familiar and strange. It is familiar because like the modern world, the medieval world is both multilingual, a term suggesting the coexistence of many languages, and translingual, a term suggesting interaction between many languages.[6] It is strange because the multilingual, translingual world of the Middle Ages manifested itself in fundamentally and radically different ways than now. Language was largely oral. The use of the technologies of reading and writing was limited, although growing rapidly by the fourteenth century. The territory around Wilsnack in northern Germany provides an excellent example of this combination of familiarity and strangeness. The language spoken in and around Wilsnack was Low German. Today Low German exists chiefly as a spoken dialect in the northernmost parts of Germany, with a decidedly rural character, but in the late Middle Ages it was spoken across a much wider geographical region. More importantly, Low German was then the leading written language of northern Europe, being the preferred vernacular of the elites (nobles and merchants) of the powerful, long-lived political and economic alliance known as the Hansa (sometimes called in English the Hanseatic League) and hence the lingua franca for those who traded with them.[7]

There was no standardization of spelling in the vernacular languages in the Middle Ages, for that was a by-product of the reorganization of linguistic registers that is part of the long process of national state formation in the eighteenth and nineteenth centuries. (The seventh- and eighth-century writers and translators who first wrote West Germanic languages struggled rather with the problems of adapting the Latin alphabet to the very different sound systems of the Germanic languages.) The vernacular languages of medieval Europe, forbearers of today's Danish, Dutch, English, French, German High and Low, Italian, Yiddish, and so on can be understood as assemblages of language variations that are mutually intelligible or are connected by a series of mutually intelligible dialects, with any speaker's speech revealing to other speakers easily identifiable markers of locality that went beyond accent to include syntax, word choice, and distinct morphological and phonological features, much as is the situation in German-speaking lands, for example, German-speaking Switzerland, even today.[8] In the Middle Ages, however, the nation-state as we know it did not yet exist, and so there was no strong connection between, on the one hand, specific languages and registers within those languages and, on the other, nationalistic political agendas. Connections between specific sociological groups and specific forms of language variation within a language group were emerging, however, and these could become associated with what was then perceived as that group's shared political interests. For example, for well over three hundred years (from 1066 until well into the fourteenth century) the noble elites of England spoke as their birth tongue a distinct dialect of Northern French, called by scholars to the infinite confusion of students everywhere, Anglo-Norman.

When written, vernacular languages retained these strong markers of linguistic locality, often in complex ways reflecting the dialect of the patron for whom the text is being copied as well as the dialects of the scribe and the source. Yet the thousands of surviving documents written in Low German, for example—most of them still unedited—are not simple transcriptions of speech. Rather, they show scribes and the chancellories where they worked attempting rudimentary standardization or perhaps better said, rudimentary regularization of written sound patterns, deliberate choice of widely known cognates, and writing out abbreviations in order to ensure comprehension across dialect boundaries, a practice modern scholars have called the creation of *Schreibsprachen* (languages for writing).[9] The status and geographic spread of Low German changed over time, a familiar development for all languages, but in the case of Low German, the direction these trends took may surprise modern readers. The movement of premodern Low German towards standardization was halted because over the course of the sixteenth century, written Low German itself was displaced by a written High German dialect, Luther's Saxonian, or east Middle, German, which was rapidly adopted as the preferred language for publishing and diplomacy. (Other written High German dialects, including those in which the major literary works of the long thirteenth century were composed, also did not develop further into standard, written forms of German.) At the same time, and moving from south to north, High German dialects slowly encroached into geographical areas where Low German had previously been spoken, so that by the seventeenth century, Low German had become a group of dialects spoken north of the so-called Benrath line, which runs from a suburb of Düsseldorf and the city of Aachen east to Berlin, Dessau, and Frankfurt an der Oder. Yet the endeavors of those medieval Low German scribes and chancellories surely belong to the category of translation because they show early attempts to mediate, or to translate, between oral and written forms of communication.

Yet there was a global language in the Middle Ages, unlike any in widespread use today. It was Latin, the pan-European language of the regionally strong and centrally weak institutions that make up the politically complex and religiously and culturally heterogeneous institution of medieval Catholicism. Late medieval Latin was a professional, pan-European language that was no one's native language and that belonged exclusively to the worlds of higher learning (philosophy, theology, and natural science) and liturgical practice. It was the primary language for writing. Latin is the language of the copious documentation surrounding the bleeding holy wafers of Wilsnack, the language that documents the miracles and the subsequent controversies surrounding it that simmered and roiled among local, regional, and papal ecclesiastical authorities for some one hundred years, with major campaigns launched against the holy site by rival prelates and princes in 1443 and 1453, although in 1403 Jan Hus produced the first treatise against Wilsnack. (All these campaigns failed, by the way. The Wilsnack holy site continued to attract throngs of the devout until the 1530s. Wilsnack's continued success, despite repeated attempts of prelates and theologians to curb it, contradicts modern belief in an authoritarian, omnipotent medieval church exercising near-totalitarian religious and social control over believers.)

Most importantly for our purposes, Latin was overwhelmingly the domain of elite, clerically trained men. Access to the higher reaches of the Latinate world in the universities was absolutely denied to women, although individual women became literate in Latin and gained limited access to elite learning in other ways. In fact, the surviving evidence strongly suggests that the regions in Europe with the highest number of women literate in Latin overlaps with those areas of northern Europe where Low German and Dutch were spoken.[10] Nevertheless, medieval Latin represented a historically and culturally specific, homo-social, collective masculine identity that contested with other forms of masculinity for prestige and power.[11] It was, in Walter J. Ong's memorable phrase, "a sex-linked language."[12]

In the late medieval world, then, choice of language meant first and foremost choice of audience, a complex issue when one considers that the late medieval world was a polyglossic world that was intensely and robustly mobile: a place where people, goods, objects, and ideas circulated constantly and in large numbers.

The holy site of Wilnack and its badges exemplify this mobility and polyglossia of the Middle Ages. Around 150 Wilsnack badges survive, and they have been found in Denmark, Sweden, England, the Netherlands, and Danzig, as well as across German-speaking lands.[13] These Wilsnack badges were most likely purchased by people who traveled to Wilsnack and took a badge home with them again (to the best of our knowledge, no evidence of long-distance trade in badges has been found). Thus, at any given moment during pilgrimage season, the church and village of Wilsnack could expect to host pilgrims speaking Danish, Swedish, English, Dutch, Flemish, Low German, and High German—a babble of mutually unintelligible Germanic languages, with a sprinkling of Polish and French thrown in. Add to this mix the Latin of the mass and the clerics, and one can begin to imagine the polyglossic soundscape of this provincial village during the pilgrimage seasons.

Travel was arduous in the Middle Ages, but nevertheless mobility was commonplace, and travels were undertaken by men, women, and children for many purposes. Beyond the traders and pilgrims we have already glimpsed, there were entire groups of people who were itinerant by profession and fortune, from soldiers to musicians and entertainers to peddlers and criminals.[14] Mobility was the rule, not the exception, in the late Middle Ages, and cross-linguistic communication and multilingualism, from the most rudimentary to fluency in multiple languages, were commonplace.[15]

Similarly, multilingualism was the rule, not the exception, in the Middle Ages. Present in rural areas such as Wilsnack, it reached its apogee in the great cities such as Paris, Rome, and London, where many linguistic groups interacted and where reading and writing had become necessary technologies facilitating intellectual, cultural, and economic exchange. (Intriguingly, urbanization is an important contributing factor to language standardization as well; cities further both standardization of dominant dialects and multilingualism.) One could find examples of multilingualism in any of these cities, and in others such as Bruges or Florence besides. To gain a flavor of a multilingual, medieval, urban context we can look to London around the year 1400, around the time when the holy site at Wilsnack was just taking off. Here, there would have been routine interactions between merchants speaking Flemish, Dutch, and Low German; local merchants, clerks, and bureaucrats speaking English; court officials and nobility speaking French; and clerics, diplomats, and notaries producing documents in Latin. All Christians, they would have encountered Latin during Mass. Those who traveled to Spain and Italy would have heard Hebrew, or even Arabic. And anyone living in London at this time would have routinely encountered trans-lingual writers, fluent in multiple languages, who chose different languages to develop distinct expressive registers, for example, French for love poetry, but English for devotional treatises.

In this intensely multilingual and trans-lingual world, translation was the energy and the creative driver of economic, social, and intellectual change.[16] The forms translation took were multiple and changed over the centuries as the balance of power between written Latin on the one hand and written vernacular languages on the other shifted slowly yet inexorably towards vernacular dominance. Translation practices of all kinds, from the freest to the most bound, flourished, encompassing practices that we might be more likely to term adaption and appropriation. The circulation of texts through translation was the fundamental shaping force of the intellectual world, driving philosophical, theological, and historical thought (think of Geoffrey of Monmouth's *History of the Kings of Britain*, which contains one version of the Arthur legend) written in Latin into the burgeoning vernaculars. Everywhere Latin-based learning was being shared and disseminated to the laity, including women, through adaptation and translation. Especially important in this regard were the communities of lay and religious women in northern Germany, whose native tongue would have been Low German, and who produced a sizable body of writing, much of it only now receiving the scholarly attention it deserves, in both Latin and Low German.[17] The trends in translation went the other way as well, from the vernaculars back into Latin. Into this latter category falls the widely influential thought of the mystic Mechthild of Magdeburg (d. ca. 1285), whose spiritual autobiography, written in Low German, survives only in two works of translation, one into Middle High German, and one into Latin. Nor is Latin necessary to this process.[18] Texts and translation circulated in huge numbers between the vernacular languages, as is attested by the traffic in tales of King Arthur and his knights crisscrossing every linguistic boundary of the high and late Middle Ages.[19]

In the Middle Ages, as I said earlier, choice of language meant choice of audience. The act of translation usually went beyond a narrow, rhetorical definition that focused on transferring meaning from one word to another. It meant adapting the text being translated to its new social and cultural environment. It is no accident that the Middle High German word commonly used to render the act of translation is the verb *diuten*, ancestor of the modern German word *deuten*, meaning "to interpret." The meanings of Middle High German *diuten* move freely between "to mean," "to tell a story," and "to translate." In the preface to his short story "Der Arme Heinrich," for example, from around the year 1200, the poet Hartmann von Aue famously states that he has read "many books" looking for the story that he now tells and translates for the reader.[20] Hartmann's preamble conveys the complexity of translation in the medieval world (in fact, it was also fashionable for medieval German authors to invoke foreign sources for their German-language works). To translate in the Middle Ages meant making knowledge and stories available, accessible, and immediate.

The Wilsnack badge reminds us that the processes of translation and adaptation crossed over the text-image divide as well. Each disk represents a wafer, and each image invokes an episode in the story of Christ's Passion, the central miracle and narrative of this faith. The wafers themselves are key actors and agents in a foundational sacrament of Christianity, Holy Communion, also known as the Eucharist, in which the Last Supper is reenacted liturgically. These iconic images would have been immediately intelligible to anyone familiar with Christianity: in late medieval Europe, more or less everyone. The memorable images on the badge present a pious Christian with an indelible and immediately legible version of the central miracle story of the Passion and of the foundational, Eucharistic liturgy of Christianity. The images are arranged in a fixed order that when read clockwise produces the holiest of Christian narratives. Yet at the same time, the images are arranged in a circle, so the story of Christ's passion is ceaselessly repeated, just as the eternity promised in Christianity is symbolically evoked and reenacted in the Mass of the Eucharist.

The imbrication of image, narrative, and liturgy is not unique to this badge. Most badges, whether secular or religious, employ a kind of iconic semiosis. This way of making meaning, common in the Middle Ages, entails a specific motif becoming, in Michael Curschmann's words, "the dominant visual emblem of the whole."[21] Such pictorial encapsulations of a widely known story could gain independence from their literary contexts, while continuing to transport meanings and messages derived or adapted from the still-circulating stories. In the case of the Wilsnack badge, iconic semiosis makes the story of Christ's Passion legible and meaningful across and beyond linguistic realms. Many mutually unintelligible languages mingled in pilgrimage at Wilsnack, not the least of them Latin, which would have been meaningful to all but intelligible only to a select few. Yet this badge transcended linguistic barriers and spoke, as it were, to everyone there, triggering via these potent, selected scenes a master narrative that was the focus of intense devotion.

Material Translations

The manifestations of translation discussed above may be largely familiar to modern readers. There are medieval concepts of translation, however, that pertain to the concrete, material dimension of translation. Though foreign to our present way of thinking about materiality, they belong to what Jeffrey Jerome Cohen and Lowell Duckert have called the past's "rich archive for thinking ecology differently" that can inspire rethinking matter in our present moment.[22]

Trans-latio means quite literally bearing, transporting, or carrying something from one place to another. It figured in medieval political theory as the concept of *translatio imperii*, meaning transfer of rule, which refers to a notion of historical change that placed Christian Europe in a divine political lineage of virtuous government.[23] Of key importance for the purpose of this chapter, however, is a different medieval notion of translation, namely the translation of the saints, meaning the ceremonial movement of saints' bodies. These fragments (there were very few whole-body saints in the medieval period) are called relics. Held to emit divine power, they were much sought after and treated with great solemnity by the medieval church and the communities it served. The processes of finding, elevating, and preparing, and then ceremoniously moving, receiving, and depositing saints' relics are together often referred to as the translation of saints, which is also the generic name given to the texts describing these processes.[24] Each process of *translatio* tells an ideologically and politically charged story. It proudly proclaims that what is in effect a radical new beginning is nothing but a stage in an unfolding, preordained narrative of divine, Christian power through the divinely and unchangingly self-identical relic.

The badges produced at Wilsnack interact with and refer to this kind of holiness, although the wafers to which they refer are a special kind of relic. The Wilsnack wafers are neither fragments of a holy corpse nor material items once in contact with a holy body, such as the tunic of the Virgin Mary or fragments of the true cross. Rather the wafers are material objects made doubly miraculous, their Eucharistic trans-substantiation proven and made manifest by their bleeding and by their miraculous survival of a fire. There was no agreement among late medieval theologians about the theology of Christ's presence that underlies the Eucharist, but whatever their understanding of the theology of Christ's blood, most still probably rejected the claim to sacred status advanced for the holy wafers of Wilsnack. Yet it seems that the pious pilgrims who thronged to Wilsnack were largely indifferent to these learned quarrels. For them, the holy wafers of Wilsnack, tortured and purified by fire, bled with the blood of Christ. The holy wafers were therefore relics that manifested the miracle of the Eucharist and channeled sacred power and divinity from Christ to humankind. For them, a holy wafer badge obtained at this sacred place, when activated by the pious journey undertaken to acquire it and (most likely) by a process in which the badge was touched to the shrine and blessed by the priest, became a holy relic, too. In this way, the Wilsnack badges participated fully in the sacred power emanating from the site.

Trans-latio refers both to the rituals and processes by which relics were ceremoniously installed in new homes, and as well to the belief that relics capture and channel divine power. Although the practices attached to relic translation differ widely across time and space, modern readers should understand that medieval objects such as the Wilsnack badges are not tangible memorials or souvenirs. They emanate power and have to be handled with great care. They are animate. They may not be living but they are alive.

The idea of *translatio* has introduced materiality into this discussion. I want to return to the Wilsnack badge again, in order to add another dimension of materiality and to gesture towards what might be theorized as a second, unfamiliar aspect of translation in the Middle Ages. The badges as they survive are but shadows of their former selves. The images and the surviving badges are often dark, nearly black in color. Yet originally, the lead-tin alloy out of which they were made would have been nearly white. Originally, badges were bright, eye-catching objects that would have shone in the sun. The images of Wilsnack badges surviving on medieval painted altarpieces show them sewn onto pilgrims' hats and as being entirely or partially red, surrounded by shiny metal. This means that they were painted (a very few, surviving badges still bear minute traces of red paint). All this confirms that shape and color together were the design hallmarks of Wilsnack badge.

The original badges, then, used red to highlight the central feature of the Wilsnack miracle story: the holy wafers, transformed by the liturgy and ceremony of the Mass into Christ's body, had been purified in the torture of fire and, being Christ's body, bled just as Christ bled in the Passion. The holy wafers of Wilsnack did not simply represent Christ; they were Christ.

The materials of the Wilsnack badge, lead alloy and red paint, also took part in what we might call another form of translation, now quite foreign to the modern mind: the mixing and tempering based in humoral theory. The theory of the four humors or temperaments, known in medieval German as the four complexions, is what we might call a vernacular science of matter. It holds that four elements—air, fire, water, and earth—make up all matter. Each element has specific properties that impart specific qualities and characteristics to matter. Air is sanguine, that is to say, hot and moist. Fire is choleric, that is to say, hot and dry. Water is phlegmatic, that is to say, cold and moist. Earth is melancholic, that is to say, cold and dry. All forms of life and matter mix and combine these elements and their influences.[25]

If my reader looks up the concept of the four humors on *Wikipedia*, she will find it described as an early, now-discredited way of understanding human psychology, physiology, and temperament, that is to say, as a theory of human medicine and proto-psychology. This finding is true enough. However, it somewhat obscures the fact that medieval humoral theory was not limited to human beings and the human body. Because it was understood that the whole of the material world—both beings and things—consisted of humor-based matter, humoral theory could explain the properties of all things: crystals, ores, plants, beasts, humans, stars. Medieval medicine and proto-psychology arose from the application of humoral theory to the human body, thus embedding the human body in a larger, cosmic framework. Thus, a human body is no more like, or unlike, a canine body than an oak tree or an emerald or lead, and all are interrelated, cosmic phenomena (if one reads contemporary ecocriticsm, this idea seems not archaic but rather very modern).

Let us return then to the lead and vermilion paint out of which the Wilsnack badge was fashioned. Humoral theory teaches that materials such as metal were not inanimate as such, but rather participated, as did everything else that existed, in the elemental forces and humors that shaped the world. Metals, too, consisted of elements whose qualities were connected to astral, cosmic influences. Each had a place in the natural and physical hierarchies that constituted the cosmos. Lead was an earth element. It was thus dry and cold, associated with Saturn, and with melancholy. These qualities placed it at the bottom of the cosmic hierarchy—not a value judgment, but rather a known fact.

In this vernacular science of matter, lead is a lowly, earthy, and base element. This is not simply allegory, although clearly it could function as such. Recall, rather, that all elements are in motion and influence one another and that all materials, including metals, have a temper which can be translated and balanced by mixing, often with agents that are linked to the desired quality by association. Let us take, for example, the red paint of the Wilsnack badges. It does not merely depict or represent blood. Rather, the paint pigment, being red, partakes in the elemental qualities of blood, which is humorally hot and moist, and associated with air. The red pigment is hot and wet, in the same way blood is hot and wet. The lead is cold and dry, in the same way that the earth is cold and dry. With its heat and moistness, the red pigment tempers the lead's coldness and dryness. Together, they approach an ideal balance of matter.

This process of tempering, of balancing is not limited to the material of the badge alone. The image, too, partakes in this vernacular science of matter, channeling cosmic forces that interact with the humoral nature of these materials, lead and pigment. In the case of the Wilsnack badge, the holiness of the image imbues it with sacred power. The image tempers the earthiness of lead, leavened and uplifted by the airiness of red pigment and the holiness of the image. Here can be glimpsed a fundamental, and from the perspective of the Middle Ages, rational and scientific reason for the use of precious materials—gold, silver, ivory, crystals, gemstones—in religious objects. It is not solely about appropriate veneration. Rather, these materials temper the sacred forces flowing through the divine images and relics, heightening those forces and making them even more efficacious and powerful.

The materials out of which the badge is fashioned, lead and pigment, were not believed to be inert. Rather, their living qualities were understood to become a part of the entire object and its force. In a way, the Wilsnack holy wafer badges are Christological. Not only do the images on the badges narrate the miracle story of the son of God who assumed human form and suffered that all Christians might live. The badges translate that story into material form, transmuting the lowly material substance out of which they are manufactured into sacred wafers that bleed human blood, that enact the living word, and that promise eternal life.

Finally, in the medieval imagination, the tempered Wilsnack badge also bodies forth the translation of matter. Such translation is an act in which matter and all its elements coexist forever in uneasy, constantly shifting relationships. Though different in substance from the bodies of warm-blooded creatures, the holy wafer badges of Wilsnack are forever entwined in, open to, acting upon and translating between the forces of nature, the cosmos, and the divine.

Notes

1. The most important reference work for all badges, both religious and profane, is the excellent, online Kunera database maintained by Radboud Universiteit Nijmegen, www.kunera.nl. Also extremely useful is the German database of religious badges, the Pilgerzeichendatenbank (Database of Pilgrim Badges), Kunstgewerbemuseum, Staatliche Museen zu Berlin (Museum of Decorative Arts, Berlin), www.pilgerzeichen.de. Indispensable are also the three catalogs published by H. J. E. van Beuningen and A. M. Koldeweij, eds., *Heilig en Profaan: 1000 Laat-Middeleeuwse Insignes Uit de Collectie H. J. E. Van Beuningen*, 3 vols. (Cothen: Stichting Middeleeuwse Religieuze en Profane Insignes, 1993, 2001, and 2012). Foundational studies on badges are Denis Bruna, *Enseignes de plomb et autres menues chosettes du Moyen Âge* (Paris: Éditions du Léopard d'Or, 2006); Denis Bruna, *Saints et diables au chapeau: Bijoux obliés du Moyen Âge* (Paris: Seuil, 2007); and Brian Spencer, *Pilgrim Souvenirs and Secular Badges* (Woodbridge, Eng.: Boydell, 2010). Finally, I refer readers to the website of the Medieval Badges Foundation (Stichting Middeleeuwse Religieuze en Profane Insignes), www.medievalbadges.org.

2. Carina Brumme, "Pilgerzeichen: Erhaltungsbedingungen und Verbreitungsräume," in *Das Zeichen am Hut im Mittelalter: Europäische Reisemarkierungen*, ed. Hartmut Kühne, Lothar Lambacher, and Konrad Vanja (Frankfurt am Main: Peter Lang, 2008), 127–42.

3. Caroline Walker Bynum, *Wonderful Blood: Theology and Practice in Late Medieval Northern Germany and Beyond* (Philadelphia: University of Pennsylvania Press, 2007), 25–26.

4. Ibid., 26.

5. For a thorough consideration of Wilsnack in the context of medieval pilgrimage, see the excellent essays in Felix Escher and Hartmut Kühne, eds., *Die Wilsnackfahrt: Ein Wallfahrts- und Kommunikationszentrum Nord- und Mitteleuropas im Spätmittelalter*, Europäische Wallfahrtstudien (Frankfurt am Main: Peter Lang, 2006).

6. See for example the outstanding new study by Jonathan Hsy, *Trading Tongues: Merchants, Multilingualism, and Medieval Literature* (Columbus: Ohio State University Press, 2013). This book explores the multilingual nature of the late medieval world, treating especially code switching and cross-linguistic exchanges and encounters in medieval contact zones, with a focus on that great,

polyglot city, medieval London. It examines the ways in which multilingualism and commerce shape texts written in medieval contact zones.

7. On the Hansa, see Philippe Dollinger, *The German Hansa* (Stanford, Calif.: Stanford University Press, 1970); Johannes Schildhauer, *The Hansa: History and Culture* (Leipzig: Edition Leipzig, 1985) and *Die Hanse: Geschichte und Kultur* (Stuttgart: Kohlhammer, 1984); and Rolf Hammel-Kiesow, *Die Hanse* (Munich: Beck, 2000).

8. Mastering two distinct dialects of the same language is known as heteroglossia, a form of linguistic mastery that must have been quite common in the Middle Ages and that still characterizes the linguistic situation of native speakers of Swiss German, for example, who have been known to describe themselves as being bilingual in a single language.

9. For more information about late medieval, Low German *Schreibsprachen* see, for example, Robert Peter, *Atlas spätmittelalterlicher Schreibsprachen des niederdeutschen Altlandes und angrenzender Gebiete* (Berlin: de Gruyter, 2009). For an excellent bibliography and information on all aspects of Low German, visit the website of the Verein für niederdeutsche Sprachforschung (Union for Language Research in Low German) at http://www.vnds.de.

10. For extensive bibliography and discussion of this topic, see Elizabeth A. Andersen, Henrike Lähnemann, and Anne Simon, eds., *A Companion to Mysticism and Devotion in Northern Germany in the Late Middle Ages* (Leiden: Brill, 2013).

11. See, for example, the essays in the edited collection by P. H. Cullum and Katherine J. Lewis, *Religious Men and Masculine Identity in the Middle Ages* (Woodbridge, Eng.: Boydell and Brewer, 2013), which provide further bibliography for this field of historical gender studies research.

12. Walter J. Ong, "Latin Learning as a Renaissance Puberty Rite," *Studies in Philology* 56 (April 1959): 106–9.

13. This is the number in the Pilgerzeichendatenbank. The Kunera database lists 185 instances. Alongside actual badges or badge fragments, the surviving medieval witnesses to this badge include bell embossments, depictions in paintings, and previously unknown written references.

14. The standard work is Ernst Schubert, *Fahrendes Volk im Mittelalter* (Bielefeld: Universitätsverlag, 1995).

15. Relevant titles appear in the notes below. See also, for example, Michael Baldzuhn and Christine Putzo, eds., *Mehrsprachigkeit im Mittelalter: Kulturelle, literarische, sprachliche und didaktische Konstellationen in europäischer Perspektive, mit Fallstudien zu den 'Disticha Catonis'* (Berlin: de Gruyter, 2011).

16. The foundational study is Rita Copeland, *Rhetoric, Hermeneutics, and Translation in the Middle Ages: Academic Traditions and Vernacular Texts* (Cambridge: Cambridge University Press, 1991). See also the annual journal devoted to issues of medieval translation, *The Medieval Translator: Traduire au Moyen Age*, 13 volumes to date (Turnhout, Belgium: Brepols, 1989 to current). Vols. 1 (1989), 2 (1991), and 4 (1994) issued as *The Medieval Translator* (Turnhout, Belgium: Brepols); volume 3 (1999) titled *Translation in the Middle Ages* and issued as volume 12 of *New Comparison: A Journal of Comparative and General Literary Studies* (Norwich, Eng.: University of Warwick).

17. The best introduction to the topic is Andersen, Lähnemann, and Simon, eds., *Companion to Mysticism*, note 10.

18. See the brilliant study by Sif Rikharddóttir, *Medieval Translations and Cultural Discourse: The Movement of Texts in England, France and Scandinavia* (Cambridge: D. S. Brewer, 2012), which traces the circulation of vernacular texts between Old French, Latin, Middle English, and Norse.

19. For example, Chrétien de Troyes's Old French texts were adapted and translated into Old Norse and into Middle High German; the Old French prose Arthurian compilations were adapted and translated by Malory into Middle English, and so on. See Rikarddottir, *Medieval Translations*, note 18.

20. "Er nam im manige schouwe an mislichen buochen . . . . nu beginnet er iu diuten ein rede die er geschriben vant" (He undertook much study of different books [this probably refers to foreign languages such as Latin or Old French] . . . Now he begins translating for you a story that he found written there), *Altdeutsche Textbibliothek*, vol. 3, *Der arme Heinrich*, ed. Paul Hermann (Tübingen: Niemeyer, 2001), lines 6–7, 16–17.

21. "From Myth to Emblem to Panorama," in *Visuality and Materiality in the Story of Tristan and Isolde*, ed. Jutta Eming, Ann Marie Rasmussen, and Kathryn Starkey (Notre Dame, Ind.: University of Notre Dame Press, 2012), 107–29. See also the classic study by André Grabar, *Christian Iconography: A Study of Its Origins* (Princeton, N.J.: Princeton University Press, 1968).

22. Introduction to *Elemental Ecocriticism: Thinking with Earth, Air, Water, and Fire*, ed. Jeffrey Jerome Cohen and Lowell Duckert (Minneapolis, MN: University of Minnesota Press, 2015,

23. For an introduction to *translatio imperii* as a political concept in the context of medieval European debates about political theory, see Janet Coleman, *A History of Political Thought: From the Middle Ages to the Renaissance* (Malden, Mass: Blackwell, 2000). For a discussion of the history of the concept and its influence into nineteenth-century political theory, see Cary J. Nederman, *Lineages of European Political Thought: Exploration along the Medieval/Modern Divide from John of Salisbury to Hegel* (Washington, D.C.: Catholic University of America Press, 2009). For a unique work that studies the ways in which medieval notions of *translatio* have shaped modern literary criticism and scholarship, see Zrinka Stahuljak, *Bloodless Genealogies of the French Middle Ages: Translatio[n], Kinship, and Metaphor* (Gainesville: University Press of Florida, 2005).

24. The foundational study is Peter Brown, *The Cult of the Saints: Its Rise and Function in Latin Christianity* (Chicago: University of Chicago Press, 1981). On relics see Patrick Geary, *Furta sacra: Thefts of Relics in the Central Middle Ages* (Princeton, N.J.: Princeton University Press, 1990); and the recent study by Cynthia Hahn, *Strange Beauty: Issues in the Making and Meaning of Reliquaries, 400–circa 1204* (College Park: Pennsylvania State University Press, 2012).

25. For an introduction to medieval understandings of matter and humoral theory, see Roberta Gilchrist, *Medieval Life: Archaeology and the Life Course* (Woodbridge, Eng.: Boydell, 2012); see also Valerie Flint, "A Magic Universe," in *A Social History of England 1200–1500*, ed. Rosemary Horrox and W. Mark Ormrod (Cambridge: Cambridge University Press, 2006), 340–55 and 497–98; and Kellie Robertson, "Medieval Materialism: A Manifesto," in *Exemplaria* 22, no. 2 (2010): 99–118.

Chapter 14

Between the Visual and the Sonic

Rewriting Rilke's "Ur-Geräusch"

Andrea Bachner

As critics thinking in the aftermath of post-structuralism, we have been taught to take one tale of translation for granted: the shift from sound to visuality. Jacques Derrida's critique of the phonocentric complex in Western philosophy replaced the privileging of speech with a generalized metaphor of writing (or *écriture*). While writing, understood in this way, was meant to encompass all types of signification, Derrida's prevalent imaginary of the trace and the mark promoted a graphic, and thus visual, regime to the status of prime object of theoretical interest.[1] For W. J. T. Mitchell, Derrida's philosophical intervention constituted one symptomatic example of a sea change in the media politics of our cultural unconscious, which he dubbed the pictorial turn: a profound shift from sound to visuality, and from language to image.[2]

Undoubtedly, this is only the bare outline of a much more complicated, nuanced, and entangled story—not least because the theorists who claimed to diagnose these changes were themselves interested parties, instead of mere cultural seismographs, and told their particular versions or parts of a larger tale. And yet, this simplified account can help us understand some of the theoretical, as well as aesthetic, consequences of the larger phenomenon. For instance, it allows us to appraise the wave of renewed interest in sound in the last two decades as a symptom of theoretical discontent with, as well as an inheritor of post-structuralist paradigms. The fact that many of these "sonic interventions" focus on the margins of signification, on music, inarticulate human sounds, or glossolalia, testifies to the apparent need to venture into insufficiently theorized media spectra, while steering clear of speech and its phonocentric stigma.[3]

With the revolution of digital media, the conceptual interest in sound is not just the first ripple before yet another shift in the way in which we imagine mediality, this time from the visual to the aural. Instead, reflections on sound—as well as media theoretical approaches in general—increasingly begin to rethink the link between different media. In the age of digitalization, the difference between media is no longer based on ontological grounds, but has become a question of input and output. Consequently, media metaphors that privilege one medium over another begin to lose much of their appeal and distinctness, since they are no longer equally able to essentialize differences between media. More simply put, when both sonic and visual information are processed as sequences of ones and zeros, elaborate theories based on the supposed gulf between sound and vision, or speech and writing, often with their concomitant value judgments, garner less interest. Rather, we might pay more attention to the nodal points at which different media meet and interact. But if—to rephrase Emily Apter's dictum—digitalization makes everything translatable, it also underscores the fact that everything has to be translated.[4] Consequently, reflections on mediality are still concerned with questions of translation—perhaps now more than ever. Instead of being mere symptoms of broader paradigmatic processes of translation, media are increasingly becoming important test cases for the limits, possibilities, and meaning of translation.

One important nodal point at which multiple processes of translation happen at the interstices between different media systems assumed surprising prevalence in the German culture of the late 1980s and 1990s. It emerged at a time marked by the fall of the Berlin Wall and German reunification, and its cultural and aesthetic challenges. It also roughly coincided with and was clearly inspired by another conceptual turn, namely the emergence of and increasing visibility of media studies as proposed by Friedrich Kittler. The medial interface I am referring to consists of an imaginary that weds sound and visuality through a process of inscription inspired by the gramophone. It hearkens back to Rainer Maria Rilke's essay "Ur-Geräusch" ("Primal Sound") of 1919, in which a gramophone-like contraption is imagined as tracing the human skull sutures and thus producing a primal sound of corporeality.

After Kittler's influential book *Gramophone—Film—Typewriter* included Rilke's essay in 1986, a range of contemporary German writers began to draw on and to rewrite Rilke's imaginary of the reversed gramophone.[5] In what follows, I will explore different "citations" of Rilke's medial imaginary with a view to processes of translation between different rewritings, as well as between the visual, the sonic, and the literary. I will focus specifically on the echoes of Rilke's model in the work of Durs Grünbein and Marcel Beyer. Rilke's short essay "Ur- Geräusch" lends itself particularly well to rewritings in the 1990s, since it links a medial, we could even say transmedial, imaginary to corporeality as captured by anatomical science—two important discourses for German writers sometimes described as part of a trend of "new new interiority" ("neue Neue Innerlichkeit").[6]

Rilke's text itself already marks various processes of translation, not least in its regressive timeline. Conjured up in Rilke's textual remembrance of 1919, two scenes appear. One is set in Rilke's schooldays, in which, shortly after Thomas Edison's invention of the phonograph, young Rilke's physics class consisted in the reconstruction of the apparatus through homely means: a cardboard funnel is equipped with a paper membrane to which a bristle has been affixed. Upon the production of sound close to the funnel, the membrane transfers its vibrations to the bristle that inscribes the sound as traces into a wax-covered, revolving cylinder. Upon reversion, when the bristle "reads" the inscription it produced earlier, a remote echo of the original sound makes itself heard. The second scene happens during Rilke's studies in Paris, when he becomes fascinated with the structure of the human skull. Putting both fascinations together results in a model that seems risqué to its own author: what would happen if a gramophone needle were made to retrace not a mark as a result of a mediated sound inscription, but rather a naturally occurring trace: the cranial sutures? Rilke imagines the output of this experiment as an eerie sound, an "Ur-Geräusch" (primal sound).[7]

At first glance, Rilke's model seems to limit translation, not least because of his self-avowed infatuation with inscription at the expense of sound. Whereas the gramophone involves a double transcription, from sound to trace, and back to sound, unmediated by any agent other than the technological apparatus, the very concept of a primal sound implies the capture of something original and indeed originary. It is "eine Spur . . . die nicht aus der graphischen Übersetzung eines Tons [stammt], sondern ein an sich und natürlich Bestehendes [wäre]" (a trace . . . that was not derived from the graphic translations of sound, but existed of itself naturally).[8] And yet, Rilke's new application of the gramophone model also appears to think translation in a more radical way, not as a mere transfer between different media or systems of representation, but rather as a means of access to the material reality of the world.

Instead of articulating the marks of the cranial sutures, of making them amenable to reading, and thus understandable, the primal sound remains as ineffable as the markings it renders sonically. For Rilke, the translation between the mysterious bone folds of the human skull and their eerie music made audible by a gramophone-like contraption consists of the mediation between two different realms of the senses. It does not translate a cryptic message into an understandable one. The added value of Rilke's process and its possible transfer to other surfaces does not lie in an increase in meaning, but in an increase of sensual stimuli. As such, Rilke's thought experiment is a pseudoscientific test case for the functioning of poetry as a generalized and heightened synesthesia. Poetry is translation. It renders reality not by opening it up to signification, but by expressing it in a different medium. To this end, poetry is not only a medium in its own right, but it has to function as a node for a multiplicity of media. Poetry can only do justice to reality by not being slave to visuality only, but by capturing the whole spectrum of possible sense perceptions.[9]

The application of "craniophony" to poetry evidences the paradoxical desires linked to mediation and translation in Rilke's essay. The primal sound, and, by analogy, poetry, embody the desire for the perfect translation of ineffable reality, a translation so perfect that it would not really be a translation so much as an alternative expression or manifestation of that same reality. And yet, the primal sound itself is already secondary with respect to the cranial sutures, which, following Rilke's own model of the gramophone, would just be another mark of an even more primal content. In a series of risky maneuvers in analogy, poetry is both framed as a direct expression of and multiply removed from reality. Where translation is most perfect, it is also most precarious.

The conjunction between writing and media, between the visible and the audible, between corporeality and representation in Rilke's essay found strong resonances in German literature of the 1990s. Its complex tale of translation, compressed into a short text, seemed to make it a particularly apt material for intertextuality. In what follows, I want to focus on two cases that are particularly revealing for thinking about medial translation, namely the work of Durs Grünbein and Marcel Beyer.[10]

In the essay "Drei Briefe" ("Three Letters"), published in 1991, and originally (and tellingly) part of a correspondence with Marcel Beyer, Durs Grünbein calls Rilke's piece a "[süchtigmachenden] Aufsatz" (an addictive essay).[11] This description of Rilke's essay by one of Germany's foremost contemporary poets does not come as a surprise. Given Grünbein's interest in literature and science as two potentially interconnected analyses of reality and especially of human nature, we can surely understand the poet's excitement at the possibility to rewrite Rilke in terms of a literary anatomy or an anatomical literature. After all, we are talking about a writer who highlighted Georg Büchner's work "Über Schädelnerven" ("On Skull Nerves") in his speech upon being awarded the Büchner Prize in 1995, tellingly entitled "Den Körper zerbrechen" ("Breaking the Body").[12]

Grünbein's direct reference to Rilke's "Primal Sound" occurs in the context of a reflection on the links between literature and corporeality, between poets and doctors. Availing himself of the inscriptive figure of the engram, of the notion of memory traces stored in the brain, Grünbein discusses hearing as a privileged channel for the outside world to leave its imprint in the human psyche. After mentioning Rilke, however, the poet quickly diverts the reader's attention to another coupling of the body and technology: his own childhood experience of having the radiography of his skull taken. Rilke's imagery of the sounding out of bodily marks, the skull's sutures, is replaced by a visual medium of representation, photography:

> Die Vorstellung, daß man mir in Sekundenbruchteilen photographisch die Haut abziehen und mein Fleisch von den Knochen lösen konnte, beeindruckte mich tief. . . . Was mich damals beschäftigte war die technische Seite, das Verfahren selbst, der Übergriff des analytischen Blicks auf die Zusammensetzung seiner Objekte, d.h. in

> diesem Falle des menschlichen Körpers. Geht nicht das Sprechen als physiologischer Akt von dem Moment an, wo es sich nicht mehr nur deskriptiv verhält, ähnlich vor?[13]

> The thought that one could strip off my skin photographically in the split of a second and sever my flesh from the bones impressed me deeply. . . . What held my attention then was the technological aspect, the process itself, namely the analytical gaze's infringement on the composition of its object, i.e., in this case the human body. Is it not true that spoken language as a physiological act functions in a similar way, from the moment in which it proceeds not only descriptively?

Grünbein's juxtaposition of Rilke's gramophone-like model and radiography effects a shift in media metaphors: first from sound (Rilke's primal sound) to visuality (Grünbein's radiography), then back to sound, since Grünbein focuses on language as a physiological act, as speech. But the translation from primal sound to X-ray image highlights a different facet of fascination not equally at the forefront of Rilke's thoughts: if not by technological means, such as radiography, the cranial sutures are invisible, unless the flesh that covers them is cut open. If Rilke saw the cranial sutures as mysterious inscriptions that awaited, if not interpretation, at least transposition by other means, being made audible as sound, Grünbein sees them as potential openings in the human bodies, marks that can become visible again after another inscription, such as the cut of the scalpel. Instead of translating a visible trace by sound, the sutures invoke the cut of dissection. Instead of merely representing reality, a medium such as radiography, so Grünbein suggests, in its equation with dissection, actually alters the object it captures.

In the aphoristic essay "Neun Variationen zur Fontanelle" ("Nine Variations on the Fontanelle") of 1993, the cranial sutures move even more forcibly to the center of Grünbein's attention.[14] Here, Grünbein reflects more specifically on the fontanelles, the parts of the human skull that are flexible in infants and only gradually ossify, leaving the cranial sutures as their remainders. For Grünbein, the fontanelles illustrate a detour, a deviation, a one-way street of human development, perhaps we could even say its fallenness. As points where the human body, especially its top-heavy skull, remains permeable after birth, before a solid circle of bone completely encases the brain, the holes of the fontanelles, the cleavages of the sutures, trace entryways into the body. The folding-shut of the sutures and fontanelles puts an end to the brain's development, to its potential further folding and unfolding.

It is in this sense that "die Faltung erwies sich als Falle" (the folding has turned out to be a trap), a phrase in the same essay that prepares the ground for Grünbein's collection of poems of 1994 with the title *Falten und Fallen* (*Folds and Traps*, but also *Folding and Falling*).[15] Consider the writer's injunction in one of the poems in *Falten und Fallen*:

Denk von den Wundrändern her, vom Veto
Der Eingeweide, vom Schweigen
Der Schädelnähte. . . .[16]

Think from the edges of the wounds, from the veto
Of the entrails, from the silence
Of the cranial sutures. . . .

Here, the edges of the wound, a cut of the surface that probes deeper, quickly give way to the entrails' coils and the skull's sutures. Grünbein's emphasis lies on a reversal of the link between subject and object, between mind and body. Instead of making the body visible and understandable by the symbolically invasive technology of radiography and/as the cutting open of the body, the body becomes the site and the subject of thought. Unlike Rilke's fantasy of the primal sound, the cranial sutures remain silent. As Judith Ryan underlines, Grünbein insists on the "Widerstand der menschlichen Physiologie, die eigenen Geheimnisse preiszugeben" (resistance of the human physiology to reveal its own secrets).[17]

But if the body as the site of thought resists meaning, it does so figuratively by embodying impossible or negative media: the cut of the wound is and is not a meaningful mark, the entrails are and are not gestures, the cranial sutures are and are not capable of sound. The negative translation of body parts into media inscribes corporeality into language while marking it as resisting signification at the same time. Even though language, and poetry in particular, happens from the body, language also has to infringe on the object world. The multiple processes of translation between visuality and sound, between meaning and corporeality, are Grünbein's problematic solution to the paradoxical circularity that results when writing tries to take stock of the body as both subject and object, both agent and content. A thought that starts from "the silence of the cranial sutures" as an injunction for poetic work produces the body as translation, between reality and representation and between different media technologies.

In contrast to Grünbein's treatment of Rilke's paradigm with a focus on an anatomically mediated visuality, novelist Marcel Beyer's rewriting of "Primal Sound" invests heavily in sound. His 1996 novel *Flughunde* (translated as *The Karnau Tapes*) is, above all, a sonically driven text. It interlaces the voices of the sound technician Hermann Karnau and of Helga Goebbels, the daughter of Nazi propaganda minister Joseph Goebbels, to draft a soundscape of the Nazi regime. Karnau is not only instrumental in setting up the sound system for Nazi mass rallies or in taping dissident voices during the linguistic purge in occupied Alsace. He also becomes an active participant in SS experiments on the vocal organs of life subjects.

The novel's thrust to provide a soundscape of Germany's traumatic past is replicated in the text itself in Karnau's project of a sound map, a complete recorded collection of the whole sound spectrum, from the sweet voices of children at play to the death cries of soldiers in combat.[18] This *mise en abyme* already hints at a means to translate between the textual medium of the novel and its sonic contents that it can only render in writing. Beyer's focus lies as much on sound itself as on the modes of recording, storing, and replaying it, underlining the inscriptive functioning of sound media such as the record and the tape.

Beyer's direct reference to Rilke's "Primal Sound" occurs toward the end of the novel, in the form of a nightmare suffered by the novel's protagonist Karnau years after the end of the war. Karnau's dream literalizes Rilke's model as the ultimate nightmare—German-style. Tied down and silenced by a gag, Karnau remains sentient while his former SS colleagues perform an experiment on him. They remove flesh and skin from his skull in order to record the sound of his cranial sutures with the help of a gramophone needle. Unlike in Rilke's musings, where the primal sound remains an elusive, imagined possibility, here, the cranial sound becomes painfully audible:

> Das Knochensummen ist ein Geräusch menschlichen Ursprungs, das kein Mensch je zuvor gehört hat, der wirkliche Schädelklang, und doch klingt es völlig menschenfremd, flaut wieder ab, wird dumpfes Knattern, droht zu ersterben, fällt zurück in das anfängliche metallische Kratzen, mein Schädel unter diesen Vibrationen, als lösten sich schon erste Knochensplitter, ein furchtbarer Ton, der mir Gänsehaut bereitet. Soll dies tatsächlich das charakteristische Lautgeben meiner eigenen Schädelnaht sein. Das Urgeräusch?[19]

> Cranial hum: the sound of human origin never previously heard by the human ear—the authentic headnote—yet it sounds entirely inhuman. It fades to a dull rattle and almost dies away, relapsing into the initial, metallic crackle that causes my skull to vibrate as if splinters were starting to detach themselves from it, a frightful noise that gives me gooseflesh. Can this be the specific sound of my own cranial suture, the most primordial of all sounds?[20]

This scene, which will trigger a return of repressed memories as Karnau listens again to a sound recording he made of the murder of the Goebbels children by their parents, works a reversal: from the perpetrator of horrors to victim. Yet, this is by no means a novelistic sleight-of-hand to exculpate Karnau from his role during the Nazi regime. Rather, the novel is interested in cathecting the roles of listener and producer of the "primal sound" that Rilke's account had kept apart. This forms the basis for the complex coupling of the imaginary of inscription with sound. In this scene from *The Karnau Tapes*, the primal sound that results from the marks of the cranial sutures forcefully makes an impact on the human body. It resonates so strongly in the body that becomes its medium as well as its audience, that it threatens to destroy the material surface that had brought it forth to begin with.

This alters Rilke's model through a doubling of inscription that is no longer thought of as a sequence—as in the gramophone that registers sound as an inscription, then reproduces the sound through a tracing of the first inscription. In Beyer's rewriting of Rilke, the primal sound of the cranial sutures triggers an instantaneous feedback loop: the body does not only emit sound as a rendering of the natural marks on the skull, but the very sound it produces inscribes the body in its turn.

The Karnau Tapes insists on the double impact that links individual bodies and their contexts through sound. From Karnau's perspective, the human voice becomes an inscriptive medium even before its output is recorded by sound technology. Each and every one of the uses of the voice leaves its traces in the vocal apparatus, as knots and scars on the vocal cords, gradually altering the voice itself. This is especially true for extreme uses of the voice, such as the bellowing of a Hitler Youth *Scharführer* in imitation of Hitler's discursive voice that triggers Karnau's reflection:

> Weiß er denn nicht, daß jeder Schrei, jede so laut hervorgebrachte Äußerung auf den Stimmbändern eine kleine Narbe hinterläßt? Wissen die Menschen das denn nicht, die ihre Stimmen derart gewalttätig aufreiben, die so unvorsichtig umgehen mit ihrem Organ? Jedes Aufbrausen zeichnet sich in die überdehnten Stimmbänder ein, das narbt sich immer weiter fort, und solch ein Mal läßt sich nie wieder zum Verschwinden bringen, die Stimme bleibt markiert bis an das Lebensende.[21]
>
> Isn't he aware that every shout, every utterance of such volume, leaves a minuscule scar on the vocal cords? Aren't they aware of this, the people who so brutally erode their voices and subject them to such reckless treatment? Every such outburst imprints itself on the overtaxed vocal cords, steadily building up scar tissue. Marks of that kind can never be erased; the voice retains them until silenced forever by death.[22]

These corporeal impressions of the voice, however, are shaped by external factors. Individual voices are trained, they consciously or unconsciously imitate the prevalent tone required for a specific role, a context, or even an era, for instance the authoritarian commands of the Nazi regime. Much as external sounds resonate with and affect a body, forcing it to vibrate, making its entrails churn, the education of the voice offers another way in which sound determines the body, in which a body becomes the medium, not the agent of sound.

In Beyer's novel, sound in general and the human voice in particular become a symptom, an unresolved remainder of a traumatic past. Instead of allowing the co-presence of the self, of guaranteeing its individual identity, the voice turns into the medium of alienation. Even before any intervention of technological media, the site of the speaking "I" only echoes with absence. The primal sound of the cranial sutures in Beyer's *The Karnau Tapes* is inhuman not because it allows its audience access to an inaccessible part of reality. Rather, it renders the gap in the embodied self painfully audible. There where the self as body seems at its most originary, Beyer's adaptation of Rilke's thought experiment shows it to be other to itself, always in translation.

In its rewritings in Grünbein's and Beyer's works, Rilke's short essay has become a catalyst, triggering powerful models for processes of translation between different media. Rather than privileging one medium over another, or telling a tale of substitution, translation allows for a creative combination of different signifying systems and modes of perception. Both texts give an important position to inscription as the link between the visual and the sonic. Inscription is a mixed medium itself, between contact and touch on the one hand, and between writing as *graphé*, as the production of meaningful marks, on the other. Inscription in this sense also allows for the implicit integration of yet another medium: the literary text. Textuality no longer functions as the disavowed master medium in which other media are invoked, framed, and contained, but rather comes under scrutiny itself as yet another medium. On a different level, this allows for a reflection on representation—of reality, history, corporeality—as translation. This does not mean that representation can never do justice to some elusive, ungraspable, or ineffable realm of the real, nor that representation can completely and seamlessly make present and material what it represents. Rather, each representation embodies a viable translation, especially since it reminds us that there is no original.

What does this imply for our understanding of translation? Throughout this chapter, I have deployed the term "translation" somewhat sloppily, referring not to the transposition of text from one language to another, but to the transposition of sensory information from one medium to another, or to a movement of literary intertextuality. This sloppiness, however, has a conceptual justification, as an experiment that assesses the possibility of linking mediality and translation beyond a mere figurative extension of the term of translation to the movement between different media. Translation forces us to think about the medium, not only as a specific language, but rather as the concrete way—speech or writing, alphabet or logograph, book or computer archive—in which information materializes itself, in which it comes before our senses, as well as our understanding. Ultimately, it might prove as fruitful to think of media as and in translation as to conceive of translation itself as a medium.

Notes

1. See Jacques Derrida, *De la grammatologie* (Paris: Minuit, 1967).
2. See W. J. T. Mitchell, *Picture Theory: Essays on Verbal and Visual Representation* (Chicago: University of Chicago Press, 1995), 11–34.
3. See Jean-Luc Nancy's *A l'écoute* (Paris: Galilée, 2001), or Michel de Certeau's "L'économie scripturaire," in *L'invention du quotidien I: Arts de faire*, ed. Luce Giard, 2nd ed. (Paris: Gallimard, 1990), 195–224, and Michel de Certeau, "Vocal Utopias: Glossolalias," *Representations* 56 (Autumn 1996): 29–47. The title of the volume *Sonic Interventions*, ed. Sylvia Mieszkowski, Joy Smith, and Marijke de Valck (Amsterdam: Rodopi, 2007), provided me with the expression used above.
4. Emily Apter, *The Translation Zone: A New Comparative Literature* (Princeton, N.J.: Princeton University Press, 2006), xii.
5. Lisa Gitelman's book *Scripts, Grooves, and Writing Machines: Representing Technology in the Edison Era* (Stanford, Calif.: Stanford University Press, 1999) provides a suggestive study of the phonograph and its media context with a critical reappraisal of Kittler's theories.
6. For example, in Jörg Magenau's article "Der Körper als Schnittfläche," *Wespennest* 102 (1996): 12–20.
7. See Rainer Maria Rilke, "Ur-Geräusch," in Friedrich Kittler, *Grammophon—Film—Typewriter* (Berlin: Brinkmann & Bose, 1986), 63–69; Rainer Maria Rilke, "Primal Sound," in *Gramophone, Film, Typewriter*, trans. Geoffrey Winthrop-Young and Michael Wutz (Stanford, Calif.: Stanford University Press, 1999), 38–42.
8. Rilke, "Ur-Geräusch," 66; Rilke, "Primal Sound," 41.
9. Linguistic difference and specificity make a short appearance here, before disappearing again in a series of general reflections on translation and mediation: Arabic poetry becomes the example of a poetic tradition more attuned to sound than to vision. In the same year in which Rilke wrote his essay "Ur-Geräusch," Ezra Pound published an edited version of Ernest Fenollosa's famous essay "The Chinese Written Character as a Medium for Poetry"—another example of a poetic desideratum (here in the form of graphic concretion and mobility) expressed through another linguistic tradition, see Ernest Fenollosa and Ezra Pound, *The Chinese Written Character as a Medium for Poetry*, ed. Haun Saussy, Jonathan Stalling, and Lucas Klein (New York: Fordham University Press, 2008).
10. Other German authors, for instance Thomas Hettche in his 1992 short story collection *Inkubation* (Frankfurt am Main: Suhrkamp, 1992), have also paid attention to Rilke's essay.
11. Durs Grünbein, "Drei Briefe," in *Galilei vermißt Dantes Hölle und bleibt an den Maßen hängen: Aufsätze 1989–1995* (Frankfurt am Main: Suhrkamp, 1996), 40–54, quotation at 43. Where not indicated otherwise, translations are my own.
12. Durs Grünbein, "Den Körper zerbrechen," in *Galilei vermißt Dantes Hölle*, 75–86.
13. Grünbein, "Drei Briefe," 44.
14. Grünbein, "Neun Variationen zur Fontanelle," in *Galilei vermißt Dantes Hölle*, 246–259. This essay originally formed part of an exhibition catalog; see

Nike Bätzner and Christoph Tannert, eds., *Fontanelle: Kunst in (x) Zwischenfällen: Ausstellung Kunstspeicher Potsdam, 26. Juni bis 5*, September 1993 (Berlin: Reison, 1993).

15. Grünbein, "Neun Variationen zur Fontanelle,"259.

16. The poem, number 28 of "Variation auf kein Thema," has no title. Durs Grünbein, *Falten und Fallen* (Frankfurt am Main: Suhrkamp, 1994), 38.

17. Judith Ryan, "Das Motiv der Schädelnähte bei Durs Grünbein," in *Schreiben nach der Wende: Ein Jahrzehnt deutscher Literatur 1989–1999*, ed. Gerhard Fischer and David Roberts (Tübingen: Stauffenberg Verlag, 2001), 301–15, here 311.

18. For a thorough account of the novel as a soundscape of fascism, see Ulrich Schönherr, "Topophony of Fascism: On Marcel Beyer's *The Karnau Tapes*," *The Germanic Review* 73, no. 4 (1998): 328–48.

19. Marcel Beyer, *Flughunde* (Frankfurt am Main: Suhrkamp Taschenbuch, 1996), 227.

20. Marcel Beyer, *The Karnau Tapes*, trans. John Brownjohn (New York: Harcourt Brace, 1997), 182–83.

21. Beyer, *Flughunde*, 14–15.

22. Beyer, *The Karnau Tapes*, 6–7.

Chapter 15

✦

Translating Lola

Multiple Language Versions of *The Blue Angel* and Subtitles

Barbara Kosta

When Josef von Sternberg, film auteur and director of *The Blue Angel*, arrived at Bahnhof Zoo in Berlin on August 16, 1929, he was about to embark on a translation project of a grand, unparalleled dimension. At a press conference held at the Esplanade Hotel shortly after his arrival, he was reported to have said: "Mir ist als wäre ich in Hollywood gestorben, und nun bin ich im Himmel wieder aufgewacht"[1] (I feel as though I died in Hollywood and now woke up again in heaven). It was less the understanding of the mark he would leave on film history than a sense of the immense possibilities open to him in a multilingual environment that was begging for sound. A speaker of English and some German, the Austrian-born émigré von Sternberg accepted Erich Pommer's invitation to transition Ufa, Germany's largest film studio, into the new acoustic landscape. Emil Jannings initiated the invitation so that von Sternberg could escort the supercilious actor into the "talkies." Jannings had left Hollywood and an Oscar-winning career in fear of professional failure owing to the unintelligibility of his heavily accented English in the new sound medium.[2] After much negotiation between von Sternberg and Ufa, *The Blue Angel*, a complex and multifaceted translation project that evolved into an intermedial exercise that involved converting the patented art of the silent cinema into sound/dialogue, began with the loose adaptation for film of Heinrich Mann's 1905 novel *Professor Unrat*. *The Blue Angel* was to be filmed in two languages: in German and in English. In either language, Lola Lola, the nightclub entertainer, would vanquish the unsuspecting Immanuel Rath, a local high school teacher. Later on, her German-language conquest would appear multiply subtitled in English. The migration across linguistic and cultural boundaries of images, people, technological know-how, capital, and scripts in 1929 was just the beginning of the translation project in which *The Blue Angel* would participate. Of interest to me in the framework of this chapter are the various subtitled versions that emerged with each new release, and more generally the significance of the subtitle as a vehicle for entry into the filmic world of the foreign space and imagination.

Scholars have amply mined the differences between the German and English versions of *The Blue Angel* in terms of the varied linguistic performances of the actors, the plot adjustments to accommodate the English-speaking version (in the English version Lola is British and Rath is an English teacher), in addition to toning down the visual excesses for a more straightforward plot that tames the erotic vitality of the film. Peter Hogue and Patrice Petro allege that the English-language version compromised the provocative sexual innuendo and the emotional, psychological complexity of the German-language version.[3] Somewhat ironic in the context of a film that fetishizes the multiplication of Lola, the English-language version of *The Blue Angel* in most discussions never measures up the to German-language versions and as a "remake" or copy lives as an inferior by-product of the original. Like any copy, the English-language version continues to be compared to its better authentic half, even though, as Petro points out, *The Blue Angel* was intentionally designed as a "'two-originals-no copy' venture into foreign-language filmmaking."[4] Its German cast and crew, its production history and its story, arguably frame the film within a set of national and cultural affiliations, despite importing a Hollywood director, himself a transnational hybrid. Asserting its legitimacy as the original, the German-language version bears subtitles—even English subtitles, which further suggests an assumed lack on the part of the German film's lesser other. To date, at least three English-subtitled versions exist. I will focus on the 103-minute Janus VHS release of 1986, and the more recent newly restored 106-minute DVD release of 2001.[5] Curiously, neither of the English-subtitled versions of *The Blue Angel* refers back to the 1929 English-language version of the film for its subtitles—both subtitlers seem to deny the linguistic cross-dressing of the multilingual antecedent. As is the fate of many subtitlers whose names are suppressed by the expediencies of the film industry, the 1980s Janus release remains anonymously subtitled; Robert Gray is credited as the subtitler of the 2001 release.[6]

The multiple incarnations of *The Blue Angel* thus make this film particularly fertile in regard to translation studies. It is illustrative of the vagaries of translation and translatability, and of the pressures placed on an industry that has a history of depending on uninterrupted linguistic transfers and transnational flows. The undertheorized aspect of cinema—the subtitle—then and now serves as an essential vehicle for the sustainability of the international market.

Before the technological development of subtitling, however, multiple-language film versions were believed to be the most efficient means to sustain the industry's international multilingual markets and audiences.[7] Film moguls in the United States and Europe had been spoiled previously by the unencumbered linguistic border crossings of their silent cultural wares. Sometimes the production of multilanguage versions required filming with the same cast as in *The Blue Angel;* other times it required a different cast and even different directors who reproduced the same script but translated for the target audience.[8] Between 1930 and 1934, London and Paris became hubs of multilanguage productions with Berlin as an occasional site. It is interesting to note that "in Germany between 1929–1931, 22% of 251 features were MLV (mostly from UA); between 1931–1932, 20% were subtitled, 10% dubbed and 70% MLVs."[9] Actors whose voices were sound-worthy and who spoke multiple languages, like Berlin-born Marlene Dietrich, were well positioned in the new acoustic milieu of cinema. After filming *The Blue Angel*, Dietrich, in fact, left for Hollywood as a German speaker and anticipated Paramount diva. She signed a five-year contract to make six more films with von Sternberg. It is said that she was to perform in the German version of the 1930 film *Paramount on Parade*, which successfully paraded out multiple-language versions with various directors.[10] The German version, however, was never made.

Before considering two English-subtitled versions of *The Blue Angel*, I wish to draw attention to the value of the 1929 English-language version as an early polyglot film. Reflecting the film industry's struggle with multilingualism in the era of sound, the English-language version features an acoustic collage of English and German, and emerges as one of the first, albeit serendipitous, experiments in polyglot films. It yields to the foreign in ways that the "original" does not have to. Frederic M. Sacket, the newly appointed American ambassador to Germany at the time, praised the polyglot venture, after visiting the Ufa atelier in Neubabelsberg on February 13, 1930, to view portions of the English-language version of *The Blue Angel*. The reputable film journal *Film Kurier* reported that the ambassador was "Besonders erfreut . . . darüber, dass die ufa sich bei der englischen Version nicht sklavisch an eine Übersetzung gebunden und fernerhin den Mut gefunden habe, bei typisch deutschen Charakteren absichtlich darauf zu sehen, dass diese Schauspieler bewusst in ihrer Sprache den deutschen Akzent beibehielten, statt auswendig gelernte englische Sätze tadellos, aber farblos wiederzugeben" (Especially pleased that the Ufa did not slavishly bind the English-language version to the translation, and furthermore, had the courage to have actors consciously retain their German accents to represent typically German characters, instead of having them memorize English sentences that are flawlessly reproduced but spoken without color).[12] American reviews of the film's reception confirm that the American "audience accepted the German without a murmur."[13] An interesting word choice in light of the early talkie. Sacket's observation, I believe, is prescient and resonates in unexpected ways with the challenges that multilingualism presented in an international film market that was adjusting to the new sound technologies. At stake are also the larger issues of translatability, of preserving the "foreign," and an approach to translation and subtitling that until today continues to put extraordinary pressures on the film industry.

At this point, however, I yield to Lola's admonishment in the German-language version, "Mensch, hör doch auf mit dem Englischen quatsch" (Stop with the English nonsense) when Rath's rebellious student confesses his amorous inclinations toward Lola and declares "I love you," and turn to two English-subtitled versions of the German-language film.[14]

In deference to a film whose emotional center is seduction, I will forego a description of the artisanal aspects of subtitling, the mechanics of transferring text to film, which subtitler Henri Béhar submits is "about as seductive as plumbing."[15] Suffice it to say that tailoring and distilling language to fit within a set number of frames has (deceptively) subordinated the subtitle to its technological function, as a mechanical task, that some critics view as verging on violence.[16] Experienced frequently as an amputation of dialogue, especially in cases of grossly misaligned translations and located at the bottom of the screen in a perpetual state of wanting to measure up to the original, the subtitle often suffers from its own inefficiencies that add to its precarious status. Subtitles have been blamed for detracting from and presenting an obstacle to cinematic pleasure, especially among those viewers who champion dubbing. Germany, for instance, has had a long tradition of dubbing films (except for foreign films on ARTE and in film festivals). Yet, in spite of the inherent deficiencies and annoyances of the subtitle and the biases against them, the subtitle plays a significant role. Its value results from attitudes toward cultural differences and the sustainability of the original language. Indeed, the subtitle, I argue, acknowledges "the foreign" and positions the spectator at the threshold of the profilmic event.

What is more, it provides entry into a "foreign" world that is conveyed as much in language production as it is in images and tonalities. With subtitles the foreign world maintains its integrity, remains intact and even resistant to appropriation. The subtitle acts as both a productive barrier and point of entry into the world represented in the film that retains its "foreign" signification. It acknowledges the world's cultural and linguistic diversity, an aspect especially important in light of the long history of exclusions implicit in the promotion of monolingualism. In *Subtitles: On the Foreignness of Film*, a collection of articles, the editors, filmmaker Atom Egoyan (director of *The Sweet Hereafter* and *Ararat*) and critic Ian Balfour, astutely recognize the complex function of subtitles and their significance beyond the needs of the global market. Subtitles, they contend, "are only the most visual markers of the way in which films engage, in direct and oblique fashion, pressing matters of difference, otherness, and translation."[17]

Acutely aware of the subtitle's extratextual significance and the vast qualitative differences in subtitling practices, Abé Nornes in *Cinema Babel* urges that we become more attentive to the value of subtitles and "reconsider the mode of translation through which our cinematic experiences with the foreign are mediated."[18] His meditation on subtitles begins with the figurative killing of the incompetent subtitler who relishes a shorthand approach and whose audiences intuit that something is amiss. Bill Murray's character, Bob Harris, in Sofia Coppola's 2003 *Lost in Translation*, for instance, replicates the bewilderment of the cinematic spectator/subtitle reader, who, after observing a lengthy conversation in Japanese, must make do with the linguistic morsel served that whets his appetite for a felicitous translation.[19] In disbelief Murray's character asks, "Is that all he said?"

In an effort to offer an analytical framework for the much undertheorized subtitle and draw subtitles out of the backwaters of film studies, Nornes identifies two classes of subtitles: the corrupt and the abusive. "Corrupt subtitles," according to Nornes, strive to domesticate the foreign and overlay the film with the cultural foil of the target language. "Abusive subtitles," in contrast, reflect the inner spirit of the text and are attuned to the connotative operations of translation instead of fetishizing the literal transfer of language. The abusive subtitles are more intuitive and bold. More ambitiously and more relevantly, the abusive subtitles acknowledge and maintain the foreign "accent"; they defer to the untranslatable while providing access. The abusive subtitle relies on an innovative, less inhibited translation, a daring rewrite that simultaneously preserves and promotes the encounter with difference. "Corrupt subtitlers," Nornes contends, "disavow the violence of the subtitle while abusive translators revel in it."[20] Despite my reservations about Nornes's word selection and the arguable ironic mistranslation of the French "abuse," the descriptive distinction between the two approaches to subtitling offers a productive point of entry to my discussion of the differences in the two English-subtitled versions of *The Blue Angel*.[21]

The subtitling differences essentially lie in the relationship to the original. The 2001 English subtitled version, I argue, harnesses the 1929 classic Weimar film in a contemporary idiom, while the earlier 1980s version maintains a textual openness that preserves and elicits the film's seductive innuendo. Recalling the American ambassador's appreciation of the English-language version of *The Blue Angel*, it may be said that the more creative subtitles of the 1980s resist the impulse to translate in a way that "enslaves" the translated text to the original. These qualitative differences in the English subtitling of *The Blue Angel* could be seen as just as divergent as Lola's role as mass culture entertainer and her self-identification as artiste on the stage of the cabaret. As to her notion of herself as artiste, Kiepert quips: "She has a funny notion of her profession."

Consequently, the 2001 subtitles provide the contemporary audience with a complete translation of the text. Even the most remote catcalls from Lola's audience during her performances are translated. Converting each translatable utterance into easily consumable meaning by serving linguistic equivalents in an effort to be loyal, and "smoothing the rough edges of foreignness" for the sake of readability, the 2001 DVD release insists on transparency, and forfeits ambiguity and that certain "je ne sais quoi"—about which Lola sings in "Ich bin von Kopf bis Fuss auf Liebe eingestellt" / "Falling in Love Again." Accordingly, all of the songs in the 2001 English-subtitled version are translated.[22] So vested in the process of transparency and translatability, this release also features a commentary by the Dietrich Collection impresario Werner Sudendorf. His running interpretation and description of the images for English-speaking audiences attempts to convey the flavor of the 1920s setting, the historical context and subtexts.

The 2001 English subtitled release drives Lola's cabaret milieu into an underworld that is punctuated by the use of urban slang. When Lola catches Rath staring at her with a coy fascination, while she applies her makeup, she jocularly asks: "Schöne Augen, wa?" The 2001 subtitle translates her flirtatious query as "Pretty Peepers?" This translation presumably goes for an edgier, more piquant reproduction of Lola's Berlin dialect, as opposed to the simpler "Nice eyes, huh?" of the earlier English subtitled version. Furthermore, when an enraged Rath accuses Kiepert, the magician and cabaret troupe leader, of being a "Kuppler" after Kiepert encourages Lola to drink champagne with the inebriated Captain Thomas, the harsh accusation translates as "pimp." While capitalizing on the insult, the potential immoral milieu of the cabaret, and Lola's dubious role, the translation strips away any doubt of Lola's genre and domesticates the film at the expense of her role as vamp and agent of her own performance. Brought into proximity with the word "pimp," Lola relinquishes her feminine mystique that is made for love or her iconicity of erotic desire and is debased as a commodity exchanged between men. Admittedly, the translation projects Rath's ire and alludes to the financial arrangements of the cabaret owner and the cabaret troupe leader, but it significantly compromises Lola's image as elusive, untranslatable boundless eroticism. Equally unsatisfying is the earlier English subtitled version that tames the charged interaction between Rath and Kiepert with the translation of "Kuppler" as "matchmaker." The truth undoubtedly lies somewhere in-between these English renditions. Other examples of the divergent inflections in the two subtitled versions are the 2001 translation of "Professorchen" as "Teach," and "Weib" as the more slang, English "dame." Additionally, Rath, who is a teacher at the local high school, is promoted to college professor in the 2001 translation, dismissing the cultural and social context of his rank. When Kiepert releases Rath from a straitjacket, he states in resigned disbelief: "Komm her. Das hast du nötig gehabt. Ich verstehe dich auch nicht. Du bist ein feiner, gebildeter Mann. Alles wegen ein Weib." The earlier English subtitled versions offers: I don't get you . . . a man of culture , ... all for a woman." The 2001 release reads:

> Come on.
> You asked for it.
> I don't get it, an educated man like you . . .
> All for some dame.

The earlier 1980s subtitle conveys Kiepert's inability to decipher Rath's breakdown and shows sympathy for the misguided bourgeois who has failed. The 2001 release places the blame on Rath for degrading himself. He is at fault and must bear the consequences.[23]

The general domestication of the dialogue in the 2001 release, as the perceived task of the subtitler, reveals an approach to translation that seeks to tone down the foreign for the sake of full accessibility. It resonates somewhat with Professor Rath's insistence on his student's unaccented pronunciation of the English article "the," by forcing a pencil into a student's mouth to effect a more authentic pronunciation. This scene unwittingly plays on Jannings's own struggles with English. "Zähne auseinander," he commands in the German-language version. The 1980s subtitled release reads, "Separate your teeth"; the more recent 2001 subtitle offers "Open your mouth." Whether with separated teeth or with an open mouth, the scene rehearses the travails of translation/subtitling, the conversion from one language to another, and the irrepressible accent as the trace of the foreign, despite the effort to extinguish it.

In contrast to the domesticating impulse of the 2001 release, the 1980s subtitles appear indebted to Lola's allures. They leave open to the imagination the untranslatable and play with linguistic innuendo. The subtitles in this version seem to be more self-reflective of their own limitations and the fragility of language in view of the compelling narrative of desire that sparks Rath's tragic downfall. In this version, much of the already sparse dialogue remains untranslated. The translator/subtitler relies on the multisensory medium of cinema in this version. In contrast to the 2001 subtitles, all of Lola's songs remain untranslated in the original. The subtitle here undoubtedly lives in tandem with the larger context of the profilmic event—the scene that the camera is recording. A master of mise-en-scène, von Sternberg saturates Lola's space with the accessories of seduction, costumes, the reproduction of images that literally multiply Lola (posters and postcards), and her tantalizing performances at the Blue Angel and other nightclubs. Undeniably an emblem of love, Lola is as much promiscuous as she is singularly sincere. In this 1980s English subtitled version, Lola "bewitches" Rath's students rather than "corrupts" them. In German, her charms "verführen" the men who always return to her.

Most notably in the 1980s English-subtitled release, the subtitler opts for a stylized use of fragmented sentences followed by ellipses, an idiosyncrasy which is as remarkable sometimes as the subtitler's choice of what to leave in the original and what enters the target language.[24] When Rath drops Lola's cigarettes and climbs under the dressing table to retrieve them, Lola teases him: "When you reach your destination, drop me a card . . ." The subtitler inserts an ellipsis, effecting an invitation to coproduce meaning in the sense of Roland Barthes's writerly text, to fill in the gaps, so to speak. Quite tellingly, Barthes uses the ellipses in *A Lover's Discourse* to introduce his mediation on "I am engulfed, I succumb . . . ," which resembles Rath's own state of amorous longing and engulfment in Lola's song and aura.[25] The more creative use of ellipses may exemplify what Nornes views as an abusive subtitle that aims for a more poetic engagement with the original. Arguably, the many omissions indicate a meaning beyond what a subtitle can translate in a film whose emotional center is the intricate interplay of seduction and desire, of disavowal and amorous fantasies. Moreover, at the end of a sentence, according to a connotative iteration, the ellipsis may signal a feeling of "melancholy longing." "Melancholy longing" indeed expresses Rath's own unfilled desires as the realities of his liaison with Lola plummet him into despair, while also reflecting the state of potential impotence ascribed to subtitles. Goethe's insight on translation resonates here: "Translators are like busy matchmakers who praise half-veiled beauty as being very lovely: they arouse an irrepressible desire for the original."[26] For the subtitle, this wanting condition is more acute considering that as a translation, it is embedded in the original in a way that other translated media are not. It is measured constantly against the original and never enjoys a life of its own.

Besides, no matter how efficient they may be, subtitles are unable to convey subtle differences in the characters' accented speech, which, Naficy insists "may imply important differences in power and other relations."[27] While Naficy refers to a different type of accent, his insights are significant too in *The Blue Angel.* Indeed, the differences in Lola's and Rath's language usages convey class and cultural differences that are worlds apart and that catalyze the dramatic and tragic trajectory of their relationship. Her working-class Berlin dialect collides with Rath's somewhat archaic, but precise German diction. She is a product of modernity; Rath is a figure of nineteenth-century ideals.

Yet, in spite of the precarious status of the subtitle and its deficiencies, its performance in the complex economy of desire and difference told in the foreign stories we watch is essential. Subtitles facilitate the exploration of foreign worlds and allow for the cadences of the other world to be heard. Their status as a "foreign object" in the original text directs spectators back to the visual economy of the original as a reminder of the spectator's "otherness." Subtitles guard against the seamless domestication of the culture of the film and against appropriating the images as part of the cultural, linguistic "home" of the target culture. They allow for proximity while maintaining distance, deterritorializing specatators, placing them somewhere between home and abroad, somewhere between the translatable and the untranslatable, within a spectrum of knowledges that define cultural products that move across borders. They reside in the intersection of an essentially intercultural space.

Thus in spite of the limitations of subtitles, their intrusions and their infidelities, they engage spectators in a potential love affair with the foreign, resituating them self-reflexively, and averting the erasure of the foreign.

Subtitles allow for hearing diverse voices and for diverse places to speak. They allow for an encounter with difference and an opportunity to infuse with empathy places beyond our own familiar repertoire. They allow for border crossings. Of course, the demands of the film industry, just like those of life, exact pressures that disrupt romances and the encounter with foreign spaces. The deceptions of love that lead Rath into a downward spiral cost him his career and life in a time in which modernity called for new sensibilities. In a new incarnation of Lola in the 1959 Hollywood remake starring Curd Jürgens as Rath and May Britt as Lola, von Sternberg's lush visuals and plot are sanitized through the conventions of realism to the point of misrecognition.[28] Rath returns to his milieu rehabilitated after the sympathetic principal of his old school rescues him from the femme fatale and sends him to a sanatorium. The remake participates in a disavowal of subtitles and speaks to a preference for remaking popular foreign films as English-language films. The "foreign" in the remade *Blue Angel* resides in the actors' accents, the reconstructed space of a German town and characters' names as a perceptible, but unsatisfying nod to the early multilanguage versions and the multiply subtitled versions that followed.

Notes

1. Werner Sudendorf, "Chronik zur Entstehung des Films," in *Der blaue Engel: Die Drehbuchentwürfe*, ed. Luise Dirscherl, Gunther Nickel, and Werner Sudendorf (St. Ingbert: Röhrig Universitätsverlag, 2000), 68–69. Sudendorf provides a timeline for the various incarnations of *The Blue Angel,* which is paraphrased here to show the migration of the film and its various linguistic iterations. In 1930 Carl Winston receives 800 RM for four songs in English. In May 1930, a resynchronization and new shots of the English version are undertaken. The English version premiers in London and in August, the production of the French version of *The Blue Angel* is approved, and a subtitled version is under consideration. The French premier of *The Blue Angel* on September 22 is followed by the American premier at the Rialto in New York on December 5 with the screening of the English version.

2. In a review of Susan Orlean's book, *Rin Tin Tin: The Life and Legend,* Jennifer Schuessler points out that the German shepherd ran a stiff competition for the Oscar for best actor in 1929 with more actual votes than Jannings. The German actor, however, received the award. Jennifer Schuessler, "Best Friend Forever," review of *Rin Tin Tin: The Life and Legend* by Susan Orlean, *New York Times Book Review*, October 23, 2011, BR1.

3. See Patrice Petro's article "*The Blue Angel* in Multiple-Language Versions: The Inner Thighs of Miss Dietrich," in *Dietrich Icon,* ed. Gerd Gemünden and Mary K. Desjardins (Durham, N.C.: Duke University Press, 2007), 141–61. See also Peter Hogue, "True Blue," *Film Comment* 30, no. 2 (March 1994): 38–43. Additionally, the 2001 DVD release allows viewers to compare the two versions by placing the English and German frames side-by-side.

4. Petro, "*The Blue Angel*," 154. Petro contends that the differences in the German and English versions are a result of production practices, codes, and audience tastes.

5. In the context of this chapter, I refer to two English subtitled releases, the DVD and VHS releases: Josef von Sternberg, dir. *The Blue Angel* (Kino International Corp., 2001). This is a special two-disc release. The German version with English subtitles is 106 minutes and the English version is 94 minutes. Josef von Sternberg, dir., *The Blue Angel* (Janus 1986). Yet another English subtitled version is the 1993 VHS Kino International release subtitled by Tassilo Schneider. The subtitles appear in orange print with different word choices for many scenes than the subtitles discussed in the scope of this chapter.

6. Robert Gray, subtitler, works for Kinograph and Vicomedia 10/2001.

7. See Chris Wahl, "Babel's Business—On Ufa's Multiple Language Film Versions, 1929–1933," in *The Many Faces of Weimar Cinema: Rediscovering Germany's Film Legacy*, ed. Christian Rogowski (Rochester, N.Y.: Camden House, 2010), 235–49.

8. Abé Mark Nornes, *Cinema Babel: Translating Global Cinema* (Minneapolis: University of Minnesota Press, 2007), 137.

9. Ibid., 139.

10. Malene Sheppard Skæved, *Dietrich* (London: House, 2003), 66.

12. Sudendorf, "Chronik," 64 (my translation).

13. "*The Blue Angel*," *Foreign Film News* (December 10, 1930), 7.

14. The 2001 subtitle reads "stop the English drivel," while the other subtitle offers "cut that English nonsense."

15. Henri Béhar, "Cultural Ventriloquism," in *Subtitles: On the Foreignness of Film*, ed. Atom Egoyan and Ian Balfour (Cambridge, Mass.: MIT Press and Alphabet City, 2004), 79–88, here 81. There are rules that must be followed so that the subtitle appears within a set number of frames. Subtitles must therefore be kept short, succinct, and paradoxically invisible. Some subtitles require speed reading. For those who understand both the original language and the subtitled language—they become amateur translators who more often than not shake their heads at the word choices—or raise their eyelashes [*sic*] as a subtitle I once read claimed.

16. See Nornes, "For an Abusive Subtitling," *Film Quarterly* 52, no. 3 (Spring 1999): 17–34.

17. Egoyan and Balfour, introduction to *Subtitles: On the Foreignness of Film*, 21.

18. Nornes, *Cinema Babel*, 447.

19. Sofia Coppola, director, *Lost in Translation* (2003).

20. Nornes, *Cinema Babel*, 448.

21. Philip E. Lewis, in fact, points to the flawed translation of Derrida's term "abuse" when insisting "a good translation must always commit abuses" ("Une 'bonne' traduction doit toujour abuser"). Quoted in Amresh Sinha, "The Use and Abuse of Subtitles," in *Subtitles: On the Foreignness of Film*, 188. The English translation lacks the sensibility evoked in the French connotation of "false, deceptive, and misleading." Additionally, the association with harm and injury presents an insurmountable obstacle to the creative act for which he calls.

22. Lola's songs yield to linguistic control in this subtitled version of her performances. She seeks a regular man in the English subtitled version—in the German-language version, she actually desires "einen richtigen Mann"—a real man. "Ich bin von Kopf bis Fuss auf Liebe eingestellt" is subtitled using songwriter Sammy Lerner's lyrics "Falling in Love Again," which Dietrich occasionally took on tour. The translation/subtitle conveys the propensity for serial love affairs. Yet, how can one expect loyalty of the subtitle when the performance confesses to infidelity? In contrast, Lola's songs in the earlier version remain unsubtitled. The spectator is bathed in the pure sound of the siren, her voice is nature, pleasure, and temptation, all of which threaten the quotidian male.

23. In the 1993 Kino release, the subtitler Tassilo Schneider offers the following translation: "Come on. Was that necessary? I don't understand you . . . a fine, well-educated man. All this because of a woman."

24. It is quite amusing that this sparsely subtitled version, so attentive to the dramatic arc of the film, provides a subtitle for a customer's order, which is yelled out, to convey perhaps the flavor of the setting: "Liverwurst with trimmings."

25. Roland Barthes, *A Lover's Discourse: Fragments*, trans. Richard Howard (New York: Hill and Wang, 1978), 10. For a discussion of Rath's surrender to Lola's performance, see Barbara Kosta, *Willing Seduction: The Blue Angel, Marlene Dietrich and Mass Culture* (New York: Berghahn, 2009).

26. Quoted as an epigraph from Goethe's *Maxims and Reflections* (1826) in Abé Mark Nornes, "For an Abusive Subtitling," 17. The original reads: "Übersetzer sind als geschäftige Kuppler anzusehen die uns eine halbverschleierte Schöne als höchst liebenswürdig anpreisen, sie erregen eine unwiderstehliche Neigung nach dem Original." Johann Wolfgang von Goethe, *Sämtliche Werke nach Epochen seines Schuffens*, ed. Karl Richter (Munich: Hanser Verlag, 1997), 17: 773.

27. Hamid Naficy, "Epistolarity and Textuality in Accented Films," in Egoyan and Balfour, *Subtitles: On the Foreignness of Film*, 131–52.

28. Edward Dmytryk, director, *The Blue Angel* (1959).

Chapter 16

Five Maps of Translations of Shakespeare

Tom Cheesman, Kevin Flanagan,
Jan Rybicki, and Stephan Thiel

For Eddy Cheesman

SHAKESPEARE:
. . . Iagogogo!

—James Joyce, *Ulysses*[1]

Si correctes et légitimes qu'elles soient, et quelque *droit* qu'on leur reconnaisse, [les traductions] sont toutes désajustées, comme injustes dans l'écart qui les *affecte* . . . (The translations themselves thus find themselves "out of joint." However correct and legitimate they may be and whatever right one may acknowledge them to have, they are all disadjusted, since unjust in the gap that affects them.)

—Jacques Derrida, *Spectres de Marx*[2]

Shakespeare's works present a paradigmatic case of "the untranslatable," as defined by Barbara Cassin: "that which we don't stop (not) translating."[3] Everything is translatable; everything *can* be translated, but always with both loss and gain. Cassin's "(not)" refers to quanta of potential meaning which *are* in the original, but *not* in the translation, *and* which are *not* in the original, but *are* in the translation. This applies to all translating. However, only certain works *must* be translated, as a matter of target culture fact, *again and again*, with correspondingly greater losses and gains, on each occasion, accruing over time. The untranslatable is this subset of the translatable, marked by compulsive repetition. Repetition-with-difference in acts of *re*translation displays, in Sharon Deane-Cox's words, "a mercurial inconstancy with regard to frequency, behaviour and motivations," and since retranslation's multiples "relate not only to the source text but to each other," they present "an intricate, entangled network of influences and agents."[4] Theorizing and studying multiple translations of literary, philosophical, religious or other works is challenging. In Shakespeare's case the "field" is more like an ocean, vast, deep, of infinite variegation.[5] Retranslations of his work in the German language alone—where his cult devotees long since proclaimed him to *be* German: "ours," the "third national classic" with Goethe and Schiller—defy oversight.[6] This chapter introduces some experimental digital aids to navigation: "maps" in various formats to help us explore, think about, and analyze large sets of retranslations in new ways.[7]

The standard approach to (re)translations is to delineate the context of origin of each one, so as to understand its raisons d'être (intercultural and cultural, social, institutional, personal) before proceeding to the text itself, and its relation to its original(s). Deane-Cox's study in English retranslations of Flaubert and Sand, in this mode, refutes the simplistic, optimistic view that over time they tend to get better, or "closer" to the source text. She finally calls for genetic criticism, in order to understand each retranslation as its own "unfolding process of creation" (*Retranslation,* 233), documented in drafts. But where retranslations are multitudinous, larger-scale commonalities, differences and transformations will be lost from view, if we focus ever closer on singularities. Close reading is a sine qua non in humanities work, but never sufficient. Where retranslations are multitudinous, they can make a corpus, and corpora call for digital approaches.

This chapter presents a website collecting retranslations of a crux, and five corpus "maps": (1) a table comparing language-cultures' decisions at that crux; (2) an interactive time-map of retranslations corpus metadata; (3) a stylometric comparison of retranslations; (4) maps of segment alignments between an original and retranslations; and (5) an interface which maps diversity among retranslations, segment by segment, and maps this diversity back onto the original. These maps have been produced in the course of work with a corpus of some forty German versions of *Othello* dating from 1766 to 2010.[8] The corpus includes various genres: print-published reading editions and study editions, and unpublished theater scripts;[9] a majority of "close" (speech-by-speech) translations, and several "free" adaptations. "Version" is a handy term for what may need to be generically distinguished as "translations," "adaptations," "rewritings," "appropriations," "rescriptings," and so on.[10] Hence the project name: "Version Variation Visualization."

Each version of any utterance "recodes in the target language *only part* of the initial translatability potential of the utterance vis-à-vis that language, and a *different part*, at that."[11] What Gideon Toury means here by "translatability potential" is a theoretical range of possible translations, in a given target context. Changes in that context—a new poetics, new stage language conventions, new political ideologies, new media affordances—will change a work's translatability. Translatability is a theoretical construct based in intercultural traffic, but oriented to the target culture. It has a material correlate. In any language at any moment, the sum of actual, extant retranslations, far greater than its parts, maps the actual dimensions of translatability within the space of translatability potential. It is an invisible map, until we can see retranslations as a corpus.[12]

Lawrence Venuti and others restrict the concept "retranslation" to new versions created in awareness of others.[13] In English first of all (historically), every new edition or production of a work of Shakespeare is a new "translation," bearing traces of its creators' return—however cursory—to what they know of the archive of previous versions, in order to lodge something different in the future's archive. Likewise in languages other than English, retranslations are explicitly or implicitly in dialogue with precursors—"antagonistic, revelatory or reverential" dialogue (Deane-Cox, *Retranslation*, 21)—through marked or unmarked textual differences. But the empirical dialogues of translators are less than the material dialogues of translations.

Shakespeare translators and adaptors working in a language such as German might consult several scholarly English-language editions, and several preexisting translations; or they might not even look at an English text, but compile an existing version and their own invention. Questions of plagiarism aside,[14] these are all in principle "legitimate" strategies for creating a new version, for whatever purpose, whether it innovates or reinscribes prior interpretations.[15] Digital maps of a corpus can reveal traces of creators' reworkings of precursors' versions: genealogies. But versions also differ from *all* other versions, past and future, in their textual materiality. The network of *material* differences and similarities among version-texts is distinct from and far larger than the networks of *empirical* affiliation among them and their creators. So corpus study offers a wider perspective on target cultures: how they are or were differentiated, how they changed and are changing, irrespective of individual agents' knowledge.

More controversially, if corpus study can map a work's actualized translatability potential in several language-cultural contexts, then we can conceive of mapping its cross-cultural translatability potential: its general translatability. At the same time, making digital retranslations corpora at least in part publicly accessible will not only open up new research directions. It will change the conditions in which retranslators and re-adaptors work by giving them a far larger archive, explorable in new ways.[16] Digital tools can also help us read texts in languages we do not know—both though machine translation and by connecting us with people to ask—so an archive of retranslations can transform work in any target language. But we need good archive maps, to help us read both closely and at distance; perhaps above all, to let us shift smoothly between different reading scales. The first "map" shown here reads very closely—just two lines–but on a global scale.

At www.delightedbeauty.org, worldwide translations of one Shakespeare couplet are being collected: the Duke of Venice's parting couplet in *Othello*, addressed to Brabantio, drawing a line under the senator's protest against his daughter Desdemona's marriage to the hero:

If virtue no delighted beauty lack,
Your son-in-law is far more fair than black.[17]

These fourteen (or sixteen) words, dense with puns, make a fascinating study in (un)translatability: the way translations can be both idiosyncratic and overdetermined by shifts in language, discourse, and ideology, pertaining in this case not just to race, but also to gender, social rank, and national politics—and that in every translating language, including English. Crowd-sourcing has so far gathered some two hundred versions, in thirty languages. The site maps an emergent global Shakespeare translation community as much as translations of the couplet.[18] Many of the fifty or so contributors—such as Bahman Zarrinjooee and Leila Baradaran Jamili, based in Iran—supply translations of their own as well as versions from their bookshelves, all with English back-translations, and context and comments. Some contributors debate the interpretation of the translations or the accuracy of back-translations. Polish and Korean, Romani and Mandarin versions, and their readers and rewriters, are in visible virtual proximity.

Translators' choices not only refract national and local cultural histories.[19] They express a far greater diversity of interpretations than would occur to any one reader, especially a monoglot. In Ruth Morse's words: "the translation of metaphor may help the native speaker to alert herself to secondary (or even primary) associations in a text"; translations "can be just as thought-provoking when they arouse reservations"; and they can "preserve what has been lost from the original" by change in English (the you/thou distinction is among her examples).[20] Dirk Delabastita asks: "Can a translation unearth new meanings in the source text and so become constitutive of it?"[21] In this case, clearly they can. Different translations, in mining the Duke's couplet for meanings, cast the Duke, Brabantio, Desdemona, Othello, and not least the audience as different characters, in different relations, in different imagined Venices, in different theaters and different present-day real worlds. To understand each translator's decisions fully, of course we must closely read their whole text, and learn about its contexts of production and use, just as in English we must decode and recode the whole play, and its history, to say what the couplet "means," how it should or can be read or acted. But this does not preclude considering the diversity of translators' choices as a phenomenon in itself, and using digital technical and social resources to map this phenomenon.

A couple of examples here will set up the argument of the next section. In most German translations of the couplet, the Duke's utterance is that of an idealized, or more rarely satirized, sovereign. He calls on his subjects and the audience to unite against race prejudice, or he lends it his sanction, or he seems to do both at once. The version by Wolf Graf Baudissin, first published in 1832 in the quasi-canonical "Schlegel-Tieck" edition, adopted a strategy of de-coloring and de-humoring (which had been pioneered by Schiller and

Voss, collaborating in 1805)[22] in order to establish a dignified, idealized sovereign:

> Wenn man die Tugend muß als schön erkennen, Dürft Ihr nicht häßlich Euren Eidam nennen.[23]
>
> If one must recognize virtue as beautiful, you may not call your son-in-law ugly.

The choice "häßlich" (ugly) for "black" activates the theme of Othello's blackness as visible horror which runs through many of Iago's, Roderigo's, and Brabantio's speeches, and is also implied in Desdemona's line: "I saw Othello's visage in his mind." But Baudissin avoids explicit reference to color and race, and couples this with a shift in the Duke's rhetoric. Rather than making witty-clumsy, quasi-syllogistic wordplay,[24] he issues a firm ethical command. This strategy had consequences for other retranslations.

The most lauded living German Shakespeare retranslator, Frank Günther, gives us an *Othello* committed to antiracism. Günther shifts the rhetoric differently, to a conditional. His Duke speaks as an idealized contemporary liberal German head of state, giving what he knows to be toxic racist doxa a sarcastic twist:

> Gäbs helle Haut für Edelmut als Preis, Dann wär Ihr Schwiegersohn statt schwarz reinweiß.[25]
>
> If light skin were a prize for noble-mindedness, then your son-in-law would be pure white instead of black.

Versions by leftist writers, critical of the state, such as Erich Fried or Feridun Zaimoglu, posit a far from liberal Duke. The anticolonialist Fried has: "nicht dunkel sondern Gold" ("not dark but gold")—the noun implying a valued commodity at least as much as a valued man.[26] Zaimoglu and Senkel, whose 2003 adaptation references contemporary European neo-fascist movements, has "eher edel als schwarz" ("more noble than black"), at once offering and denying membership in the elite in-group.[27] We can see historical sense in such individual mutations, but do they collectively tell us anything about the culture in which they occur?

Given a corpus such as is displayed online at "Delighted Beauty," we can "map" choices and so discover patterns of synchronic difference between language-cultures. Figure 16.1 compares twenty-two different French and thirty-five different German translations of the keywords "fair" and "black" in the Duke's couplet. Apparently significant differences in proportions are highlighted in bold (empty cells, meaning absence of examples, are also significant). What do we see? The wider range of choices in German

'... far more fair than black'

'BLACK'	French famous (11)	French obscure (11)	German famous (11)	German obscure (21)
<null>	1	1	5	2
black	10	10	4	18
dark			2	1
ugly			1	

'FAIR'	French famous (11)	French obscure (11)	German famous (11)	German obscure (21)
<null>	2		2	1
beautiful	4	3	1	12
white		2	4	4
bright	1	3	1	2
agreeable	2	2	1	
blond				2
other	2	1	4	1

Figure 16.1. Comparing translation cultures: a table of choices for a crux

("black" = "dark," "black" = "ugly," "fair" = "blond," "fair" = "*other*")[28] might be accounted for by the larger sample. Consider the totals: the narrow columns. There is a disproportion in "fair"= "white": much commoner in all German (8/35: 0.22) than in all French translations (2/20: 0.1). But the distributions of choices are largely similar. A further analytic step reveals a far bigger difference.

In both languages, translators were sorted into two groups: "authors" (those with a reputation, a "name" in institutionalized cultural memory, or currently celebrated), and "others" (the obscure).[29] This division is not watertight, but it is analytically useful. It reveals no difference within French, but very significant differences within German. Reputed German author-translators are much more likely not to translate "black" at all ("black" = "*null*"), and far more likely to choose alternatives to "black" = "black" or "fair" = "beautiful," which are by far the commonest choices of "other" translators.

What accounts for the difference between the *dividedness* of German translation culture and the *consistency* of French translation culture? Two explanations can be suggested. First, retranslation studies inspired by Bourdieu emphasize agonistic struggles for cultural capital.[30] Shakespeare's status is very different in the two cultures: in German, a "national classic"; in French, an admired but inessential import. Therefore German author-translators' reputations are more at stake in rewriting Shakespeare, so they work harder to appropriate him in original ways.

Second, just as plausibly, Baudissin's translation of the couplet, in becoming canonical, dictated its future: it radically changed the translatability of this moment within the text. The decisions which tend to differentiate German "authors" from German "others" are all features of the canonical version. No such canonical version exists in French, and the couplets in such "classic" versions as de Vigny's or Hugo's are much less unexpected and therefore challenging. Baudissin's creativity at this point in *Othello* established two rules: first, that the Duke is an ideal sovereign; second, that retranslators should take liberties here, should find a creative solution. "Other" translators fail to respond to the second rule.

Both explanations are plausible. But then, mapping versions of this crux has only confirmed what we knew: that Shakespeare is always differently translatable in German, and that Schlegel-Tieck—here: Baudissin—had and still has colossal influence on his translatability. We need to work with much bigger samples.

We need maps of whole texts. But before that, we need corpus overviews.[31] A list (for example, a bibliography) is all very well, but a poor way of presenting basic metadata: the who what where and when and the how (by genre and by reception) of retranslating. Make the list into a database, and we can create visualizations of corpus metadata. We can see how many items there are, of what kinds, when they were created, where, by whom and for whom; and when and where and in what kinds of ways they were reused (republished, revised, performed, and so on). The prototype interactive time-map pictured (figure 16.2) is based on very basic metadata for our forty German versions of *Othello*.[32] The metadata classes are genres (print-published text or theatre script); places and dates of creation; places and dates of first publication; and translators' names. From the map interface we can access pages with further information about each version and translator, and the digitized texts (or a portion, subject to copyright constraints). The scale of view can be altered. We can operate a slider in order to "time-travel" from 1766 to the present: *Othello* versions "appear" before us on the map. This kind of data visualization will come into its own when we have a far larger dataset.[33]

Figure 16.3 is a "network map," created by Jan Rybicki, which visualizes the outputs of a stylometric analysis of our German *Othello* corpus.[34] The analysis compares the statistical distributions of the most frequent words (MFW) in each text.[35] Texts differ in their use of frequent, semantically lightweight words such as conjunctions, prepositions, and pronouns; these "stylistic fingerprints" differentiate writers, genres, and periods. MFW can be defined in many different ways for any given corpus. Hundreds of differently scaled, multifactorial "cluster analyses" are run, and this map depicts a statistical "consensus" of results. A distance on the map between any two versions indexes their stylistic (dis)similarity, relative to other (dis)similarities. Lines linking versions indicate common stylometric properties or "affinities." The thickness of a line indexes the prominence of such affinities.[36] On the labels, a name beginning "Baud" indicates a revision of Baudissin's *Othello* by the named editor(s) or adaptor(s). The suffix "T" indicates a theater script

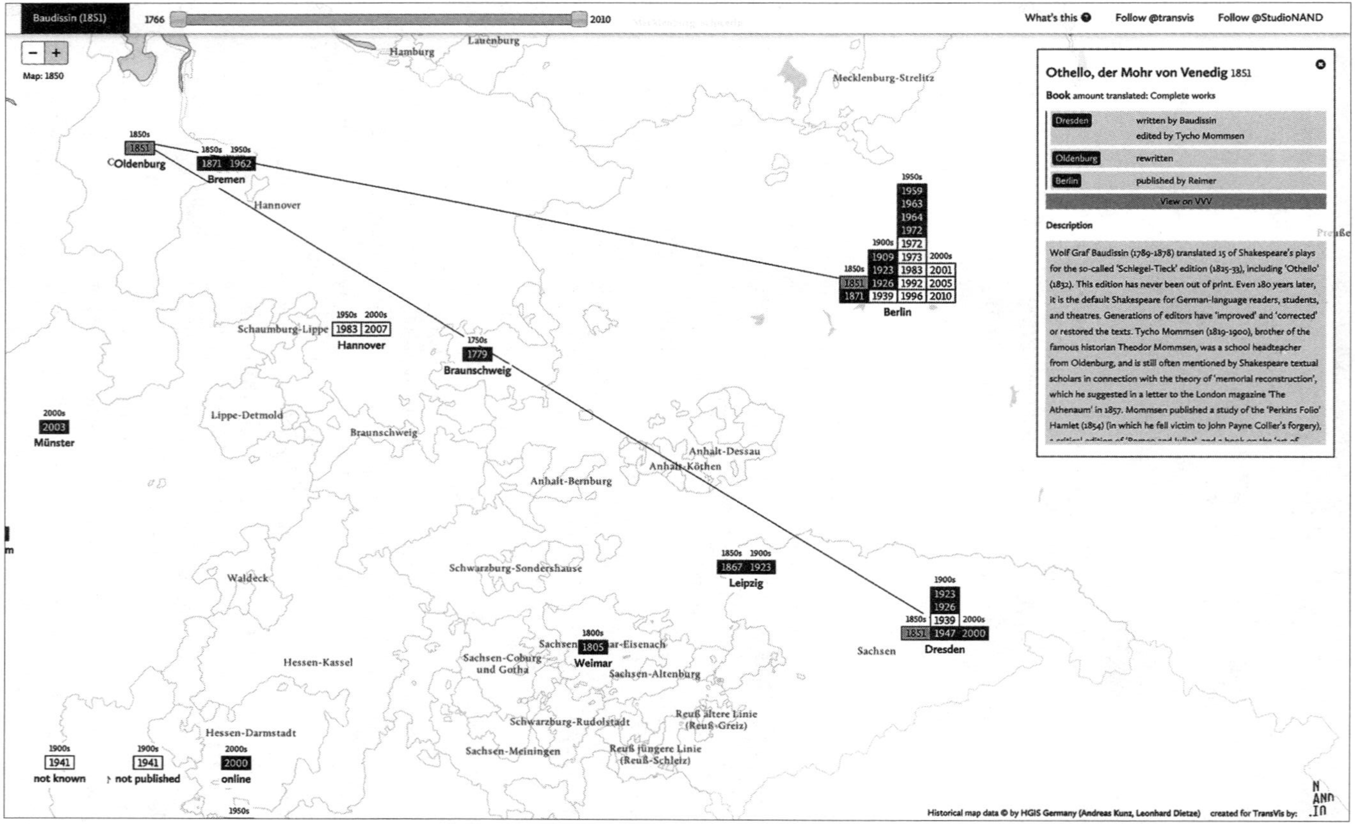

Figure 16.2. A translations metadata time map

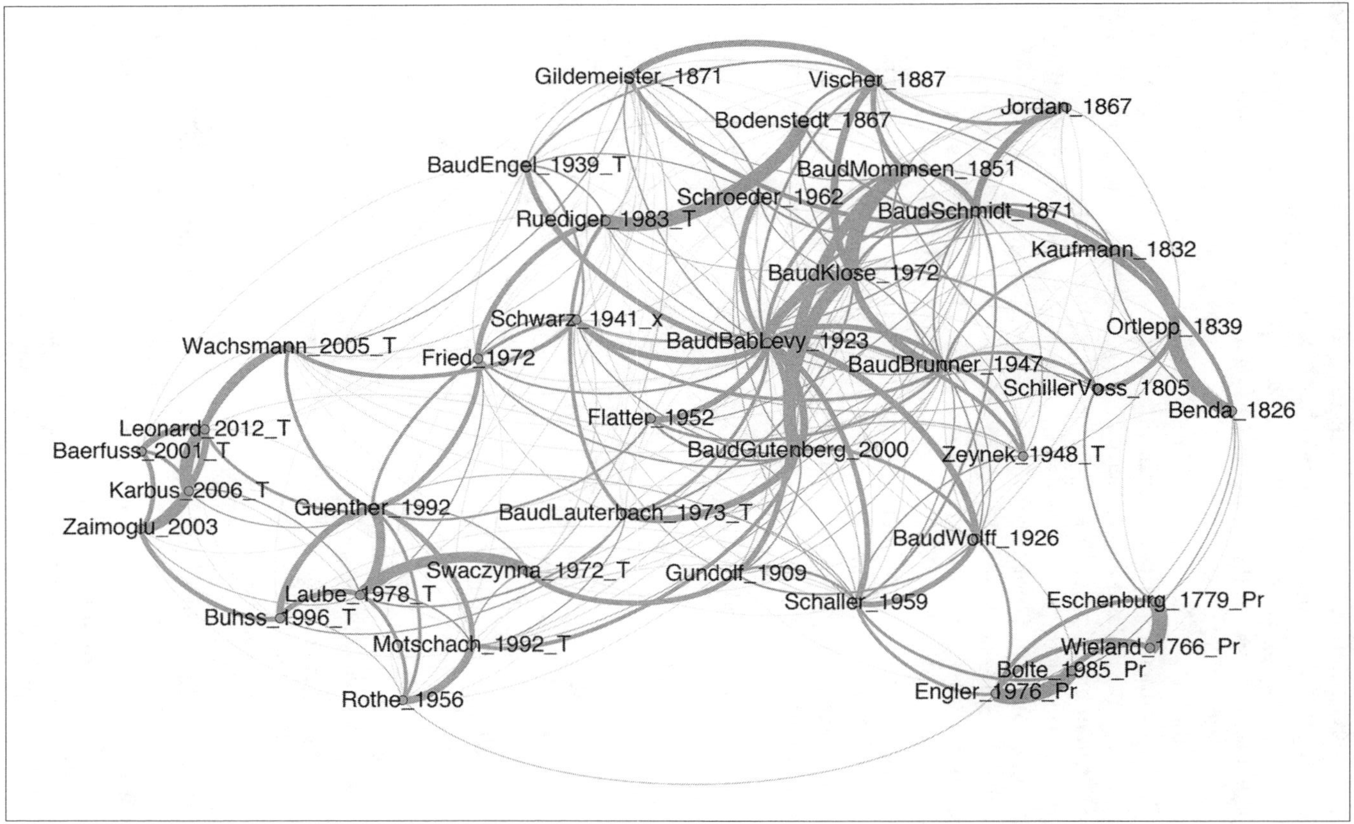

Figure 16.3. Stylometric comparison of retranslations

(others were published in book form; of course, many of these were also used in theatrical productions). The suffix "Pr" indicates a prose study text, not designed for performance. All others are "poetic" versions, using iambic verse, or, in some recent theater scripts, using a poetically charged prose. Versions labeled "Pr" make up the most obvious cluster: they all form an island to the southeast, off the "continent" of poetic versions.

The two-dimensional space on this map represents the space of *Othello*'s actualized (un)translatability in German cultural history, 1766–2010. We can read the map historically: clusters on the western and eastern peripheries are strongly period-defined. We can also read the map in genre terms. To the east and central are translations primarily for readers. To the west we find theater scripts—the "T" labels—and performance-oriented versions published in book form (Rothe, Fried, Günther, and Zaimoglu). Period and genre (or purpose) are interlinked here: this is a feature of our corpus. But the "Pr" cluster to the southeast, set apart and tightly interconnected, shows that an explanatory translation aimed at students and scholars stylistically resembles another explanatory translation, even when they are two hundred years apart, much more than it resembles any poetic translation.[37] Genre can trump period. On the other hand, all our twenty-first-century versions, which also happen to be adaptations, form a tightly interconnected "island" cluster to the far west: is this genre or period or both?

The main bulk of versions is a large tangle centred on Baudissin or "Schlegel-Tieck." The revision by Bab and Levy (1923) is most central, and has most affinities with other versions. Dozens of other revisions of Baudissin (and earlier versions of his text) might be added to our corpus, changing this part of the picture. What is striking is how stylistically diverse revisions of Baudissin can be. The German "set text" of Shakespeare is "canonical, but tacitly evolving" (Morse, "Reflections," 79). We would expect performance scripts adapted from Baudissin's text to be distinctive: thus Engel (for the Deutsches Theater, Berlin, in 1939), and Lauterbach and Gleisberg (GDR, 1973), are positioned furthest west of other Baudissin versions. But the gaps between our earliest Baudissin for readers (Mommsen in 1851) and our latest (a "Gutenberg" e- text, c. 2000),[38] or Wolff's 1926 revision far to the southeast, are surprisingly large.

East of Baudissin lies a well-defined period cluster: Schiller and Voss, Benda, Ortlepp, and Kaufmann, proximate and interlinked by lines of affinity. These are early nineteenth-century poetic versions of *Othello*, which all came to be eclipsed by Baudissin's. Not clustered, but all out on the northern periphery are the later nineteenth-century would-be alternatives to Schlegel-Tieck: Gildemeister, Bodenstedt, Vischer, Jordan. The most distinct clusters lie over to the west. All the twenty-first-century versions in our corpus are stylometrically surprisingly close, and densely interlinked. They are structurally varied adaptations: Bärfuss a radically condensed version; Karbus, Leonard, and Wachsmann making cuts; Zaimoglu cutting and also adding material.

This "island" is distinct from another: the southwesterly, densely interlinked cluster consisting of several later twentieth-century "full" versions (making no or very minor cuts), together with Rothe (1956). Rothe made enemies in conservative quarters with his populist, liberty-taking, modernizing approach.[39] This map tells us he was uniquely far ahead of his time. It also tells us that in "catching up" with Rothe, the nature of Shakespeare translating has changed since about 1970—in fact, since Fried's publication and Swaczynna's script (both 1972). Their versions opened up the new westerly space, which appears to be centered on Günther, the best candidate for twenty-first-century canonicity as a German Shakespeare translator. He occupies a central position in relation to the two westerly, "postmodern" clusters. Just what it is that changed around 2000, dividing these clusters—not only the "fullness" of versions but their styles—is another question.

Versions of Baudissin, and other versions of the later nineteenth and twentieth centuries, occupy a roughly circular area around Bab and Levy. It is as if Baudissin were a center of gravity, with revisers and rivals equally pulling away in various directions. The later twentieth- century versions on the northern periphery, Schröder's version of 1962, Rüdiger's of 1983, Zeynek's of 1948, Schaller's of 1959 (the "official" East German Shakespeare): all were or became anachronisms. But if Rothe's and Fried's direction turned out to be the stylistic future, then the versions published by Gundolf (in 1909) and Flatter (1952) also pointed roughly the "right" way, as did the unpublished scripts by Lauterbach and Gleisberg (1973) and Schwarz (1941)—of whom more in a moment.

We conclude that, in "poetic" German *Othello* translation, a strong stylistic consensus formed in the early nineteenth century, to be displaced by a weaker consensus around Baudissin. Late nineteenth- and early- to mid-twentieth-century translators edged away from this consensus, pushing stylistically in several different directions. Rothe was by far the boldest of these, and he anticipated a new kind of style which emerged in the late twentieth century, in the form of a new, surprisingly narrow consensus. Then in the twenty-first century, a different, less Rothe-like, but again surprisingly narrow stylistic consensus formed.

One might assume that the well-known published versions by Fried and Günther helped to define this new stylistic space. The affinity line between Fried and Günther also suggests possible "influence." But remarkably, this is the only line linking Fried to any later version, and links from Günther to later versions are also surprisingly few. Proximities and affinities, read together, give much food for thought. The map speaks of possible retranslation genealogies, independently of documentary evidence. Rüdiger's title page makes plain his improbable rewriting of Bodenstedt (up north, the longest thick line shown). Vischer acknowledges debts to Baudissin, Jordan, and Gildemeister in his annotations. But Ortlepp admits to no uses of Benda, Kaufmann, or Schiller and Voss. Was this plagiarism, or innocent stylistic convergence? Eschenburg is known to have revised Wieland. Perhaps Bolte reused Engler likewise? Did Schmidt, in revising Baudissin for the Deutsche Shakespeare-Gesellschaft edition in 1871, draw upon Jordan and Kaufmann? What lies behind the lines interlinking all the twenty-first-century versions, or Motschach back to Rothe, or Günther back to Laube, him back to Swaczynna, him back to Gundolf? Only close reading—or only further computational analysis *and* close reading—will tell.

Swaczynna links back to Gundolf, but Fried, the other innovator of 1972, is scarcely connected with any precursors. He occupies a distinct space of his own—except for the proximity to Schwarz. Günther has strong precursor affinities with Laube, Fried, Rothe, and—less strong, but still distinct—also with Schwarz. This is remarkable because, in this corpus, Hedwig Schwarz is not only the only female sole translator:[40] her *Othello* is also the only one which was neither published in print for the book trade, nor included in the repertory of any theater script publisher.[41] Did Fried or Günther consult her typescript, *Othello, der Maure von Venedig*, held in the Munich Shakespeare Library? Schwarz's style links back in time to Bab and Levy, and other versions of Baudissin; forward in time to Wachsmann (2005) as well as to Günther. Positioned close to Fried, near-central between Baudissin-centric tradition and Günther-centric innovation, the forgotten Schwarz might almost be seen as a stylistic paradigm of this corpus.[42]

Rybicki's map is apt to stimulate new explorations. But South to North, East to West, what positive differences underlie the different relative positions? What do the axes index? If we say that the map ranges from archaism far left to postmodernism far right, what exactly are we saying? Do affinity-lines represent close-readable similarities? There is no space to answer these questions here. This kind of analysis also demands comparative extension, outwards and inwards. Outwards: will maps of other Shakespeare translations corpora show similar patterns? What other styles, in yet other text corpora, do translator styles resemble and differ from? What spaces do Shakespeare translations occupy in literary universes? Rybicki has revealed (in "The Great Mystery") the Venutian "invisibility of the translator" in stylometric comparisons of multiple retranslations of classic English novels in Polish. Different translators' versions of the same originals are more similar than one translator's versions of different originals. In other words, translators have (almost) no style: they mimic the original's, such that different translations of a novel converge stylistically.[43] There must be far more stylistic diversity in Shakespeare translations than in translations of novels: this the map above shows, for poetic versus prose translations. Still, if we compared Shakespeare retranslation corpora with other corpora (such as the same translators' translations from other authors, and their non-translated works), we might see whether, and in which translations, a "Shakespeare-in-translation" fingerprint is stronger than that of translators. But then, we would also expect such differences to be distributed differently along the flow of a text. We need to move "inwards," to explore differentiation within versions.[44] The Duke's couplet poses different challenges from neighboring speeches. Iago's style differs from Othello's. Can stylometry and other digital, algorithmic aids help us read more closely, across corpora and within particular texts?

Consider Jan Matthijsen's study of seventy Dutch retranslations of *Hamlet*. He uses four scales of differentiation to plot each version's place intuitively on a visual grid, on a master scale from "source text" to "target culture" ("The Breach," 26). His scale (1) runs from "invisible translator" to "visible translator" (from subservience to freely creative rewriting); scale (2) from "text over performance" to "performance over text" (from "full version," via "reduction" and "emendation," to "addition"); scale (3) from "source culture oriented" language to "target culture oriented" language (from "archaicization" to "modernization"); scale (4) from "poetic function" to "communicative function" (from "musicality, rhythm" to prosaic "clarification"). Three of these scales are at least partially captured by stylometry, as we have just seen. But Matthijsen's scale (2)—from a version which reproduces the original's structure, speech by speech, to one which makes cuts, resequences segments, and adds new material—needs a different kind of map.

The sample "alignment maps" in figure 16.4 are drawn by an algorithm which retrieves data from a database of German *Othello* versions, aligned speech-by-speech to an English "base text." The database for holding versions corpora, and the tool for aligning multiple versions, were built by Kevin Flanagan.[45] The visual interface design is by Stephan Thiel.[46] The maps depict versions of *Othello*, act 1, scene 3. In each map, the left column represents the English base text; the right column represents the version. Read top to bottom, each horizontal bar represents a speech; its thickness, the length of that speech. The thickest, darker bar is Othello's great speech to the Senate: "Her father loved me . . ." We can see at a glance which versions, where, expand or condense, omit, transpose, or add material.[47] The principle behind this visualization is powerfully extensible to any set of structurally comparable, differentiated versions (not just of texts). In our VVV database, not only speeches but speech-prefixes are aligned. Therefore these alignment maps also serve as navigational aids in close reading: we can travel within or filter parallel texts by speaker-names, as demonstrated in VVV interfaces.[48]

The last "map" was also designed by Thiel as a visual interface with Flanagan's database, based on Tom Cheesman's ideas.[49] The VVV interface shown in figure 16.5 offers close readings of multiple retranslations, and of the original "through" them. Any database can sort versions of a text or part of it, by metadata values (translator name, date, genre, etc.), reduction/expansion, or the presence/absence of certain terms. This VVV interface does something different and new. It displays the base text in full and retrieves from the corpus all translations of any selected segment (here, the line "I saw Othello's visage in his mind"), plus Google "backtranslations." It can display the translations sorted by author or date—or by predictability: how unusual they are,

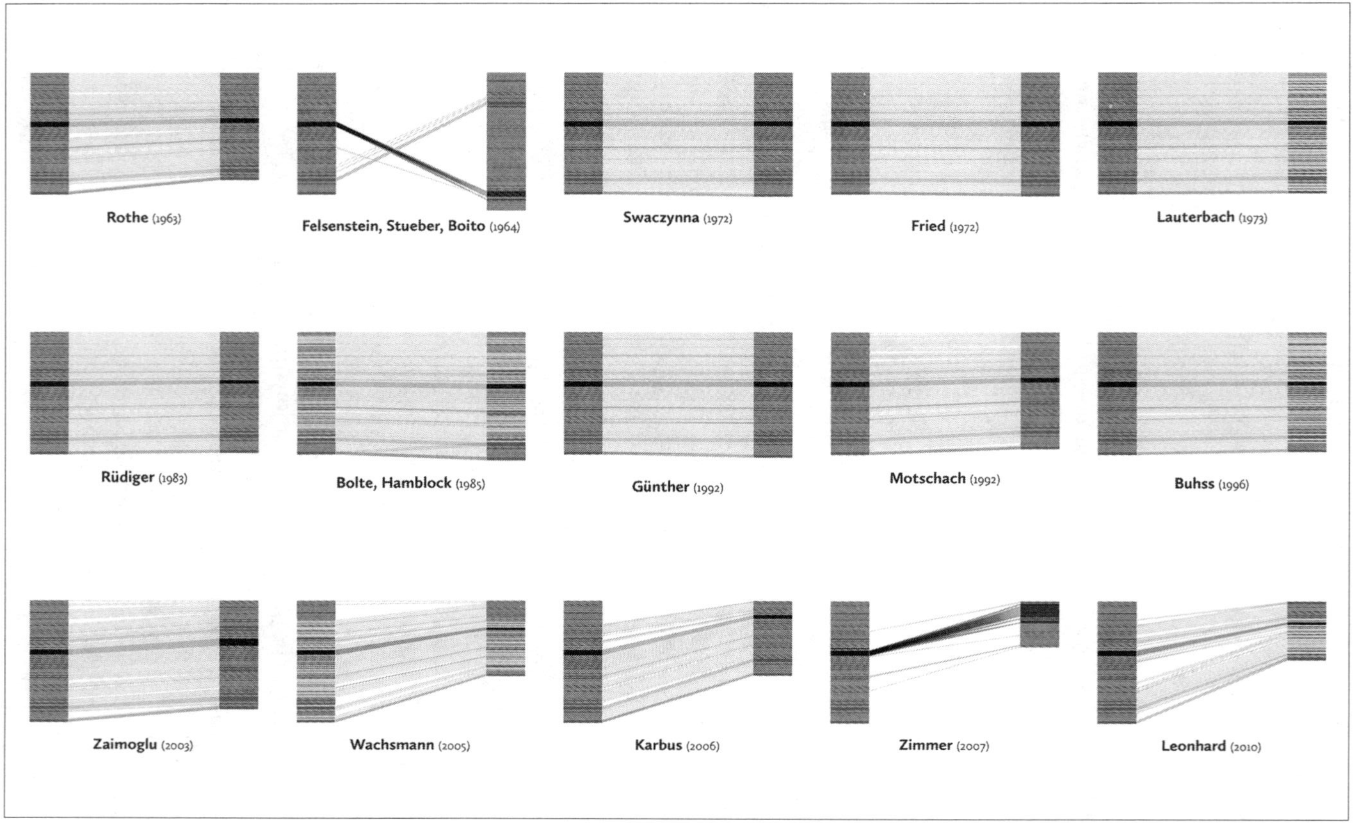

Figure 16.4. Maps of segment alignments between versions and an original

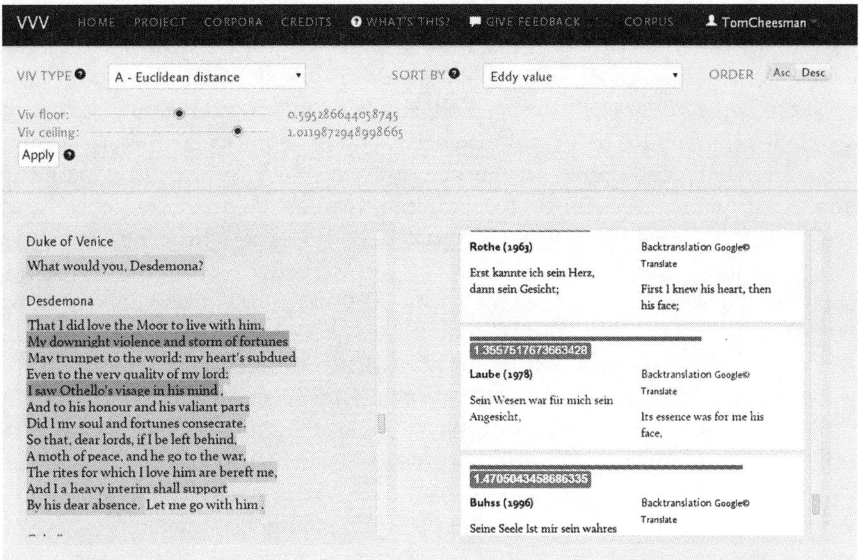

Figure 16.5. Eddy and Viv: diversity in retranslations sorted and mapped back onto the original

compared to the others. In figure 16.5 we see some of the most unusual translations of Desdemona's line in our *Othello* corpus—versions with the highest "Eddy value," so called because this "mapping" is carried out by an algorithm called Eddy. Eddy begets an algorithm called "Viv" ("variation in versions").[50] The "Eddy and Viv" interface (a.k.a. "Translation Array") makes visible that any translation is just one raid on the untranslatable.

Eddy sorts versions of a given segment by counting all the word forms in the segment- versions corpus, and assigning a frequency value to each word form: the more frequent the word form, the lower the value. A version using the same words as many other versions will be assigned a low Eddy value; a version consisting of unique words (within the segment-versions corpus) has a very high Eddy value. This explanation simplifies the mathematics; the algorithm must also adjust for segments' different lengths, because versions of (say) a four-word speech differ less than versions of a hundred-word speech.[51] But what we are after is not "precision": we want an intuitively usable, *helpful* tool for seeing and exploring how translations vary. Eddy measures a proxy for what Derrida calls the "gap" ("l'écart") between one translation and others, "in the relation among them and thus in their multiplicity."[52] What words are used is the proxy, enabling us to sort versions from least to most unexpected. Much more sophisticated proxies can be imagined. A more advanced Eddy could distinguish the presence/absence of semantic fields (with semantic tagging) and rhetorical structures (with part-of-speech tagging combined with analysis of syntax). We can already use VVV tools to investigate the coherence of translators' decisions along the flow of a text, for example in the dozen or so other passages in *Othello* which resonate most with the Duke's couplet.[53] Rather than single segments, Eddy could sort such segment-groups: sites of metaphoric networks, or rhetorical tropes, or scenes, character parts, and conversations across scenes. In VVV we can scale Eddy analysis down to subcorpora (for example, versions by period or genre), and create graphs showing versions' averaged Eddys over a timeline, or Eddys along the flow of text for each version. Thus Eddy lets us consider questions such as: Do versions (all or some of them) differ most in certain scenes or character parts? Do they differ in regular ways, along the flow of the text, in terms of the translator's investment of effort to differentiate her style from other translators', or the speech of one character from others?

The Viv algorithm, finally, returns us to close reading of the *original*. Viv takes Eddy's mapping of the gaps between segment-versions and maps the products of those gaps onto the translated text, segment by segment. The Viv value for a segment in the original expresses how much variation it provokes among the versions. These values are shown as a varying color layer under the base text: the darker the color, the more the translators disagreed about translating that segment. In figure 16.5 we can see that "Let me go with him" (unsurprisingly) has provoked less disagreement than "I saw Othello's visage in his mind." Algorithmic reading through translations becomes a way of reading Shakespeare, even if you cannot read the other language(s). We can test our knowledge or intuitions about which elements in Shakespeare's language make for ambiguity or controversy in interpretation, against the evidence of translators' choices. In principle, with multilingual versions corpora, Viv might filter out positive or negative constraints on variation which are specific to translating language-cultures. We can envisage mapping a work's original or "general translatability," along the flow of text, as the product of multiple, cross-cultural "actual translatabilities."

VVV maps are language-neutral: they will work just as well with Confucius and the Quran, Balzac and the Bhagavad Gita, in principle. Displayed, arrayed in their variety, translators' versions can be made to tell us things we never knew about "all the virtualities of the original" (Derrida, *Specters,* 21). They also make us wonder about translation's creative freedom, the diverse interpretations of its "task." Where do divergent readings of cruxes, or of characters, events, or governing metaphors, come from? What is the interplay between the forces of historical cultural contexts (ideologies, histories of ideas), institutional frameworks (practices in publishing, education, or theater), literary influences, and individual, idiosyncratic agency? Corpus work, and making digital maps of computable differences, will not answer such questions. But it will help us ask them much better, and answer them much more fully. Eventually we will even use algorithms to help us understand what makes one version better than others: how gains offset losses; maybe even what makes some translations better than their originals.[54] Maps create territories—spaces for exploration. They can help us get from A to B, or envisage adventures. Maps of the gaps among versions—to paraphrase Derrida: "cartes d'écarts"—open new vistas for textual-cultural research.

Notes

This chapter draws on the work of the "Version Variation Visualization" (VVV) project team, especially research assistants Kevin Flanagan (software engineering), Stephan Thiel of Studio Nand, Berlin (software and interface design), Zhao Geng (software experiments), and Alison Ehrmann (initial text preparation). The team also includes David M. Berry, Pavel Drábek, Jonathan Hope, Robert S. Laramee, Márta Minier, Andrew J. Rothwell, and Jan Rybicki. The work has been generously funded by Swansea University (2011–14) and the Arts and Humanities Research Council (2012). See www.delightedbeauty.org/vvvclosed (Credits page).

1. James Joyce, *Ulysses*, ed. Hans Walter Gabler (New York: First Vintage, 1986), 463.

2. Jacques Derrida, *Spectres de Marx: L'État de la dette, le travail du deuil et la nouvelle Internationale* (Paris: Galilée, 1993), 43, from a passage on French versions of Hamlet's remark: "The time is out of joint." Translation adapted by Tom Cheesman from Jacques Derrida, *Specters of Marx: The State of the Debt, the Work of Mourning, and the New International*, trans. Peggy Kamuf (New York: Routledge, 1994), 21.

3. ". . . ce qu'on ne cesse pas de (ne pas) traduire": Barbara Cassin, ed., *Vocabulaire européen des philosophes: Dictionnaire des intraduisibles* (Paris: Seuil, 2004), xvii.

4. Sharon Deane-Cox, *Retranslation* (London: Bloomsbury, 2014), 1 and 14.

5. See Dirk Delabastita, "Shakespeare," in *Routledge Encyclopedia of Translation Studies*, ed. Mona Baker and Gabriela Saldanha, 2nd ed. (London: Routledge, 2009): 263–69, and "Shakespeare and Translation. A Guide to Further Reading," in *Shakespeare and the Language of Translation*, ed. Ton Hoenselaars, rev. ed. (London: Arden Shakespeare, 2012), 289–316.

6. For further reading on Shakespeare in/as German, see Andreas Höfele, "Re-educating Germany: BBC Shakespeare 1945," in *Shakespeare and European Politics*, ed. Dirk Delabastita, Jozef de Vos, and Paul Franssen (Cranbury, N.J.: Rosemont, 2008), 255–77 (273, note 35). The sonnets illustrate the multitudinous variety of German re-versioning well: see Manfred Pfister, "Made in Germany: Shakespeare's Sonnets," *Angermion* 5 (2012): 29–57. Key resources include the *Shakespeare Jahrbuch*, or *Jahrbuch der Deutschen Shakespeare-Gesellschaft* (since 1865); Hansjürgen Blinn, *Der deutsche Shakespeare = The German Shakespeare: Eine annotierte Bibliographie zur Shakespeare-Rezeption des deutschsprachigen Kulturraums (Literatur, Theater, Film, Funk, Fernsehen, Musik und bildende Kunst)* (Berlin: Erich Schmidt, 1993); and Hansjürgen Blinn and Wolf Gerhard Schmidt, *Shakespeare—deutsch: Bibliographie der Übersetzungen und Bearbeitungen* (Berlin: Erich Schmidt, 2003).

7. Franco Moretti's work is inspirational, especially *Graphs, Maps, Trees: Abstract Models for a Literary History* (London: Verso, 2005). See also Jonathan Goodwin and John Holbo, eds., *Reading Graphs, Maps, Trees: Responses to Franco Moretti* (Anderson, S.C.: Parlor, 2011).

8. See further note 1 and below. All the German translations and adaptations of *Othello* used in this study are listed in the "Appendix" to this chapter.

9. The bibliographical starting point is Blinn and Schmidt, *Shakespeare—deutsch*. Theater script publishers' stock (often not in that bibliography) was accessed through www.theatertexte.de.

10. On "rescriptings," see Alan C. Dessen, *Rescripting Shakespeare: The Text, the Director, and Modern Productions* (Cambridge: Cambridge University Press, 2002).

11. Gideon Toury, "What Is It That Renders a Spoonerism (Un)Translatable?" in *Traductio: Essays on Punning and Translation*, ed. Dirk Delabastita (Manchester: St Jerome, 1997), 271–91, here 283. For a useful discussion of Toury's translatability concept, see Edoardo Crisafulli, "The Adequate Translation as a Methodological Tool: The Case of Dante's Onomastic Wordplay in English," *Target* 13, no. 1 (2002): 1–28.

12. Related work with retranslations corpora includes Kemal Altintas, Fazli Can, and John Patton, "Language Change Quantification Using Time-Separated Parallel Translations," *Literary and Linguistic Computing* 22, no. 4 (2007): 375–93; Sara Castagnoli, "A New Approach to the Analysis of Explicitation in Translation: Multiple (Learner) Translation Corpora," *International Journal of Translation* 21, no. 1 (2009): 89–105, and Sara Castagnoli, "Exploring Variation and Regularities in Translation with Multiple Translation Corpora," *Rassegna Italiana di Linguistica Applicata* 1–2 (2011): 311–32; Stig Johansson, "Between Scylla and Charybdis: On Individual Variation in Translation," *Languages in Contrast* 11, no. 1 (2011): 3–19; and Pekka Kujamaki, "Finnish Comet in German Skies: Translation, Retranslation and Norms," *Target* 13, no. 1 (2002): 45–70.

13. Lawrence Venuti, "Retranslations: The Creation of Value," in *Translation and Culture*, ed. Katherine M. Faull (Lewisburg, Pa.: Bucknell University Press, 2004), 25–38; Sehnaz Tahir Gürcaglar, "Retranslation," in *Routledge Encyclopedia of Translation Studies*, ed. Mona Baker and Gabriela Saldanha, 233–36.

14. On unedifying practices, see Maik Hamburger, "Translating and Copyright," in *Shakespeare and the Language of Translation*, ed. Ton Hoenselaars, 148–67.

15. Anthony Pym introduced a distinction between "active" versus "passive" retranslations—those which innovate versus those which merely update—in *Method in Translation History* (Manchester: St. Jerome, 1998), 82–83. For critique, see: Deane-Cox, *Retranslation*, 14–20: no retranslation is ever merely "passive."

16. On the broader issues raised, see, for example, Gregory Crane et al., "Classics in the Million Book Library," *Digital Humanities Quarterly* 3, no. 1 (2009), www.digitalhumanities.org/dhq/vol/003/1/000034/000034.html; Kate Rumbold, "From 'Access' to 'Creativity': Shakespeare Institutions, New Media, and the Language of Cultural Value," *Shakespeare Quarterly* 61, no. 3 (2010): 313–36.

17. William Shakespeare, *Othello, The Moor of Venice,* ed. Michael Neill (Oxford: Oxford University Press, 2006), 233 (act 1, scene 3, lines 287–88).

18. Special thanks to Jürgen Gutsch for animating the Shakespeare translator network associated with Manfred Pfister and Jürgen Gutsch, eds., *William Shakespeare's Sonnets: For the First Time Globally Reprinted: A Quartercentenary Anthology 1609–2009* (Dozwil: Edition Signathur, 2009, repr. 2010).

19. See Tom Cheesman, "Thirty Times 'More Fair Than Black': *Othello* Re-Translation as Political Re-Statement," *Angermion* 4 (2012): 1–52 (on German versions); Tom Cheesman, "Mutations of a Difficult Moment," in *The Cambridge Guide to the Worlds of Shakespeare*, ed. Bruce R. Smith, vol. 2 (Cambridge: Cambridge University Press, 2016) (on German and French versions); and Tom Cheesman, Kevin Flanagan, Stephan Thiel, Jan Rybicki, Jonathan Hope, and Avraham Roos, "Multi-Retranslation Corpora: Visibility, Variation, Value and Virtue," *Digital Scholarship in the Humanities*, forthcoming.

20. Ruth Morse, "Reflections in Shakespeare Translation," *The Yearbook of English Studies* 36, no. 1 (2006): 79–89, here 79, 81, 82.

21. Dirk Delabastita, "Focus on the Pun: Wordplay as a Special Problem in Translation Studies," *Target* 6, no. 2 (1994): 223–43, here 225.

22. Schiller died before the collaborative work with Voss, documented in the *Nationalausgabe*, was complete; Voss published *Othello* under his sole name in 1806. The VVV digital corpus currently only includes the *Nationalausgabe* text. See "Appendix" for source details.

23. Wolf Graf Baudissin, *Othello*, first published in *Shakespeares Dramatische Werke*, ed. August Wilhelm von Schlegel and Ludwig Tieck (Berlin: Reimer, 1825–33), vol. 8 (of 9) (1832). The VVV corpus includes eight revised editions of Baudissin's text and two scripts based on such editions.

24. The couplet is an example of enthymeme: an incomplete syllogism. Translation must deal with the unspoken proposition(s). See Glyn Pursglove, "Some Observations on the Uses of Rhetoric in a Couplet from Othello" (2011) at www.delightedbeauty.org ("Outputs and Events" page).

25. Frank Günther, *William Shakespeare: Othello,* bilingual edition (Munich: DTV, 2006 [1995]), 51. Günther advocates antiracist translation choices for "Moor" in his essay appended to the translation, "Aus der Übersetzerwerkstatt: 'The Moor'—der Mohr—der Neger" (271–74), but his note on "fair" and "black" in the couplet (278) does not explicate his translation of it.

26. Erich Fried, *William Shakespeare: Hamlet / Othello* (Berlin: Wagenbach, 1999 [1972]), 140.

27. Feridun Zaimoglu and Günter Senkel, *William Shakespeare: Othello* (Münster: Monsenstein und Vannerdat, 2004) (first performed in 2003), 26. See Tom Cheesman, "Shakespeare and Othello in Filthy Hell: Zaimoglu and Senkel's Politico-Religious Tradaptation," *Forum for Modern Language Studies* 46, no. 2 (2010): 207–20.

28. "Fair" = "*other*": these are the versions by Fried and Zaimoglu/Senkel quoted above. Note that Baudissin's version is classified "fair" = "*null*," since his "schön" translates "beauty."

29. German "authors" are Baudissin (a.k.a. "Schlegel-Tieck"), Fried, Günther, Gundolf (collaborating with Stefan George), Rothe, Schiller, Voss (three alternative versions), Wieland, and Zaimoglu/Senkel. French "authors" are Aicard,

Bonnefoy, Déprats, Hugo (2), LeTourneur (2), Robin, de Vigny (2). For further names and details see www.delightedbeauty.org. My thanks to Matthias Zach for supplying most of the French repertoire.

30. Deane-Cox (*Retranslation*), like much of the recent work she surveys, deploys Bourdieu's model. Jan Mathijssen, without mentioning Bourdieu, proposes a very similar model: "The Breach and the Observance: Theatre Retranslation as a Strategy of Artistic Differentiation, with Special Reference to Retranslations of Shakespeare's *Hamlet* (1777–2001)" (Ph.D. diss., Utrecht, 2007).

31. Shneidermann's influential "visual information seeking mantra" is: "overview first, zoom and filter, then details-on-demand," in Ben Shneiderman, "The Eyes Have It: A Task by Data Type Taxonomy for Information Visualizations," *Proceedings of the IEEE Symposium on Visual Languages* (Washington: IEEE Computer Society, 1996): 336–43, here 337.

32. Design by Stephan Thiel (2013): see www.nand.io/othellomap. See also Valentina Palladino, "'Othello Time Map' Tracks, Charts 250 Years of Translations," *Wired* 2 (2013), http://www.wired.com/design/2013/02/othello-time-map.

33. Projects are under discussion with Wikimedia Education (UK) to collect translations metadata for all Shakespeare's works in all languages, and with Shakespeare's Globe Theatre, London, to combine a time-map interface with video of "To be or not to be" performed in multiple languages, collected during the global tour of the Globe's *Hamlet* in 2014–16.

34. This *Othello* corpus analysis is based on c. 8,000 words of each copyedited digital text (normally up to act 2, scene 2); the corpus differs slightly from the online VVV corpus (Felsenstein and Zimmer were excluded, Kaufmann and Schmidt added).

35. The method of multivariate analysis, typically used in forensic authorship attribution, is described in Jan Rybicki, "The Great Mystery of the (Almost) Invisible Translator: Stylometry in Translation," in *Quantitative Methods in Corpus-Based Translation Studies. A Practical Guide to Descriptive Translation Research*, ed. Michael Oakley and Meng Ji (Amsterdam: John Benjamins, 2012), 231–48. For the network map visualization technique, using GEPHI software, see Rybicki, "Visualizing Literature: Artistic Statistics," in *The Art of Literature, Art in Literature*, ed. Bożena Bucała, Izabela Curyło-Klag, and Magdalena Bleinert (Kraków: Wydawnictwo Uniwersytetu Jagiellońskiego, 2014), 137–46.

36. Rybicki, "Visualizing." Also: "The lines are based on the number of times one text comes as the 1st, 2nd or 3rd closest (with different weights attached) to another text in very many iterations of cluster analysis of the most frequent words in the whole corpus. The more often two texts are shown to be similar, the thicker the line. In turn, the thickness of the lines determines the distances between texts on the graphs—imagine that they are rubber bands: the thicker the band, the less expanded it can get." Rybicki, personal correspondence, February 6, 2014.

37. The digital texts were not modernized. Happily, the orthography of most MFW has not changed in German since the eighteenth century.

38. The Baudissin text in the German Gutenberg collection (http://gutenberg.spiegel.de/buch/2185/1) appears to be identical, aside from lacking color-coding of interpolations, with a text prepared c. 2000 and posted at www.william-shakespeare.de, a site run by Ruediger Wenig. The scans are said to come from

a three-volume set of the "Schlegel-Tieck" texts, published by Sigbert Mohn Verlag (presumably a reprint of Hans Jürgen Meinerts's edition, first published in 6 volumes in 1958) and interpolations to be based on comparison with the English "Project Gutenberg" e-text. Wenig does not reply to e-mails.

39. Hans Rothe, a very successful Shakespeare rewriter for stages and publication in the 1920s, was persecuted by the Nazis, and went into exile, resuming his career in Germany in the 1950s. See Ruth Freifrau von Ledebur, "'The Country That Gave Birth to You a Second Time': An Essay about the Political History of the German Shakespeare Society 1918–1945," in *German Shakespeare Studies at the Turn of the Twentieth Century*, ed. Christa Jansohn (Newark: University of Delaware Press, 2006), 255–71. Rothe's work was always disparaged by guardians of the German Shakespeare cult, and still is; his "eminently speakable" versions "now merely cause readers to shake their heads": Hamburger, "Translating and Copyright," 163–64.

40. Woman co-translators named on title pages are E. [Elisabeth] Levy with Julius Bab in 1923, and Benita Gleisberg with "E. S. Lauterbach" (pen-name of Erich Selbmann) in 1973.

41. Hence the map label suffix "x." Eight other Shakespeare translations by Schwarz (dated between 1938 and 1941, or 1955) are listed in Blinn and Schmidt, *Shakespeare—deutsch*; seven are available from Steyer Verlag, www.steyer-verlag.de. A 1955 recording of her *Maß für Maß*, directed by Hans-Günther von Klöden for Radio Bremen, was released on CD in 2006.

42. Schwarz's version of the Duke's parting couplet, uniquely, places Desdemona center stage: "Wenn nie der Tugend lichte Schönheit fehlt, / ist Eure Tochter hell, nicht schwarz, vermählt" ("If virtue never lacks radiant beauty, your daughter is brightly, not blackly, married") (*Othello* [typescript, 1941], 14). Biographical information is scant. She published "Neue Shakespeare-Übersetzungen in Selbstanzeigen," *Shakespeare Jahrbuch* 82–83 (1948): 199–206, and "Arbeit für Shakespeare durch Shakespeare-Bearbeitungen," *Shakespeare-Jahrbuch* 92 (1956): 175–83. The delightful *35 lyrische Variationen*, ed. Uta Schwarz and Paul-Christian Dressler (Norderstedt: Books on Demand, 2010) is by Hedwig Schwarz (1898–1983). Hedwig Schwarz-Rowe published *Des Kindes Stimme: Ein Weihnachtsspiel aus der Gegenwart* (Berlin: Arbeiterjugend-Verlag, 1924); Hedwig Rowe published *Maispiel für die Arbeiterjugend* (Berlin: Arbeiterjugend-Verlag, 1924) and was "eine der ersten Frauenrechtlerinnen bei den Jusos" in Cologne in 1923; Jürgen Seitz, "Jungsozialisten heraus!" (1996), *Sozialistisches Forum Rheinland*, www.sf-rheinland.de/75-jahre-koelner-jusos/artikel/jungsozialisten-heraus.

43. Nevertheless, different translators' fingerprints can still be distinguished: see Jan Rybicki and Magda Heydel, "The Stylistics and Stylometry of Collaborative Translation: Woolf's *Night and Day* in Polish," *Literary and Linguistic Computing* 28, no. 4 (2013): 708–17.

44. See, for example, Stephen Ramsay, on characters' vocabularies in Virginia Woolf's *The Waves*: "Algorithmic Criticism," in *A Companion to Digital Literary Studies*, ed. Susan Schreibman and Ray Siemens (Oxford: Blackwell, 2008), 477–91, http://www.digitalhumanities.org/companionDLS/.

45. For details of Flanagan's segmentation and alignment tool ("Prism") and the database it populates ("Ebla"), see Tom Cheesman, Kevin Flanagan, and

Stephan Thiel, "Translation Array Prototype1: Project Overview" (2012–13), at www.delightedbeauty.org/vvvclosed/Home/Project.

46. See also Thiel's "Understanding Shakespeare" (2010), www.understanding-shakespeare.com.

47. Mommsen was one prominent editor of the "Schlegel-Tieck" Shakespeare. Engel adapted Baudissin's text for the production he directed in 1939 at the Deutsches Theater, Berlin. Felsenstein and Stueber translated into German Boito's libretto for Verdi's *Otello*. Zimmer's *Othello steht im Sturm* (2007) is a play for young people, extensively reusing Baudissin's text.

48. There are two online installations of VVV. At both, guest users can try out the range of navigational aids. At www.delightedbeauty.org/vvv, you can also try out the alignment and editing tools, that is, alter the contents of the database. At www.delightedbeauty.org/vvvclosed, you cannot alter the data. We welcome inquiries from researchers wishing to use the tools with their own corpora.

49. The principles of algorithmic reading with Eddy and Viv were first presented by Cheesman at the 2011 "Un/Translatables" conference. Handmade draft visualizations and crude mathematical formulae are archived in Tom Cheesman and the VVV Project Team, "Translation Sorting with Eddy and Viv" (2011), www.scribd.com/doc/101114673/Eddy-and-Viv. See also Zhao Geng et al., "Visualizing Translation Variation: Shakespeare's *Othello*," *Advances in Visual Computing: Lecture Notes in Computer Science* 6938 (2011): 653–63. On related problems, see Carlos Monroy et al., "Visualization of Variants in Textual Collations to Analyze the Evolution of Literary Works in the Cervantes Project," *Research and Advanced Technology for Digital Libraries: Lecture Notes in Computer Science* 2458 (2002): 199–211; Desmond Schmidt and Robert Colomb, "A Data Structure for Representing Multi-version Texts Online," *International Journal of Human-Computer Studies* 67, no. 6 (2009): 497–514.

50. The name Eddy derives from a wilful misreading of the symbols Σ and D, as used in the mathematics of information retrieval, stylometry, and natural language processing: Σ "the sum of," D: "document(s)." It also evokes "eddy," as in local turbulence: "Eddy is the disturbance created when the flows of cultural histories intersect with the flows of individual re-translation decisions"; and Viv evokes "vivacity": "the energy in the relation between the translated text and all its translations: all those disturbances, cultural changes and individual decisions" (Cheesman, Flanagan and Thiel, "Translation Array").

51. For a fuller account of the Eddy algorithm, see Flanagan's section, "6.2. Eddy and Viv Formulae," in Cheesman, Flanagan, and Thiel, "Translation Array." See also Tom Cheesman, "Reading Originals by the Light of Translations," *Shakespeare Survey* 68 (2015): 87–98.

52. Jacques Derrida, *Specters of Marx*, trans. Peggy Kamuf (New York: Routledge, 1994), 21.

53. A "Table" function, added to VVV by Flanagan in 2013, enables users to select any set of versions and segments, and display the texts for comparative reading in a table, together with scatterplot representations of all the Eddy values for each segment, calculated for the selected subcorpus.

54. See "The Riddle of Literary Quality," a research project directed by Karina van Dalen-Oskam, at http://literaryquality.huygens.knaw.nl/.

Appendix: Some German Translations and Adaptations of *Othello*

Bab, Julius, and E[lisabeth] Levy, trans. and eds.; Wolf Graf Baudissin, trans. *Othello*. In *William Shakespeare: Sämtliche Werke*. Vol. 7 (of 9, 1923–24). *Die großen Tragödien: Lear Macbeth Othello Coriolanus: Nach der Schlegel-Tieckschen Übersetzung neu bearbeitet*. Stuttgart: Union Deutsche Verlagsgesellschaft, 1923.

Bärfuss, Lukas, trans. *Othello—Kurze Fassung. Stück in 5 Akten nach William Shakespeare*. Cologne: Hartmann & Stauffacher Verlag, 2001.

Baudissin, Wolf Graf, trans. *Othello, der Mohr von Venedig*. In *Shakespeares Dramatische Werke*, ed. August Wilhelm von Schlegel and Ludwig Tieck, vol. 8 (of 9) (1832). Berlin: Reimer, 1825–33.

Benda, Johann Wilhelm Otto, trans. *Othello*. In *Shakespear's dramatische Werke*. Vol. 19 (of 19, 1825–26). Hanover: Georg Joachim Göschen, 1826. (Text used: Harvard College Library copy, facsimile at http://books.google.co.uk/books?id=bV8oAAAAYAAJ&dq=benda+shakespear%27s+dramatische+othello&source=gbs_navlinks_s.)

Bodenstedt, Friedrich, trans. and ed. *Othello*. In *William Shakespeare's Dramatische Werke*. Uebersetzt von Friedrich Bodenstedt, Nicolaus Delius, Otto Gildemeister, Georg Herwegh, Paul Heyse, Hermann Kurz, Adolf Wilbrandt. Ed. Friedrich Bodenstedt. Vol. 7 (of 9, 1872). Leipzig: F. A. Brockhaus, 1872. (Copy used includes with its own title page: *Othello, der Mohr von Venedig*. Translated by Friedrich Bodenstedt. Leipzig: F. A. Brockhaus, 1867, i.e., part of the first edition, 38 vols, 1867–71, vol. 1, 1867.)

Bolte, Hanno, and Dieter Hamblock, trans. *William Shakespeare: Othello: Englisch-Deutsch*. Stuttgart: Philipp Reclam jun., 1985.

Brunner, Karl, trans. and ed.; Wolf Graf Baudissin, trans. William Shakespeare, *Othello, der Mohr von Venedig*. English text with German translation by Ludwig Tieck (Wolf Graf Baudissin). Linz: Österreichischer Verlag für Belletristik und Wissenschaft, 1947.

Buhss, Werner, trans. *William Shakespeare: Othello, Venedigs Neger*. Typescript. Berlin: Henschel Schauspiel Theaterverlag Berlin, 1996.

Engel, Erich, trans. *William Shakespeare Othello: Weitgehend neu übersetzt und bearbeitet von Erich Engel (Unter Benutzung der Übersetzung von Baudissin)*. Typescript. Berlin: Felix Bloch Erben, 1939.

Engler, Balz, trans. and ed. *Othello: Englisch-deutsche Studienausgabe*. Munich: Franke, 1976. (Repr.: Tübingen: Stauffenberg, 1989.)

Eschenburg, Johann Joachim, trans. and ed.; Gabriel Eckert, trans. and ed. *Othello*. In *Willhelm Shakespears Schauspiele* (ed. Johann Joachim Eschenburg), new and improved edition by Gabriel Eckert. Vol. 9 (of 22, 1778–83). Mannheim: [Gegel], 1779. (Text used: Bayerische Staatsbibliothek copy, facsimile at http://reader.digitale-sammlungen.de/resolve/display/bsb10749635.html.)

Felsenstein, Walter, and Carl Stueber, trans. *Giuseppe Verdi: Othello: "Otello": In der Originalsprache (Italienisch mit deutscher Übersetzung), Opernführer*, ed. Kurt Pahlen and Rosemarie König. Munich: Wilhelm Goldmann Verlag and Musik Verlag B Schott's Söhne, 1980. (Translation first published: Milan.: Ricordi, 1964.)

Flatter, Richard, trans. *Othello der Mohr von Venedig: Sonderabdruck für Bühnenzwecke.* Vienna: Walter Krieg Verlag, 1952. Offprint: Theater-Verlag Desch. From Flatter, trans., *Shakespeare: Neu übersetzt.* 6 vols. Vienna: Walter Krieg Verlag, 1952–55.

Fried, Erich, trans. *Othello.* In *Shakespeare-Übersetzungen: Hamlet, Othello.* Berlin: Wagenbach, 1972. (Text used: repr. 1999).

Gildemeister, Otto, trans. *Othello.* In *Shakespearedramen (Romeo und Julia, Othello, Lear, Macbeth): Nachgelassene Übersetzungen.* Ed. Heinrich Spies. Berlin: Georg Reimer, 1904. (*Othello* translated c. 1871.)

Gundolf, Friedrich, trans. *Othello.* In *Shakespeare in deutscher Sprache.* Vol. 2 (of 10, 1908–18). Berlin: Georg Bondi, 1909. (Text used: repr. in 6 vols, 1920–22, vol. 1, 1920.)

Günther, Frank, trans. *William Shakespeare: Othello, Zweisprachige Ausgabe, Mit einem Essay von Dieter Mehl.* Munich: Deutscher Taschenbuch Verlag, 4th edition, 2006. (First edition: 1995. First production: Hildesheim, 1992).

[Gutenberg]; Wenig, Ruediger, ed.; Hans-Jürgen Meinerts, ed.; Wolf Graf Baudissin, trans. *William Shakespeare: Othello.* Electronic file at www.william-shakespeare.de/othello1/othello.htm and at http://gutenberg.spiegel.de/buch/2185/1. (Created by Ruediger Wenig [?], c. 2000. Derived [?] from Meinerts.)

Karbus, Oliver, trans. *William Shakespeare, Othello.* Typescript. Vienna: Thomas Sessler Verlag, Bühnen- und Musikverlag, 2006.

Kaufmann, Philipp, trans. *Othello.* In *Shakespeares dramatische Werke, nach der Uebersetzung von August Wilhelm Schlegel, Philipp Kaufmann und Voß.* Ed. Max Koch. Vol. 8 (of 12, 1882–84). Stuttgart: Cotta, c. 1883. (Translation first published in Philipp Kaufmann, trans., *Shakespeares dramatische Werke.* Vol. 2 [of 4, 1830–36]. Berlin: Nicolai, 1832.)

Klose, Dietrich, ed.; Wolf Graf Baudissin, trans. *Othello, der Mohr von Venedig: Trauerspiel in fünf Aufzügen.* Stuttgart: Reclam, 1993.

Laube, Horst, trans. *William Shakespeare Othello Der Mohr von Venedig.* Typescript. Frankfurt am Main: Verlag der Autoren, 2005.

Lauterbach, E. S. [Erich Selbmann], and Benita Gleisberg, ed. and trans.; Wolf Graf Baudissin, trans. *William Shakespeare, Othello, der Mohr von Venedig* (Originaltitel: *Othello, the Moor of Venice*). Typescript. Berlin: Henschel Schauspiel Theaterverlag, 1996. (Created 1973.)

Leonard, Christian, trans. *Othello! Theaterproduktion von Shakespeare Company Berlin.* Typescript (pdf), Shakespeare Company Berlin. Berlin, 2010.

Meinerts, Hans Jürgen, ed. Wolf Graf Baudissin, trans. *Othello.* In *William Shakespeare Gesammelte Werke in drei Bänden.* Vol. 3: *Tragödien.* Notizen. Gütersloh: Bertelsmann and Sigbert Mohn, n.d. (First edition: 6 vols, 1958.)

Mommsen, Carl Johannes Tycho, trans. and ed.; Wolf Graf Baudissin, trans. *Othello.* In *William Shakespeare: Dramatische Werke. Übersetzt von A.W. von Schlegel und Ludwig Tieck.* Vol. 9 (of 9). *Ende gut, Alles gut; Othello; Cymbeline; Macbeth.* Berlin: Reimer, 1867. (First edition: 12 vols, 1850–51; repr. 9 vols, 1853–55.)

Motschach, Hermann, trans. *William Shakespeare Othello (Othello, The Moor of Venice).* Typescript. Munich: Drei Masken Verlag, 2004. (First production: Cottbus, 1993. Created: 1992.)

Ortlepp, Ernst, trans. *Othello*. In *W. Shakspeare's dramatische Werke*. Vol. 5 (of 16, 1838–39). Stuttgart: Rieger, 1839.

Rothe, Hans, trans. *Othello*. In *William Shakespeare. Dramen*. Vol. 3 (of 4). Munich: Langen and Müller, 1963. (Revised edition of: *Der Elisabethanische Shakespeare: Das dramatische Werk*. Vol. 4 [of 9, 1955–59]. *Othello, Komödie der Irrungen, König John*. Baden-Baden: Holle, 1956.)

Rüdiger, Reinhold, trans. *William Shakespeare Othello, der Mohr von Venedig Tragödie: In Anlehnung an die Übersetzung von Friedrich von Bodenstedt Nach dem Original neu übersetzt*. Typescript. Berlin: Felix Bloch Erben, 1983.

Schaller, Rudolf, trans. *Othello*. In *Shakespeares Werke*. Vol. 2 (of 4, 1964–70). Berlin (DDR): Rütten & Loening, 3rd edition 1964. First edition: 1960–62. (Othello text used: photocopy Verlag Autorenagentur. First production: Cottbus, 1959.)

Schiller, Friedrich, and Johann Heinrich Voß, trans. *Othello*. In *Friedrich Schiller: Werke, Nationalausgabe*. Vol. 14 (of 46). *Bühnenbearbeitungen, Zweiter Teil*. Ed. Hans Heinrich Borcherdt. Weimar: Böhlau, 1949. (*Othello* text pp. 147–264, introduction 267–289, variants and notes 343–77.)

Schmidt, Alexander, trans. and ed.; Wolf Graf Baudissin, trans. *Othello*. In *Shakespeare's dramatische Werke nach der Uebersetzung von August Wilhelm Schlegel und Ludwig Tieck*. Ed. Hermann Ulrici. Vol. 12 (of 12, 1876–77). 2nd rev. ed. (Deutsche Shakespeare-Gesellschaft). Berlin: Reimer, 1877. (First edition: 1867–71.)

Schröder, Rudolf Alexander, trans. *Othello*. In *Shakespeare: Deutsch*. Berlin: Suhrkamp, 1963.

Schwarz, Hedwig, trans. *Othello, der Maure von Venedig: Trauerspiel in fünf Aufzügen von William Shakespeare*. Typescript. Shakespeare-Bibliothek München: Sh Üz 25. MS date on the folder: 1941.

Swaczynna, Wolfgang, trans. [*William Shakespeare,*] *Die Tragödie von Othello, dem Mohren von Venedig (The Tragedie of Othello, the Moore of Venice)*. Typescript. Cologne: Jussenhoven & Fischer, 1972.

Vischer, Friedrich Theodor, trans. *Othello*. In *Vorträge: Zweite Reihe: Shakespeare-Vorträge*. Ed. Robert Fischer. Vol. 3 (of 6). *Othello, König Lear*. Stuttgart: Cotta, 1901. (Posthumous. Lectures delivered, with translations, in 1869–87.)

Voß, Johann Heinrich, trans. *Othello*. Jena: Frommann, 1806.

Wachsmann, Michael, trans. *William Shakespeare, Die Tragödie von Othello, dem Mohr von Venedig*. Typescript. Berlin: Gustav Kiepenheuer Bühnenvertriebs-Gmbh, 2005.

Wieland, Christoph Martin, trans. *Othello*. In *William Shakespeare Theatralische Werke in 21 Einzelbänden*. (Zurich: Orell, Geßner & Comp.: 1762–66). Reprint edited by Hans and Johanna Radspieler. Vol. 18. Zürich: Haffmans, 1995. (Text used: Gutenberg ebook 7185, produced by Delphine Lettau, 2003. http://www.gutenberg.org/ebooks/7185.)

Wolff, Max J., trans. and ed.; Wolf Graf Baudissin, trans. *Othello*. In *Shakespeares Werke übertragen nach Schlegel-Tieck*. Vol. 14 (of 22). *Hamlet, Othello*. Berlin: Volksverband der Bücherfreunde, Wegweiser-Verlag, (1926).

Zaimoglu, Feridun, and Günter Senkel, trans. *William Shakespeare Othello*. Münster: Monsenstein und Vannerdat, 2004. (First production: Munich, 2003.)

Zeynek, Theodor von, trans. *Shakespeare: Othello Der Mohr von Venedig*. Typescript. Munich: Ahn und Simrock Bühnen- und Musikverlag, n.d. (Zeynek: b. 1873–d. 1948.)

Zimmer, Hans. *Othello steht im Sturm: Jugendstück frei nach Shakespeare. Vertonung der Lieder von Anja Neideck*. Weinheim: Deutscher Theaterverlag Weinheim, 2007.

Part VI

✦

Translingual Travels

Chapter 17

Rusty Rails and Parallel Tracks

Trans-Latio in Yoko Tawada's *Das nackte Auge* (2004)

Leslie A. Adelson

Travel and translation are the two most common points of entry for a growing field of international scholarship on the contemporary literary author Yoko Tawada, who writes primarily in German and Japanese to probe—in writing—structures of language and forms of innovation that might properly be called productive in one sense or another.[1] As I have summarized elsewhere, for example, "Tawada scholars generally regard spatial movement and translational turns of various sorts as crucially and productively linked to a reinvention of subjectivity as a conjoined literary and social project in the author's oeuvre."[2] A prominent scholar of new translation studies in Germany, Doris Bachmann-Medick calls for more refined critical attention to specific "forms of movement" in contemporary literary texts more generally in order to understand cultural transformations in subjectivity under way as social life in Europe is transformed by diverse new technologies of "spatial appropriation" around 2000.[3] While travel and translation frequently appear linked in both Tawada scholarship and the author's literary projects, and while the linkage does serve the writer's explicit and repeatedly invoked passion for transformation in the German sense of *Verwandlung*, I will argue here that the linkage is neither casual nor coincidental but pivotal for the very form that transformation takes in key passages from Tawada's German-language novel of 2004, *Das nackte Auge* (*The Naked Eye*), a Japanese version of which appeared simultaneously with a title referencing a "traveling" naked eye.[4] However, because the argument advanced in this chapter concerns something related to train travel in particular—yet another ubiquitous motif in Tawada's many literary experiments and countless biographical descriptions of the author's arrival in Europe via the Trans-Siberian Railway in 1979—it is important to clarify that the argument will not pivot on the trope of trains as such but on the figure of the rails.[5] In this sense I am less interested in train travel as a mode of human movement in *Das nackte Auge* than in analyzing specific forms with which this novel configures the means by which movement by train is rendered possible. This requires attention to the rails, which appear as parallel tracks in a world of Euclidean geometry where parallel lines never meet though they do go somewhere.[6] Shifting our attention from the protagonist-narrator's train travels as such to Tawada's literary configuration of the rails by which real and imagined movement becomes possible may change the way we think of the author's writing projects in relation to transnational migration through space, cosmopolitan values over time, and Tawada's thought-image (*Denkbild*) of translation. At the very least it will offer some new perspectives for assessing a pivotal link between travel and translation in *Das nackte Auge*, on the one hand, and possible consequences for understanding one of the operative forms of transformation in Tawada's literary prose, on the other.[7]

Petra Fachinger has called *Das nackte Auge* Tawada's "most plot-centred work to date," and Hansjörg Bay ascribes "a decidedly political dimension" to the novel's transnational travel narrative, originating in Ho Chi Minh City and proceeding via East Berlin (when it was still the capital of the German Democratic Republic), the West German city of Bochum, Paris (where the main figure spends ten years as an illegal immigrant), and occasional thoughts of Moscow, back eventually to Berlin, albeit one transformed by the end of the Cold War. Delegated to represent communist Vietnam at a youth conference in East Berlin in 1988, Tawada's protagonist-narrator is rendered unconscious for purposes of abduction by a West German man intending to save her and then escapes "unwittingly" from Bochum to Paris while intending to catch a train to Moscow.[8] Much like Zafer Şenocak's first-person narrator in *Gefährliche Verwandtschaft* in this respect, Tawada's traveling figure too "misses" ("verpaßt") the historic events of 1989 in the European city most symbolically associated with Cold War divisions and their ostensible erasure.[9] While in Paris, she spends most of her time cultivating a filmic obsession with Catherine Deneuve on screen, and the novel's chapters are organized around the communist schoolgirl's encounters with screen images of Deneuve in films such as *Indochine* (dir. Régis Wargnier, 1992), which addresses French colonial regimes in Vietnam, *Est-Ouest* (dir. Régis Wargnier, 1999), which features encounters with Stalinism through the eyes of a Russian doctor and his French wife, and more. Tawada's story as such thus suggests a tale of mobility and multilingualism embedded in palimpsestic spatial and temporal metanarratives of postcolonialism and postcommunism, which in this case connote a cosmopolitanism more "rootless" than "rooted" in any geographic or social sense.[10] Traces of these parallel metanarratives run through *Das nackte Auge* much like the railroad tracks enabling the main figure's transition from Bochum to Paris. Her abductor describes these tracks as "die Verlängerung der Transsibirischen Eisenbahn durch Bochum" (the extension of the Trans-Siberian Railway through Bochum) and the Trans-Siberian Railway as an "Eisenbahnlinie" (railway line) linking

Moscow "direkt" (directly) to Paris (*Das nackte Auge,* 27). In Susan Bernofsky's English translation this is rendered as "the Trans-Siberian Railroad extension passing through Bochum" and providing "a direct link between Moscow and Paris" (*NE* 26). Part of my subsequent argument will hinge on Tawada's exact wording in German.

Despite the plot-driven and overtly political elements of the German novel, scholars generally agree that the text is ultimately—and far more characteristically for Tawada's work overall—about writing, though they account for the convergence of travel, writing, and history in *Das nackte Auge* in a range of ways. Commenting on the many textual instantiations of the novel in different languages and time frames, Yumiko Saito refers to this textual corpus as writing that is itself on the move ("ein sich bewegendes Werk") and thus—or so we might extrapolate—as writing that produces its own history in flux.[11] For Petra Fachinger, one of the few scholars to address the novel's postcolonial and postcommunist motifs in any sustained sense, *Das nackte Auge* deploys a "hybrid" form of writing to reflect cultural shifts away from national identities to more global vectors of orientation, especially through stylistic recourse to the literary tradition of the picaresque.[12] Claiming that the novel "refuses to be read as German *Migrantenliteratur*" (which she defines as literature depicting migrants' experience of "being the Other in German society"), Fachinger stresses in her reading the processual nature of becoming transnational, "not by moving physically from one continent to another, but by making this transition in and through writing." Tawada's figure of the *pícara* is pivotal for Fachinger's emphasis on a contemporary poetics "not between, but across locations, cultures, and languages," and this shift in prepositions allows Fachinger to distance herself from earlier critical models of intercultural dialogue while still accounting through the picaresque perspective for those marginalized by capitalism and colonialism. For Fachinger, the fundamentally performative nature of identity is "a central theme" of the novel (297, 299–300, and 304, respectively).

Volker Wehdeking observes parallels between the main character's life story and the many film stories she absorbs in Parisian movie theaters (without her understanding much French) and concludes that Tawada's "Filmfreak" suffers a "diffusion" of identity instead, albeit one he finds "subversive" in a Foucauldian reading of her cinema as "heterotopia."[13] Although Hansjörg Bay argues more insistently than most that *Das nackte Auge* entails a political critique of "capitalist ideology" after 1989, he sees a largely "autopoetological" significance in the many "parallels" between life and film in the world of the text. By his account, *Das nackte Auge* marks a distinct departure in Tawada's oeuvre from her earliest intertextual "journey into writing" ("Reise ins Schreiben") to a pointedly intermedial "journey into cinema" ("Reise ins Kino"). However, this "journey into cinema" is something that Bay in the end ascribes to Tawada's traveling protagonist, whose extreme "passivity" fails to counter the ideological force of the culture industry exerted by the films that consume her. In his assessment, the counterforce to such ideology is Tawada's writing style in *Das nackte Auge*, which pivots on "translations between film and text," that is to say, as an intermedial writerly journey "into the language of literature" ("in die Sprache der Literatur").[14] By contrast, Monika Schmitz-Emans considers the main figure's passivity not as a character flaw but as a linchpin for understanding both the novel's engagement with the history of early film theory (by writers such as Hugo von Hofmannsthal, Viktor Sklovskij, Hugo Münsterberg, and Béla Balász, for example) and Tawada's contributions to "new forms of linguistic representation" amidst a more general medial turn to images of various sorts in contemporary literature.[15] In her reading, "the naked eye" of Tawada's title signals an "I" that can be understood only as the eye of a camera, for which the narrator's lived reality and film world are necessarily "congruent."[16] Here one might add an intertextual and intermedial reference to the 1955 film *I Am a Camera* (dir. Henry Cornelius), based on Christopher Isherwood's story collection *Goodbye to Berlin* (1939), which opens with a first-person narrator presenting as a camera: "shutter open, quite passive."[17]

What happened to the railroad tracks, and why are they important for understanding a pivotal link between travel and translation in the service of transformation in *Das nackte Auge*? Whereas others foreground the novel's transnational movements and intermedial translations in one form or another, I will focus on Tawada's particular mobilization of train tracks in a cluster of scenes that I too—like Hansjörg Bay but for different reasons—would call key to one form of transformation operating in this text.[18] The scenes I have in mind involve the unwitting protagonist-narrator's point of departure from Bochum, and I propose to read these scenes as a text-to-text translation of isolated elements from Walter Benjamin's 1923 essay, "The Task of the Translator."[19] While there is nothing new in claiming Benjaminian influences on Tawada's writerly projects in general or even the general importance for her of Benjamin's thoughts on "the task of the translator"—as reflected in her own essay on reading Paul Celan's poetry in Japanese translation, for example—the aspect I hope to illuminate here does contribute something new to critical discussions of the nexus of travel, translation, and transformation in Tawada's literary work.[20] My analysis additionally resonates with Christine Ivanovic's astute observation that Tawada's allusions to Benjamin in works such as the novel *Schwager in Bordeaux* and the play *Sancho Pansa* remain "fragmentary." According to Ivanovic, Tawada "focuses above all on a few selected features of Benjamin's oeuvre while largely bracketing out central aspects of his thought." At the same time Ivanovic ascribes "constitutive significance" to Benjamin's translation essay for Tawada's poetics.[21]

Benjamin famously defines translation in this essay as "a form," but what form does transformation take when travel and translation converge in *Das nackte Auge*? The crucial scene in this regard marks a moment—not in Saigon, Moscow, Berlin, or Paris but Bochum—where two different sets of train tracks also converge. In so doing they allow the main figure to escape her abductor by boarding an imaginary train that nonetheless takes her to Paris. This scene constitutes a decisive turning point and relay station in the novel, but not only because the protagonist-narrator first encounters a screen version of Catherine Deneuve at the former's "favorite spot by the rusty tracks" (*DnA* 36; *NE* 37).[22] Beyond this, real and imagined means of travel merge here to the point of becoming indistinguishable in their novelistic effects, and this successful fusion in chapter 1 sets the tone for everything that follows.[23] In this sense Tawada's rusty-rail scene can be understood in relation to Tzvetan Todorov's critical category of the fantastic, which he defines as "that hesitation experienced by a person who knows only the laws of nature, confronting an apparently supernatural event," in literary terms "an ambiguous perception shared by the reader and one of the characters."[24] As Todorov elaborates in his distinction between the fantastic-uncanny and the fantastic-marvelous, "the laws of reality remain intact" in the first instance, while readers must entertain "new laws of nature" in the second. However, we might consider Tawada's approach to the fantastic-marvelous in *Das nackte Auge* as "exophonic" rather than "exotic" in the way Todorov applies the latter term to a subcategory of the marvelous.[25] Tawada's transnational readership may not be familiar with Bochum as such but is certainly called upon to be surprised—as the main figure is—when a working train arrives on "the rusty tracks" described earlier in the text as an "extension" of the Trans-Siberian Railroad (*DnA* 27; *NE* 26). As Dorothea E. von Mücke has trenchantly argued in her account of the fantastic as an intervention in "the cultural history of reading," the literary form signals changing historical relations between text and reader. This too applies, I would suggest, to the productive interventions that *Das nackte Auge* seeks to mobilize.[26]

Rust does not merely connote diminished functional value in an everyday sense but advanced chemical transformation too. The rusty rails in *Das nackte Auge* acquire special significance not only because of what transpires at a key moment but also because the narrative structure introduces them in stages, and with each successive stage the linkage to motifs of transformation is heightened.[27] When the main figure's West German abductor first tells her about the train tracks in disuse running through Bochum, he appears to take pity on her by stressing a factual "direct link [in the German: an "Eisenbahnlinie" or railway line] between Moscow and Paris," even "suddenly" speaking Russian to impart this information to his communist interlocutor (*DnA* 27; *NE* 26). Another couple involved in this conversation includes a woman from Moscow who speaks only German to the woman from Vietnam, and the German-speaking Muscovite confirms the factual nature of the rails by identifying their location in Bochum as Sieben Planeten (Seven Planets), an area once known for a coal mine.[28] This prompts someone else to mention an American film about a coal miner's son who was inspired to become an astronaut when he once saw Sputnik in the night sky. To this the dejected abductee protests, "'I like Tarkovsky,'" thus alluding to an acclaimed Soviet film director known for his experimental cinematography of derealization effects (*DnA* 28, *NE* 26). If the later scene at the tracks signals a "journey into cinema" as Hansjörg Bay proposes, different cinematic languages are already invoked when the facticity of the train tracks is asserted in the text.

In a second stage the "I" of the narrative underscores that *Sieben Planeten* are "the first two German words I consciously learned" (*DnA* 28; *NE* 26). This is striking from a figure that the text more commonly depicts as refusing to learn or unable to learn various languages, not knowing or even unlearning them. The German words *Sieben Planeten* are thus highlighted in more ways than one, and I would suggest that Benjamin's many allusions to things planetary and cosmic are loosely in play here. Specifically, the narrative voice tells us that she conjures these words—and with them "the planets in the cosmos"—to dispel her fears and especially her fear "of an enormous distance" (*DnA* 28; *NE* 27). A later instantiation of this occurs when she is able to banish her fears in a rainstorm of "inky clouds" by saying "Sieben Planeten" out loud (*DnA* 36; *NE* 36).

The motifs of writing and travel are thus close at hand, and yet the term *Sieben Planeten* more importantly interposes forms of metamorphosis and temporality into the second stage of train-track narrative. In Greek mythology the Seven Planets are the Pleiades, the seven daughters of Atlas transformed by Zeus into a constellation of stars in order to save them from Orion's pursuit on earth. For ancients with no access to telescopes, a different configuration of Seven Planets consisted of seven celestial bodies for which days of the week would be named.[29] Attempting to articulate a Benjaminian "'task of the reader'" on the basis of Benjamin's "divergent models of language," Irving Wohlfarth gives an especially incisive account of astrological, theological, and historical-anthropological structures as reflected in Benjamin's writings over time on language.[30] Wohlfarth builds the argument in this endeavor on his own translational turn of phrase "zwischen den Linien—*between the lines*" (298), which is inspired by Benjamin's use of "zwischen den Zeilen" in reference to interlinear translation in "The Task of the Translator." More will be said about that below. Here I wish only to underscore three of Wohlfarth's observations as arguably relevant to a reading of Tawada's rusty rails: (1) that reading "between the lines" for Benjamin disrupts a linear "continuum" and allows something else to happen, through reading, in the space "between the lines"; (2) that language for Benjamin is "a medium" for contrapuntal encounters between disjunctive temporalities ("ein Medium, in dem unterschiedliche Zeitrhythmen einander kontrapunktieren" [314, 315]); and (3) that Benjamin's astrologers among the ancients had to rely on their "naked eyes" (320) to read the stars.[31] Benjamin seems a far cry from Bochum, however, when Tawada's West German character claims simply that one can ride the rails anywhere from Bochum but is unsure whether the Trans-Siberian Railroad "ever stopped" there. The second stage of the train-track narrative closes by pointing—through train sounds that the restless woman hears approaching at night—to the oncoming convergence of real and imagined dimensions. "From a distance I could hear the faint grating sound of the drive axle, the clatter of the couplings, and a long, howling reverberation from the train tracks. Somewhere not far from my pillow a train was passing" (*DnA* 28; *NE* 27).

The third stage of train-track narrative entails considerably heightened effects when the protagonist-narrator makes a conscious decision to follow her abductor's directions to a street called Sieben Planeten. There she feels torn between the physical pull of a radiant field of rapeseed—"The rapeseed field was tugging at my hair with invisible hands" (*DnA* 33; *NE* 34)—and the shadow realm of a small forest. At this crossroads, which is also textually marked by a real crossing sign, she eventually discovers "the grass-covered railway tracks" (*DnA* 34; *NE* 34). In another turn of phrase recalling Benjamin (this time in his second thesis on the philosophy of history) the rusty rails bring back to life "a secret link" to times not lost after all ("die doch nicht vergangen und abhanden gekommen waren") (*DnA* 34; *NE* 35).[32] Explicitly "excited" by the prospect of railway lines that could take her to Moscow and facilitate a return to Saigon, Tawada's traveling figure desperately wants to board an eastbound train but cannot find a train station or even "a trace" of one. She never sees a train go by and only hears "the sound of a train far off in the distance" when she lies awake at night, her "eyelashes on fire" (*DnA* 35; *NE* 35).

The fourth stage of train-track narrative is both decisive and crucial for the novel overall for reasons adduced above. Real and imagined means of train travel converge here, and Tawada's main figure both encounters an unnamed version of Catherine Deneuve and leaves Bochum at this juncture.[33] The "other woman" standing by the rusty rails seems to appear with an unspecified mission, and the protagonist-narrator's heart beats faster because of it. Motifs of transformation proliferate through rhetorical likenesses in relation to parallel tracks, for example, when the Deneuve figure's collar is compared to "the gills of a tropical fish," the mysterious woman herself is likened to an immovable "spire of a temple" when she lies down on the tracks, or when the lever that the "I" must activate to stop the train in Bochum appears "like the tail of a dragon" (*DnA* 36–37; *NE* 37–38). Something out of the ordinary is clearly in play when the figure of the other woman is described as wearing "ornaments that looked somehow extraterrestrial," as if she had escaped from a "futuristic" opera set. The protagonist-narrator recognizes "something extraordinary" in the figure at the tracks (*DnA* 36; *NE* 37). Recalling "extraordinary voyages" (Jules Verne) associated with science fiction, these aspects of the wordless apparition even seem to change "the consistency of the air around her" (*DnA* 36; *NE* 37). When she lies down on the rusty rails and refuses to be moved, her figural counterpart hears a train approaching and wonders whether the sound could be coming from a city tram or perhaps a domestic refrigerator humming in her brain. This question marks the terrain of the fantastic, and the narrative voice answers it by asserting: "The heavy iron wheels continued to turn, coming closer and closer" (*DnA* 37; *NE* 38). This assertion of the real is followed by decisive action on the part of the "I," who activates the lever with all her might to save the woman and stop the train. A siren blares and then we read: "Innumerable tiny red blinking lights set in a line at regular intervals into the distance began flashing on and off" (*DnA* 37; *NE* 38). With this the rusty rails of the "Eisenbahnlinie" (railway line) and a more abstract line leading far away fuse, and this line is rendered as noncontinuous or interrupted in its very linearity. Here too Benjamin is along for the ride as Tawada configures it.

Translation is thematized in this segment when Tawada's first-person narrator feels her heart beat "even louder" with a question she is afraid "to translate . . . into a language" (*DnA* 38; *NE* 39). This question too is answered by action, which the "I" undertakes at just the right moment to travel—or so she imagines—to Moscow and from there home to Vietnam. Instead she will find "Indochina," which as she observes much later in Paris, exists as "no country" but only "on the screen" (*DnA* 84; *NE* 98). In her moment of heightened decisiveness at the rusty rails of Sieben Planeten, however, she crawls "parallel to the train through the bushes" ("parallel zu dem Zug durch den Busch") in order to reach the door through which she boards the train (*DnA* 38).[34] Her movement at this vital juncture is encoded as "parallel to the train," which itself requires parallel tracks or lines to move. As the discussion of Wohlfarth's article on Benjamin has underscored, "between the lines" ("zwischen den Zeilen") is a key trope in Benjamin's "The Task of the Translator," and these lines are understood to be parallel. There Benjamin writes, "to some degree all great texts contain their potential translation between the lines; this is true to the highest degree in sacred writings. The interlinear version of the Scriptures is the prototype or ideal of all translation." (In the German this reads: "in irgendeinem Grade enthalten alle großen Schriften, im höchsten aber die heiligen, zwischen den Zeilen ihre virtuelle Übersetzung. Die Interlinearversion des heiligen Textes ist das Urbild oder Ideal aller Übersetzung.")[35]

The phrases "zwischen den Zeilen" and "interlinear" themselves stand in translational relation to each other, even in Benjamin's German essay, and I would like to suggest that Tawada's configuration of parallel lines enabling movement picks up this Benjaminian cipher so important for his concept of translation and carries it over into *Das nackte Auge* without rendering it as metaphor. This is *trans-latio* not "across" the space between two lines of writing or thought but off to the side in another direction altogether. I am not suggesting that Tawada's text entails systematic engagement with Benjamin's philosophical treatment of translation but quite the contrary in this instance. Unlike other elements of her writing projects that do seem to be in systematic dialogue with Benjamin's body of thought—as elaborated, for example, through figures of reading discussed elsewhere[36]—the parallel tracks in *Das nackte Auge* literally trans-late a translational moment from his work on translation and mobilize it in the service of Tawada's work on transformation in and through literature. Lateral movement rather than direct confrontation is key to all that transpires in this novel and to forms of reading it would seem to require, even in reference to postcolonialism and postcommunism as parallel tracks of narrative.[37] Although the protagonist-narrator of *Das nackte Auge* does find her "rusty rails" and makes them operate in her favor, albeit with completely unpredictable results, the real and imagined train tracks that converge here can also not be understood as "found objects" in a surrealist sense. As Bettina Brandt elaborates in an illuminating analysis of Tawada's reworking of a seminal image from the historical archive of surrealism, the German novel *Ein Gast* (*A Guest*, 1993) both invokes and alters Lautréamont's version of a chance encounter between a sewing machine and an umbrella in systematic ways.[38] *Das nackte Auge* by contrast toys with an arsenal and even a vocabulary of "found words" and "found objects" in some passages—notably having to do with air travel—and many others are oneiric in tenor.[39] Yet the finding of the indispensable train tracks is far too deliberate and the incremental narrative staging of the pivotal scene too directed for any surrealist image of a chance encounter to apply in this critical instance. Tawada's treatment of translation "between the lines" ("zwischen den Zeilen") likewise signals no chance encounter with Benjamin but renders his phrasing a translatable and trans-lated object in *Das nackte Auge* instead.

Addressing Tawada's overall body of work in an article titled "Surface Translations," Susan C. Anderson stresses "Tawada's emphasis on the literal" as a category that she both shares and does not share with Benjamin's translation essay in particular.[40] Yasemin Yildiz speaks similarly but for different reasons of many "literalized formulations of metaphorical language" in Tawada's literary prose.[41] Tawada's configuration of a favored place by the "rusty rails" is not a literalized rendition of Benjamin's rhetorical usage *zwischen den Zeilen*, though one might make a case of sorts for the literalization of his "interlinear version" (*Interlinearversion*) instead, even though Benjamin himself uses this particular phrase in its literal rather than metaphorical sense. More to the point, the parallel lines of *Das nackte Auge* give us a trans-lated likeness of textual phenomena that simultaneously defies the comparability of their forms and their claims on us as readers. In this sense I would also suggest that the parallel configurations of postcolonialism and postcommunism running alongside the textual tracks in this novel aim less at a critique of comparable historical conditions of oppression associated with colonial and communist regimes. To put it more accurately, these parallels derail the critical lingua franca for thinking about twenty-first-century legacies of such regimes as historiographical categories of collective experience and comparative analysis.[42] Tawada's well-known predilection for *Verwandlung* is not always felicitously translated as "transformation," which obscures the sense of something going awry or askew entailed in the prefix *ver-*. After all, says Benjamin, "method is detour" ("Methode ist Umweg").[43] At the same time, what interests me about the word "transformation" in relation to *Das nackte Auge* is not merely the "trans" but in an acute sense the "form." If we ask what form transformation takes in this novel, one key answer gleaned from this reading of the rails is a trans-lated likeness—beyond metaphor—that yields grounds for more movement still but no stable comparisons.[44] Benjamin too takes recourse to a geometric likeness in "The Task of the Translator" to explain the "law" ("Gesetz") of motion that literary translation can take. For him this involves the "touch" ("Berührung") of a tangent and a circle.[45] Tawada's geometric likeness of parallel lines that never meet—but do go somewhere and also enable lateral and diffracted movement that they do not control or dictate—is itself a trans-lation that encourages us to read, not between the lines but running alongside them and staying alert to paths that lead elsewhere. The "rusty rails" of *Das nackte Auge* are at once singular in their articulation and plural in their invitation to consider the nexus of travel, translation, and transformation in ever-changing ways.[46] Tawada's singular *Denkbild* of parallelism in this novel arguably signals a sea change in critical options for understanding movement and migration as transnational tropes of collective experience and transformation.

Notes

1. See for example Susan C. Anderson, "Surface Translations: Meaning and Difference in Yoko Tawada's German Prose," *Seminar* 46, no. 1 (2010): 50–70; Julia Genz, "Yoko Tawadas Poetik des Übersetzens am Beispiel von *Überseezungen*," *Études Germaniques* 65, no. 3 (2010): 467–82; or Gizem Arslan's recent study of the larger stakes of Tawada's literary experiments with letters and ideograms as orthographic symbols ("Metamorphoses of the Letter in Paul Celan, Georges Perec, and Yoko Tawada," diss. Cornell University, 2013). Anthologies addressing Tawada's oeuvre from various transnational and translational perspectives include *Études Germaniques* 65, no. 3 (2010), special issue on "L'oreiller occidental-oriental de Yoko Tawada," ed. Bernard Banoun and Linda Koiran; Heinz Ludwig Arnold, ed., *Literatur und Migration* (Munich: text + kritik, 2006); Christine Ivanovic, ed., *Yoko Tawada: Poetik der Transformation* (Tübingen: Stauffenburg, 2010); Doug Slaymaker, ed., *Yōko Tawada: Voices from Everywhere* (Lanham, Md.: Lexington Books, 2007); and Heinz Ludwig Arnold, ed., *Yoko Tawada* (Munich: text + kritik, 2011). Appearing too late to be addressed in the present chapter, a volume titled *Die Lücke im Sinn: Vergleichende Studien zu Yoko Tawada*, ed. Barbara Agnese, Christine Ivanovic, and Sandra Vlasta, appeared in 2014 with Stauffenburg Verlag. See also Yasemin Yildiz's chapter on Tawada in her monograph, *Beyond the Mother Tongue: The Postmonolingual Condition* (New York: Fordham University Press, 2011), 109–42. Accompanied by several scholarly analyses, Tawada's Hamburg poetics lectures of 2011 appeared under the title *Yoko Tawada: Fremde Wasser, Vorlesungen und wissenschaftliche Beiträge,* ed. Ortrud Gutjahr (Tübingen:

konkursbuch Verlag Claudia Gehrke, 2012). John Namjun Kim's forthcoming monograph on Yoko Tawada and Paul de Man, tentatively titled *Ethnic Irony: Autobiographies of the Living Dead—Translation and Migration from the Great Beyond,* will be of keen interest on structures of rhetoric in particular. See also John Namjun Kim, "Ethnic Irony," *The German Quarterly* 83, no. 3 (2010): 333–52, as well as Kim's "Die Poetik einer transzendentalen Deduktion: Das Ich bei Tawada und Kant," in *Yoko Tawada*, ed. Heinz Ludwig Arnold, 94–98. For a particularly lucid discussion of productive aspects of Tawada's poetics, see Christine Ivanovic's individual contribution to her edited volume *Yoko Tawada: Poetik der Transformation*, "Exophonie und Kulturanalyse: Tawadas Transformationen Benjamins," 171–206, esp. 177. For critical work on Tawada's poetry in particular, see Marjorie Perloff, *Unoriginal Genius: Poetry by Other Means in the New Century* (Chicago: University of Chicago Press, 2010), 123–45.

2. See Leslie A. Adelson, "The Future of Futurity: Alexander Kluge and Yoko Tawada," *The Germanic Review* 86, no. 3 (2011): 153–84, here 158. That piece compares time travel and parallel worlds in twenty-first-century writing by Kluge and Tawada rather than focusing (in Tawada's case) on movement through either space or language.

3. See Doris Bachmann-Medick, "Fort-Schritte, Gedanken-Gänge, Ab-Stürze: Bewegungshorizonte und Subjektverortung in literarischen Beispielen," in *Raum und Bewegung in der Literatur: Die Literaturwissenschaft und der Spatial Turn*, ed. Wolfgang Hallet and Birgit Neumann (Bielefeld: Transcript, 2009), 257–79, here especially 257–58. One might loosely say that new translation studies approach even literary modes of translation as a form of social labor, in part, rather than a linguistic or artistic enterprise in any strictly delimited sense. See for example Doris Bachmann-Medick's chapter on the "Translational Turn" in *Cultural Turns: Neuorientierungen in den Kulturwissenschaften*, 3rd rev. ed. (Hamburg: Rowohlt, 2009), 238–83; *The Translational Turn* [special issue of *Translation Studies* 2, no. 1], ed. Doris Bachmann-Medick (London: Routledge, 2009); Brett de Bary, "Dislocation, Deixis, and Suspense in Translation," in *Translation and the Senses of the Wor(l)d*, ed. Stephanie Shu-ling Tsai, special issue of *Tamkang Studies of Foreign Languages and Literatures* (*Danjiang wai yu lun cong*) 9 (2007): 17–29; and Naoki Sakai, "How Do We Count a Language? Translation and Discontinuity," *Translation Studies* 2, no. 1 (2009): 71–88. See also *The Politics of Culture: Around the Work of Naoki Sakai*, ed. Richard F. Calichman and John Namjun Kim (New York: Routledge, 2010). Some of the theoretical work in translation studies undertaken by Asian Studies scholars such as Brett de Bary and Naoki Sakai is explicitly inspired by their readings of literary work by Tawada.

4. This does not necessarily but might conceivably involve transformations of subjectivity. The Japanese title is provided here in transliteration only and not the Japanese kanji of the publication by Kôdansha Publishers in Tokyo. For the German version of the novel, see Yoko Tawada, *Das nackte Auge: Erzählung* (Tübingen: Konkursbuchverlag, 2004). An English translation by Susan Bernofsky appeared as *The Naked Eye* (New York: New Directions, 2009), in the preface to which the translator describes the novel as Tawada's "first truly bilingual book" (n.p.) inasmuch as the German and Japanese versions were written in tandem. As Bernofsky explains, her English translation "is based solely on the German version of the novel" (n.p.). On the Japanese version, see Yumiko

Saito, "Zur Genese der japanischen Textphasen von *Das nackte Auge*," in *Yoko Tawada: Poetik der Transformation*, 285–96. Page references for the German and English versions will be provided parenthetically in this article as relevant, with the German title abbreviated as *DnA* and the English title as *NE*. (With one exception all English citations from the novel are drawn from Bernofsky's translation. Unless otherwise indicated, all other translations in this chapter are my own.) Tawada's early poetic lectures were published under the rubric and title *Verwandlungen: Tübinger Poetik-Vorlesungen* (Tübingen: Konkursbuchverlag, 1998), and both the term and the motif figure prominently in subsequent works as well. Transformation is not tied to questions of subjectivity alone for Tawada.

5. Petra Fachinger persuasively situates *Das nackte Auge* in intertextual dialogue with Tawada's text "Wo Europa anfängt" (1991), especially in relation to the Trans-Siberian Railway, to argue that the German novel "playfully undermine[s] critics' attempts to mythologize the beginning of [Tawada's] literary career as a Japanese German writer." See Petra Fachinger, "Postcolonial/Postcommunist Picaresque and the Logic of 'trans' in Yoko Tawada's *Das nackte Auge*," in *Yoko Tawada: Poetik der Transformation*, 297–308. For Suzuko Mousel Knott's thoughtful discussion of train motifs in German and Japanese versions of another Tawada text, see Knott's "Sign Language: Reading Culture and Identity in Tawada Yōko's 'The Gotthard Railway,'" in *Yōko Tawada: Voices from Everywhere*, 137–51. Both scholars link Tawada's use of train motifs to transformation through writing—Fachinger through recourse to the picaresque and Knott through an emphasis on semiotics. Neither addresses the aspect of the rails to be discussed here, which has less to do with language or writing as such than with particular aspects of translation. This also targets something other than what Miho Matsunaga has discussed as Tawada's self-declared bent for "'Übersetzung ohne Original' als literarisches Programm." See Matsunaga, "'Schreiben als Übersetzung': Die Dimension der Übersetzung in den Werken von Yoko Tawada," *Zeitschrift für Germanistik* 12, no. 3 (2002): 532–46, here 544.

6. In an especially interesting reading of mobile geographies in the writings of both Roland Barthes and Yoko Tawada, Ottmar Ette invokes the "post-Euclidean geometry" of fractals to highlight infinite discontinuities through which transitional spaces for Tawada become mobile sites of experimentation in language and translation. Focusing on texts drawn from Tawada's *Talisman* (1996) and *Überseezungen* (2002), Ette develops a critical concept of "interstitial space" (*Zwischenraum*) in contradistinction to the static "between" of so-called intercultural dialogue. By this account, frequent references to the Trans-Siberian Railway in Tawada's prose index "die längste einzelne Bahnstrecke der Erde" and thus "eine infrastrukturelle Kontinuität" that Tawada's mobile geographies in text undercut. See Ottmar Ette, "Zeichenreiche: Insel-Texte und Text-Inseln bei Roland Barthes und Yoko Tawada," in *Yoko Tawada: Poetik der Transformation*, 207–30, here esp. 216, 223, and 228–29. For additional but differently configured critiques of static tropes of betweenness in reference to literatures of migration, see Leslie A. Adelson, *The Turkish Turn in Contemporary German Literature: Toward a New Critical Grammar of Migration* (New York: Palgrave Macmillan, 2005), and Adelson, "Against Between: A Manifesto," in *Unpacking Europe: Towards a Critical Reading*, ed. Salah Hassan and Iftikhar Dadi (Rotterdam: NAi Publishers, 2001), 244–55.

7. Because the trope of train travel is also volatile in Tawada's hands, I do not claim comprehensive applicability for the argument advanced here about the role of the rails in *Das nackte Auge*. However, the reading I propose does shed some light on the extent of Tawada's literary experimentation with train travel and also underscores its relevance for our thoughts on translation as transformation in her work. On "real and imagined transnational mobility" in relation to Tawada's particular approach to literary bilingualism, see Yildiz, in *Beyond the Mother Tongue*.

8. As Daniel Medin observes, this character "unwittingly boards a train to Paris." See Daniel Medin, "The Woman Who Disappeared: Traces of Kafka in Yoko Tawada's *Das nackte Auge*," *Études Germaniques* 65, no. 3 (2010): 627–36, here 630. To be more precise, the woman wittingly escapes her abductor and wittingly boards a train but "unwittingly" boards a Paris-bound train. While the direction of the train's movement eludes her, her boarding of the Paris-bound train is no mistake as Petra Fachinger suggests with the adverb "mistakenly." For the Fachinger and Bay quotations, see Fachinger, "Postcolonial/Postcommunist Picaresque," 297 and 300; and Hansjörg Bay, "'Eyes Wide Shut': Mediale Übersetzungen in Yoko Tawadas *Das nackte Auge*," *Études Germaniques* 65, no. 3 (2010): 553–68, here 558.

9. The word "verpaßt" is quoted from Zafer Şenocak, *Gefährliche Verwandtschaft* (Munich: Babel, 1998), 121. Tom Cheesman translates this as "misses" on p. 77 of *Perilous Kinship* (Swansea: Hafan, 2009), his English translation of the Şenocak novel. For a discussion of Şenocak's figure of belatedness in a familial narrative of transnational genocide, see Adelson, *The Turkish Turn*, 114–15.

10. On "rooted cosmopolitanism," see especially Kwame Anthony Appiah, *The Ethics of Identity* (Princeton, N.J.: Princeton University Press, 2004); and Sidney Tarrow, *The New Transnational Activism* (Cambridge: Cambridge University Press, 2005). On place as "temporally layered" in Tawada's work, see also Christina Kränzle, "The Limits of Travel: Yoko Tawada's Fictional Travelogues," *German Life and Letters* 61, no. 2 (2008): 244–60, here 254. For insights into Tawada's multilingual "transnational imaginary" through the lens of "historical considerations" in particular, see Yasemin Yildiz, "Tawada's Multilingual Moves: A Transnational Imaginary," in *Yōko Tawada: Voices from Everywhere*, 77–89, and her especially trenchant chapter on Tawada in *Beyond the Mother Tongue*.

11. See Yumiko Saito, "Zur Genese der japanischen Textphasen von *Das nackte Auge*," on the Japanese phases of writing *Das nackte Auge*, 286.

12. See Petra Fachinger, "Postcolonial/Postcommunist Picaresque." Karl Esselborn makes a related argument concerning hybridity and globalization in "Übersetzungen aus der Sprache, die es nicht gibt: Interkulturalität, Globalisierung und Postmoderne in den Texten Yoko Tawadas," *Arcadia* 42, no. 2 (2007): 240–62. A shifting emphasis from "intercultural" to "transcultural" analysis can be observed more generally in recent years, especially in Germany under the influence of Wolfgang Welsch. See for example Wolfgang Welsch, "Transculturality—the Puzzling Form of Cultures Today," in *Spaces of Culture: City, Nation, World*, ed. Mike Featherstone and Scott Lash (London: Sage, 1999), 194–213. For a rigorous rejection of the static presuppositions of "intercultural dialogue" in specific reference to Tawada's writing, see Ottmar Ette, "Zeichenreiche." Partly through

his comparison of micro-textual geographies in Tawada and Barthes, Ette reconfigures the notion of "Zwischenraum," which can then be understood "gerade nicht als stabiler Raum eines Dazwischen, sondern nur als ein hochdynamischer Bewegungs-Raum" (222). In her essay "Tawada's Multilingual Moves," Yasemin Yildiz also addresses other ways in which Tawada's approach to literary bilingualism departs from a communicative model of intercultural dialogue. For an approach to literatures of migration that diverges from both Fachinger's definition and intercultural paradigms, see Adelson, *The Turkish Turn*.

13. See Volker Wehdeking's final chapter of *Generationenwechsel: Intermedialität in der deutschen Gegenwartsliteratur* (Berlin: Erich Schmidt, 2007), where he discusses *Das nackte Auge* (207–19, here 210–11 and 214–15).

14. See Hansjörg Bay, "Eyes Wide Shut," 553–55, 567. In my view Tawada's stylistic interest in intermediality begins much earlier than with *Das nackte Auge*. Bettina Brandt and Tawada also discuss the political settings of *Das nackte Auge* in Bettina Brandt, "The Postcommunist Eye: An Interview with Yoko Tawada," *World Literature Today* (January-February 2006): 43–45. There Tawada recounts a conversation with a writer from the former East Germany pointing out that East Germany is "'a country that has actually disappeared'" (45).

15. See Monika Schmitz-Emans, "Entgrenzungsphantasien und Derealisierungserfahrungen—Das Kino im Spiegel des Romans bei Thomas Mann, Luigi Pirandello, José Saramago und Yoko Tawada," in *Literarische Medienreflexionen: Künste und Medien im Fokus moderner und postmoderner Literatur*, ed. Sandra Poppe and Sascha Seiler (Berlin: Erich Schmidt, 2008), 185–204, here 185. For a relevant study of intermedial networks influencing German literature early in the twentieth century, see Stefanie Harris, *Mediating Modernity: German Literature and the "New" Media, 1895–1930* (University Park: Pennsylvania State University Press, 2009).

16. See Monika Schmitz-Emans, "Entgrenzungsphantasien und Derealisierungserfahrungen": "die Idee eines Ichs . . . , das sich auf ein Auge reduziert, welches nichts anderes als ein Kameraauge ist und für das darum Wirklichkeit und Filmwelt kongruent sind" (201). Schmitz-Emans specifically mentions Hofmannsthal's thoughts on "Kino als Traum," Münsterberg's concept of derealization, Sklovskij's approach to agency, and Balász's notion of spectatorship (200–201).

17. Volker Wehdeking in *Generationenwechsel* understands Tawada's "naked eye" as an allusion to Luis Buñuel's 1928 film, *Un chien andalou* (216). See also Bettina Brandt, "Schnitt durchs Auge: Surrealistische Bilder bei Yoko Tawada, Emine Sevgi Özdamar und Herta Müller," *Text + Kritik* 9 (2006), special issue on *Literatur und Migration*, 74–83.

18. Bay calls one scene that appears on p. 36 of the German version and p. 37 in Bernofsky's English translation the "Dreh- und Angelpunkt" of the intermedial "Übersetzungen" he has in mind because the scene marks what he understands to be the first appearance of Catherine Deneuve. See Bay, "Eyes Wide Shut," 554.

19. See Walter Benjamin, "Die Aufgabe des Übersetzers," in *Illuminationen: Ausgewählte Schriften*, ed. Siegfried Unseld, 2nd ed. (Frankfurt am Main: Suhrkamp, 1980), 50–62. The English translation used here is "The Task of the Translator," trans. Harry Zohn, in *Illuminations* (New York: Schocken, 2007), 69–82.

20. See Adelson, "The Future of Futurity," for discussion of one way in which Tawada's writing in two other literary works significantly diverges from Benjamin's dismissal of the figure of the reader in "The Task of the Translator." See also Christine Ivanovic's insightful overview of the difference between Tawada's poetics of exophony and Benjamin's approach to cultural analysis, "Exophonie und Kulturanalyse." For Ivanovic, the key difference concerns Tawada's departure from "Verfahren von Aneignung und Kritik" that were still relevant for Benjamin, and she ties this difference in part to the centrality of the figure of the reader for Tawada (177). She additionally sees Tawada's structural interest in a "Moment der Befreiung" as dispensing with Benjamin's cultural-critical attention to "die Erkenntnis der Geschichte" (190). Tawada's parallel invocation of colonial and communist histories in *Das nackte Auge*, I suggest, might demand a different reading of her literary work on historical material. Ivanovic furthermore notes that Tawada reads Benjamin's essay on translation "gegen den Strich" by dispensing with his concern for "die reine Sprache" (195). Through her analysis of Tawada's reworked Japanese version of Anne Duden's prose piece on St George and the dragon, Ivanovic understands Tawada's writing "als eine Art Realisation von Lektüre- *und* Textproduktionsverfahren" in a Benjaminian sense and as "Erlösung" from violence "qua Übersetzung" albeit without a Benjaminian "Sprachkonzept" that could be understood as metaphysical (198). On Tawada's essay "Das Tor des Übersetzers oder Celan liest Japanisch," which appears in *Talisman* (Tübingen: Konkursbuchverlag, 1996 [121–34]), see John Namjun Kim, "Writing the Cleft: Tawada Translates Celan," in *Yōko Tawada: Poetik der Transformation*, 233–39. Commenting on a Japanese poem by Tawada ("Shitai no nai sôshiki") "as a poetic rewriting of Celan's 'Die Todesfuge,' " Kim offers a rather different reading of historical violence in Tawada's poetics than Ivanovic, especially in reference to "the legacy of Japanese imperialism" (234). Since both scholars tie their understanding of Tawada's translational poetics at least in part to a reading of history and violence, the contrast is instructive.

21. See Ivanovic, "Exophonie und Kulturanalyse," 177–78. Like Fachinger but for different reasons, Ivanovic also argues that Tawada's writing (by which she means especially Tawada's writing as "exophony") exceeds "das ästhetische Paradigma einer Poetik der Migration" (205).

22. Hansjörg Bay in "Eyes Wide Shut" attributes the importance of the scene to the appearance of Catherine Deneuve in conjunction with the main character's "Reise ins Kino" (554, 567).

23. There are certainly fantastic elements in the pages preceding the decisive scene at the rusty rails, but these elements—often rendered rhetorically in simile or metaphor—can ultimately be accounted for in realist terms. As Petra Fachinger has observed in "Postcolonial/Postcommunist Picaresque" in reference to the novel's overall "transgression of the boundaries between fantasy and reality," the passages concerning the train trip to Paris are "the least realistic" (297, 301).

24. Tzvetan Todorov, *The Fantastic: A Structural Approach to a Literary Genre*, trans. Richard Howard (Cleveland, Ohio: Case Western Reserve University Press, 1973); see pp. 25, 41, and 46 for the relevant quotations offered here.

25. For Todorov, the "*exotic marvelous*" entails implied readers who are "ignorant of the regions where the events take place" and thus have "no reason for calling them into question" (*The Fantastic*, 55). For an especially lucid account

of "exophony" in Tawada's oeuvre and scholarly discussions of it, see Ivanovic, "Exophonie und Kulturanalyse." So many scholars now reference this term in discussions of Tawada's work that a complete list cannot be provided here.

26. See Dorothea E. von Mücke, *The Seduction of the Occult and the Rise of the Fantastic Tale* (Stanford, Calif.: Stanford University Press, 2003), 2. For von Mücke, gender and sexuality are key to understanding the linkage between changing cultures of reading and literary form in the nineteenth century. This is very likely true for Tawada's engagement with the fantastic in the twenty-first century too. Yildiz's book chapter on Tawada in *Beyond the Mother Tongue* is instructive also in this regard.

27. Allusions to modes of transportation associated with rust crop up elsewhere in the novel as well. For example, we encounter "a rusty bicycle" ("ein verrostetes Fahrrad") in a cellar (*DnA* 47; *NE* 51), and a motorcycle in Vietnam is described as "nothing but a rusty ox full of dents and scratches" ("nichts anderes als ein verrosteter Ochse voller Beulen und Kratzer") (*DnA* 8; *NE* 3). These rusty vehicles do not acquire the narrative status of the rusty rails in Bochum.

28. Susan Bernofsky retains the German *Sieben Planeten* in her English translation, presumably because the words refer to an actual name designation for part of Bochum.

29. See Eviatar Zerubavel, *The Seven Day Circle: The History and Meaning of the Week* (Chicago: University of Chicago Press, 1985), 12–19; and Georg-Karl Bauer, *Sternkunde und Sterndeutung der Deutschen im 9.-14. Jahrhundert* (Berlin: Ebering, 1937), 30–31. Christine Ivanovic also discusses "zahlreiche aus der Mythologie bekannte Verwandlungen" related to violence towards women in her discussion of Tawada. See Ivanovic, "Exophonie und Kulturanalyse," 190.

30. See Irving Wohlfarth, "'Was nie geschrieben wurde, lesen': Walter Benjamins Theorie des Lesens," in *Walter Benjamin 1892–1940 zum 100. Geburtstag*, ed. Uwe Steiner (Bern: Peter Lang, 1992), 297–344. See also Eric Downing, "Magic Reading," in *Literary Studies and the Pursuits of Reading*, ed. Eric Downing, Jonathan M. Hess, and Richard Benson (Rochester, N.Y.: Camden House, 2012), 189–215, on Benjamin and "divinatory reading."

31. See Wohlfarth, "Was nie geschrieben wurde," whose analysis addresses four pivotal essays by Benjamin: "Über Sprache überhaupt und über die Sprache des Menschen," "Die Aufgabe des Übersetzers," "Über das mimetische Vermögen," and "Die Lehre vom Ähnlichen."

32. Benjamin refers to "eine geheime Verabredung zwischen den gewesenen Geschlechtern und unserem." See Benjamin, "Über den Begriff der Geschichte," in *Illuminationen*, ed. Siegfried Unseld, 252–61, here 252. In stage four of the train-track narrative the first encounter with Catherine Deneuve is characterized in terms of an implied "Vereinbarung" rather than "Verabredung" (*DnA* 36).

33. One might also note a fifth but much briefer stage of the train-track narrative much later in the novel. At that point mention of *Sieben Planeten* and the rails is tied to the protagonist-narrator's direct address of the figure of Deneuve (*DnA* 174–75; *NE* 214–15).

34. Here my translation deviates from that provided by Susan Bernofsky, whose English yields: "I crept through the bushes that ran alongside the train" (*NE* 39). The "parallel" in the German text is important for the analysis developed in this essay.

35. In Harry Zohn's English translation the internal translation indicated by Benjamin's use of "zwischen den Zeilen" and "interlinear" is effaced. Compare Benjamin, "Die Aufgabe des Übersetzers," 62, and "The Task of the Translator," 82.

36. On the figure of the reader in Tawada's reception of Benjamin, see especially Ivanovic, "Exophonie und Kulturanalyse" and Adelson, "The Future of Futurity." Adelson's discussion of Tawada's "Eine Heidin in einem Heidekloster" (2009) addresses the author's treatment of reading "zwischen den Zeilen" in yet another way there. For additional commentary making systematic claims about Tawada's writing in relation to Benjamin's theoretical oeuvre, see for example Claudia Breger, "'Meine Herren, spielt in meinem Gesicht ein Affe?': Strategien der Mimikry in Texten von Emine Sevgi Özdamar und Yoko Tawada," in *AufBrüche: Kulturelle Produktionen von Migrantinnen, Schwarzen und jüdischen Frauen in Deutschland*, ed. Cathy S. Gelbin, Kader Konuk, and Peggy Piesche (Königstein: Ulrike Helmer, 1999), 30–59; Susan C. Anderson, "Surface Translations"; Ivanovic, "Exophonie und Kulturanalyse"; and Hiltrud Arens, "Das kurze Leuchten unter dem Tor oder auf dem Weg zur geträumten Sprache: Poetological Reflections in Works by Yoko Tawada," in *Yōko Tawada: Voices from Everywhere*, 59–76. Writing on Tawada's essay on reading Celan in Japanese, John Namjun Kim speaks presciently of Tawada "borrowing an image from Walter Benjamin" with the word "arcade." See Kim, "Writing the Cleft, 234.

37. In relation to contemporary visual arts, Lutz Koepnick discusses ways "in which the lateral and the trajectorial, sideways and forward glances, go hand in hand, not in order to screen out what possibly might diminish one's attention, but to allow the unanticipated and forgotten, the invisible and unspoken to (re)enter the frame of attention." See Koepnick, *On Slowness: Toward an Aesthetic of the Contemporary* (New York: Columbia University Press, 2014), 200.

38. See Bettina Brandt, "The Unknown Character: Traces of the Surreal in Yoko Tawada's Writing," in *Yōko Tawada: Voices from Everywhere*, ed. Doug Slaymaker, 111–24. Brandt refers here to Isidore Ducasse Lautréamont, *Les Chants de Maldoror*, as published in English translation by New Directions in 1965. In "The Unknown Character" Brandt additionally analyzes Tawada's treatment of an image of an alarm clock drawn from Benjamin's 1929 essay on surrealism. See also Bettina Brandt, "Schnitt durchs Auge: Surrealistische Bilder bei Yoko Tawada, Emine Sevgi Özdamar und Herta Müller," *Text + Kritik* 9 (2006), special issue on "Literatur und Migration," 74–83, which blazed important new trails in the scholarly discussion of surrealism as an aesthetic category in contemporary German literature in an age of intensified transnational migration. Brandt is preparing a book on the subject as well.

39. Attempting to fly with an illegal passport, for example, the protagonist-narrator arms herself, we read, with "found words" ("gefundenen Wörtern") (*DnA* 128; *NE* 153). Taken into custody and passing by the "'Bureau for Found Objects'" ("'Das Büro für gefundene Objekte'"), she is not allowed to enter it (*DnA* 129; *NE* 154). In an earlier scene she finds herself hidden in a cellar among discarded objects including "a deformed leather handbag" ("eine deformierte Handtasche"). When she sorts out other discarded items inside the bag, she for the first time encounters Deneuve's name in print on an old movie advertisement (*DnA* 47; *NE* 51).

40. See Susan C. Anderson, "Surface Translations," 53. Anderson is particularly concerned with Tawada's aesthetics of "playing with the surface phenomena of language" such as the "shapes and sounds of letters and syllables" (57). For Anderson, this play "questions . . . the distinction between native and foreign culture" on the basis of any putative origins, and translation becomes this "play of surfaces, as hyperattentiveness to form and literality" in Tawada's German prose (50). Marjorie Perloff in *Unoriginal Genius* refers to the "stubborn literalism of Tawada's logic" (143).

41. See Yildiz's Tawada chapter in *Beyond the Mother Tongue*. There Yildiz discusses "Bioskoop der Nacht" from *Überseezungen* (2002) and likens certain aspects of Tawada's writing to dreams as described by Freud, which transform rhetorical tropes "into scenes and narratives" (136).

42. For innovative approaches to the concept of comparison in relation to comparative literature and postcolonial studies, see especially Natalie Melas, *All the Difference in the World: The Ends of Comparison* (Stanford, Calif.: Stanford University Press, 2007). See also Emily Apter, "Comparative Exile: Competing Margins in the History of Comparative Literature," in *Comparative Literature in the Age of Multiculturalism*, ed. Charles Bernheimer (Baltimore: Johns Hopkins University Press, 1995), 86–98, and Apter, *The Translation Zone: A New Comparative Literature* (Princeton, N.J.: Princeton University Press, 2005). See also diverse entries in *Comparative Literature in an Age of Globalization*, ed. Haun Saussy (Baltimore, Md.: Johns Hopkins University Press, 2006).

43. See Walter Benjamin, "Epistemo-Critical Prologue," in *The Origin of German Tragic Drama*, trans. John Osborne (London: Verso, 2009), 28. Osborne translates "Methode ist Umweg" as "Method is a digression." In relation to Tawada, "detour" rather than "digression" strikes me as the better translation. For Benjamin's original phrasing, see his "Erkenntnistheoretische Vorrede," in *Ursprung des deutschen Trauerspiels*, ed. Rolf Tiedemann (Frankfurt am Main: Suhrkamp, 1978), 9–39, here 10.

44. Further discussion would have to address the complex status of likeness and comparison in Benjamin's writing and thought. See especially his essays "Doctrine of the Similar" ("Lehre vom Ähnlichen") and "On the Mimetic Faculty" ("Über das mimetische Vermögen"), both written in 1933.

45. Benjamin, "Die Aufgabe des Übersetzers," 60; Benjamin, "The Task of the Translator," 80. For detailed insights into the importance of mathematics for Benjamin's consideration of language and time, see Peter Fenves, *The Messianic Reduction: Walter Benjamin and the Shape of Time* (Stanford, Calif.: Stanford University Press, 2011), and especially his section on "interpolation" and the drawing of lines (235–38). Ivanovic discusses other likenesses that play a role in "The Task of the Translator"—such as the "Königsmantel" and "Scherben"—and their relevance for a reading of other works by Tawada. See Ivanovic, "Exophonie und Kulturanalyse," 194.

46. For additional thoughts on Tawada and "singularity" in relation to cultural analysis, see Ivanovic, "Exophonie und Kulturanalyse," 174. For more general philosophical reflections on "being singular plural," see Jean-Luc Nancy, *Being Singular Plural*, trans. Robert D. Richardson and Anne E. O'Byrne (Stanford, Calif.: Stanford University Press, 2000).

Chapter 18

✦

Yoko Tawada's "Tongue Dance," or The Failed Domestication of a Tongue in Furs

Bettina Brandt

When I asked Yoko Tawada in an interview later published in *World Literature Today* according to which work method she composes her texts, the author answered:

> A single word can inspire me. When this happens, I want to create a whole text out of that one word, which seems to contain the entire microcosm. That is my dream, and it is how I often start writing. I use variations of this word, place associations next to each other, create word chains like branches of a tree, and play with different forms and shapes. Finally, I realize that I have to create an ending, but I don't find an ending because I don't want to and cannot have a result. A text is a weird and wonderful plant that has grown in all directions out of a single word knot.[1]

In this chapter I will identify and analyze specific word knots in Tawada's "Zungentanz" ("Tongue Dance") and demonstrate that having found these word knots the reader finds herself or himself at the entrance of a rhizomatic labyrinth for the curious, where at each fork in the road the dialectical imagination is at work. Next I will argue that in Tawada's texts a word knot functions as a site where "a scene is being enacted simultaneously on several levels with reversals and reduplications in the allocation of roles and discourse," to borrow Gilles Deleuze's words.[2] To make matters more complex, a Tawadian word knot, when unraveled, breaks down into a multitude of different languages, both natural and technical, written and spoken.[3] As Tawada's Dutch translator I can also tell you that word knots are particularly difficult to translate and that each translator will inevitably overlook or drop some. Since the word knots are embedded in larger networks of connotations disseminated throughout the text, however, a reader engaging with Tawada's work in translation can still find enough fragments of the word chains to create his or her own interpretive map for reading Tawada's texts, presuming of course that the meshwork between word knots is, by and large, carried over in translation. My reading will particularly demonstrate how and to what purpose the word knots in Tawada's "Tongue Dance," the opening text of a 2002 collection entitled *Überseezungen,* incorporate metaphors from two seminal texts in the history of psychoanalysis: Sigmund Freud's *The Interpretation of Dreams* (*Traumdeutung*) and Leopold von Sacher-Masoch's *Venus in Furs* (*Venus im Pelz*), a text of importance to Krafft-Ebing. But before we approach "Überseezungen"—a witty neologism made up of the words "Übersee," or overseas, "Seezunge," or an edible fish known in English as "sole," and "übersetzen," or to translate—let us take a quick detour to the year 1909, a deviation which will expedite our analysis in the end. 1909 is the year in which Sigmund Freud added the, by now classic, sentence to the second edition of the *Traumdeutung* in which he declared: "the interpretation of dreams is the royal road to a knowledge of the unconscious activities of the mind."[4] Freud did not write this sentence in English, of course, and therefore did not mention a "royal road." Instead, he spoke of a "Via regia," thereby introducing two Latin words into his German sentence: "Die Traumdeutung ist die Via regia zur Kenntnis des Unbewussten im Seelenleben." In translations of Freud's *Traumdeutung* the *Via regia* is, typically, carried over as a metaphor while the two actual Latin words tend to drop out of sight. In the standard English translation of James Beaumont Strachey, the British psychoanalyst and editor of the *Standard Edition of the Complete Psychological Works of Sigmund Freud*, for instance, there is no sign of the *Via regia*—the reader stumbles over the already mentioned royal road instead.[5]

With Lawrence Venuti in mind, we can call this translation strategy, commonly adopted in the United States and in the United Kingdom, a "domesticated" translation: a translation in which most cultural, stylistic, or linguistic peculiarities of the foreign are erased in the name of fluency and transparency.[6] This translation practice is heralded as being natural and reader-friendly: it offers a helping hand to the reader by moving the source text (or original) to the target culture. Of course, this type of translation strategy comes at a cost as well. It masks what Venuti (advocate of a different translation strategy which he dubbed "foreignization") calls the "ethnocentric violence" done to the source text.[7] But it does more: it also renders the translator "invisible" and, as we have seen in the Freud example, leads to a flattening of the source text, especially its multilingual aspect. A domesticated translation, therefore, resembles a taming in more ways than one.

Through the domestication of the Latin expression in Freud's sentence the reader loses in fact something specific: the conceptual connection to the oldest and longest European two-lane road system that for centuries connected the East and the West.[8] One such *via regia*, for instance, started in Santiago de Compostella, Spain, and ended in Constantinople. Nowadays connecting "8 European countries through a length of 4,000 km," the *via regia* is marketed in the twenty-first century as a cultural symbol for European unification and persists as a tourist attraction.[9] The course of a historical *via regia*, however, was frequently altered due to changing political situations, but key locations (river crossings or mountain passes) would stay the same over long periods of time.

On a *via regia* like the one that ran outside of Freud's house in Vienna where he wrote the *Traumdeutung*, and that continued on to Lviv (then Lemberg) in the western Ukraine—former capital of the kingdom of Galicia and birthplace of Leopold von Sacher-Masoch who in his writings frequently returned to the region's (folk) history—imperial spaces were being constituted and many languages were spoken.[10] Typically, travellers on this type of road had to rely on interpreters and local guides to do their business, whether they were princes or kings, traders, pilgrims, soldiers, wandering scholars, refugees, or migrants. The Habsburg Empire was, of course, also famous for its multilingual inhabitants, and travelers would no doubt have been able to negotiate more than a few different languages on their own. A *via regia*, therefore, can also be interpreted as a multilingual road—a road on which (original) discourses and translations are being negotiated.

Traveling along the *Via Regia* in Yoko Tawada's "Tongue Dance"

Tawada's "Tongue Dance," I propose, can be interpreted as unfolding along the *via regia*, both in the literal sense—that is to say, as taking place along specific parts of the actual historical road—and metaphorically, in other words as a narrative consisting of (marked and unmarked) dream fragments that provide an insight into "the unconscious activities" of the narrator's mind and its linguistic desires. Freud's Latin *via regia*, I suggest, appears in "Tongue Dance" disguised as a German autobahn. It is a word knot that marks the threshold to the narrative's dreamscape.

In pursuing our analysis, we will now first examine the narrator's literal travel along the *via regia*. "Tongue Dance," the first story of the first section of *Überseezungen* called "Euroasiatische Zungen," or "Eurasian Tongues," evolves around a traveling figure from overseas who has a good ear for languages and a good eye for script. The figure speaks Japanese, but is also fluent in German though she experiences occasional difficulties articulating words. Pronouncing the letter "n" in the middle of a word is a particular challenge and only possible if the "n" is followed by a consonant. Another problem that the narrator figure faces is that when reading out loud, that is to say when translating the written into a spoken word, a wall is suddenly erected, forming a blockage that the narrator tries to climb over with the help of her Gregor Samsa-like minuscule feet.[11] How exactly the narrator overcomes these difficulties with spoken articulation will be addressed in the last part of this chapter.

During her travels, the narrator encounters a number of languages spoken on the historical *via regia*, including Latin, Greek, German, Hungarian, and Hebrew. More modern, specialized languages also play a role in "Tongue Dance," such as the language of psychoanalysis, the technical terminology of speech therapy, or well-known *Denkbilder* in the history of translation theory. Both the older and the newer languages, however, appear in the text only as cleverly disguised fragments and composites. A *via regia* dressed up as an autobahn is a case in point. A reader interested in deciphering these dream figures and language fragments will have to translate them without having access to an original text because, as we know from Freud, the language of dreams comes to us as a translation whose original has been lost.

The autobahn in Tawada's "Tongue Dance" signposts the entrance to Freud's *via regia*, the highway into the unconscious. The first dream sequence in Tawada's short text begins at the moment when the narrator remarks: "Damals in einem Traum stand ich auf einer unbefahrenen Autobahn,"[12] or, in my translation, "Once in a dream I was standing on an untraveled highway."

Translating Freud's *via regia* as an autobahn has, first of all, a specific mimetic function, for the text recounts the travels of the narrator who earns a living as a writer on a book tour. Given that the narrator is a migratory figure, the word "autobahn" highlights that the narrator is traveling along a specifically German network, both spatially and linguistically.

> Meine ganze Person bestand aus einer Zunge. So bekam ich keine Arbeitsstelle. Dann schrieb ich eine Autobiogaphie. Die Lebensgeschichte einer Zunge. Ich trug sie dem Publikum vor: in Melsungen, in Hemmelsdorf, in Winsen, in Bad Hersfeld, in Bendesdorf, in Reutlingen und in Ittingen.[13]

> My entire person now consisted of one huge tongue. I was unable to find work. Then I wrote an autobiography. The life story of a tongue. I read it aloud to audiences in Melsungen, Hemmelsdorf, Winsen, Bad Hersfeld, Bendestorf, Reutlingen, and Ittingen.[14]

There is, of course, a cartographic connection between Tawada's text and the historical *via regia*, for the town in the middle of Tawada's reading tour, Bad Hersfeld in Hessen, has a recorded history that dates back to the eighth century, when the town's abbey was first built. Tawada's inclusion of Bad Hersfeld in the sequence of her travels makes the connection between the *via regia* and the autobahn explicit: the actual "Via Regia" once ran through Bad Hersfeld. Today a remnant of the old road survives in the shape of a contemporary autobahn, known within Germany as the A4 and further east as the E4.

The word "autobahn" also references the historical period when the word and the object originated in Germany, the Weimar Republic and Hitler's Third

Reich, when the autobahn system was expanded under Fritz Todt. As part of the Nazis' larger military strategy, the autobahn's rapid construction was enabled by the conscription of laborers, including ultimately prisoners of war and concentration camp inmates. In "Tongue Dance," the word "autobahn" also reminds us that the *via regia*, far from simply being a peaceful trade route, was also always a strategic passage for a sequence of ever-changing armies. "Tongue Dance" references the bloodshed on the *via regia* and the autobahn explicitly through the inclusion of a murdered man in uniform ("ein uniformierter Rücken") on the road.[15] As we will see, the violent character of the *via regia* particularly comes to the fore in the last part of this chapter which deals with the narrator's linguistic education.

Thirdly, on a semantic level, "autobahn" can equally be read as a composite word made up of two different languages: the Greek word αὐτό (or self) and the German word *Bahn* (path, track, network). Hence, the autobahn in Tawada's "Tongue Dance" can, by the same token, be interpreted as both "a path to or through the self" as well as a "path that takes on a life of its own," that is to say, a word knot that spontaneously generates further networks of word knots. In "Tongue Dance" both translations are operative: on the lexical level the autobahn produces a string of associations, including the earlier mentioned "Autobiographie," as well as several implicit ones, ones that are not referenced as words in the text but occur as detailed descriptions of (dislocated) actions such as "Autoerotik" (the practice of becoming stimulated through stimuli of one's own body) or "Autoanalysis" (the psychoanalytic practice which in Tawada's dream text, as we will see, produces a specifically linguistic form of wish fulfillment), which is connected to self-translation.

Let us take an even closer look at this interpretative sequence. Since the "autobahn" in "Tongue Dance" is "unbefahren," or untraveled (". . . stand ich auf einer unbefahrenen Autobahn"), Tawada's "autobahn" can also be read as a road on which there is no "Verkehr," that is to say, no traffic or sexual intercourse, though there certainly is a lot of sexual imagery in the short text. On close examination, "Tongue Dance" can also be read as an "autoerotic" game, one which gets played when certain words are formed in the mouth through the act of pressing the tongue upon the palate. The importance of *where* to place the tongue becomes important later in Tawada's narrative when the narrator seeks help from a speech therapist in order to learn how to enunciate German words properly. The narrator's ensuing tongue game on the roof of the mouth has the effect in Tawada's text of turning the mouth, specifically the tongue and the palate, into an erotic, disciplinary zone against which the narrator ultimately rebels.

If, to reiterate Deleuze's definition already cited above, the autobahn can be read as a site where "a scene is being enacted simultaneously on several levels with reversals and reduplications in the allocation of roles and discourse," then it can be interpreted as a translation of the *via regia*, and as a "Road to the Self." The later interpretation, "the Road to the Self," includes in Tawada's text an explicitly phonetic aspect, so that the road runs along the roof of the mouth on which the tongue has to be trained to position itself. To shift the position of the tongue, to move it along a different path in the mouth, amounts to producing original tones for a newly imagined language.

The Failed Domestication of a Tongue in Furs

"Zungentanz" recounts the modifications that the narrator undergoes as the story unfolds: first a partial, then a complete bodily metamorphosis. Tawada's text opens, in a passage suggestive of Kafka's "The Metamorphosis," with its description and acknowledgment of a bodily change upon awakening. Unlike Gregor Samsa's metamorphosis, the Tongue's modification is temporary and a seemingly minor one, though in both cases the bodies are transformed into much larger objects. The bodily scale of Kafka's insect is overly large, as is Tawada's Tongue: "Wenn ich aufwache, ist meine Zunge immer etwas geschwollen und viel zu groß, um sich in der Mundhöhle bewegen zu können"[16] (My tongue is always somewhat swollen when I wake up, much too large to move easily within my mouth).[17] Indeed, the narrator's tongue initially shrinks back to its regular size, retreating into the esophagus while dragging the rest of the narrator's head behind it. The next modification, which occurs in the very next paragraph, is by contrast explicitly marked as a dream: "Damals in einem Traum . . . Mein Körper bestand aus einer einzigen Zunge"[18] (Once in a dream . . . My entire body was one huge tongue). "Nackt, rosa und unerträglich feucht" (naked, pink and unbearably moist),[19] the Tongue steps out of the house (and outside the mother tongue) and turns to writing. With her newly produced autobiography entitled "The Life Story of a Tongue," the narrator then commences a lecture tour through Germany.[20] While on the road, the Tongue diagnoses herself as feeling sick. During her final transformation, connected to a state of illness, the Tongue turns into a "Venus in furs." To "see" the Tongue in this particular meaningful guise, it will be helpful to draw attention to the fact that a number of German expressions having to do with the tongue occur in the text. Because "Tongue Dance" is embedded in a dreamscape, these figurative expressions are translated literally and visually rendered in this literal form. The expression most relevant to my particular analysis of "Tongue Dance," occurs in a dream in which the sick and shivering Tongue finds herself in a dark room in which the air is "eisig," "chilly" (Bernofsky's choice), or perhaps "freezing." Then the Tongue casually remarks: "Ich bin froh, daß ich einen Pelzmantel anhabe," or in the translation of Susan Bernofsky, "I'm glad I have on a fur coat."[21] Stumbling upon a tongue wearing a fur coat, an attentive German reader might think of the expression: "eine pelzige Zunge," or what medically in English is referred to as a "coated tongue." Hence Bernofsky's translation works beautifully since both the "Pelzmantel" or "fur coat" and the underlying connection to sickness ("eine pelzige Zunge" or "a coated tongue") are carried over.

In the remainder of this chapter, I will read Yoko Tawada's "Tongue Dance" in tandem with Leopold von Sacher-Masoch's *Venus in Furs* (1870) to suggest that Tawada's text can be interpreted as a critical commentary on and a humorous description of a particular type of domestication: that of the failed training of a tongue in furs. Tawada's "Tongue Dance" transfers the erotics of Masoch's story onto speech therapy, whereby the tongue is subjected to a disciplinary training comparable to the way Masoch's protagonist Severin von Kusiemski is lashed and humiliated by Wanda von Dunajew, whose slave he had voluntarily become. The tongue in Tawada is a metonym for Sacher-Masoch's body, speech therapy thereby operating as one of the "new micro-physics" of power that Foucault described in *Discipline and Punish* as a "political anatomy of detail" that, in Tawada's story, focuses disciplinary training and supervision specifically on the apparatus of the mouth.[22] In Tawada's "Tongue Dance," in other words, the entire drama of Sacher-Masoch's *Venus in Furs* is concentrated on the tongue: from its initial willing subjugation to speech therapy to its ultimate refusal to be cured of its mispronunciations.

The correspondences between "Tongue Dance" and *Venus in Furs* are striking indeed.[23] Particularly interesting are the aesthetic correspondences between the two texts, which I will draw out first. As Gilles Deleuze reminds us, in Leopold von Sacher-Masoch's writings "everything is suggestive of coldness," from the sneezing heroines to the women of stone and the marble bodies" and the cold light of the moon.[24] Tawada mimicked Sacher-Masoch's glacial atmosphere in the final dream sequence of "Tongue Dance" in which the Tongue (in furs) meets Zoltán "in der eisigen Luft des düsteren Zimmers" (in the chilly air of the dark room) where his skin becomes more and more transparent "wie von einer Eisschicht bedeckt" (as if it were covered with ice).[25] But Tawada does more than simply imitate Sacher-Masoch's style: she critically alters it as well. Let us look at one example. Significantly, for instance, Tawada does not employ Sacher-Masoch's romantic moonlight descriptions in "Tongue Dance," but instead sets the masochistic scene in a "Neonlicht" (or the "light of a neon lamp").[26] This modification is critical not only because the "natural" moonlight has been replaced by the "artificial" light of the neon lamp, but also because it is referred to as "cold light." This alteration I suggest can be understood as a direct critique of Sacher-Masoch's philosophy in which the relations between the sexes, between north and south, or between Christians and atheists is described as static and as having its cause in nature. As Deleuze points out, Sacher-Masoch grounds human behavior in nature: so many examples abound in *Venus in Furs*—"Die Natur des Weibes" (Woman's true nature), "geben Sie sich dem Zuge Ihrer Natur hin" (follow your natural bent), "deine Natur is viel zu gut" (you are far too good)—that Deleuze lists the many different "natures" Sacher-Masoch references.[27]

While Sacher-Masoch may ultimately have undermined the epistemological certainty of nature by inventing so many different types of nature, Tawada opposes all manner of "natural" *epistemés* by stressing the artificial character of conventions, including anthropologically naturalized ones, such as the belief in the naturalness or superiority of one's own mother tongue. A second major feature characteristic of Sacher-Masoch's aesthetic can be found in Tawada's "Tongue Dance" as well—what Deleuze has called Sacher-Masoch's novelistic preoccupation with "arrested movement" where scenes have "a frozen quality, like statues or portraits."[28] But whereas in Sacher-Masoch the narrative stagnation often is centered on the plastic arts, in Tawada's text the "arrested movement" can be seen in "close-ups" of selected soft body parts (a tongue, a palate) reminiscent of surrealist photographs.[29]

The frozen, arrested movement manifests itself furthermore on the level of the narrators' broken bodily relationship to the spoken word. In both Tawada and Sacher-Masoch, the protagonists are writers who struggle with the physical mechanics of speaking: Tawada's Tongue has difficulties with word stress, whereas Severin von Kusiemski has an actual speech impediment—he is a stutterer ("wieder das fatale, eselhafte Stottern," or "once again the stupid, despicable stuttering").[30] Both authors call attention to the heightened operation of the sensory organs. *Venus in Furs* is centered around Severin von Kusiemski, author of a manuscript entitled "Bekenntnisse eines Übersinnlichen" (Confessions of a Supersensualist). Tawada's "Tongue Dance" revolves around an anthropomorphized "sensory organ" (that is, a protagonist whose entire body consists of only one huge tongue), who is reading from her autobiography entitled "Lebensgeschichte einer Zunge" (Autobiography of a Tongue) on tour in Germany. Both Tawada and Sacher-Masoch organize their narratives around the possibility of a "cure" for their protagonist's displaced expressions, though Tawada's Tongue ultimately refuses the disciplinary treatment imposed upon her. In the frame narrative to *Venus in Furs*, Severin claims to have been finally "cured" of his "Übersinnlichkeit," or "supersensuality" through the merciless whippings of a man by the name of Alexis Papadopolis but who throughout Sacher-Masoch's novel is typically only referred to as the "Greek."[31] For Tawada Sacher-Masoch's "Greek" character opens up an additional level of signification—the Greek language—that she will exploit in her own linguistic account of discipline and pleasure.

Tawada's protagonist, whose "sickness" lies in the realm of the mouth, turns to a "Spracharzt," or "language doctor," yet finally resists his training and the implied cultural domestication.[32] This man in a "white smock," whom the narrator had located with the help of a phone book, shortly after having stumbled upon an "Internist," is presumably a speech therapist. This kind of therapist is in German also referred to as a "Logopäde," a Greek compound word consisting of the word "logos," or "word," and "paideia," or "education or lesson." This "Greek" speech therapist, in other words, attempts to cure the Tongue through a specific training of the organs of articulation.[33] The trainer in question is in fact a Freudian composite (dream) figure split into two. Two trainers attempt to teach the Tongue how to correctly position itself inside the mouth in order to speak German without an accent: the speech therapist from the phone book and a second man by the name of Zoltán (which in Hungarian means "Ruler"), whom the tongue encounters "auf der Strasse" (in the street) in a later dream sequence.[34] For now let us examine the Tongue's visit to the "Logopäde." Once in the doctor's office, the "Greek" interrupts ("unter*bricht*") the sick patient who is explaining her symptoms ("Sprachschmerz," or "language pain," being one of them) and immediately starts giving "Ratschläge," or practical advice. The German word "Ratschläge" can be translated as "recommendation" or "advice." What is at stake here, however, is the fact that the word "Ratschläge" contains the word "Schläge" or "beatings or thrashings."[35] Hence the doctor's "Ratschläge" can be simultaneously read as "advice" and as a "thrashing." The anonymous doctor from the phone book expresses his recommendations with the following words:

> Ich solle mir in jedem Satz, den ich sage, ein Wort aussuchen, das ich betonen will. Dieses Wort solle über die restlichen Wörter *herrsche*n und den ganzen Satz *unter seiner Gewalt haben*. Sonst gebe es eine Anarchie im Mundbereich. Ich sollte nur dieses eine Wort ins Auge fassen und allen anderen Wörter nur mit einem leichten Atem*schlag* streifen. (emphasis mine)[36]

> In each sentence I say, I am to select a single word I wish to emphasize. This word, he says, should dominate over the others and take complete control of the sentence, otherwise anarchy will reign in my oral cavity. I am to focus on this single word and skim over all the others with a light breath.[37]

A second (body) part (besides the anthropomorphized tongue) rears its head in the later dream sequence: what in the text is called "ein weiches Glied" or, literally, "a soft member." Initially, this "weiches Glied," which appears in a narrative in which the reader earlier encountered "Plastikfrauen ohne Geschlechtsorgane," or "plastic women who lacked sexual organs," seems to have purely sexual connotations.[38] In Susan Bernofsky's English translation the "weiches Glied" hence becomes "a soft penis," which seems to belong to Zoltán, At first glance, therefore, the "Glied" seems to have a purely sexual connotation indeed.

In this dream sequence of "Tongue Dance," the roles played in Sacher-Masoch's story by the dominatrix Wanda and the pathological narrator, Severin, are switched. Tawada's text reenacts a displaced version of *Venus in Furs* by reversing and reduplicating the original character roles while folding in the technical languages of psychoanalysis and speech therapy. Zoltán functions as Severin who is trying to teach Tawada/Wanda to become a Venus in furs. In Tawada's text Zoltán is a mixed figure, for he himself has the paleness of the Venus statue in Sacher-Masoch. Deleuze has pointed out that in *Venus in Furs*, erotic relationships are structured in terms of a contract. This written contract in Tawada's dream story has been displaced onto Zoltán's body, which is covered with red and blue veins that have the appearance of "Schriftzüge," or "lettering." Tawada's Tongue is attracted to the letter "N" which she sees shining through Zoltán's skin. When she asks whether the "N" is a tattoo, he mumbles, "Nein. Das ist meine Natur"(No, it's just my nature), an answer that the Tongue receives skeptically. Zoltán then takes on the position of the instructor correcting the movement of tongue and mouth. "Er meint, ich solle bei dem Laut 'n' nicht den hinteren Teil der Zunge gegen den Gaumen drücken, sondern die Zungenspitze müsse sich gegen die Rückseite der Vorderzähne pressen"[39] (He says that when I say "N," I shouldn't press the back of my tongue against my palate; the tip of my tongue is supposed to press against the back of my front teeth).[40] Here Zoltán in fact suggests that the protagonist retrain her tongue: it should stop hitting what is called "the soft palate" (the velum or muscular palate) and find the "hard palate," the part of the palate involved in speech, instead. The Tongue concludes that her mouth is just not organically shaped to make the proper "N" sound. As she struggles to pronounce the letter, the sexual imagery stands out. The palate and the tongue are described in terms of a soft and hard "Glied." On the level of Sacher-Masoch, the Tongue's hitting the right spot on the palate produces the equivalent of an ejaculation; on the level of speech, the Tongue's *Zungenschlag* creates a unique enunciation: the word "Menosch" which sounds familiar but does not belong to any official language. The Tongue literally breaks the word "Mensch" in two, inserts an "O" after the "N," and then fuses together her own irregular phoneme. The rules of speech production are thus rerouted. Unlike the masochist Severin, who obsessively follows the rules of his contract with Wanda, the Tongue breaks the word literally. By failing to live up to the language community's contract, she refuses to domesticate her speech.

"Glied" has in German a number of other connotations with which the text engages as well. Given that "Zungentanz" largely revolves around the visual and acoustic differences between two language and sign systems, and that enunciation is one of the key subjects of this narrative, the word "Glied" can equally and simultaneously be interpreted as the second part of the compound word "Satzglied" (sentence part). In Tawada's "Tongue Dance," the "Satzglied" separates into a "Satz," which is camouflaged as a wall, and a "Glied" which presents itself as a penis. The "Satzglied," like autobahn, is, in other words, another strategic word knot that leads us down various paths.[41]

The concluding dream of "Tongue Dance" functions, as Freud argued for most dreams, as a personal wish fulfillment for the narrator, who now is finally able to create a new word that allows her to survive into the future:

> Ich bin aber kein Mensch, sondern eine Zunge. Außerdem kann ich das Wort "Mensch" nicht aussprechen, weil ein einsames "n" in ihm steht. "Menosch" rufe ich![42]

> I am a tongue. In any case, I can't produce the word "friend" because there is a single "n" in the middle of it. "Frienod"! I cry out.[43]

This new word is the tongue's very own "Zungen*schlag*," a term that means "dialect" or "accent." The word "Menosch," which carries within itself traces of the past in the form of distorted echoes (acoustic remains from words such as "Masoch," for example) but also introduces one more language—Hebrew—in which "Enosch" means "human being,"[44] might just hold the key for a design of the future or "ein Entwurf für die Zukunft, " a future in which an O is introduced—an O that stands for the mouth itself, for curiosity and for new beginnings.[45]

The narrator of "Tongue Dance" is, at the end, neither "domesticated" nor "educated" within the structure of a bildungsroman. Quite on the contrary, the Tongue's education has failed on purpose. Structurally, however, the ending of Tawada's narrative develops in formal analogy to Sacher-Masoch's text while simultaneously altering the terms of the masochistic contract by breaking a word. "Tongue Dance," in fact, ends namely with a "Wortbruch," in its literal, not in its figurative sense, that is to say with the "breaking of a word" and not with a "betrayal."

Notes

1. Bettina Brandt, "The Post-Communist Eye: An Interview with Yoko Tawada," in *World Literature Today* 80:1 (2006), 41–43. Because I interviewed and recorded Tawada in German and then translated her words into English, "word knot," is my translation for the German word "Wortknäuel" that Tawada used in the interview. Knäuel (a ball, a tangle, or a knot) has both organic and inorganic connotations and is also the word that Freud used when describing what he called the "Nabel," or navel of the dream: that is, the spot in the dream that shows the "limits to the possibility of interpretation of the interpretable." Sigmund Freud, *Die Traumdeutung*, in *Studienausgabe 10 Bände* (Frankfurt: Fischer, 1996), 2: 503.

2. Gilles Deleuze, *Masochism: Coldness and Cruelty*, trans. Jean McNeil (New York: Zone, 1991), 22.

3. Mousel-Knott and Koiran draw attention to the importance of the rhizome for Tawada's work in general. See Suzuko Mousel-Knott, "Yoko Tawada und das 'F-Word': Intertextuelle und intermediale Prozesse des Romans *Ein Gast* im feministischen Diskurs," in *Études Germaniques* 65, no. 3 (July–September 2010): 569–80; and Linda Koiran, "Offen und ent-ortet: Anmerkungen zur Gestalt von Yoko Tawadas Werk," in *Text und Kritik* 191/192 (2011): 14–19.

4. Sigmund Freud, *Die Traumdeutung*, 2:577; Sigmund Freud, *The Interpretation of Dreams* (1900), in *The Standard Edition of the Complete Psychological Works of Sigmund Freud*, vols. 4–5, ed. James Strachey (London: Hogarth, 1966–74), 608. Translated from the German under the general editorship of James Strachey in collaboration with Anna Freud, assisted by Alix Strachey and Alan Tyson.

5. Riccardo Steiner commented on Strachey's translation of the *via regia* as royal road in his article "Paths to Xanadu: Some Notes on the Development of Dream Displacement and Condensation in Sigmund Freud's *Interpretation of Dreams*," *International Review of Psycho-Analysis* 15 (1988): 415–54, as quoted by Susan Sherwin-White in "Freud, the Via Regia and Alexander the Great," *Psychoanalysis and History* 5 (2003): 187–93. Sherwin-White also notes that Freud spoke about the *via regia* a second time in 1909 during a talk at Clark University, part of a larger lecture tour Freud undertook in the United States to introduce psychoanalysis in that country. Again, Strachey translated these two words as "royal road." Thanks to Veronika Fuechtner for bringing to my attention that Strachey's general tendency is to Latinize and medicalize Freud's discourse and that his translation of the *via regia* can hence be seen as a counterexample to this trend.

6. Lawrence Venuti, *The Translator's Invisibility: A History of Translation* (New York: Routledge, 1995).

7. Ibid., 20.

8. Sherwin-White, in "Freud, the Via Regia and Alexander the Great," suggests that Freud had the "ancient great royal Persian road system along which Alexander and his army marched to found a new empire"(White, 192) in mind when he added the *via regia* to his *Traumdeutung*. One could, however, equally well assert (given that Freud inserted the two Latin words immediately after introducing a verse of Vergil's *Aeneid*) that he purposely juxtaposed the *via regia* to a narrative about the founding myth of the city of Rome.

9. See www.via-regia.org/eng/index/php.

10. In his essay "Lemberg, die Stadt," Joseph Roth stresses the multilinguality of Lemberg: "Man hörte Russisch, Polnisch, Rumänisch, Deutsch und Jiddisch. Es war wie eine kleine Filiale der großen Welt" (People spoke Russian, Polish, Romanian, German and Yiddish. It was like a small subsidiary of the large world). In *Joseph Roth auf Reisen*, ed. Petra Herczeg and Rainer Rosenberg (Klagenfurt: Wieser Verlag, 2011), 27.

11. Echoes of Walter Benjamin's "The Task of the Translator," in which he famously defines the "sentence" as the "wall" in front of the language of the original reverberate in this passage but cannot further be discussed. Benjamin, "Task of the Translator," trans. Harry Zohn in *Selected Writings I*, ed Marcus Bullock and Michael Jennings (Cambridge, Mass.: Harvard University Press, 2000), 253–63, here 260. I discuss the importance of this particular Benjamin essay for Tawada's overall theories of translation in Bettina Brandt, "The Bones of Translation: Tawada's Translational Poetics," in *Challenging the Myth of Monolingualism*, ed. Liesbeth Minnaards and Tim Dembeck (Amsterdam/New York: Rodopi, 2014), 183–96. This volume also contains my English translation of Tawada's "Die Schrift einer Schildkröte oder das Problem des Übersetzens" as "The Script of a Turtle or the Problem of Translation," 171–80.

12. Yoko Tawada, "Zungentanz," in *Überseezungen* (Tübingen: Konkursbuchverlag Claudia Gehrke, 2002), 9.

13. Ibid., 10.

14. Yoko Tawada, "Tongue Dance," in *Where Europe Begins*, trans. Susan Bernofsky and Yumi Selden (New York: New Directions, 2002), 115–20, here 116.

15. "Zungentanz," 9.

16. Ibid.

17. Yoko Tawada, "Tongue Dance," 115.

18. "Zungentanz," 9.

19. "Tongue Dance," 115, 116, 116, respectively; "Zungentanz," 9.

20. Christine Ivanovic, "Tawada von zwei Seiten: Eine Dialektüre in Stichworten," *Text und Kritik* 191/192 (2011): 108–57.

21. Tawada, "Zungentanz," 13; "Tongue Dance," 119.

22. Michel Foucault, *Discipline and Punish: The Birth of the Prison*, trans. Alan Sheridan (New York: Vintage Books, 1979), 139.

23. Gilles Deleuze described Sacher-Masoch's aesthetics in similar terms in *Coldness and Cruelty*, 20. For an excellent critical analysis of the function of the "tableau vivant" as self-conscious and theoretical strategy in *Venus in Pelz*, see Catriona Macleod's "Still Alive: Tableau Vivant and Narrative Suspension in Sacher-Masoch's *Venus im Pelz*," *Deutsche Vierteljahrschrift für Literaturwissenschaft und Geistesgeschichte* 80, no. 4 (2006): 640–65.

24. Deleuze, *Coldness and Cruelty*, 52.

25. Tawada, "Zungentanz," 13; Tawada, "Tongue Dance," 119.

26. "Zungentanz," 13.

27. Deleuze, *Coldness and Cruelty*, 54. All references to the German text are to Leopold von Sacher-Masoch, *Venus im Pelz* (Berlin: Zenodot, 208) and all English translations refer to *Venus in Furs* in *Masochism*, trans. Jean McNeil (New York: Zone Books, 1991). The sources for the quotations are as follows: *Venus im Pelz*, 6, 45, 65, respectively; *Venus in Furs*, 144, 182, 201.

28. Deleuze, *Coldness and Cruelty*, 69–70.

29. Famous examples of surrealist close-ups of body parts include Man Ray's photograph "Anatomies," a close-up of a reclining neck of a woman photographed in such a way that the similarities between it and a penis are stressed while simultaneously suggesting that one is slowly transforming into the other.

30. Leopold von Sacher-Masoch, *Venus im Pelz*, 21; *Venus in Furs*, 15.

31. *Venus in Furs*, 112.

32. "I have been thoroughly whipped myself and it cured me." Sacher-Masoch, *Venus in Furs*, in *Masochism*, 150; Tawada, "Zungentanz," 11; Tawada, "Tongue Dance," 117.

33. The word "Logopädie" was introduced into the German language by Emil Fröschl, a Viennese speech therapist who was a contemporary of Freud and a fellow refugee.

34. Tawada, "Zungentanz," 13; Tawada, "Tongue Dance," 119.

35. This wordplay is also at the origin of the German idiom "Ratschläge sind auch Schläge."

36. Tawada, "Zungentanz," 12.

37. Tawada, "Tongue Dance," 118.

38. Tawada, "Zungentanz," 13; Tawada, "Tongue Dance," 119.

39. Tawada, "Zungentanz," 10.
40. Tawada, "Tongue Dance," 119.
41. One of these, for instance, circles back to the earlier mentioned naked, plastic doll, commonly known as a *mannequin,* a French word which in German could also be called a "Gliederpuppe." (During his final beating Severin notices the beautiful "Glieder," i.e., arms and legs, of the Greek).
42. Tawada, "Zungentanz," 14.
43. Tawada, "Tongue Dance," 120. For a reflection about the problems related to translating this and other passages from Tawada's "Zungentanz," see Susan Bernofsky's "Disoriented Language: On Translating Yoko Tawada," in *Transforming Texts-TextTransformationen*, ed. Christine Ivanovic (Tübingen: Stauffenberg, 2010), 449–53.
44. I would like to thank Na'ama Rokem for pointing this out to me.
45. Tawada, "Zungentanz," 14.

Epilogue

✦

Vierundzwanzig

Yoko Tawada

An einem einzigen Faden hängt mein Gehirn als Päckchen, schwebt im Seitenwind und denkt nicht einmal dran, an nichts zu denken. Das Unterkieferbein, das Nasenbein und das Tränenbein: so viele Beine im Kopf. Verpackt in einer dünnen Haut. Sie werden in einem Spielzeugladen angeboten. Ich bin keine Marionette, höchstens ein Mobile. Man soll nicht einmal lügen, sondern zweimal. Die erste Lüge und ihre Freundin finden gemeinsam einen Boden unter den Füßen. Würde es mir gelingen, wieder Anfängerin zu sein, könnte ich ohne Sorgen wackelig stehen. Die Richtung des Fallens dem Zufall überlassen. Die Handflächen saugen Hitze aus der untersten Gesteinsschicht. Ich drehe meine Hüften und empfange einen Spielball wie einen Gast. Der Ball ist eine Ballung aus dichtem Nebel. Es ist immer ein Verhängnis mit einem Ball, der größer ist als mein Kopf. Wo denkt er hin? Ich kenne die Haltung, einen Ball zu halten. Aber kenne ich den Ball selbst? Das Gehaltene? Den Gehalt? Er löst sich im Nu auf, wenn ich die Mähne des Windes zu kämmen anfange. Mit schweren Gedanken soll man nicht seine Knie belasten. Im Fleisch des Oberschenkels schlafen die belastbaren Toten. Ich öffne die weibliche Grabstätte und grabe meinen Korpus mit unlackierten Fingernägeln aus. Sie buddeln und babbeln in der Nacht. Wohlschmeckende Wörter sprudeln aus den schwarzen Zellen. Ich spreche die Sprache meiner Hände, die keine Gebärden kennen. Sie bleiben still und lehnen jedes Komatrinken ab, ohne Nein zu sagen. Bist du bereit, ein Kranich zu werden? Wenn meine Flügel sich diagonal öffnen, blitzt es in der Höhe meiner Augenbrauen. Der rechte Flügel berührt die labilen Wolken, der linke das Volk. Den lästigen Busch und das weitere Gebüsch abästen und einen kleinen Strand erreichen. In einer heißen, salzigen Strömung mit tiefen Farben und Falten findet der letzte Kampftanz der Wale statt. Siebzig Prozent für die Zukunft, dreißig für die Vergangenheit. Immer mehr Politiker ziehen einen Sportanzug an. Ich spanne die Saiten auf einer alten Birnenharfe und halte sie zweideutig. Als eine Waffe und als ein Musikinstrument. Ein Aufklärer mit ausgeschältem Apfelgesicht greift mich an. Unerwartet, von vorne. Vier Schritte zurück. Bei einem stillen Rückzug bin ich meines Sieges gewiss. Die rechte Hand überholt den Stundenzeiger, während die linke die Zeit zurückdreht. Der zweite Spielball, den ich dabei fange, heißt nicht mehr Erdkugel, sondern Globus. Er duftet nach Kaffee. Oder ist es dasselbe grüne Ei vom alten Phönix? Meine Zuneigung ist beflügelt und einseitig. Ein schwangerer Vogel weigerte sich einst, aus mir einen Baum zu machen. Die kopflose Erinnerung flog mir weg und ich zog an ihren Schwanzfedern. Jeder Abschied kann später als Tanz variiert werden. Halte keinen Vogel fest, der ein Nest braucht! Denn du bist selber der Pfau, mehr als jeder Pfau. Die Peitsche der Verwandlung pfeift. In ihrer Schwingung werde ich von mir selbst abgerissen, befreit. Ich verspinne die Zuckerwattefäden: die Lieblingsbeschäftigung aller Müßiggänger. Auch die Wolken schmecken süß: kein Wunder, denn sie sind die Träumereien des Wassers. Ich lese seine Wirbel und Parabeln von rechts nach links. Sie sind weiß auf weiß geschrieben. Die Peitsche pfeift zum zweiten Mal. Aus der Zeit aussteigen. Jedes Portrait ist eine Haltestelle für einen Gesichtszug. Was liegt auf der zurückgelassenen rechten Hand? Eine verschwitzte Landkarte eines Schlachtfeldes. Erneut nach vorne orientieren und den schläfrigen Turm besteigen: nicht für die Bande des Bluts, sondern für die Band der Straßenmusiker mit ihren Hunden. Ich verhandle nicht mit ihnen, ich spiele bedingungslos mit. Aus der Ferne nähern sich Feinde der Freunde und Freunde der Feinde. Ich springe vom Turm hinunter, lande unverletzt auf einem gepflegten Familienrasen. Mit meinem Fußtritt wollte ich niemanden treffen. Es war bloß eine Übung, Gleichgewicht zu halten. Der Montag versucht mich einzuschüchtern und ich packe ihn an den Ohren. Er verwandelt sich zurück in den vertrauten Mond, der seine Tage und Sternstunden hat. Ein zweiter Herausforderer schleicht sich von hinten an. Er heißt Dienstag oder Dienstreise. Ich schraube mein rechtes Bein in die Matte und gebe mit dem linken der Arbeitswoche einen Tritt in die Mitte. Es donnert und der Himmel zittert samt Wolken und der abwesenden Sonne. Die Woche ist um. Ich rieche plötzlich das Wort Schlange in mir, gehe in die Hocke mit gestreckten Beinen. Wer ist halb Tier, halb Schiff? Der Hafen öffnet sich nach hinten. Kommt meine beleidigte Ladung mit? Das Wort Kranich zieht mich hoch. Jeder Vogelname macht mich stolz im Bereich zwischen dem Hals und der Brust. Es gehört zum Menschenrecht, ein Tier zu sein. Die Richtung wechseln und die Kehrseite durchspielen. Dabei nicht an die nächste Form denken. Auch nicht an das Ich, denn das Ich ist oft das Vergangene. Die Bauchbinde umkreist den Schwerpunkt meines Schreibens. Wer mit der linken Hand radikal nach vorne denkt, soll nicht die rechte Schläfe vergessen. Den Osten gibt es schon längst nicht mehr. Auf einer Kugel ist jeder Richtungswechsel eine Ausrede. Ein Wind von rechts, dann ein anderer von links. Ich kenne sie, ich bin in einem Luftzug schwarzgefahren. Dann habe ich meinen Schriftzug gedichtet, gelockert, gelüftet, gesponnen und gewebt. Als Kind hatte ich eine untreue Weberin als Amme. Sie ließ ihr Webschiffchen fallen und schlüpfte ins geheime Loch hinein. Sie war nackt und nicht politisch. Damals noch nicht. Die flatternden

Webstoffe: das sind meine Hände. Der Seidenfaden schimmert blau und laut. Eine Nadel liegt unter dunkelgrünem Meereswasser. Sie ist die Zaubernadel, mit der der Affenheld einst die stürmischen Wellen besänftigt hat. Ich verbeuge mich höflich mit lockeren Ellbogen, um sie aufzuheben. Achtung! Ein romantischer Faustschlag! Er schlägt ins Leere. Meine rechte Elle kippt nach vorne und die Faust trifft mein Selbstbild. Eine Hebelwirkung. Das Loch in meinem Bewusstsein hat jetzt die Form meiner Faust. Ich lasse meine Hand einfühlsam ins Loch schlüpfen und ziehe es als Handschuh an. Wo ist aber meine Krisentasche? Es ist Zeit zum Aufbrechen. Den linken und dann den rechten Kontinent noch einmal kurz ansprechen, um den letzen Kreis des Ausatmens zu betreten. Ich werde zu einem Strich, zu einem Punkt und zu einer Stille, einer Lebensstille.

Twenty-Four

Yoko Tawada

My brain dangles from a single thread, a small parcel borne aloft in the crossbreeze, thinking not even of thinking of nothing. Jawbone, nose bone, tear bone: so many bones in the head. Packaged in a thin skin. You can buy them at a toy store. I'm not a marionette, at most I'm a mobile. Don't lie once, lie twice. The first lie and its friend will find their footing together. If I were to succeed in becoming a beginner again, I could wobble on my feet without a care in the world. Leave the direction you fall in up to chance. Your palms absorb heat from the stone's bottommost layer. I turn my hips to receive a ball like a special guest. This ball is just dense fog that has thickened and become round. When a ball is bigger than my head, nothing good can come of it. What could this ball be thinking? I know the proper stance for holding a ball. But do I know the ball itself? What is being held? What are its holdings? It dissolves instantly once I start combing the wind's mane. Do not burden your knees with heavy thoughts. The dead, slumbering in the flesh of your thighs, are more resilient. I open this female grave and dig out my own body with unpolished nails. They burrow and babble in the night. Delicious words bubble up from the black cells. I speak the language of my hands, which know no gestures. They keep still, rejecting all binge drinking without saying no. Are you ready to become a crane? When my wings open diagonally, lightning flashes about my eyebrows. The right wing grazes the unstable clouds, the left, the populace. Lop the branches from that annoying bush and then the other bush as well to arrive at a small beach. In a hot, salty current deep with colors and folds, the final battle dance of the whales is taking place. Seventy percent for the future, thirty for the past. More and more politicians are putting on track suits. I tighten the strings on an old pear harp and hold it ambiguously. As both weapon and musical instrument. A rationalist with a freshly peeled apple face attacks me. An unexpected frontal attack. Four steps backward. By quietly withdrawing, I am ensuring my victory. My right arm overtakes the hour hand, while my left turns back time. The second ball that I catch as I am doing so is no longer called the terrestrial sphere, now it's a globe. It smells of coffee. Or is it that same green egg from the old phoenix? My affections are winged, one-sided. A pregnant bird once refused to make me a tree. This headless memory flew away from me, and I grasped at its tail feathers. Every parting can recur in the form of a dance. Don't hold on to a bird that needs a nest. For you yourself are the peacock, more than any peacock. The whip of transformation is whistling. Its oscillations tear me away from myself to freedom. I spin the threads of cotton candy: a favorite pastime of all idlers. Even the clouds taste sweet: no wonder, for they are the daydreams of water. I read its whorls and its parables from right to left. They are written white on white. The whip whistles once more. Disembark from time. Every portrait is a bus stop for a facial feature. What lies upon the right hand, which has been left behind? The sweaty map of a battlefield. Reorient to face front and then ascend the sleepy tower: not for a bond of blood, but for the band of street musicians with their dogs. I don't haggle with them, I follow their lead. In the distance, enemies of friends and friends of enemies approach. I leap down from the tower, landing uninjured upon a well-tended family-friendly lawn. I had no wish to strike anyone with my kick. It was just an exercise in keeping my balance. Monday is trying to intimidate me, so I seize it by the ears. It changes back into the familiar moon that has its days and its hours of glory. A second challenger is creeping up from behind. Its name is Tuesday or toothpick. I screw my right leg into the mat and jab my left into the gut of the workweek. Thunder. The sky trembles with all its clouds and the absent sun. The week is over. Suddenly I smell the word snake inside me, I crouch down with legs extended. Who is half animal, half ship?

The harbor opens toward the rear. Will my affronted freight accompany me? The word crane draws me to my feet. The name of any bird makes me proud in the region between neck and chest. It is a human right to be an animal. Change direction and play out the reverse. Without thinking of the next form. Nor even of the self, for often the self belongs to the past. The waist sash circles the focal point of my writing. One who thinks his way forward radically with his left hand should not neglect his right temple. The East vanished long ago. On a sphere, every change of direction is just an excuse. A breeze from the right, then another from the left. I know them, I've traveled without a ticket on a breath of air. Then I thickened my script, loosened it, aired it out, spun it and wove it. As a child, I had a faithless weaver for a wet nurse. She forsook her shuttle and slipped into a secret hole. She was naked, not political. At least not yet. The flutterings of woven fabric: these are my hands. The silk thread shimmers blue and loud. A needle lies beneath dark green seawater. It is the magic needle that the monkey hero once used to calm the stormy seas. I bow down politely, elbows loose, to pick it up. Look out! A romantic fisticuff! The blow misses its mark. My right ulna tips forward, and the fist strikes my self-image. An example of lever action. The hole in my consciousness now has the shape of my fist. I let my hand slip into this hole insightfully, pulling it on like a glove. But where is my crisis satchel? It's time to set off. Let me briefly address the left and right continents once more, so as to enter the last circle of exhalation. I become a line, a dot, and then a stillness, the stillness of life standing still.

Translated by Susan Bernofsky

CONTRIBUTORS

Leslie A. Adelson is the Jacob Gould Schurman Professor of German Studies at Cornell University, where she previously directed the Institute for German Cultural Studies. Her monographs include *Crisis of Subjectivity* (1984), *Making Bodies, Making History: Feminism and German Identity* (1993), and *The Turkish Turn in Contemporary German Literature: Toward a New Critical Grammar of Migration* (2005). Her edited volumes include *Atlas of a Tropical Germany* (2000) and *The Cultural After-Life of East Germany: New Transnational Perspectives* (2002). She was the coeditor of "Futurity Now," a special issue of *Germanic Review* (2013). Adelson is currently writing on the narrative status of futurity and hope in Alexander Kluge's experimental prose for the twenty-first century. An article comparing time travel in works by Kluge and Tawada appeared in *Germanic Review* (2011) as "The Future of Futurity."

Doris Bachmann-Medick is a senior research fellow at the International Graduate Centre for the Study of Culture (GCSC), Justus-Liebig Universität Giessen (Germany). The author of *Cultural Turns: Neuorientierungen in den Kulturwissenschaften* (5th ed., 2015; revised English ed., *Cultural Turns: New Orientations in the Study of Culture* (2016)), she has also edited *The Trans/National Study of Culture: A Translational Perspective* (2014), a special issue on "The Translational Turn" of *Translation Studies* 2, no. 1 (2009), *Kultur als Text: Die anthropologische Wende in der Literaturwissenschaft* (2004), and *Übersetzung als Repräsentation fremder Kulturen* (1997). She writes regularly on cultural theory and questions of translation. She has been a member of the editorial board of *Translation Studies* since 2008.

Andrea Bachner is associate professor of comparative literature at Cornell University. Her research explores comparative intersections between Sinophone, Latin American, and European cultural productions in dialogue with theories of interculturality, sexuality, and mediality. She is the author of *Beyond Sinology: Chinese Writing and the Scripts of Cultures* (2014) and the coeditor (with Carlos Rojas) of the *Oxford Handbook of Modern Chinese Literatures* (forthcoming 2016).

Heike Bauer is a senior lecturer in English and gender studies at Birkbeck, University of London. She has published widely on the history of sexuality, nineteenth and twentieth-century literary culture, and on translation. Her books include *English Literary Sexology, 1860–1930* (2009), *Women and Cross-Dressing, 1800–1939*, 3 vols. (2006), and the edited collections *Queer 1950s: Rethinking Sexuality in the Postwar Years* (2012, with Matt Cook) and *Sexology and Translation: Cultural and Scientific Encounters across the Modern World* (2015). She coedited with Churnjeet Mahn a special issue on "Transnational Lesbian

Cultures" for the *Journal of Lesbian Studies* (2014); and with Sarah Lightman and Andrea Greenbaum a special issue on "Contemporary Comics by Jewish Women" for *Studies in Comics* (2015). Her forthcoming monograph is titled *The Hirschfeld Archives: Violence, Death, and Modern Queer Culture*.

Nina Berman is director of the School of International Letters and Cultures at Arizona State University. She is the author of *German Literature on the Middle East: Discourses and Practices, 1000–1989* (2011), *Impossible Missions? German Economic, Military, and Humanitarian Efforts in Africa* (2004), and *Orientalismus, Kolonialismus und Moderne: Zum Bild des Orients in der deutschsprachigen Kultur um 1900* (1997), as well as the coedited anthology *German Colonialism Revisited: African, Asian, and Oceanic Experiences* (2014). She has written articles on colonialism, minority literature, orientalism, German activities in Kenya, and intercultural contact. Her study *Land, Charity, and Romance* about the presence of Germans on the coast south of Mombasa is forthcoming in 2017 with Indiana University Press.

Susan Bernofsky is a translator and author and past chair of the Translation Committee of the PEN American Center. She directs the literary translation program in the School of the Arts MFA Program in Writing at Columbia University. She has translated over twenty books, including seven by the great Swiss-German modernist author Robert Walser, Kafka's *The Metamorphosis*, Hesse's *Siddhartha*, and *The End of Days* by Jenny Erpenbeck. Her prizes and awards include a Guggenheim Fellowship in 2014, as well as the 2006 Helen and Kurt Wolff Translation Prize, the 2012 Hermann Hesse Translation Prize, the 2015 Independent Foreign Fiction Prize, Schlegel-Tieck Translation Prize, and Oxford-Weidenfeld Translation Prize. She blogs about translation at www.translationista.net and is writing a biography of Robert Walser for Yale University Press.

Charles Bernstein is author of *Recalculating* (2013), *Attack of the Difficult Poems: Essays and Inventions* (2011), and *All the Whiskey in Heaven: Selected Poems* (2010). He is Donald T. Regan Professor of English and Comparative Literature at the University of Pennsylvania, where he is codirector of PennSound at writing.upenn.edu/pennsound.

Bettina Brandt is on the faculty of the Department of German and Slavic Languages and Literatures at Pennsylvania State University. She is coeditor of *Herta Müller: Politics and Aesthetics* (2013) and well as of *China in the German Enlightenment* (2016). Moreover, she is the Dutch co-translator of Yoko Tawada's *De Berghollander* (2010). Brandt has also written numerous articles on topics such as women and the avant-garde, the literatures of migration, literary multilingualism and translation studies, theater and performance studies, German-Jewish literature, and early modern global relations. She has published on authors and artists such as Barbara Honigmann, Elfriede Jelinek, Marguerite Duras, Herta Müller, Emine Sevgi Özdamar, Meret Oppenheim, Dorothea Tanning, Yoko Tawada, and Rahel Varnhagen.

Tom Cheesman is reader in German and founding co-director of the Centre on Digital Arts and Humanities at Swansea University. His books include *Novels of Turkish German Settlement* (2008), *German Text Crimes* (ed., 2013), and

Feridun Zaimoglu (co-ed., 2013). He conceived the "Version Variation Visualization" project, first presented at the Un/Translatables conference in 2011 (www.delightedbeauty.org, 2010ff.). The VVV "Translation Array" system was realized by software developers Kevin Flanagan and Stephan Thiel (www.delightedbeauty.org/vvv, 2012–). Cheesman's ongoing work involves VVV applications for translation research, training, and competitions; a computer-assisted history of German *Othellos;* a study of the social democrat and feminist Hedwig Schwarz, and her Shakespeare translations under the Third Reich; and projects on the public understanding of translating.

Daniel DiMassa is a postdoctoral scholar in the Department of Humanities and Arts at Worcester Polytechnic Institute. He has written on Dante, Goethe, Stefan George, and Thomas Mann, and he is currently completing a manuscript on *Dante's German Modernity: Art, Myth, and the Limits of Romanticism.*

Kevin Flanagan is architect and technical specialist at SDL International and a senior associate teacher at the University of Bristol. His software development career has been complemented by his skills as a linguist, and he also works as a freelance technical translator. Having used a number of translation memory (TM) systems in that capacity, he developed a prototype TM system providing more effective sub-sentential recall. This research constituted the core of his Ph.D. at Swansea University, and the resulting technology was acquired by SDL for integration into their products.

Ken Frieden is the B. G. Rudolph Professor of Judaic Studies at Syracuse University. His most recent publication is *Travels in Translation: Sea Tales at the Source of Jewish Fiction* (2016). Prior books include *Classic Yiddish Fiction* (1995) and anthologies of Yiddish literature in translation, such as *Tales of Mendele the Book Peddler* (1996) and *Classic Yiddish Stories* (2004). At Syracuse University Press, Frieden edits the series on *Judaic Traditions in Literature, Music, and Art.* He translates from Yiddish and Hebrew and has edited collections by the Israeli authors Etgar Keret (*Four Stories*) and David Ehrlich (*Who Will Die Last: Stories of Life in Israel*).

Willi Goetschel is professor of German and philosophy at the University of Toronto. He is the author of *Constituting Critique: Kant's Writing as Critical Praxis* (1994), *Spinoza's Modernity: Mendelssohn, Lessing, and Heine* (2004), and *The Discipline of Philosophy and the Invention of Modern Jewish Thought* (2012). He is the editor of the collected works of Hermann Levin Goldschmidt in nine volumes (1993–2014), the general editor of *Bamidbar: Journal for Jewish Thought and Philosophy,* and the executive editor of *The Germanic Review: Literature, Culture, Theory.*

Kathryn Hellerstein is associate professor of Yiddish at the University of Pennsylvania. Her books include a translation and study of Moyshe-Leyb Halpern's poems, *In New York: A Selection* (1982), *Paper Bridges: Selected Poems of Kadya Molodowsky* (1999), and *Jewish American Literature: A Norton Anthology*, of which she was coeditor (2001). Her new book, *A Question of Tradition: Women Poets in Yiddish, 1586–1987* (2014), won the National Jewish Book Award in Women's Studies. Hellerstein's poems and many scholarly articles on Yiddish and

Jewish American literature have appeared in journals and anthologies, including *American Yiddish Poetry: A Bilingual Anthology* (1986), to which she was a major contributor. Hellerstein has received grants from the NEA, the NEH, and the Guggenheim Foundation. Her *Women Yiddish Poets: An Anthology* is forthcoming.

Barbara Kosta is the head of the Department of German Studies at the University of Arizona. She is the author of *Recasting Autobiography: Women's Counterfictions in Contemporary German Literature and Film* (1994), *Willing Seduction: "The Blue Angel," Marlene Dietrich, and Mass Culture* (2009), and a coedited volume, *Writing Against Boundaries: Gender, Ethnicity and Nationality in the German-Speaking Context* (2003). She publishes widely on contemporary German film and literature as well as on the literature and visual culture of the Weimar Republic. At present she is coediting a volume on *Women Writing World War I* and working on a monograph on Hollywood's German remake.

Catriona MacLeod is Edmund J. and Louise W. Kahn Term Professor of German at the University of Pennsylvania. She is the author of *Embodying Ambiguity: Androgyny and Aesthetics from Winckelmann to Keller* (1998) and *Fugitive Objects: Sculpture and Literature in the German Nineteenth Century* (2013), which was awarded the 2014 Jean-Pierre Barricelli Prize for best book in romanticism studies. The coeditor of two volumes of collected essays in *Word and Image Interactions*, *Elective Affinities: Testing Word and Image Relationships* (2009) and *Efficacité/Efficacy: How To Do Things With Words and Images?* (2011), she is also senior editor of the journal *Word & Image*. Her work focuses on theories of intermediality, especially in the romantic period, and she is currently completing a monograph on *Romantic Scraps: Cutouts, Collages, and Inkblots*.

Ann Marie Rasmussen joined the University of Waterloo, Canada, as the John G. Diefenbaker Memorial Chair in German Literary Studies in 2015 after working for twenty-five years at Duke University where the Graduate School awarded her in 2014 the Dean's Award for Excellence in Mentoring. Her numerous articles treat medieval literature and culture from the twelfth century to the Reformation, combining gender studies with a variety of other approaches including manuscript studies, the anthropology of gift-giving, visuality studies, and, most recently, material culture. Her books include *Mothers and Daughter in Medieval German Literature* (1997), *Ladies, Whores, and Holy Women: A Sourcebook in Courtly, Religious, and Urban Cultures of Late Medieval Germany, with Introductory Essays* (coedited, 2010), and *Visuality and Materiality in the Story of Tristan and Isolde* (coedited, 2012). She is currently completing a study of medieval badges.

Simon Richter is a professor in the Department of Germanic Languages and Literatures at the University of Pennsylvania. He is the author of *Women, Pleasure, Film: What Lolas Want* (2013), *Missing the Breast: Gender, Fantasy, and the Body in the German Enlightenment* (2006), and *Laocoon's Body and the Aesthetics of Pain* (1992).

Jan Rybicki is assistant professor (*adiunkt*) at the Institute of English Studies, Jagiellonian University, Kraków. He has also taught at Rice University in Houston, and at Kraków's Pedagogical University. His research combines translation studies, comparative literature, and computational stylistics to produce quantitative and qualitative analyses of literary language in the original and in translations. He has authored a number of publications on the stylometry of literary translations (Sienkiewicz, Woolf, Conrad, Ford), on stylometric methods, and on the visibility of various signals. He serves on the Executive Committee of the European Association for Digital Humanities. He has translated some thirty novels into Polish by authors including Amis, Coupland, Fitzgerald, Golding, Gordimer, Ishiguro, le Carré, and Winterson.

Gerhild Scholz Williams is the Barbara Thomas and Thomas M. Thomas Professor in the Humanities in Arts and Sciences at Washington University in St. Louis. She is also vice provost and associate vice chancellor of academic affairs. As a member of the German Department and Comparative Literature, her research and teaching explore early modern German and French literature and culture, translation, magic and witchcraft, and more recently, seventeenth-century news media and novels. Alongside many articles, she has published books and translations: *Mediating Culture in the Seventeenth-Century German Novel, Eberhard Werner Happel, 1647–1690 (*2014); *Ways of Knowing in Early Modern Germany: Johannes Praetorius as a Witness to His Time* (2006); *Mothering Baby: On Being a Woman in Early Modern Germany: Johannes Praetorius's Apocalypsis Myteriorum Cybeles. Das ist Eine Schnackische Wochen-Comedie, 1662 (*2010); *On the Inconstancy of Witches: Pierre de Lancre's Tableau de l'inconstance des mauvais anges et demons, 1612* (with Harriet Stone, 2006).

Azade Seyhan is the Fairbank Professor in the Humanities, professor of German and comparative literature, and affiliated faculty in philosophy at Bryn Mawr College. She is the author of *Representation and Its Discontents: The Critical Legacy of German Romanticism* (1992); *Writing Outside the Nation* (2001); and *Tales of Crossed Destinies: The Modern Turkish Novel in a Comparative Context* (2008), which appeared in Turkish translation in 2014. She has published and lectured extensively on German idealism and romanticism, critical theory, exile narratives, Turkish-German literature, and the modern Turkish novel. She is completing a book-length study, *Exile in Translation: Legacies of a Disrupted Century*.

Yoko Tawada is a contemporary Japanese-German writer. Born in Tokyo in 1960, she moved to Hamburg when she was twenty-two, and then to Berlin in 2006. She writes in both Japanese and German, and so far has published more than forty titles—stories, novels, poems, plays, essays—in both languages. She has received numerous awards for her writing, including the Akutagawa Prize, the Adelbert von Chamisso Prize, the Tanizaki Prize, and the Goethe Medal. English translations of her German work include *Where Europe Begins* (2007),*The Naked Eye* (2009), and *Memoirs of a Polar Bear*, forthcoming November 2016. English translations from the Japanese include *Facing the Bridge* (2007) and the prizewinning *The Bridegroom Was a Dog* (2003, first published in Japanese in 1993).

Nicholas Theis is a graduate student in the Department of Germanic Languages and Literatures at the University of Pennsylvania. His dissertation, "Epic, Enlightenment, and the Empowerment of the German Mind: Versified Legitimacy from Leibniz to Goethe," examines the roles of genre, aesthetic theory, and philosophy in the emergence of the German *Versepos* in the eighteenth century. He has presented work on figures ranging from Bodmer and Breitinger to Mauthner and Morgenstern regarding the significance of philosophy and translation in German literary history.

Stephan Thiel is managing director at Studio NAND, a design company in Berlin focused on data visualization and interaction design which he cofounded in 2011. At NAND, Thiel puts cultural data to use via the design of user interfaces, visualizations, and via workshops for people interested in technology. He also actively pushes the inclusion of coding literacy in education as a board member and cofounder of the German nonprofit Start Coding. Thiel holds a B.A. in interface design from the University of Applied Sciences Potsdam and an M.F.A. in media art and design from the Bauhaus University Weimar.

Lawrence Venuti is professor of English at Temple University. He is the author of *The Translator's Invisibility: A History of Translation* (2nd ed., 2008), *The Scandals of Translation: Towards an Ethics of Difference* (1998), and *Translation Changes Everything: Theory and Practice* (2013), as well as the editor of *Rethinking Translation: Discourse, Subjectivity, Ideology* (1992) and *The Translation Studies Reader* (3rd ed., 2012). His translations from Italian include Antonia Pozzi's *Breath: Poems and Letters* (2002), Massimo Carlotto's *The Goodbye Kiss* (2006), and I. U. Tarchetti's *Fantastic Tales* (2014). His version of the Catalan poet Ernest Farrés's collection, *Edward Hopper* (2009), won the Robert Fagles Translation Prize. The recipient of awards from the PEN American Center, the NEA, the NEH, and the Guggenheim Foundation, he held a Fulbright Senior Lectureship at the Universitat de Vic (Catalonia).

Xiaojue Wang is associate professor of Chinese literature in the Department of Asian Languages and Cultures at Rutgers University. She is the author of *Modernity with a Cold War Face: Reimagining the Nation in Chinese Literature across the 1949 Divide* (2013) and the coeditor of the forthcoming *Lu Xun and Sinophone Asia*. She is the author of articles on modern Chinese literature, the cultural Cold War, film and visual studies, German literature, and comparative literature. She is also the Chinese translator and co-translator of Jürgen Habermas, Max Horkheimer, and Peter Weiss, among others.

Bethany Wiggin is associate professor of German and associate faculty in English and comparative literatures at the University of Pennsylvania. She is the author of *Novel Translations: The European Novel and the German Book* (2011). At present she is completing *Germanopolis: Utopia Found and Lost in Penn's Woods* and is editing an essay collection, *Babel of the Eighteenth-Century Atlantic*, and co-editing, with David Gramling, a special issue of *German Studies Review* on monolingualism. Her articles range in topic from the birth of fashion and commodity culture, to world literature and early modern globalization, to early transnational writing against slavery. Wiggin is the founding director of the Penn Program in Environmental Humanities (ppehlab.org) and will direct the Penn Humanities Forum in 2016–17 in a year devoted to the theme of translation.